RUSSIA Under PUTIN

RUSSIA
UNDER
PUTIN

FRAGILE STATE AND
REVISIONIST POWER

EDITED BY
Andrew S. Natsios

Johns Hopkins University Press
Baltimore

© 2025 Johns Hopkins University Press
All rights reserved. Published 2025
Printed in the United States of America on acid-free paper
9 8 7 6 5 4 3 2 1

Johns Hopkins University Press
2715 North Charles Street
Baltimore, Maryland 21218
www.press.jhu.edu

Library of Congress Cataloging-in-Publication Data

Names: Natsios, Andrew S., editor.
Title: Russia under Putin : fragile state and revisionist power / edited by
    Andrew S. Natsios.
Description: Baltimore : Johns Hopkins University Press, 2025. | Includes
    bibliographical references and index.
Identifiers: LCCN 2024042539 | ISBN 9781421451923 (paperback) |
    ISBN 9781421451930 (ebook)
Subjects: LCSH: Russia (Federation)—Politics and government—1991– |
    Russia (Federation)—Foreign relations. | Putin, Vladimir Vladimirovich,
    1952– | Russian invasion of Ukraine, 2022.
Classification: LCC DK510.763 .R87135 2025 | DDC 947.086/4—dc23
    /eng/20250219
LC record available at https://lccn.loc.gov/2024042539

A catalog record for this book is available from the British Library.

Special discounts are available for bulk purchases of this book. For more
information, please contact Special Sales at specialsales@jh.edu.

EU GPSR Authorized Representative
LOGOS EUROPE, 9 rue Nicolas Poussin, 17000, La Rochelle, France
E-mail: Contact@logoseurope.eu

Contents

	Introduction	1
	Andrew S. Natsios	

PART I: THE RUSSIAN STATE UNDER PUTIN

1.	Russia's Domestic Politics Under Putin	23
	Kathryn Stoner	
2.	The Role of Power and Wealth in Putin's Russia	47
	Anders Åslund	
3.	Vladimir Putin and the Russian Military	65
	Alexandra Chinchilla and Raymond C. Finch III	
4.	Russian Cyber Warfare	94
	Scott Jasper	
5.	Putin's Economy: On the Road to Ukraine and Empire?	120
	Paul Gregory	
6.	Russian Power in Decline: A Demographic and Human Resource Perspective	143
	Nicholas Eberstadt	

PART II: THE MYTHOLOGY OF THE PUTIN STATE

7.	The End of Glory? Putin's Use and Abuse of the Legacy of the Second World War	186
	Roger R. Reese	
8.	*Project Russia*: The Bestselling Book Series of Putin's Kremlin	221
	Lynn Corum	

vi   *Contents*

PART III: THE RUSSIAN REVISIONIST FOREIGN POLICY

9. The Russo-Ukrainian War in the Historical Perspective   245
    Serhii Plokhy

10. Russia, Demography, and Putin's Hidden Agenda   264
    Andrew S. Natsios

11. A View from Northeastern Europe: The Baltic States
    and the Russian Regime   291
    James S. Corum

12. Economic Implications of the Russian Invasion of Ukraine   314
    Todd J. Lefko and Raymond Robertson

    Contributor Biographies   331
    Index   335

RUSSIA Under PUTIN

Introduction

Andrew S. Natsios

Some essays in this collection, previously published in the 2018 *South Central Review*, were originally presented by scholars and journalists at a September 2015 conference and subsequent talks on Vladimir Putin's Russia at the Bush School of Government at Texas A&M University. The essays have all been updated to include the 2022 Russian invasion of Ukraine (henceforth known as the second invasion). Several essays that did not appear in that issue of *SCR* are included in this book, including those by Anders Åslund, Kathryn Stoner, Scott Jasper, Raymond Robertson and Todd Lefko, and my chapter. This book fills a gap in our understanding of Putin's Russia by answering the question: is Russia under Putin a revisionist power that seeks to undermine or destroy the existing international order, or is it a fragile state with profound dysfunctions? The essays in this book argue that Russia is both. These essays took a more ominous view of Russia under Putin's leadership at the time they were published, a position criticized by some scholars and analysts who saw Putin as a pragmatist.

These essays suggest that Russia is an increasingly well-armed, declining power. But it is also a revisionist power that seeks—with its Chinese, North Korean, and Iranian allies (henceforth CRIN)—to undermine or even destroy the existing international order. A declining, revisionist power can be as dangerous and destabilizing as a rising power, particularly if it has a large land army, cyber warfare capability, new advanced conventional weapons, and a modernized nuclear arsenal. Russia's second Ukraine invasion represents the gravest threat to the European security system since World War II and is striking evidence for what a declining power (with its powerful ally, China) can do to undermine the international system. Since the first Ukraine invasion, the Kremlin has boasted publicly that it can incinerate European countries with its nuclear arsenal, rhetoric more inflammatory than that used even during the Cold War. The long-term prospects are not good for Russia. Its public services, military power, and economic system rest on an unstable foundation of volatile oil, gas, and mineral revenues, a propaganda machine that grossly distorts external reality for the Russian people, a severe demographic decline, corrupted institutions lacking legitimacy and resilience, and a predatory governing elite of oligarchs and the Siloviki (the military and security services) who make up Putin's elite support base. Perhaps more ominously for the Russian government's balance sheet are international efforts to de-carbonize the world economy, which will make Russian oil and gas reserves of dwindling significance strategically and economically as demand for fossil fuels (and thus prices) decline.

Putin's History

When Boris Yeltsin named Vladimir Putin as acting president in December 1999, many in the Western capitals hurriedly attempted to determine who he was and how he rose in three years from being an obscure municipal official to acting president of Russia. In his earlier career, Putin served 16 years in the KGB, the Soviet secret police, rising to become a lieutenant colonel assigned to East Germany. After retiring from the KGB, he went to work in St. Petersburg city government in several posts, including deputy mayor, where he was deeply involved in organized crime, according to Karen Dawisha's research in *Putin's Kleptocracy: Who Owns Russia?* Boris Yeltsin brought him to Moscow, where he held several positions before being appointed director of the Federal Security Service (FSB), the new name for the KGB. He then became prime minister and acting president, and was elected in his own right on March 26, 2000.

Much of the initial Western perception of Vladimir Putin was based on his early years as president, when he was an economic reformer who sought to bring Russia into the international economic order. For the first fourteen years of Putin's presidency, the leaders of the industrial democracies treated Russia as a great power and one of the select countries in the G8. Beginning in the late 2000s, Putin abandoned his economic reform agenda and shifted the direction of his government, ending Russia's integration into the world economy, weakening civil society, gaining control of the Russian electronic news media, and seizing the territory of neighboring states such as Georgia and Ukraine, all the while aggressively re-arming. Russia began its withdrawal from global economic integration well before the first invasion of Ukraine. Expelled from the G8 by the other industrial democracies after the first Ukraine invasion, Russia became more isolated in international bodies and the global economy while forming an alliance with China, North Korea, and Iran.

European and US policymakers were slow to acknowledge and react to the reality of Putin's revisionist policies and the threat to its neighbors until after the shock of the second invasion.[1] Since the end of the Cold War, many European countries had defunded their militaries and thus virtually disarmed themselves; it appeared that as their militaries shrank and fell into disrepair, they became more tolerant of Russian aggression. When Russia launched its second invasion of Ukraine in February 2022, European policymakers and journalists abandoned their characterizations of Putin as a pragmatist. No European leader could ignore the invasion the way they had the first, despite these other crises. (Eastern European countries—the Baltic states, Moldova, Poland, Czech Republic, and Slovak Republic, among others—have long seen Russia as a revanchist threat, whereas Western European political leaders took a less alarmist view.) The televised images of the Russian army invading Ukraine evoked memories of Hitler's aggression in the late 1930s and the failure of the European powers then to acknowledge the grave danger Nazi Germany posed to European civilization until it was too late.

The Putin State System

Putin has gradually either infiltrated, intimidated, or shut down most of the nascent institutions of Russian democratic pluralism, as described by Kathryn Stoner in chapter 1. Putin has done this to ensure he faces no competing centers of domestic power, which has made him stronger personally even as it made Russian society weaker, as Anne Applebaum pointed out in her essay in the *South Central Review* issue of Spring 2018. Russia has neither the rule of law, civil society, nor an independent court system, and its police are corrupt and a tool of repression rather than law enforcement. Russia has gradually evolved into what Russians call a "managed democracy," a democracy in appearance, but not reality.[2]

Since the second Ukrainian invasion, any pretense of Russia even being a managed democracy has been abandoned: it is simply an old-style autocracy. Russia under Putin is a classic case of a patronal state as described by Stoner, which goes a long way toward explaining his behavior and the behavior of Russia governing elites.[3] Clientelistic or patronal states are often (but not always) unstable and can face succession crises. Russia experienced a collapse of its clientelist system twice in the twentieth century, leaving chaos in its wake: once under Tsar Nicholas II in 1917–1918 and then under Mikhail Gorbachev in 1990–1991. Thus, should Putin die in office or resign, Russia could face a succession crisis because of this highly personalized system for governing.

Russian institutional weakness may be found in the retarded level of internal development and the dysfunctional characteristics of its governance structure. Douglass North, Barry Weingast, and John Joseph Wallis argued in their book *Violence and Social Orders* that what distinguishes wealthy, advanced, and stable countries from those in the developing world is the density, legitimacy, resilience, and robustness of their government, private corporate, and civil society institutions.[4] Russia has a weak private sector of formally incorporated businesses, a rapidly disappearing network of civil society organizations, and a highly centralized, massive state sector controlled by a small oligarchy in Moscow. North, Weingast, and Wallis call these states *limited access orders* or *natural orders*. These types of states, they write, are held together—and violence suppressed—through governing coalitions of political bosses whose loyalty is rewarded through no-bid government contracts, patronage government jobs, monopoly access to natural resources and government regulatory systems, and limiting access to resources and public services by the general public based on political loyalties. This is in contrast to advanced industrial democracies, which North, Weingast, and Wallis call *open access orders*, where institutions and the rule of law organize societies, not personal loyalties, where government contracts and permits to access natural resources are competitively bid, where merit-based civil service systems manage public services that are available to every eligible person, and where power is widely disbursed among the population, which has control over the government through democratic elections. Nick Eberstadt argues that, judged by its health indicators, Russia has more in common with the least developing countries than even middle-income countries, another sign of institutional weakness.[5]

Paul Collier suggests in his book *The Bottom Billion* that abundant natural resources can be a curse more than a blessing in a country with fragile institutions.[6] In such a country, these resources will corrupt and undermine the legitimacy of the state and hamper the development of accountable institutions. Russia is a poster child for the "resource curse," and thus its luxuriant natural resources are a source of weakness, but they are also simultaneously a source of strength because they allow Moscow to fund activities it could not otherwise do. Some of this wealth has been squandered on mismanaged show-and-tell projects such as the $51 billion spent to prepare for the Sochi Olympics.[7] And a portion of the oil and gas infrastructure revenues have been siphoned off to enrich Putin's inner circle of former KGB agents who now control perhaps a third of the mineral, oil, and gas wealth of the country.[8] According to Anders Åslund in chapter 2, more than $1 trillion of oligarch wealth has been moved outside the country because it is insecure when invested in Russia.

Oil and gas wealth, which makes up about 50% of the Russian government's revenues with another 15% generated by mineral income, has been used by Putin to ensure pension and paychecks have been paid on time after the chaos of the 1990s. That oil and gas wealth also provides Russians with stable government jobs in exchange for the public's tacit acceptance of Putin's growing centralized, autocratic power, but they have done little to transform Russia into an advanced industrial economy and a lot to hinder it.[9]

Putin, perhaps anticipating public hostility to the election corruption, expelled the US Agency for International Development (USAID) Mission in Moscow months before the 2012 elections. He correctly believed USAID (which I ran from 2001 to 2005) supported the development of Russian civil society over the previous two decades, along with other Western aid agencies. Putin feared Russian civil society might have led the protests against election abuses.

Putin rules through a system of security agencies, including the FSB and the military, called collectively the Siloviki, and has certainly been the most powerful Russian leader since Joseph Stalin (though he has not exercised anywhere near the same level of control over Russian society as Stalin did). When Russian Foreign Minister Sergey Lavrov was asked who Putin's inner circle of advisors was, he replied, "He has three advisers, Ivan the Terrible, Catherine the Great, and Peter the Great."[10] This suggests Putin is reverting to traditional Russian autocracy as a governance model with an aggressive expansionist foreign policy.

Putin has a fear of public uprisings, which was why he gradually took control of Russia's electronic news media. He has emasculated these major media outlets, tried to block Internet access from outside Russia, and suppressed dissent. These efforts have substantially accelerated since the second invasion of Ukraine. The Kremlin has been accused of assassinating prominent journalists, civil society leaders, hostile oligarchs, and political opponents. According to a report from the Center for Strategic and International Studies (CSIS), between the time Putin took office and 2007, twenty-two Russian journalists were murdered and three disappeared.[11] Opposition leader Boris Nemtsov was assassinated on a bridge in sight of the Kremlin the day before he was to release a report in February 2015 with evidence that Russian troops were fighting alongside separatists in Ukraine. We don't have hard evidence Putin himself gave orders to assassinate Nemtsov, nor are we likely to find it, but the five men convicted of killing him and sentenced in July 2017 in a Moscow court were Chechens with ties to Chechnya's leader, Ramzan Kadyrov, a mafia-like acolyte of Putin's, heavily subsidized by Moscow.[12]

In the first year after the second invasion of Ukraine, thirty-nine oligarchs and journalists who were critical of the invasion died mysteriously, most likely assassinated.[13] We do not have hard evidence Putin gave a direct order to kill Alexei Navalny, the celebrated opposition figure who died from what appeared to be wounds from torture in February 2024 in a penal colony in the Arctic north, but many Western political leaders and analysts believe Navalny would not have been killed without his approval.

Putin's Grand Economic Bargain with the Russian People

According to Paul Gregory, Putin's legitimacy as a ruler has been based on a tacit agreement with the Russian people that traded individual freedom and democracy for economic security. Following the severe economic contraction after mid-2014, that tacit agreement ended. In response, Putin reformulated this grand bargain when he promised to bring back the glorious days of the Soviet Union and earlier Tsarist empires in exchange for the Russian public's acceptance of his autocratic rule and a lower living standard.[14]

As Paul Gregory argues in chapter 5, Putin's ability to use oil and gas resources has been curtailed since 2014, when oil prices collapsed from $117 a barrel to $27 at the beginning of 2016 before rising to $68 a barrel in 2018, $71 by December 2021, and $120 by May 2022. Oil prices stood at $76 a barrel in May 2024. Because of this earlier price collapse, Russia suffered a significant drop in state revenues between 2014 and 2017, particularly after Western economic sanctions were imposed because of the first invasion of Ukraine.[15]

After the 2014 drop in oil prices, the central government was forced to shore up Russia's fragile banking system. The country then faced a serious risk of internal economic implosion. This was due to cuts in public services and pensions, growing unrest among the Russian elites due to Moscow's policies, rising unemployment and declining family incomes, and the Russian military's discomfort with the first and second invasions of Ukraine and (earlier) Georgia.[16] The Soviet Union collapsed for many reasons in 1990, but one immediate cause was its bankruptcy. During the West German–Soviet negotiations over the reunification of East and West Germany, Mikhail Gorbachev, then-president of the Soviet Union, repeatedly asked Helmut Kohl, the West German chancellor, for tens of billions of dollars in loans (which the German government provided) to remedy the Soviet Union's internal financial crisis.[17] Perhaps the memory of this bankruptcy has driven Putin's conservatism in managing Russian debt, which was at 15.5% of GDP, the seventeenth lowest in the world, in 2022 and has since risen to 20% as the Ukraine war has unfolded.[18] One of the reasons for the timing of the second Russian invasion of Ukraine may have been high oil and gas prices, which allowed Russia to build a $650 billion sovereign wealth fund, perhaps as insurance against the risk of future sanctions by the West, which were actually imposed after the second invasion.[19] Many of those funds were invested in Western banks and were quickly frozen after the second invasion, with two-thirds of those funds "very difficult to utilize, if not completely blocked off" because of Western sanctions, as reported by Richard Nephew.[20]

The Mythology of the Putin State

Putin has positioned himself and Russia as a culturally and religiously reactionary alternative to Western liberal democracies. This world view is described in chapter 8, Lynn Corum's essay on *Project Russia*, which is a curious, if alarming, bestselling collection of essays published in four volumes as a semi-official government publication that describes the political ideology of the state, the Russian Orthodox Church's theology (other Orthodox church leaders outside Russia have condemned the Moscow Patriarchate's ultra-nationalist ideology and support for Russia's attack on Ukraine), geographic determinism, and reactionary social analysis shared by Putin, the Siloviki, and his circle of oligarchs who rule Russia. These essays form a strange amalgam of anti-democratic, ultra-nationalist attacks on Western democratic values, combined with an unhealthy dose of conspiracy theories, paranoia, xenophobia, and a defense of autocratic government and dictatorship with roots in nineteenth-century Russian intellectual traditions. These volumes represent Russia's grand strategy, and are evidence of a revisionist power seeking to destroy the existing international order and replace it with a Russian Orthodox religious vision and an autocratic political system.

The Cold War certainly involved the arming of US and Russian client states against each other, but after the collapse of the Soviet Union in 1991, US policy changed to one of facilitating the integration of Russia into the international system and its conversion into a democratic capitalist system. The United States spent $28 billion ($60 billion in 2024 dollars) in foreign aid to Russia and the twelve former Soviet states as of 2007; Europe spent even more in aid programs to help Moscow implement these political and economic reforms.[21] Fritz Bartel argues in his book, *The Triumph of Broken Promises*, that the Russian elites were expecting far more assistance from the West than the aid they received after the collapse of the Soviet Union. Nevertheless, if the Western democracies intended to destroy Russia permanently, why did they make these substantial investments?

Vladimir Putin has had to explain to the Russian people why the country has been so far behind the Western democracies in its standard of living, as did his predecessors in the Soviet Union. According to Roger R. Reese in chapter 7, Putin continues to pursue the Brezhnev-era Soviet strategy of keeping the memory of World War II alive to stir up Russian nationalism among the population, but also as an explanation for Russia's underdevelopment. This strategy faces growing skepticism by the younger generation of Russians. The Soviet Union's epic and extraordinary sacrifices during World War II—when, according to Stephen Kotkin, 27 million Soviet citizens died[22]—no longer have much resonance with younger people, who know little about the war, and the older generation, and who tire of a war fought seventy-five years ago being used to explain Russia's inability to match Western living standards today. Thus, what had been a powerful historical experience of collective suffering and sacrifice during World War II has now become a fading memory that lacks the magnetic power it previously held over the Russian people.

Understanding Russian Foreign Policy

George Kennan and John Mearsheimer argued in the late 1990s that the expansion of NATO (North Atlantic Treaty Organization) membership to former members of the Soviet bloc in Eastern Europe and the Balkans would eventually provoke a Russian backlash, and potentially a war.[23] Stephen Kotkin, the preeminent biographer of Stalin and historian of the Soviet Union and Russia, disagreed with this view in a 2022 interview with David Remnick in *The New Yorker*.[24] He argued that Putin would have invaded Ukraine even if NATO never existed, that Putin's ambitions and worldview is similar to those of his Communist and Tsarist predecessors. Russian journalist and scholar Sergei Medvedev asserts in his book, *The Return of the Russian Leviathan*, written before the second invasion, that the Siloviki need an outside threat, in this case NATO, even if it is entirely invented, to justify their "bureaucratic domination" of the Russian system.[25]

Introduction 9

The expansion of NATO was a convenient excuse for the invasion of Ukraine, not the cause. Some writers such as Anne Applebaum have argued elsewhere that Putin has no grand strategy, but manages an improvised foreign policy. Thus, Russia's aggression in Georgia, Ukraine, and Syria, and its threats to the Baltic States and Moldova, may be seen not as a carefully designed and executed strategy of conquest, but as symptomatic of Putin's ad hoc, opportunistic foreign policy. He has probed for Western weakness, irresolution, and indecision, and then, if there was no resistance, he has intervened to extend Russia's reach by absorbing more territory. Russia's aggression, some claim, is driven by the fear of Western alternate models of democratic governance, the rule of law, and the protection of human rights and individual freedom. In the March/April 2024 issue of *Foreign Affairs*, Nicholas Eberstadt predicted Russia's population will decline 9% by 2050, which will reduce its (increasingly aged) population to 130 million. Putin is attempting to restore Russia as a great power. The downward trajectory of Russian demography makes that ambition unreachable without military conquest, which I describe in chapter 10.

In the case of the second Ukraine invasion, Russian intelligence services badly misjudged the conditions on the ground. Putin believed his reforms had successfully rebuilt the Russian military, as described by Raymond Finch and Alexandra Chinchilla in chapter 3. Some argue that Putin's intelligence chiefs told him the Ukraine military would not or could not fight and thought NATO had devolved into a squabbling group of pacifist European states who would ignore an invasion of Ukraine as they did the first invasion in 2014. Moscow believed that European nations' dependence on Russian oil and gas, particularly Germany's, had neutralized them, and that the United States, after an embarrassingly chaotic withdrawal from Afghanistan, was in no mood to risk another military engagement, directly or indirectly, this time with a major nuclear power. All of these assumptions proved to be wrong.

However, Russia has learned from its early mistakes in the first two years of the war and rebooted its command structure, weapons systems, propaganda machine, and economy to fight a protracted conflict. Many European leaders, such as President Emmanuel Macron of France, do not believe the Russian Army will stop if it overruns Ukraine. The cover page of *The Economist* for May 4, 2024, featuring a photograph of Macron, bore the cover line "Europe in Mortal Danger," which suggests European elites are now more frightened by Russian aggression than at any time since the 1940s.

For years, the Western democracies ignored the Kremlin's expansionary ambitions, the worldwide reach of Russian cyber warfare and black operations, and the grievances that Putin himself has expressed multiple times against the West, particularly at the Munich Security Conferences as described in Michael Stuermer's book *Putin and the Rise of Russia*. These grievances were rooted in, among other factors, Putin's personal experience in East Germany. He and other mid-level KGB operatives were traumatized as the USSR and its satellite Communist states in Eastern Europe and Central Asia collapsed in 1990 and 1991. Putin and his fellow operatives watched with horror as their world disappeared overnight; they destroyed their police files in East Germany and fled the country. In a matter of a year, the population of the Soviet Union itself shrank by more than 50% from 290 million to 142 million people in Russia proper. The borders of the Russian state that Vladimir Putin inherited resembled Russia before the reign of Catherine the Great in the second half of the eighteenth century rather than the Russia of the nineteenth and twentieth centuries, whether Tsarist or Communist. Russia's Warsaw Pact with occupied "allies" in Central and Eastern Europe dissolved as these countries threw off Soviet control in a chain of uprisings that swept across the region in little more than a year. Most of these states later joined the NATO alliance and the European Union as newly independent democratic capitalist nations because they feared a future revanchist Russian expansionism, fears now being realized with the second invasion of Ukraine.

Putin has sought to return Russia to great power status by weakening other competing powers or annexing neighboring states *rather* than risking reforms that could be destabilizing in the short term, but that would strengthen Russia as a nation state over the long term. The immediate objectives of Russian foreign policy are not mysterious if one examines Putin's public rhetoric, and Moscow's published documents and external behavior. A study of eleven European countries' intelligence services assessments (from 2014 to 2018) concluded that Moscow's strategic objectives include neutralizing or breaking up the NATO alliance and the European Union, destabilizing European democracies by interfering in their elections, initiating cyberattacks against Western businesses and energy infrastructure, and spreading disinformation that damages public confidence in Western institutions.[26]

As this book will show, Russia's foreign policy seeks to

- dismantle the existing liberal international political and economic order;
- gain military parity with the United States;

- create an alternate illiberal, authoritarian, reactionary governance model of statehood for which Russia is trying to gain adherents among far-right and far-left parties in Europe (and around the world); and
- reconstruct the historic Russian empire by annexing neighboring states.

Putin has ruthlessly pursued these objectives, using some of Russia's vast natural resources to rebuild the Russian military and create a powerful cyber warfare capacity (as described by Scott Jasper in chapter 4) to pursue asymmetrical attacks against the West, neighboring independent states, and other vulnerable countries.

Did Russia face a serious threat from the Western democracies prior to the first Ukraine invasion? US military presence in Europe in 2014 before the first invasion of Ukraine was at its lowest level since before World War II, down from a high of 400,000 during the peak of the Cold War.[27] After the first invasion of Ukraine, US troops in Europe rose from approximately 30,000 at the end of 2016 to 100,000 by 2024. Even more significant than any real or imagined threat Putin saw coming from the United States before the first Ukraine invasion is that the American military under President Barack Obama was going through major budget cuts. By the end of the Obama administration, the US defense budget had been cut by nearly 25%.[28] Although it increased substantially under Donald Trump, most of the additional spending was for increased salaries and maintenance. The defense budget modestly increased under the Biden administration until the second invasion of Ukraine, after which the increases rose more rapidly. Thus, the United States was not engaged prior to the second Ukraine invasion in an arms race to bankrupt Russia as it was during the Reagan administration.

Many European countries' military forces had been scaled back to such a degree they had undertaken virtually unilateral disarmament. Russia's aggressive expansionism with the first and second invasions of Ukraine, its rapid increase in its defense budget, the annexation of Crimea, the rebuilding of its nuclear arsenal, and its military intervention in Syria have all been undertaken with no self-evident threat to Russia's survival or vital national interests until the second invasion of Ukraine mobilized most of the industrialized Western democracies against Russia.

As Medvedev has argued in *The Return of the Russian Leviathan*, if Putin's strategic objective was to minimize or reduce external threats to Russia, the second invasion of Ukraine was a major strategic blunder because it mobilized the previously docile and distracted Western alliance to counter the new threat. NATO member states began to rearm. Within months of the second invasion, Sweden and Finland abandoned a historic policy of neutrality and began the process of joining NATO.

The Russian foreign policy riddle may in fact be better explained, per some essays in this book, as a response to the power dynamics domestically and its demographic crisis rather than by external actors. These dynamics are internal, not external, threats to Putin's rule. Moscow's policies may be driven by the insecurity and illegitimacy of the small circle of oligarchs and Siloviki surrounding Putin who fear their own people more than they fear any outside threat—evidence of profound, if disguised, weakness.[29] After Putin rigged the 2012 presidential elections to ensure his return to power (he would likely have won anyway),[30] hundreds of thousands of Russians took to the streets of major cities in months of protest which Putin blamed the United States (and Hillary Clinton while she was secretary of state) for orchestrating.

Russia's Military and Cyber Warfare Buildup

Prior to the second Ukraine invasion, the two instruments of national power— Russia's military strength and the Kremlin's cyber warfare capacity—appeared on the ascendancy, according to chapters 3 and 4.[31] But when the war came Russia's strategic planning was weak, coordination among the services nearly nonexistent, and its manpower pool for its army seriously constrained. Its air force failed to dominate the skies, and its command and control proved problematic. The Russian losses of tanks, Armored Personnel Carriers (APCs), trucks, and aircraft in the early phases of the second invasion were staggering (see chapter 3).

Even the much-feared, supposedly invincible hypersonic missiles Russia developed, known as the Kinzhal, turned out to be a lot less of a threat after the Ukrainian Air Defense shot down six of them in May 2023 using US-made Patriot anti-aircraft missiles. The three Russian scientists who developed the hypersonic missile were subsequently arrested on charges of treason, once again to send a message to the public that secret conspiracies were responsible for Russian failures instead of Putin's policies or the superiority of Western defense technologies.

The rising Russian military threat was on display in the country's two invasions of Ukraine and annexation of Crimea, but Moscow miscalculated in several critical respects. According to Moscow's propaganda, a corrupt and illegitimate government had taken power in Ukraine through street demonstrations while Putin's democratically elected ally in Kyiv was driven from office by mob rule funded by billionaire George Soros and Western civil society groups. Putin expected to be greeted by much of Ukraine as a Slavic liberating hero because eastern Ukraine has historically been more oriented toward Russia. Instead, Russia met Ukrainian resistance and united what had been a divided country into one mobilized to resist the second Russian invasion (see chapter 9). Multiple independent surveys of Ukrainian public opinion show more than 90% of the population opposed the Russian invasion and wanted Russian troops to leave the country. President Volodymyr Zelensky showed a 91% approval rating[32] in Ukraine weeks into the second invasion, compared with public support at 24.7% in late 2021.[33]

The Russian military showed more weaknesses than strengths in the first two years of the second Russo-Ukrainian war, but that changed in later 2023 when Putin took the decision to mobilize Russia for a long-term war, a term Putin did not use in the first year but did in 2023 and 2024.

Russia's new cyber warfare capabilities, described in chapter 4, were on display in 2016 during the US presidential election, the Dutch and French elections, and German parliament hacking incidents. Perhaps the most authoritative public document describing Russian attempts to influence the 2016 US elections may be found in the indictment submitted in federal court by US Special Counsel Robert Mueller on February 16, 2018, against three Russian corporations and thirteen individuals employed by or affiliated with those corporations.

One of these corporations, Internet Research Agency, owned by Wagner Group founder and commander Yevgeny Prigozhin (now deceased), sought to manipulate American voters by creating social media pages that were focused on divisive issues such as immigration, race, and religion and appeared to be controlled by US political activists. Starting in 2014, Internet Research Agency's employees created false personas on Facebook, Twitter, and other platforms to post on these pages. The company also purchased advertisements online to direct individuals to these pages (funded through US Bank and PayPal accounts established under stolen US identities), and posed as US grassroots organizations to stage political rallies.

Closer to the election, employees were instructed to post material supporting Donald Trump and Bernie Sanders and to disparage Hillary Clinton, Marco Rubio, and Ted Cruz, who were much more hostile to Russia under Putin. Even after the election, the company coordinated rallies to protest the results and stir up political discord. It was an effort to use the open society, open information, and public discourse of the United States against itself, not simply to support one candidate over another. One of the statutes that the Russian operatives were accused of violating was the Foreign Agents Registration Act (FARA), a law enacted in 1938 to uncover and prosecute Nazi propaganda efforts in the United States. The use of this anti-Nazi law to charge the Russians was one more indication of the state of Russian–American relations, and the threat Russian interference posed.

Destabilizing Russia's Neighbors

Prior to the second Ukraine invasion, Russia encouraged and facilitated refugee flows from the Middle East to the borders of Europe, presumably to destabilize the Western democracies. NATO Supreme Allied Commander General Philip M. Breedlove, in testimony before a US Senate Committee in March 2016, declared, "Together, Russia and the Assad regime are deliberately weaponizing migration in an attempt to overwhelm European structures and break European resolve." Breedlove said that he could see no purpose behind the Russian bombing of purely civilian targets in Syria. He argued these attacks were a tactic to increase refugee flows to Europe in order to destabilize the European political system and strengthen extremist political movements on the continent, many of which are pro-Putin. In 2015 and 2016, Russia facilitated the movement of Syrian and Iraqi refugees to the borders of Finland, and later Norway, where they were pushed across. A similar Russian strategy may have been at work, according to chapter 10, in causing massive refugee flows from Ukraine to Europe during the second Russian invasion. One of the major forces driving European voters to embrace far right-wing and neo-Nazi fringe parties has been the influx of refugees and migrants, more than 2 million of whom arrived in European countries (well before the Ukraine invasions), as well as the subsequent violent terrorist incidents or attacks against women that are being blamed on these migrants.[34]

Domestic Threats to Putin's Rule

Prior to the second invasion of Ukraine, Vladimir Putin appeared to be a towering figure of autocratic and decisive strength amidst a field of weak, diminished, and distracted Western democratic leaders. The second Ukraine War has tarnished that image.

The collapse of Russia as a state because of an unresolved succession crisis or infighting within the Siloviki, should Putin die or be removed from power, could unleash chaos and have terrible humanitarian consequences for the Russian people. It could also increase the risk of its weapons of mass destruction getting into the wrong hands. Because the second invasion of Ukraine has gone so poorly for the Russian forces, at least initially, fissures in the security apparatus have made their way into the public arena, which could be an early sign of an unravel-

Introduction 15

ing of central government control. In May 2023, Yevgeny Prigozhin, the founder and then-leader of the Wagner Group—a force of 50,000 private mercenary troops outside the command structure of the Russian armed forces—publicly and repeatedly attacked the (now former) defense minister, Sergei Shoigu, and chief of the general staff, Valery Gerasimov. He called them incompetent and denigrated their supposedly plush lifestyle and failure to provide adequate weapons and ammunition to his soldiers. *The Washington Post* reported the CIA had intelligence that Prigozhin offered Ukrainian forces the location of Russian troop emplacements if they would allow his army to take Bakhmut, a story Prigozhin denied.[35] In early June, Prigozhin accused Russian troops of planting landmines and firing on Wagner troops withdrawing from Bakhmut, and by July 2023, his troops marched on Moscow, coming within 125 miles of the city. They finally ended their short rebellion after Putin went on national television to condemn their actions.[36]

The nascent institutions Putin has weakened or destroyed under his tenure may be unable to stabilize the country in the event of such an internal crisis. Because there are no permanent governing institutions or norms in Russia, few outsiders know who Putin's real successor would be (the Constitution says that the prime minister would assume power if the president dies in office, but Russian governments often do not follow the provisions of their constitutions).

Western policymakers and opinion-makers have focused much analytical attention on the idiosyncratic rule of Putin as the leader of Russia, but they have devoted limited attention to who will likely be his successor. One thing is for certain: it will not be a Russian version of Thomas Jefferson or Abraham Lincoln. It most likely will be someone from the Siloviki, who could be more hardline and autocratic than Putin. The Putinist state system has elevated the size, power, and influence of the Siloviki, which will have heavy influence on who becomes Putin's successor. As Stephen Kotkin has pointed out, Russia has been cursed with malevolent leaders for much of its history. And thus this book's analysis will not change much when Putin leaves office, however that happens.

Russia's future will be to some degree determined by how Putin's invasion of Ukraine ends. If the United States and the European democracies abandon Ukraine to the Russian military, it will be an invitation to Putin for more aggression. If the Russian military overruns Ukraine despite Western support and then turns its sights on Moldova, and then to the NATO members, the Baltic states and Poland, a Great Power war in Europe may ensue as Article 5 of the NATO treaty will then be operative. Under the NATO treaty, if one member state is attacked, all are attacked, and the other states are obligated to intervene to defend. If the

NATO member states fail to respond to such an attack, the European security architecture that has kept the peace for seventy-five years will collapse. A treaty is a piece of paper, and has force only if the signatories have the political will to enforce its provisions. Tim Snyder, historian of central Europe, the Soviet Union, and Russia, made these very arguments in a lecture at a conference in Estonia on May 2024. If Ukraine's front line holds and the Russian military is held back, a new Great War may be avoided. If Ukraine wins back all the territory it lost during the second Russian invasion (or even the first invasion, however unlikely that may be), the Siloviki networks may remove Putin from office as his gamble in starting the second war has come at a terrible cost in Russian blood and treasure. By its third year, the conflict has devolved into a war of attrition. Given that Russia has more than three times the population of Ukraine (and North Korea is now sending troops to the front supporting Russian forces), they will be able to absorb far more casualties—which Putin appears willing to do. Only time will tell how it ends.

Thus, in response to the question posed by this book—is Russia a fragile or dysfunctional state or a twenty-first-century revisionist power?—the answer is that it is both. The issue for Vladimir Putin and his successors is and will be that the gap between Russian grand strategy and its internal fragility is growing more pronounced as the Russo-Ukrainian War has unfolded. But to paraphrase Nicholas Eberstadt at the conclusion of chapter 6, a great many things can happen that are not pleasant to contemplate before this gap leads to Russia's failure.

Thanks to many people who played important roles in the reviewing, editing and production of this book. Laura Davulis, editor at Johns Hopkins University Press, has been instrumental in seeing this book through to publication. Kassandra Maduzia, the Scowcroft Institute's administrative coordinator, served as a preliminary production editor for this book, ensuring each of the stages were completed properly on time. Monica Holder, assistant director of the Scowcroft Institute, has skillfully managed the Bush School contracting and financing processes internally to finish the book. Professor Joe Golsan, the editor of the *South Central Review*, encouraged me to transform the journal essays he'd previously published there into a book and introduced me to Hopkins Press editors to facilitate the process. Professor Nicholas Lawrence at the University of South Carolina Lancaster served as copy editor for the manuscript on late notice. Cate Stackhouse, Hayden Upchurch, Jake Brien, Kathrine Carwile, and other graduate students at the Bush School, as well as my graduate assistants, did extensive research for chapter 10 and for this introduction. Thanks also goes to Dr. Sarah Misemer, who served as coeditor with me of the 2018 essays in the *South Central Review*, for her fine editing skills. Thanks also to Dr. Raymond Robertson and Ambassador Larry Napper, professors at the Bush School, and Dr. Desaix "Terry" Myers, retired senior foreign service officer who also served as USAID Mission Director in Russia in the mid-2000s, all of whom commented on some of the chapters, and Nick Eberstadt, who inspired my argument through his scholarship and analysis. None of them are responsible for my errors or misjudgments.

NOTES

1. See Pascal Bruckner, "The Return of the Enemy," *South Central Review* 35, no. 1 (2018): 35–47.

2. This was the term used by Russian human rights and NGO leaders I met with (as USAID administrator) in November 2005 in Moscow.

3. Kimberly Marten, "Putin's Choices: Explaining Russian Foreign Policy and Intervention in Ukraine," *Washington Quarterly* 38, no. 2 (2015): 189–204.

4. Douglass C. North, John Joseph Wallis, and Barry R. Weingast, "Introduction," in *Violence and Social Orders: A Conceptual Framework for Interpreting Recorded Human History* (New York: Cambridge University Press, 2009).

5. See Nicholas Eberstadt's essay, "A Statistical Glimpse at Russia's Multiple Demographic and Human Resource Problems," *South Central Review* 35, no. 1 (2018): 147–174.

6. Paul Collier, *The Bottom Billion: Why the Poorest Countries Are Failing and What Can Be Done About It*, 1st ed. (New York: Oxford University Press, 2008). Also see Steven Lee Myers, *The New Tsar: The Rise and Reign of Vladimir Putin* (New York: Alfred A. Knopf, 2015), 364–368.

7. Karen Dawisha, *Putin's Kleptocracy: Who Owns Russia?* (New York: Simon & Schuster Paperbacks, 2014).

8. Collier, *The Bottom Billion*.

9. Paul Gregory, "A Reassessment of Putin's Russia: The Economy," *South Central Review* 35, no. 1 (2018): 175–195.

10. Max Seddon, Christopher Miller, and Felicia Schwartz, "How Putin Blundered into Ukraine—Then Doubled Down," *Financial Times*, February 23, 2023, https://www .ft.com/content/80002564-33e8-48fb-b734-44810afb7a49?s=09.

11. Andrew C. Kuchins, "Dead Journalists in Putin's Russia," *Center for Strategic and International Studies*, March 19, 2007, https://www.csis.org/analysis/dead-journalists -putins-russia.

12. Connor Surmonte, "At Least 39 Russian Oligarchs, Scientists & Generals Dead under Mysterious Circumstances after Criticizing Putin's War in Ukraine," *Radar*, March 13, 2023, https://radaronline.com/p/39-russian-oligarchs-scientists-generals-dead -mysterious-circumstances-criticizing-putin-war-ukraine/.

13. Aria Bendix, "Gunman Who Killed Boris Nemtsov Receives 20-Year Prison Sentence," *The Atlantic*, July 13, 2017, https://www.theatlantic.com/news/archive/2017/07/gunman-who-killed-boris-nemtsov-sentenced-to-20-years-in-prison/533652/.

14. Gregory, "A Reassessment of Putin's Russia."

15. "Russia GDP Annual Growth Rate," *Trading Economics*, 2017, https://tradingeconomics.com/russia/gdp-growth-annual.

16. Anders Åslund, "How Russia Stays Afloat," *Project Syndicate*, November 28, 2016, https://www.project-syndicate.org/commentary/putin-russian-sanctions-economy-by-anders-aslund-2016-11.

17. During a conference at the Bush School of Government at Texas A&M University titled The Fall of the Berlin Wall, the Reunification of Germany, and the End of the Cold War, German Chancellor Helmut Kohl's national security advisor, Horst Teltschik, described these requests by Gorbachev to Kohl.

18. "Russia," in *The World Factbook* (Central Intelligence Agency, May 31, 2022), https://www.cia.gov/the-world-factbook/countries/russia/#economy.

19. Daniel Yergin, "The Struggle Behind Oil's Ups and Downs," *Wall Street Journal*, May 16, 2017, https://www.wsj.com/articles/the-struggle-behind-oils-ups-and-downs-1494976842.

20. Joseph Zeballos-Roig, "The U.S. Rolls Out Fresh Sanctions Meant to Block Putin from Accessing a $630 Billion 'War Chest' He Could Use to Prop Up a Battered Economy," *Business Insider*, February 28, 2022, https://www.businessinsider.com/us-putin-sanctions-russia-central-bank-war-chest-ukraine-crisis-2022-2.

21. Curt Tarnoff, "U.S. Assistance to the Former Soviet Union," vol. RL32866 (Congressional Research Service, Library of Congress, 2007), https://sgp.fas.org/crs/row/RL32866.pdf.

22. See, for instance, Philip D. Zelikow, "A Reply to President Putin," *The American Interest*, July 31, 2020, https://www.the-american-interest.com/2020/07/31/a-reply-to-president-putin/.

23. See John J. Mearsheimer, "Why the Ukraine Crisis Is the West's Fault," *Foreign Affairs*, September/October 2014, https://www.foreignaffairs.com/articles/russia-fsu/2014-08-18/why-ukraine-crisis-west-s-fault.

24. David Remnick, "The Weakness of the Despot: An Expert on Stalin Discusses Putin, Russia, and the West," *New Yorker*, March 11, 2022, https://www.newyorker.com/news/q-and-a/stephen-kotkin-putin-russia-ukraine-stalin.

25. Sergei Medvedev, *The Return of the Russian Leviathan* (New York: Polity, 2019).

26. Geir Hågen Karlsen, "Divide and Rule: Ten Lessons about Russian Political Influence Activities in Europe," *Palgrave Communications* 5, no. 1 (Feb. 2019), https://www.nature.com/articles/s41599-019-0227-8.

27. Becky Sullivan, "Explaining the U.S. Military Presence in Europe as 2,000 More Troops Deploy," *NPR.org*, February 4, 2022, https://www.npr.org/2022/02/04/1078241901/us-troops-europe-ukraine-russia-crisis.

28. James Carafano, "Yes: Obama-Era Cuts Left U.S. Too Weak to Deal with Multiple Global Menaces," Heritage Foundation, March 24, 2017, https://www.heritage.org/defense/commentary/yes-obama-era-cuts-left-us-too-weak-deal-multiple-global-menaces.

29. See Anne Applebaum, "Putin's Grand Strategy," *South Central Review* 35, no. 1 (2018): 22–34.

30. John Hudson, "How Putin Tipped the Scales of the Russian Election," *The Atlantic*, March 6, 2012, https://www.theatlantic.com/international/archive/2012/03/how-putin-tipped-scales-russian-election/330916/.

31. See Dave Majumdar, "Did Russia Just Cut Its Defense Budget by a Whopping 25 Percent?," *The National Interest*, March 20, 2017, https://nationalinterest.org/blog/the-buzz/did-russia-just-cut-its-defense-budget-by-whopping-25-19831.

32. Afiq Fitri, "How President Zelensky's Approval Ratings Have Surged," *New Statesman*, March 1, 2022, https://www.newstatesman.com/chart-of-the-day/2022/03/how-president-zelenskys-approval-ratings-have-surged.

33. Mykhailo Minakov, "Just Like All the Others: The End of the Zelensky Alternative?", Wilson Center, November 2, 2021, https://www.wilsoncenter.org/blog-post/just-all-others-end-zelensky-alternative.

34. Ann-Sofie Dahl, "A Continent in Chaos: The Security Implications of the European Migrant Crisis," Scowcroft Institute of International Affairs, June 2016, https://oaktrust.library.tamu.edu/server/api/core/bitstreams/286ef526-41a9-4106-87ea-eb91ab05a175/content.

35. Shane Harris and Isabelle Khurshudyan, "Wagner Chief Offered to Give Russian Troop Locations to Ukraine, Leak Says." *Washington Post*, May 15, 2023, https://www.washingtonpost.com/national-security/2023/05/14/prigozhin-wagner-ukraine-leaked-documents/.

36. Matthew Loh, "Wagner Boss Yevgeny Prigozhin Is Accusing the Kremlin of Planting Landmines to Blow Up his Troops as They Left Bakhmut," *Business Insider*, June 5, 2023, https://www.businessinsider.com/wagner-boss-prigozhin-kremlin-planted-mines-blow-up-troops-bakhmut-2023-6.

PART I / The Russian State Under Putin

Chapter One

Russia's Domestic Politics Under Putin

Kathryn Stoner

R ussia's domestic political system has been both a help and a hindrance in realizing its foreign policy aims over the last two decades. On the one hand, the increasingly personalistic autocratic system of governance that has evolved under Vladimir Putin since 2000 has enabled quick decision-making (the seizure of Crimea from Ukraine in 2014, military mobilization in Syria in 2015, and the full invasion of Ukraine beginning in 2022) in a bid to remake the international system. Inevitably, however, many of those decisions were bad for the promotion of Russian national interests. Therefore, in addressing the question as to whether Russia under Putin is a revolutionary power seeking to alter the international system or a dysfunctional state, the answer is that it is both. The fact that the state is dysfunctional and governed by a corrupt, now highly centralized and personalistic autocracy necessarily thwarts the regime's aspirations to recast the post–Cold War international system. As a result, Putin's Russia is at best a disruptive global force, but not a transformational one.

Despite the presence on paper of formal institutions of accountable government, like political parties, regular elections, the separation of executive, legislative, and judicial branches of government, and freedom of speech and the press, in practice, all of these trappings of transparency, equity, and accountability have eroded steadily since Putin succeeded Boris Yeltsin as Russia's president in 2000. By 2012, after castling the positions of president and prime minister, respectively, with his protégé, Dmitry Medvedev, Putin returned to the Kremlin with a vigorous new attack on civil society, the media, and what remained of a true political opposition. Evidently still nervous about any form of potential opposition to his regime, in 2020, he reframed the constitution to restrict civil liberties even further and to extend his presidency for an additional two terms. His reelection (with an improbable 87.3% of the vote) in March 2024 over Kremlin-approved opponents gave him the first of those two six-year terms, keeping him in office through 2030. He could, however, serve an additional term and rule to 2036, at which time he will be eighty-three years old.

In the almost quarter-century that Putin has served at the apex of the political system, Russia has become a consolidated, highly personalistic authoritarian system based on a complicated network of patron-client ties. The lack of accountability and transparency in the political system has meant rife corruption in many (though not all) Russian bureaucracies, little resistance to presidential decisions in the face of a now fully disemboweled civil society, nonexistent opposition parties, the elimination of a free press, and a truly rubber-stamp legislative branch in the Duma.

Although the trajectory toward autocracy began early in Putin's long tenure as Russia's leader, its downward slope toward a highly repressive form of authoritarianism has intensified dramatically since Russia invaded Ukraine on February 24, 2022, after the initial seizure of Crimea in 2014. The Economist Intelligence Unit (EIU) reported that Russia suffered "the biggest democratic decline of any country in the world" in 2022, tumbling twenty-two places to the rank of 146 (just ahead of Venezuela) out of 167 countries on the EIU's Democracy Index.[1]

In what follows, this chapter examines how Russia's political system has evolved since the collapse of the Soviet Union in 1991 and its deepening autocratization under Putin since he first rose to the Russian presidency in 2000. It concludes with an evaluation of the relative strengths and vulnerabilities of Putin's regime.

From the Disordered 1990s to the Dictatorship of Law . . . and Then to Dictatorship

When the Soviet Union collapsed in December 1991, Russia's first elected president, Boris Yeltsin, prepared to launch massive political, economic, and social reforms in what was then and remains the largest country, geographically speaking, on the planet. Unsurprisingly, given the challenges that he had inherited from seventy-four years of communism and six years of halting reform under the last general secretary of the Communist Party of the Soviet Union, Mikhail Gorbachev, the ensuing eight years of his leadership of the new Russian Federation were tumultuous to say the least. Yeltsin initially faced a fractious Congress of People's Deputies, elected under an old Soviet-era constitution that was dominated by the new Communist Party of the Russian Federation (CPRF), which opposed his initial reform attempts at almost every turn. By the autumn of 1993, he had had enough and used the Russian military to disband the congress such that by early December of that year, Russian voters were asked to ratify a new constitution as well as vote for the newly created lower house of parliament (the Duma). To avoid the intransigence Yeltsin faced in the previous parliament, the new constitution created a strong presidential system, where the president could dismiss the legislature if its members failed on the third attempt to accept the president's proposed candidate for the post of prime minister. The constitution also allowed the president to rule by decree in some policy areas, as well as to directly appoint the "power ministries" (including the Federal Security Service, the Foreign Intelligence Service, the Ministry of the Interior, and the Ministry of Defense) without the need for Duma oversight, to name but a few of its provisions.

Despite the sweeping authority granted to the presidency, Yeltsin nonetheless faced a new parliament in the Duma that was also dominated by opposition parties intent on thwarting many of his reform efforts. Politics and elections were fractious, fueled by a newly enabled media environment and a civil society that had grown quickly and become highly mobilized, partly on the back of Gorbachev's 1980s-era glasnost reforms. Civil society organizations also thrived as a result of an influx of foreign support from private foundations in the European Union and the United States, as well as developed democratic governments anxious to shore up the nascent democracy that seemed to be developing under Yeltsin. These funds went toward attempts to create a rule of law, including training judges and developing a jury trial system, for example, as well as training political parties on organization, electoral tactics, and strategy. Other funding was directed toward ensuring free and fair elections and providing other forms of transparency of state functions.

Political parties proliferated in Yeltsin's early years; elections took place regularly, and while not perfect, they were largely free and fair. By 1996 and Yeltsin's second run for the presidency, however, there was concern that he might not triumph over the Communist Party candidate, Gennady Zyuganov, at a time when massive neoliberal-based economic reforms were causing tremendous economic difficulty for all but a few Russian voters. The economic transformation was deep, sometimes radical, and unquestionably painful for the average citizen. Russia's short-lived attempt at "shock therapy," which began with price liberalization in

January 1992, has been well-documented elsewhere.[2] The high percentages of the population living at or below the official poverty level between 1992 and 2000 varied from 20% to 30%. State-sector pensions and wages in the early 1990s went unpaid for months at a time as the Russian government struggled to impose a stiffer macroeconomic policy and fiscal constraints. Also well known is the story of Russia's controversial privatization program for small and medium enterprises between 1994 and 1996, which benefited the few at the expense of the many and caused major disillusion among the Russian citizenry regarding capitalism and democracy.

This period also bred an oligarchical class of Russian businessmen, a group that operated under largely unregulated economic conditions, some of whom were linked to political decision-making through the types of shady deals that were endemic in the period. A prime example is the Yeltsin government's 1996 loans-for-shares program, which transformed a small cadre of oligarchs who helped bail out the government into billionaires by giving them major shares in the gems of the Russian economy.[3] They owned media conglomerates and other valuable formerly state assets, had created banks that helped them further amass tremendous personal riches, and extended loans to the deeply indebted Yeltsin government, which used some of the Russian economy's most valuable assets as collateral. This enabled them to become even wealthier when the government ultimately defaulted on the loans. The funding may have, however, ensured Yeltsin's reelection in 1996, but he appeared to have transferred control of the jewels of the Russian economy to the oligarchs as part of the deal. All of this happened just as the government defaulted in 1998 on its domestic international loan commitments, causing the crash of the ruble and regular people to lose most of their savings as a result.[4]

Thus, when Vladimir Putin emerged from relative political obscurity in the autumn of 1999 as Russia's newly appointed prime minister under the ailing Boris Yeltsin and was then named by Yeltsin as his preferred successor for president, Russians were ready for political and economic stability. But as much as Yeltsin thought Putin would be a competent leader, he was also looking for a reliable successor possibly to protect himself and his family (rumored to be under investigation themselves for corruption) once out of office. In a surprise telecast at midnight on December 31, 1999, Yeltsin announced that he would be resigning the presidency effective January 1, 2000, and that Vladimir Putin would become acting president until an election could be held later in the year. In his own New Year's address very shortly thereafter, and in subsequent speeches and articles, Putin promised stability, and it was a welcome change for most Russians at the time.[5]

Putin also appeared to understand what ailed the Russian system. Just before he unexpectedly assumed the acting presidency in 2000, he published his economic dreams for Russia in the short paper "Russia at the Turn of the Millennium."[6] Putin was acutely aware of the economic challenges Russia faced at the time and began this remarkable essay by noting how far backward Russia had fallen in the 1990s, lamenting its former status as a global power in the Imperial and Soviet eras. He recognized Russia's dangerous economic dependence on raw materials extraction. Consistently measuring Russia in relation to China and the United States, he noted, "Labor productivity in the real economy sector is extremely low. While our production of raw materials and electricity is close to the world average, our productivity in other industries is much lower—for instance, at 20–24% of US indicators." Another issue was low foreign investment, which, as he stated, amounted to slightly more than $11.5 billion, whereas China received as much as $43 billion.[7]

He also pointed to the low proportion and low output of enterprises engaged in innovative production, noting that "Foreign competitors have pushed Russia especially far back in the market of high-tech civilian commodities. Russia accounts for less than 1% of such products on the world market, whereas the US provides 36% and Japan 30%." He recognized the dramatic fall in Russian living standards, stating, "There has been a steady decline in real incomes since the beginning of reforms. The greatest plummet was registered after the August 1998 crisis . . . Currently, Russians' total monetary income, calculated by UN methods, adds up to less than 10% of the analogous figure for a US resident."

At least in 1999, Putin blamed not the flaws of Yeltsin's governments in the 1990s, as he would later, but rather the "excesses" of the Soviet system—its distortions and excessive reliance on revenues from oil, gas, gold, diamonds, and other raw materials; its focus on heavy industry as opposed to consumer products and services; and the fact that it did not require competition among producers, thus hindering scientific and technological progress that could have boosted the Russian economy's competitiveness in world markets after the Soviet system ultimately collapsed in 1991.

To the average Russian, Putin's diagnosis of what ailed the Russian economy, coupled with his emphasis on restoring a strong state and social stability, sounded right on the mark. Remarkably, in about eight months between autumn of 1999 and spring of 2000, Vladimir Putin went from a political unknown who had never contested an election—national or regional—to the president of the country, garnering almost 53% of the vote, avoiding a second-round runoff with Zyuganov of the Communists.[8] A new political party, Unity (now known as United Russia), was created in December 1999 to boost legislative support in anticipation of the new president. It did surprisingly well, although it fell short of a majority in the Duma. Over time, however, United Russia would come to dominate the legislature. Gone forever would be the days of a Russian president facing a recalcitrant parliament.

Promising a "dictatorship of law," Putin's initial emphasis was on rebuilding Russian state capacity and governing competence. This was to some degree a response to popular demand and acceptance for a time that "any order is better than disorder."[9] Aleksandar Matovski has convincingly argued that a majority of Russians consistently expressed clear preferences for order and stability, especially given the "extraordinary trauma that stemmed from Russia's cataclysmic decline since the late 1980s."[10] Yet stability came in exchange for a narrowing of the civic rights and social and political freedoms that had been introduced in the 1990s under Yeltsin, as well as the gradual curtailment of freedom of the press and a reduction in the number of contested electoral offices at all levels of the political system.

In Russia under Putin in the early 2000s, regime legitimacy came initially from the contrast between Putin's leadership and Yeltsin's, as a younger, seemingly more capable and decisive president. But the biggest contrast was in the economic performance of the 1990s under Yeltsin's uneven reforms, including a privatization process that was largely viewed as unfair by a majority of Russian citizens, versus the tremendous economic boom of 2003–2008 during Putin's first two presidential terms.[11] In a sense, an implicit social contract developed between the people and the emerging autocracy under Putin: "You tolerate a rollback of rights and freedoms of the 1990s and I will ensure that the country is stable and the economy is growing."[12] Revenues from the rise in global oil prices pumped money through the economy, Russian standards of living increased, while freedoms of the press, of speech, of association and rule of law steadily declined without much in the way of popular opposition.[13] This would change, however, by 2012, as explained later in this chapter.

The initial winnowing of the already weak representative institutions that existed when Boris Yeltsin left the Kremlin in December 1999 began not long after Putin's first inauguration in 2000. Indeed, the methodical approach to dissembling checks on the state's control over society during Putin's first administration (2000–2004) reads like an autocrat's "playbook" on how to undermine institutions of democracy and accountability. The first target was the Russian media, which, in the 1990s, had been bought up by a small group of wealthy businessmen (the original Russian oligarchs) who had made their money through the vagaries of the privatization process. They benefited in particular from the loans-for-shares scheme in 1996, as noted above. Two of them, Boris Berezovsky, who ironically had helped to bring Vladimir Putin to the attention of Yeltsin's inner circle in 1996, and Vladimir Gusinsky, created huge media conglomerates from what had formerly been Soviet state-owned TV channels and newspapers. Naturally, they used their positions to influence the editorial line and ideally bend policy in their favor.

Days after Vladimir Putin's inauguration in the spring of 2000, Gusinsky's Media Most conglomerate, which included a leading independent television station (NTV), was raided by armed battle-ready tax police.[14] Gusinsky himself was arrested on fraud charges. By the fall of 2000, he had left Russia permanently, handing over control of his assets to the state-owned gas conglomerate, Gazprom. The following year, Berezovsky was indicted himself and eventually sold off his remaining shares in ORT, his television station. He fled Russia, eventually landing in the United Kingdom, where he died in his ex-wife's bathroom in 2013.[15]

Not only did the Kremlin's actions serve to emasculate two powerful oligarchs who, in Putin's estimation, had become far too influential over Russian politics and the economy, but it also enabled the increasingly centralized Russian state to reestablish control of the traditional mass media and thus to control the flow of information from the regime to the Russian public. In addition, this initial curbing of the authority of many of Russia's richest men proved popular to many Russians who felt they had been ripped off by the economic reforms of the 1990s while others had prospered by taking advantage of a vague legal environment. So, when Putin used not only the interior ministry but tax authorities to raid oligarchs' media conglomerates and banks, the general public supported what seemed initially to be the correction of some of the wrongs of the previous decade.

Other wealthy Russian businessmen were brought to heel by similar means. In two meetings with the new president, the oligarchs of the 1990s (Russia's richest men) were told that the rules of business influencing politics were now changing under Putin's administration. If they stayed out of politics, then the regime Putin was constructing would stay out of their businesses.[16] It was too late for Gusinsky, but others got the message and managed to survive, businesses largely intact. The wealthiest among them, Mikhail Khodorkovsky, however, continued to finance opposition political parties and civil society organizations in addition to owning some of the most valuable companies in the Russian economy. He was taken down by the regime's selective application of the law. In October 2003, he was arrested and charged with tax evasion, fraud, and embezzlement. The state quickly dismantled his Yukos empire and effectively repossessed most of the rest of his businesses, including oil and gas holdings, banks, and media. Khodorkovsky's subsequent ten-year sentence to a labor colony in Siberia served as an example to others who had made their money in exactly the same way in the 1990s: if they failed to comply with the unofficial rules of the new regime, then they would lose everything too.[17]

Khodorkovsky was released in December 2013 just prior to the Sochi Winter Olympics, and now leads an opposition movement to Putin from outside the country. Others like Mikhail Fridman, Vladimir Potanin, Roman Abramovich, Mikhail Prokhorov, and Oleg Deripaska managed to retain their fortunes by maintaining good relations with the Kremlin, which has become more or less their only option for retaining any of their wealth since coming under international sanctions and freezes on their assets held abroad since the start of the February 2022 invasion of Ukraine.

Most average Russians felt no sympathy for Khodorkovsky, Gusinsky, Berezovsky, and other so-called oligarchs, who had made billions while most of the rest of society suffered the full financial brunt of the collapse of communism and Yeltsin's uneven reforms.[18] On the back of this strike against this group of ultra-wealthy men, and in a stroke of luck for Putin's young regime, by 2003, global oil prices began a multiyear climb. The revenue that flowed into the country's economy rapidly increased economic growth and the incomes of ordinary Russians, and Putin's personal public approval soared in this period, reaching a high for the preceding three years of 86% only a month or so after Khodorkovsky's arrest in late October of 2003.[19]

After bringing much, but not all (at least not yet) of the independently owned media under state control and bringing the oligarchs under control, Putin's next move targeted political pluralism by establishing the supremacy of a ruling party that would tame any recalcitrance against the executive branch of government in the Duma, Russia's lower house of parliament. The Russian constitution, forged in a particularly fraught moment for Yeltsin, as noted earlier, gave the executive branch extraordinary powers relative to the legislature.[20] But Yeltsin faced stiff opposition throughout his presidency, even from the new weaker parliament, and this effectively held his presidency in check. Beyond the Duma, Yeltsin also had to battle for political and economic control against the powerful governors of the then eighty-nine subnational units of the Russian Federation. Neither problem would arise for Putin, however.

Through administrative measures that made it increasingly difficult for opposition parties to gain representation in the legislature and via manipulation of election rules and outcomes themselves, Putin's party of choice, first known as Unity in 2000, as noted above, and then United Russia by 2003, managed to dominate the Duma too, eventually gaining overwhelming majorities. Whereas Yeltsin ruled against the Duma, Putin, through United Russia and vast executive power, rendered it largely irrelevant as a separate branch of government. This eliminated an alternative locus of political influence to the Kremlin.

Forms of political accountability, like opposition parties, were systematically undermined throughout the early to mid-2000s. This was accomplished through the creation of administrative hurdles for more liberally leaning opposition candidates to register in elections at the local and federal levels, the unequal access to the media for approved versus opposition candidates, and the co-optation of parties to remaining in the legislature, like the Liberal Democratic Party of Russia (neither actually liberal nor democratic) and Communist Party of the Russian Federation. When necessary, there was also sometimes outright fraud at the polls in favor of United Russia. So bad had the problem become by 2021 that even the long-loyal opposition Communists complained.[21]

Step three of the dissolution of accountable government was to eradicate the patchwork system of Russian federalism that had evolved under Yeltsin. In the 1990s, with little else to offer them, powerful elected governors had wrestled preferential tax arrangements and other special privileges from Yeltsin's administration. Under Putin, a new layer of central bureaucracy (federal districts) was put in place to prevent governors from dealing directly with the president and his administration, blocking their efforts to cut special deals for their regions. Further, no more would the upper house of parliament, the Federation Council, be populated by governors and held hostage to their agendas. Instead, the presidential administration would appoint full-time "senators" in consultation with regional legislatures and governors. In practice, this meant that senators became more dependent on the Kremlin than on the regions that they were appointed to represent.

The final blow to Russian federalism involved the selection process of governors themselves. Using the pretext of a 2004 domestic terrorist attack in the southern Caucasus town of Beslan, which was badly handled by local authorities (tragically resulting in the deaths of hundreds of children and their parents), governors would no longer be elected. Instead, they too would be appointed by the presidential administration in what was called a "vertical of power." This reform was rolled back in most regions by 2012 where reliable clients of the Kremlin could be assuredly elected, and by 2022, all but seven of the now eighty-three elected regional executives in Russia were members of United Russia or Kremlin-backed independents. The remainder were from the other three loyal opposition parties in the Duma: A Just Russia, the Liberal Democratic Party of Russia, and of course the CPRF (the Communist Party).[22] The president of Russia can also remove regional executives and appoint acting replacements. Regional legislatures are still elected, although United Russia dominates most regional parliaments.[23] There are no longer direct elections for mayors.

In parallel with the derailment of Russia's already-flagging democratic development, Putin assumed the task of rearranging the economy to construct a patronal system of control over state resources in his first two terms as president (2000–2008). With the original oligarchs swept aside, his closest associates— some from his childhood and university days in St. Petersburg, others from his career in the KGB—moved into plum positions controlling huge portions of the re-nationalizing economy. They moved freely between government and business in the absence (or in open violation) of conflict-of-interest laws that may have inhibited them privately benefiting from holding public office. Moreover, Putin's curbing of the oligarchs of the 1990s did not lead to a redistribution of what many Russians considered their ill-gotten gains stolen from the public trust. Instead, he effectively replaced one system of cronyism with another that was more firmly under his control.

The Rise of Putin's Patronal System

Putin's biography is well known.[24] Speculations on how his youth in St. Petersburg or stationing in Dresden as a lieutenant colonel in the KGB in the mid-1980s may have shaped his worldview are important, of course; but what is more important to understanding how Russia's political system has come to function is the network that he developed upon his return to St. Petersburg a few months after the collapse of the Berlin Wall in 1990.[25] It is this network that formed the basis of contemporary Russia's patronal political economy.[26]

Putin returned to his hometown from Dresden in 1990 and was hired in May of that year to advise his old law professor, Anatoly Sobchak, on his work on the Leningrad City Council. When Sobchak was elected mayor in 1991, Putin was promoted to deputy and then first deputy mayor, an unelected position he held until June 1996, when Sobchak lost his bid for reelection. With Sobchak out of the

Russia's Domestic Politics Under Putin   33

mayor's office, Putin found himself out of work. He landed an enviable job in Moscow thanks to some of his St. Petersburg contacts, however. His first position in Yeltsin's administration was to serve as deputy director of the presidential administration's international property division. From this position, he moved to serve briefly as head of the FSB (one of the Russian successor agencies to the Soviet-era KGB), a year before he was unexpectedly catapulted to the office of prime minister in August 1999. Seven months later, as already described, Putin was formally elected to the presidency—a little more than three years after he had first arrived in Moscow from St. Petersburg.

With him to the Kremlin came the network of friends from St. Petersburg. Many already had used their proximity to Putin and his position in the deputy mayor's office (which enabled him to control licenses for foreign trade) to enrich themselves and Putin too, as is strongly suspected by most observers.[27] But with their arrival in Moscow and his rapid rise to the presidency, the opportunity to control the resources of the entire Russian state now lay before them. Having removed obstacles to control, including the oligarchs of the 1990s, Putin installed his friends as heads of new quasi-state entities like Rosneft (which has long been run by his former St. Petersburg assistant, Igor Sechin) and Gazprom, where the CEO became Alexei Miller, who had served on the external relations committee with Putin in St. Petersburg. Others with KGB backgrounds oversee the vast resources of the presidential administration or have been given control over powerful agencies like the Security Council (Nikolai Patrushev, the former head of the FSB), as well as investigative agencies (Alexander Bortnikov, who has served since 2008 as head of the FSB) and the foreign intelligence agency (Sergei Naryshkin, the head of Russia's foreign intelligence agency, SVR, and who purportedly went to the KGB Higher School in St. Petersburg at the same time as Putin).

A third group of Putin's close friends from his youth in St. Petersburg became owners of sprawling conglomerates that gained preferential access to state contracts that would make them billionaires over Putin's long reign.[28] These are now some of Russia's wealthiest men (and there are no women in this group), including Arkady and Boris Rotenberg, Gennady Timchenko, and Yurii Kovalchuk. As Karen Dawisha explains, "It is this kleptocratic tribute system underlying Russia's authoritarian regime that the US government sought to expose and punish beginning in March 2014. The names of the sanctions list read like a Who's Who of Team Putin."[29] In sum, she observes, "Political leaders close to Putin have become multimillionaires, and the oligarchs around them . . . have become billionaires. . . . And these billionaires, far from being titans of industry motoring the modernization of the Russian economy, have secured and increased their wealth by relying on and bolstering the centralized power of the state."[30]

Dawisha continues, "Under this system, the state absorbs the risk, provides state funds for investment, and gives those close to the Kremlin massive monetary rewards . . . the state nationalizes the risk but continues to privatize the rewards to those closest to the president in return for their loyalty."[31] Alena Ledeneva refers to the regime as "Sistema," and Brian Taylor describes it as operating according to "The Code of Putinism."[32] Regardless of the terminology, descriptions of the system converge on one key point: "Its inner logic was focused on the protection of the wealth of those closest to the Russian president."[33]

Although Dawisha characterizes this system as a kleptocracy designed to steal assets from the state for private gain, a more fitting term to describe the entire system is *patronalism*. Patronal systems are defined not by formal institutions so much as a "politics of individual reward and punishment."[34] Power is distributed through a complex web of patron-client networks. In the Russian case, Vladimir Putin sits at the top of a pyramidal network comprised of elite relationships that divide state resources among themselves and control who gets what. Further, as Henry Hale argues, "Ultimate power in patronalistic societies can be used not only to push for policies one supports, but to direct favors to allies and to target opponents for punishment."[35] But this system is inherently fragile—and herein lies its dysfunction. Its main vulnerability is at the summit of power—if the head of state were to change, then the value of networks and their access to state resources might well decline. Thus, there is every incentive to maintain the status quo. This requires the support of clients within the network and a steady flow of favors from patrons to clients, with a share of financial rewards flowing back to patrons. But patronal systems also require stability within elite groups and within society more broadly; instability caused by social mobilization against the inequalities of wealth and access to state resources that patronalism generates is the biggest potential threat to such a system of rule. And so, as the system matured and generated sharper wealth inequalities, and as social discontent with the system spilled onto the streets from 2012 onward, Putin's system has become ever more repressive, especially as the conflict with Ukraine has intensified.[36]

Vladimir Putin vs. the People

The fates of Egypt's Hosni Mubarak and Libya's Muammar Gaddafi following the Arab Spring of 2011 attest to the fact that even autocrats with the seemingly unfettered ability to use state-sponsored violence to impose their wills on their people can suddenly be overthrown. The popularity of the autocrat (or in patronal autocracies, the biggest patron in the system) is a valuable and important power resource, as Samuel Greene and Graeme Robertson have noted.[37] If public approval is genuine, either encouraged by high growth rates or a coherent and transformational ideology, a cult of personality, and state-controlled messaging through the media, for example, then social control is relatively easy to maintain without extensive use of violence. (Stalin's funeral witnessed outpourings of true loss and hysterical devotion from the Soviet people, after all.) But failing that, the use of force and selective application of the law against any opposition are other tools that are still readily available. Putin's regime also introduced an ideology of social conservatism and nationalism and a narrative that presents Russian culture, values, and the nation itself as under threat from an aggressive, liberal West, but this arose mostly after his seizure of Crimea in 2014.

There is ample evidence that autocrats are sensitive to public opinion, and Vladimir Putin is purportedly an avid consumer of his own polling data.[38] Within contemporary Russia, despite the concentration of power within his hands, there are still many good examples of Putin's autocratic regime adapting to demands from Russian society—even changing policies that provoked street demonstrations. Two notable examples are the 2005 social benefits reform and the 2018 pension reform. In the former, the federal government was attempting to eradicate social subsidies like free public transportation, subsidized housing, prescriptions, and telephone services for millions of veterans, retirees, and people with disabilities. Instead, those eligible were to receive a small monthly cash payment that was slow to arrive and insufficient to cover the costs of the previous in-kind benefits. In the face of widespread street protests against the new law led by the elderly and disabled, Putin appeared on television to quickly make modifications that softened the program's effects.[39] Similarly, in 2018, protesters came out onto the streets in the tens of thousands to oppose a law that would raise the federal pension age for both men and women. Again, the regime retreated, and the law was modified in an attempt to quell social unrest.

In both cases, the reforms were altered but not completely eliminated.[40] Still, the regime was compelled to relent from the original versions of the policies in the face of social protests across the country. Putin's popularity was also damaged significantly. In 2018, for example, it dropped fifteen points between April (82% approval) and August (67% approval) in a difficult summer for the Kremlin that was punctuated by street protests nationwide.[41] That said, however, over the course of 2022 and the regime's mismanaged invasion of Ukraine, Putin's autocracy

The Deepening of Autocratic Politics in Putin's Russia

hardened further, such that open disapproval or protests against the "special military operation" (it is illegal to refer to it as a war) were met with harsh penalties, including high fines and jail time in some cases. When all else fails to ensure a complacent society, autocracies can still resort to violence to keep society in check, and Putin's repressive regime is no exception to this tendency.

The Deepening of Autocratic Politics in Putin's Russia

In his spring 2020 address to the Duma, Vladimir Putin noted the importance of "evolutionary" and not "revolutionary" change in Russia.[42] Society must be kept compliant and complacent—ideally through performance legitimacy of the regime earned through high growth rates and rising real incomes. This is something Russia enjoyed on the back of a dramatic rise in global oil prices and decent macroeconomic policies between 2003 and 2008. But with the collapse of the global economy in 2008–2009, the high growth rates within Russia evaporated.[43] This meant that the source of social legitimacy—and thus regime stability—was in danger.

In the autumn of 2011, Vladimir Putin dramatically announced that he would be swapping places once more with Dmitry Medvedev. Putin would give up his post as prime minister to become president again in the elections scheduled for spring of 2012, and Medvedev would move back to serving as prime minister. There was technically a constitutional barrier to his return to the Kremlin in that it stipulated that no one could hold more than two consecutive terms in the presidency. However, there was nothing that forbade Vladimir Putin from taking a four-year break from the presidency to serve as prime minister in 2008 to return to the Kremlin as president in 2012.

Yet Putin's decision to return officially to run Russia from the Kremlin was not greeted with as much enthusiasm by thousands of Russians as he likely anticipated it would be. Instead, in Moscow, St. Petersburg, Ekaterinburg, and other large cities, people took to the streets in protest—not just against the decision for Putin to return, but against the results of the Duma elections of December 4, 2011, which appeared rigged in favor of United Russia when compared with exit poll results. Examples of ballot box stuffing appeared on the internet. In the street rallies that began that winter and extended through spring of 2012, tens of thousands of average Russians from across Russia—from the tiny enclave of Kaliningrad in the west to Vladivostok in the far east—marched through hundreds of cities, many carrying placards with slogans like "Russia without Putin," "The rats should go," "Swindlers and thieves, give us our elections back!" and "Putin is a thief."[44] Hundreds of protesters and some of the main leaders of Russia's weak opposition were arrested. US Secretary of State Hillary Clinton condemned the 2011 Duma election results as "dishonest and unfair," which Vladimir Putin later characterized as encouragement by the United States to the protesters to oust him from power. Putin evidently saw the hand of the CIA in sparking further social protests within Russia to prevent his return to the Kremlin, rather than a typical statement by the United States delivered to any country where election results are suspect.[45]

The rallies and marches against Putin's return to the presidency continued until his inauguration in early May 2012. One study of the change in state and society relations notes that until the spring of 2012 and Putin's return to the Kremlin, "ideological ambiguity and peaceful co-existence had been the name of the game . . . the goal was to keep politics away from the people and the people away from politics."[46] But the popular mobilization that confronted the regime in late 2011 and 2012 initiated a change in strategy to more actively marshal segments of Russian society in favor of Putin's rule. A narrative emanating from the Kremlin, one of Russia under siege by the West, began in earnest at this point. Part of this new legitimacy story was that these sorts of liberal uprisings were not indigenous to the Russian nation but were detrimental foreign influences coming from "the West."

Samuel Greene and Graeme Robertson demonstrate convincingly that Putin's strategists aimed to demobilize opposition through the exploitation and activation of existing social "wedge" issues in Russian society—specifically religion and gay rights. In 2013, a new law was passed "on the protection of feelings of religious believers" that criminalized "insulting the feelings of religious believers," which evidently included such acts as playing a video game in a church.[47] Support for the law (and for another law that was soon moved through the Duma against perpetrating positive images of the "gay lifestyle" to children) would serve to separate out a segment of the population who had supported the demonstrations against Putin from the opposition forces who had led the protests. A Pew Research survey indicated that in 2013, 74% of Russians thought homosexuality should not be accepted by society, so in adopting laws that denigrated homosexuality, the regime was following rather than leading public opinion.[48] Greene and Robertson argue that the use of religion and sexuality as wedge issues "did exactly what it was designed to do: it widened the ideological divide between the pro-Putin majority and the oppositional minority in the country."[49]

But as Putin's personal public approval ratings declined, more mechanisms of social repression were introduced.[50] These included amendments to earlier laws regulating nongovernmental organizations (NGOs) that were judged to be involved in political activities and accepting money from abroad; beginning in 2012, these organizations were required to reregister with the Ministry of Justice as "foreign agents"—a politically charged term from the Soviet era associated in Russia with espionage. Because there were few alternative funding sources for many Russian NGOs, especially those whose activity was often focused on protecting human rights and freedoms from abuse by the state, this would effectively mean closure. Russia's Civic Chamber reported that the number of civil society organizations in Russia declined from 400,000 in 2012 to 219,000 in 2019.[51] At the same time, Putin created government-backed NGOs in support of the regime, such as the youth group Nashi, to create a narrative of Russian exceptionalism and Putin's indispensability.[52]

A further strike against supporters of the liberal opposition involved harsh jail sentences for some of their key leaders and for dozens of young protesters, whose punishments were handed out slowly over a three-year period after the 2012 protests while they were held in prison without bail. Some ended up in labor camps for several years, a disturbing parallel to the treatment of dissidents in the Soviet era. The effect of these punishments would be to divide society further and to deflate enthusiasm for future public demonstrations against the regime.[53] Opposition figures were cast in the state-controlled media as out-of-touch intellectuals funded by foreigners, while a highly polished, adoring two-and-a-half-hour documentary (*President*) celebrating fifteen years of Putin's rule appeared on Russian television in April 2015.[54] Pro-Kremlin bloggers were unleashed on the internet to project the regime's message, and the state employed denial-of-service attacks against opposition websites.

The Kremlin also co-opted some of the largest internet providers and effected a takeover of the Russian version of Facebook, VKontakte. A flood of new legislation enabled regulators to block any online content that published "extremist" content (a term left largely undefined by the laws). Television content from late February 2014 through May of 2015 was devoted increasingly to coverage of Ukraine as an emerging "fascist state" in the wake of the Russian seizure of the Ukrainian peninsula of Crimea.[55]

In 2015, in the wake of US and European sanctions imposed in response to the Crimean seizure, Putin's regime introduced a new term, "Undesirable Organization," for some civil society organizations that required them to immediately cease operations. Further, the designation could be made by the Russian Ministry of Justice without a court order, and penalties for failing to shut down immediately ranged from steep fines to jail time. The first round of Undesirable Organizations in Russia included the Open Society Institute founded by George

Soros and based in the United States, the National Endowment for Democracy (including the National Democratic Institute and the International Republican Institute that had been working in Russia to train political parties and candidates to run in elections since the early 1990s), and the US Russia Foundation. The list of Undesirable Organizations grew steadily to include forty-nine organizations through early 2021, when an amendment to the Russian criminal code made more criminal prosecutions possible for any foreign or international organization that, in the judgment of the Ministry of Justice undermines "Russia's security, defense or constitutional order."

The list of organizations grew further as a result and then blossomed following Russia's invasion of Ukraine in February 2022 to include an additional thirty-six organizations from seventeen countries.[56] A number of Russian-owned and Russian-run organizations that moved abroad after the 2022 invasion have also been designated Undesirable Organizations, including nongovernmental media organizations and foundations. A person in Russia judged by the Ministry of Justice to have "continued involvement" with an organization so designated, which means working on its behalf but could also mean simply reading the organization's website or retweeting an article, can be subject to administrative and even criminal sanctions. A person deemed to have a leadership or management role in an "Undesirable Organization" could face up to five years in prison, and anyone found to be organizing financial arrangements for such an organization faces the same penalty. There have even been cases reported of people facing criminal charges because they had not known that a group they were supporting had been designated undesirable.[57]

An Ever-Hardening Autocracy

As Vladimir Putin and clients in his network have used access to the state's resources for personal gain, the real wages of Russian citizens have declined.[58] Some had begun to weary of the increasingly obvious inequalities that were growing within Russian society and corruption that many perceived as endemic. In the spring of 2017, for example, after the publication on YouTube of a video by Alexei Navalny of an estate purportedly owned by then Prime Minister Medvedev, young people took to the streets to protest inequality and graft.

Unable to risk further instability, in August 2020, the regime poisoned Navalny while he was in Siberia advocating his system Smart Voting, which provided information to voters to cast their ballots for the candidate in upcoming elections most likely to defeat the United Russia candidate. Navalny left Russia for treatment in Germany from what turned out to be the effects of exposure to a Novichok nerve agent administered, according to German authorities, through application to Navalny's undergarments. Navalny survived and later recorded himself interviewing one of the FSB agents responsible for the poisoning. Navalny returned to Russia from Germany after his recovery from the poisoning despite knowing that he would almost certainly be jailed upon arrival in Moscow for violating the terms of his probation for a previous conviction for fraud that is generally understood to be politically motivated. He died under suspicious circumstances on February 16, 2024, while serving a combined thirty-year sentence in a penal colony near the Arctic Circle.

It is Navalny's work through his Anti-Corruption Foundation that exposed the graft and network of cronyism. His series of well-produced and well-documented videos and his leadership of Russia's embattled opposition movement also made him an enemy of the regime. In a patronal autocracy, an independent and vocal civil society and its leaders are direct threats to regime longevity, so they must be controlled, jailed, or eliminated. Putin's regime has picked up the pace for all three options. The tactics of legal control and restrictions and imprisonment of the regime's critics have increased in scale and scope for social media critics within Russia of the "special military operation" in Ukraine.

Dysfunction and Vulnerability in Personalistic Patronal Autocracies

Personalistic patronal regimes such as Russia's today are inherently vulnerable because of the lack of a genuinely competitive and institutionalized succession process for the leader at the summit of the pyramid of patron-client relations. Lingering threats to the regime of alternative sources of power also could arise from society or from other elite networks when the patron in chief leaves office one way or another. This might explain the furious rush in January 2020 to initiate sweeping constitutional reforms to enable Putin to remain Russia's president until 2036, thereby demystifying what would happen to the regime after his term expired in 2024. This plan served to reassure invested wealthy cronies that there is a plan, and it is the status quo, regardless of the social disapproval they may be seeing.

Russia's descent from disorganized pluralist and unconsolidated democracy in the 1990s to consolidated personalistic and patronal autocracy happened gradually—and then suddenly. Social pacification was achieved initially through high growth rates, social prosperity, and stability, especially in contrast to the

1990s. But when growth rates trailed off and popular concerns about corruption increased, the regime became less tolerant of transparency, criticism, and dissent. Putin's ill-considered war in Ukraine sharpened the contours of a system that already existed, and it is now an unabashedly and highly repressive form of authoritarianism bent on using force and fear to gain social compliance. His regime had achieved a high degree of subjugation of society by the start of the war in Ukraine on February 24, 2022, but the new laws prohibiting freedom of speech and association and the heavier punishments issued by Russian courts for anyone articulating opposition to the "special military operation" then made Russia's autocracy grow even more repressive. What Mr. Putin fears most is not a NATO invasion of Russia via Ukraine. Russia has maintained a significant conventional and nuclear weapon deterrent to forestall that possibility. Rather, it is upheaval from within that is the greatest threat to his regime: thus, for Putin, it is truly existential to insist, as he did, that "Russia has fulfilled its plan when it comes to revolutions."[59]

Yet ironically, because the system has become so highly focused on the man at the pinnacle of the pyramid of elite relationships, it has become especially vulnerable to his removal. There is no obvious successor to Putin, and should he die suddenly (through natural or other causes), there will be some degree of political instability as elites below him battle for position. Putin has never created more cause than the faltering war in Ukraine for an attempt to be made to remove him from power. Few businesses are truly profiting from the war effort (although some of his close cronies are benefiting substantially from lucrative state contracts to supply the military), and many if not most of Russia's economic elite have lost access to their assets abroad. The Russian military is suffering tremendous reputational damage as a result of its mediocre battlefield performance against what on paper was a much less capable Ukrainian defense force in 2022. What was intended to be a rapid toppling of the Zelensky government and its replacement with a puppet regime controlled by Moscow turned into a years-long conflict that has already produced high casualty rates (an estimated 615,000 or more Russian casualties, at least 115,000 of which were deaths, according to US military assessments and others confirmed by independent agencies in the first two and a half years of fighting).[60] The dysfunctions of the Russian state under Putin's long tenure have been laid bare, and he will be remembered not for the economic growth of the 2000s but for the losses of 2022 and beyond and for the instability that he will have left in his wake.

NOTES

Parts of this chapter are drawn from chapter 8 of Kathryn Stoner, *Russia Resurrected: Its Power and Purpose in a New Global Order* (New York: Oxford University Press, 2021).

1. "The World's Least and Most Democratic Countries in 2022," *The Economist*, February 1, 2023, www.economist.com/graphic-detail/2023/02/01/the-worlds-most-and-least-democratic-countries-in-2022.

2. See, for example, Anders Åslund, *Russia's Capitalist Revolution: Why Market Reform Succeeded and Democracy Failed* (Washington, DC: Peterson Institute for Economic Studies, 2007); David Lipton and Jeffery Sachs, "Russia's Prospects for Economic Reforms," *Brookings Papers on Economic Activity*, no. 2 (1992).

3. See Åslund, *Russia's Capitalist Revolution*; Daniel Treisman, "Russia's Billionaires," *American Economic Review* 106, no. 5 (2016): 236–241; Timothy J. Colton, *Russia: What Everyone Needs to Know* (Oxford, UK: Oxford University Press, 2016); Richard Sakwa, *Putin and the Oligarch: The Khodorkovsky-Yukos Affair* (London and New York: I. B. Tauris & Co., 2014). On the loans-for-shares program, see Mikhail Zygar, *All the Kremlin's Men: Inside the Court of Vladimir Putin*, (New York: Public Affairs Press, 2016), 54–55.

4. For a short overview of the proximate causes of the 1998 financial crisis, see for example, Padma Desai, "Why Did the Ruble Collapse in 1998?", *American Economic Review* 90, no. 2 (May 2000): 48–52; and also Anders Åslund, "Russia's Financial Crisis: Causes and Possible Remedies," *Post-Soviet Economics and Geography* 39, no. 6 (1998): 309–328.

5. Boris Yeltsin's resignation speech of December 31, 1999, can be viewed here: https://www.youtube.com/watch?v=vTsqy18Mbvs; and Vladimir Putin's 1990 New Year's Address can be viewed here: https://www.youtube.com/watch?v=CJI2_lw1gIQ. Both accessed May 22, 2023.

6. Vladimir Putin, "Russia at the Turn of the Millennium" [*Rossiia na rubezhe tysiacheletii*], December 29, 1999, http://www.ng.ru/politics/1999-12-30/4_millenium.html.

7. Putin, "Russia at the Turn of the Millennium." Putin does not indicate whether these numbers refer to the volume of foreign investment in 1999 or since the collapse of the Soviet Union.

8. For full coverage of Putin's 2000 election to the presidency of Russia, see "Report on the Russian Presidential Elections, March 2000," Commission on Security and Cooperation in Europe, October 2000, https://www.csce.gov/international-impact/publications/report-russian-presidential-elections-march-2000?page=4.

9. Adam Przeworski, *Democracy and the Market: Political and Economic Reforms in Eastern Europe and Latin America* (New York: Cambridge University Press, 1991), 86.

10. Aleksandar Matovski, *Popular Dictatorships: Crises, Mass Opinion and the Rise of Electoral Authoritarianism* (New York: Cambridge University Press, 2021), 176.

11. See Matovski, *Popular Dictatorships*, 179–182, on popular support for stability relative to the 1990s.

12. In "From Boom to Bust: Hardship, Mobilization and Russia's Social Contract," *Daedalus* 146, no. 2 (Spring 2017): 113–127, Samuel Greene discusses the various

iterations and accuracy of the presumed social contract between Putin and Russian society, https://direct.mit.edu/daed/article/146/2/113/27161/From-Boom-to-Bust -Hardship-Mobilization-amp-Russia.

13. For evidence of the dramatic changes in the Russian economy in this period, see the data and charts in Stoner, *Russia Resurrected* (128–149), which draw from various international data sources like the International Monetary Fund and World Bank. On declining Russian civil liberties over time, see among many examples Michael McFaul, "Choosing Autocracy: Actors, Institutions and Revolution in the Erosion of Russian Democracy," *Comparative Politics* 50, no. 3 (April 2018): 305–325; and M. Steven Fish, "What Has Russia Become," *Comparative Politics* 50, no. 3 (April 2018): 327–346.

14. David Hoffman in *The Oligarchs: Wealth and Power in the New Russia* (New York: Public Affairs, 2002) provides a detailed account of the raid on Gusinsky in May 2000 (477–485), and on Berezovsky's downfall after promoting Putin to Yeltsin (485–489).

15. On the circumstances surrounding Berezovsky's death in the United Kingdom in 2013, see Toby Melville, "UK Coroner Records Open Verdict on Death of Russian Oligarch Berezovsky," *Reuters*, March 27, 2014, https://www.reuters.com/article/us -britain-berezovsky/uk-coroner-records-open-verdict-on-death-of-russian-oligarch -berezovsky-idUSBREA2Q25O20140327. See also the lengthy obituary in Radio Free Europe Radio Liberty on Berezovsky at https://www.rferl.org/a/boris-berezovsky -obituary/24937119.html, accessed May 22, 2023.

16. Zygar, *All the Kremlin's Men*, 48.

17. For useful insights into how Putin's regime uses the Russian legal system to disarm opponents, see Maria Popova, "Putin-Style 'Rule of Law' and Prospects for Change," *Daedalus* 146, no. 2 (Spring 2017): 64–75.

18. See Stanislav Markus, "The Atlas that Has Not Shrugged: Why Russia's Oligarchs Are an Unlikely Force for Change," *Daedalus* 146, no. 2 (Spring 2017): 101–112.

19. For Putin's approval ratings from 1999 through May 2023, see the Levada Center, "Putin's Approval Rating," https://www.levada.ru/en/ratings/.

20. Constitution of the Russian Federation, "Chapter 4: President of the Russian Federation" and "Chapter 5: Federal Assembly of the Russian Federation."

21. Maria Tsvetkova, "Defeated Candidates in Russian Election try to Annul 'Crooked' Online Results," *Reuters*, September 23, 2021, https://www.reuters.com/world /europe/defeated-candidates-russian-election-try-annul-crooked-online-results-2021-09 -23/, accessed May 22, 2023.

22. These numbers come from Corey Welt, "Russia: Domestic Politics and Economy," *Congressional Research Service*, September 9, 2020, 12.

23. Welt, *Congressional Research Service*, September 9, 2020, 12–13.

24. Natalia Gevorkian, Natalia Timakova, and Andrei Kolesnikov, *From the First Person* (New York: Public Affairs, 2000).

25. See, for example, Karen Dawisha, *Putin's Kleptocracy: Who Owns Russia?* (New York: Simon and Shuster, 2014); Fiona Hill and Cliff Gaddy, *Mr. Putin: Operative in the Kremlin* (Washington, DC: Brookings, 2015); Steven Lee Meyer, *The New Tsar: The Rise and Reign of Vladimir Putin* (New York: Knopf, 2015); and Masha Gessen, *Man Without a Face: The Unlikely Rise of Vladimir Putin* (New York: Riverhead Books, 2012).

26. Brian Taylor, *The Code of Putinism* (New York: Oxford University Press, 2018), 100.

27. See Catherine Belton, *Putin's People: How the KGB Took Back Russia and Then Took on the West* (New York: Farrar Straus and Giroux, 2021).

28. Dawisha, *Putin's Kleptocracy*; Gessen, *Man Without a Face*; Gleb Pavlovsky, "Russian Politics Under Putin: The System Will Outlast Its Master," *Foreign Affairs* 95, no. 3 (May/June 2016): 10–17; Hill and Gaddy, *Mr. Putin*; and Zygar, *All the Kremlin's Men* are but a few of many sources on Putin's networks and their influence on the system. For information on finances and the Panama Papers see also Luke Harding, "Sergei Roldugin: The Cellist Who Holds the Key to Tracing Putin's Hidden Fortune," *The Guardian*, April 3, 2016, https://www.theguardian.com/news/2016/apr/03/sergei-roldugin-the-cellist-who -holds-the-key-to-tracing-putins-hidden-fortune, accessed June 22, 2020.

29. Dawisha, *Putin's Kleptocracy*, 8.

30. Dawisha, *Putin's Kleptocracy*, 3.

31. Dawisha, *Putin's Kleptocracy*, 4–5.

32. See Alena V. Ledeneva, *Can Russia Modernise? Sistema, Power Networks and Informal Governance* (New York: Cambridge University Press, 2013); and Taylor, *The Code of Putinism*.

33. Dawisha, *Putin's Kleptocracy*, chapter 2.

34. Henry Hale, *Patronal Politics: Eurasian Regime Transitions in Comparative Perspective* (New York: Cambridge University Press, 2014), 20.

35. Hale, *Patronal Politics*, 10.

36. Kathryn Stoner, "The Putin Myth," *Journal of Democracy* 34, no. 2 (April 2023): 5–18, https://www.journalofdemocracy.org/articles/the-putin-myth/.

37. Samuel Greene and Graham Robertson, *Putin v. The People* (New Haven: Yale University Press, 2019).

38. Juliet Kaarbo, "A Foreign Policy Analysis Perspective on the Domestic Politics Turn in IR Theory," *International Studies Review* 17, no. 2 (2015): 197–199; Greene and Robertson, *Putin v. The People*, 13.

39. For more on this see Sara Wengle and Michael Rasell, "The Monetisation of L'Goty: Changing Patterns of Welfare Provision in Russia," *Europe Asia Studies* 60, no. 5 (July 2008): 739–756.

40. Sasha de Vogel, *Protest Mobilization, Concessions, and Autocracies*, University of Michigan PhD Dissertation, 2021, https://deepblue.lib.umich.edu/handle/2027.42 /169838, accessed April 12, 2023.

41. For Putin's monthly approval ratings from 1999 through May 2023, see the Levada Center, "Putin's Approval Rating," https://www.levada.ru/en/ratings/, accessed May 2023.

42. Vladimir Putin, March 10, 2020, speech at the State Duma Plenary Session, https://en.kremlin.ru/events/president/news/62964, accessed May 12, 2023.

43. These figures for Russia's annual growth rates come from The World Bank, https://data.worldbank.org/indicator/NY.GDP.MKTP.KD.ZG?locations=RU, accessed May 22, 2023.

44. Steve Gutterman and Amy Ferris-Rotman, "Thousands of Russians Protest against Putin," *Reuters*, December 10, 2011, https://www.reuters.com/article/us-russia -protests/thousands-of-russians-protest-against-putin-idUSTRE7B907W20111210, accessed June 9, 2020.

45. See, for example, Michael Crowley and Julia Ioffe, "Why Putin Hates Clinton," *Politico*, July 25, 2016, https://www.politico.com/story/2016/07/clinton-putin-226153, accessed June 9, 2020.

46. Greene and Robertson, *Putin v. The People*, 25.

47. See Carl Schreck "Holy Slight: How Russia Prosecutes For 'Insulting Religious Feelings,'" *Radio Free Europe, Radio Liberty*, August 15, 2017, https://www.rferl.org/a/russia-prosecuting-insults-to-religious-feelings/28678284.html, accessed May 22, 2023.

48. "The Global Divide on Homosexuality," Pew Research Center, 2013, https://www.pewresearch.org/global/2013/06/04/the-global-divide-on-homosexuality/, accessed May 22, 2023.

49. Greene and Robertson, *Putin v. The People*, 37. See also Katie Riley, "Russia's Anti-Gay law in Line with Public's View of Homosexuality," Pew Research Center, August 5, 2013, https://www.pewresearch.org/fact-tank/2013/08/05/russias-anti-gay-laws-in-line-with-publics-views-on-homosexuality/; and Valerie Sperling, *Sex, Politics and Putin: Political Legitimacy in Russia* (New York: Oxford University Press, 2014).

50. Again, see Levada's monthly reports on this at https://www.levada.ru/en/ratings/.

51. As cited in Vsevolod Bederson and Andrei Semenov, "Between Autonomy and Compliance: The Organizational Development of Russian Civil Society," in Z. Kravchenko et al., eds., *Resourceful Civil Society* (New York: Palgrave, 2020), 177.

52. For more on Nashi, see Eva Hartog, "A Kremlin Youth Movement Goes Rogue," *Moscow Times*, April 8, 2016, https://www.themoscowtimes.com/2016/04/08/a-kremlin-youth-movement-goes-rogue-a52435.

53. See Greene and Robertson, *Putin v. The People*, 33–39.

54. *Prezident* is available in Russian at https://russia.tv/video/show/brand_id/59329/episode_id/1193264/video_id/1165983/, accessed June 29, 2020, and on Amazon Prime in English as *President*.

55. See Maria Lipman, Anna Kachkaeva, and Michael Poyker, "Media in Russia," in Daniel Treisman, ed., *The New Autocracy: Information, Politics and Policy in Putin's Russia*, (Washington, DC: Brookings University Press, 2018), 171–172.

56. For a full list see the website of the Ministry of Justice of the Russian Federation, "List of Foreign and International Organizations the Activities of which Are Named Undesirable on the Territory of the Russian Federation," https://archive.ph/r3nfK, accessed May 15, 2023.

57. See Human Rights Watch, "Undesirables Law Expands Activists' Danger Zone," at https://www.hrw.org/news/2021/06/17/new-undesirables-law-expands-activists-danger-zone, accessed May 23, 2023.

58. See Aine Quinn, "Russian Real Incomes Fell to the Lowest in a Decade," *Bloomberg*, May 16, 2021. The chart showing quarterly declines from 2009 onward can be found at https://www.bloomberg.com/news/articles/2021-05-17/russian-real-incomes-fall-to-the-lowest-in-a-decade-chart#xj4y7vzkg, accessed 22 May 2023.

59. Vladimir Putin, March 10, 2020, speech at the State Duma Plenary Session, available at https://en.kremlin.ru/events/president/news/62964, accessed May 12, 2023.

60. This estimate comes from Eric Schmitt, "September Was Deadly Month for Russian Troops in Ukraine, U.S. Says," *New York Times*, October 10, 2024, https://www.nytimes.com/2024/10/10/us/politics/russia-casualties-ukraine-war.html. For earlier

estimates of Russian casualties, see also "Mediazona: Confirmed Losses of the Russian Federation in the War -More than 50 Thousand, Estimated About 85 Thousand Dead," in Radio Svoboda, April 12, 2024, https://www.radiosvoboda.org/a/news-mediazona -vtraty-rf-ponad-50-tysjach/32903180.html; and "At Least 50,000 Russian Military Deaths, Likely Thousands More, Recorded In Ukraine War," Radio Free Europe/Radio Liberty, April 13, 2024, https://www.rferl.org/a/russia-war-ukraine-deaths/32903736 .html, accessed May 7, 2024; and "Russia's Losses in the War with Ukraine, Media Zone's Summary," https://zona.media/casualties, which is regularly updated, but accessed May 7, 2024.

Chapter Two

The Role of Power and Wealth in Putin's Russia

Anders Åslund

Scholars of all disciplines tend to believe that rulers focus on their topics. Political scientists deal with politics, public opinion, and constitutions. Economists concentrate on macroeconomic stability and growth. Foreign policy specialists emphasize the national interest and often international stability. But real-world politicians have their own goals, and they vary with the nature of the regime.

Russian President Vladimir Putin has ruled since 2000 (with a brief intermission as prime minister from 2008 to 2012). He has persistently built his power on two bases, the KGB and organized crime.[1] Putin's views are pretty clear, and most of them were evident in his interview book *First Person* from 2000, in which Putin glorified the KGB.[2] Apart from aiming at personal power and wealth, Putin is also pursuing imperialism. His war in Georgia and his two wars in Ukraine show that he does want to "gather Russian lands," as the old Russian saying goes. His political aims may draw on the Soviet Union or the Russian Empire or both.

In the early 1990s, when Putin was St. Petersburg's first deputy mayor for international economic relations, the city was renowned as the crime capital of Russia, and Putin dealt with the most criminal part of that economy. A report by an investigative commission chaired by the liberal politician Marina Salye offers overwhelming evidence that Putin was deeply involved in organized crime from at least late 1991.[3] Salye later strangely disappeared from the public eye as a consequence of her report and reemerged only just before her presumably natural death in 2012. Crony capitalism was no late idea of Putin but an original part of his system.[4]

Putin's imperialism is not very clearly defined. He has cited two antidemocratic Russian nationalist philosophers, Ivan Ilyin and Lev Gumilev. But they are quite different. Ilyin harbored a narrow linguistic outlook, whereas Gumilev preferred an imperialist outreach. Putin has quoted each of them publicly, Ilyin five times and Gumilev six times.[5] Although not being quite a Nazi, Ilyin was close to it. Walter Laqueur assessed that Ilyin "considered Nazism a positive phenomenon that with some modifications could serve as a model for the future Russia."[6] Putin has been careful not to become firmly connected with any specific branch of nationalism.[7] He repeatedly praised Lev Gumilev, who was the father of Eurasianism, the imperial form of Russian nationalism, strongly opposed to the narrow ethnic or linguistic nationalism of Ilyin.[8] Putin has honored both kinds of Russian nationalism without taking a clear stand.

Many good books have been written on how Putin has consolidated his political power. In his first term (2000–2004), he was everything to everybody and promoted economic reform and growth. He carried out substantial structural reforms, such as land reform, tax reform, budget reform, judicial reform, and so on, but most of all he seized control of the security services and television.[9] In his second term, he defeated the oligarchs and moved to state capitalism. Yet, until May 2008, the Russian stock market went straight up because both Russian and foreign investors believed in Putin's reforms. In his third term, informal because he was prime minister, he moved on to asset stripping from the state companies. After returning to the presidential office, he has pursued arbitrary personal decision-making.[10]

Organized crime and its connection with offshore wealth, however, tend to be discussed as a separate criminal issue and not as a part of Putin's political power in Russia.

The Emergence of Russian Offshore Wealth

At the end of the Soviet Union, the main means of enrichment was commodity trade. Soviet wholesale prices of commodities, notably oil, metals, and chemicals, were extremely low, down to 1% of the world market price. Clever operators organized private exports of commodities from Russia's big state companies, acquired export licenses and quotas, and sold them to their own trading companies that they had set up in Cyprus. Then they sold the commodities on the world market at normal market prices. Through under-invoicing, they could accumulate their gains in offshore havens.[11]

The Role of Power and Wealth in Putin's Russia   49

Since 1990, almost two years before the end of the USSR, Russia has had a private net capital outflow of about $30–$40 billion a year, although it has varied greatly.[12] Until now, the total net Russian capital outflow has amounted to about $1 trillion, aggregated from 1990 to 2021. This figure presumes no return on the capital because the main point was to move the money out of Russia and keep it safe. Before Russia's invasion of Ukraine, its GDP in current US dollars amounted to about $1.5 trillion, which means that Russia's offshore wealth was two-thirds of its GDP (which is quite extreme) and was highly concentrated to about 100 billionaires.

Originally, most private Russian money went out of the country through Cyprus. Then the money would move to other offshore havens, but mostly to the British Virgin Islands, which is a shell company formation center, to the Cayman Islands, which is a major banking center, and then to Wilmington, Delaware, or to England. Seriously dirty Russian money was typically hidden in twenty to thirty shell companies on top of one another from a dozen different offshore jurisdictions.[13]

The Russian capital flight was facilitated by the far-reaching liberalization of capital markets that Prime Minister Margaret Thatcher had carried out in the United Kingdom in 1986, which was called the Big Bang. It also involved many British overseas territories, mainly in the Caribbean, and some former British territories, such as the United Arab Emirates and Singapore. For the United Kingdom, the Big Bang broke stifling regulations and facilitated higher economic growth for decades, but the sudden rise of capital flight from Russia and many other semi-free countries was an unintended consequence.

There are many offshore havens, and as Gabriel Zucman underscored, they usually do not compete with but complement one another, rendering it much more difficult to trace the money. The three key requirements for a Russian businessman who wants to hide his money abroad are good rule of law and great financial freedom (the Western legal system), secrecy (Anglo-American law), and deep financial markets.[14] By and large, Western countries and most British overseas territories comply with the rule of law requirement, but only the Anglo-American law jurisdictions fulfill the secrecy requirement. The United States and the United Kingdom are the only countries with sufficiently deep financial markets.

For the end of June 2021, the US Treasury claimed that the three biggest investors in US securities, both stocks and debt, were the United Kingdom with $2.6 trillion, the Cayman Islands with $2.5 trillion, and Luxembourg with $2.3 trillion.[15] The US Treasury has no idea who actually owns the vast amounts from the Cayman Islands and Luxembourg because these funds are by and large anonymous.

We have good reason to believe that Russian private offshore funds amount to $1 trillion (at least). Given that the United States offers the largest secret financial market, a fair guess is that some $500 billion of the Cayman Islands investment in US securities is Russian money. By comparison, the Swiss Bankers Association estimates that about $150–$200 billion of Russian money is being held by Swiss banks.[16] But the same money tends to be counted several times because it moves among several jurisdictions.[17]

The reasons to keep money abroad are many and have varied through the years. In the 1990s, Russian banks were highly unreliable, and the country faced repeated bank crises. The only safe banks were abroad. The fear of taxation has probably been less important in Russia than elsewhere, but Russia's fundamental problem is that it does not have any real property rights, and this problem has become worse over time as Putin and his officials indulge in corporate raiding. Whenever billionaires fall out with Putin, which happens all too often, they usually get forty-eight hours to flee the country, and they do. Thus, all wealthy Russians keep any significant free cash abroad.

Putin's People

During his time as first deputy mayor of St. Petersburg, from 1991 to 1996, when he was also in charge of foreign investment, Putin was involved in all kinds of unsavory business in such sectors as commodity trading and real estate, as well as the privatization of a telecommunications company and oil refinery. But he does not seem to have made much money.[18]

However, he established three circles of close friends that would stay with him and become immensely rich. The first circle consisted of his friends from the KGB, with whom he was going to take power in Russia. The most important were the four KGB generals, Sergei Ivanov, Nikolai Patrushev, Alexander Bortnikov, and Sergei Naryshkin. The first three would in turn become chairmen of the FSB, while Naryshkin is currently chairman of the Foreign Intelligence Service (SVR).

The second circle was Putin's cronies, four not very prominent private businessmen—Yuri Kovalchuk, the brothers Arkady and Boris Rotenberg, and Gennady Timchenko.

The third circle consisted of Putin's assistants in the mayor's office: Igor Sechin, who eventually became CEO of Rosneft; Alexei Miller, who became CEO of Gazprom; and German Gref, who became CEO of Sberbank, Russia's biggest state bank. They would all become billionaires doing business with Putin, but they were his servants rather than his partners.

The Role of Power and Wealth in Putin's Russia   51

The KGB generals and Putin's cronies were all of almost the same age as Putin and acted as his partners, whereas Sechin, Miller, and Gref were younger and clearly subordinate.

How Putin Made His Money

One single company appears to have been the main source of the wealth of Putin and his cronies: the state-owned gas company Gazprom. Thanks to Viktor Chernomyrdin being the last Soviet minister of the gas industry, Gazprom was never broken up. It was all-dominant in gas production and possessed a monopoly on gas transportation and exports. When Chernomyrdin became prime minister in December 1992, he started to privatize half of Gazprom, to his and his colleagues' benefit, primarily Gazprom's CEO Rem Vyakhirev. After Chernomyrdin was dismissed as prime minister, he and Vyakhirev launched large-scale asset stripping from Gazprom.

Putin appeared as a white knight, wanting to stop this robbery of the state. In May 2001, he carried out a virtual coup against the old Gazprom management and installed his former assistant Alexei Miller as CEO. Gazprom's many minority shareholders cheered because they saw this as an improvement of corporate governance. They became represented on the supervisory board. In 2006, the previously restricted trade in Gazprom shares was ended, and the stock price skyrocketed. In parallel, however, another process had started—namely, a new asset stripping, but now to Putin's friends.

In 2008, the two opposition activists Boris Nemtsov and Vladimir Milov deflated the success of Gazprom. In their book *Putin and Gazprom*, they revealed how Putin's cronies had been allowed to loot the energy company.[19] Yuri Kovalchuk took over Gazprom's main financial assets, Gazprombank and the insurance company Sogaz, and its media assets, Gazprom-Media, which included the powerful television channel NTV and radio station Ekho Moskvy, which Putin had seized from the former media oligarch Vladimir Gusinsky in a forced sale in 2000. All these transactions were complex and involved multiple offshore companies, but the principle was that Kovalchuk paid little for them. Kovalchuk, who is called Putin's banker and is considered his closest friend, went on to buy most of Russia's television channels in a number of deals.

The brothers Arkady and Boris Rotenberg bought some of Gazprom's pipeline-building companies and went on to build one pipeline after the other for Gazprom, becoming the kings of public procurement in Russia, needless to say without competition. They also acquired the biggest Russian road-constructing company,

52 Anders Åslund

Mostotrest, and became Russia's biggest road builders. Their business was asset stripping thanks to their close relations with Putin plus privileged public procurement. They also became the main contractors for the 2014 Sochi Winter Olympics, and they built the bridge over Kerch Strait to the Crimea.[20]

Unlike Putin's other cronies, Gennady Timchenko was a real businessman. In 2000, he founded Gunvor, an oil trading company in Switzerland. Putin appeared to own a minority share through a childhood friend (Petr Kolbin). Suddenly, the upstart Gunvor became the third-largest oil trader in the world, trading oil from Russian oil companies. *The Economist* made the claim that Gunvor bought oil at a discount from the Russian oil companies. Timchenko sued the magazine for libel, but the case was settled out of court.[21] When the US Treasury sanctioned Timchenko in 2014, it claimed: "Putin has investments in Gunvor and may have access to Gunvor funds."[22]

In 2009, Timchenko bought Gazprom's other pipeline-building companies and went on to build one pipeline after the other for Gazprom. He also took over Gazprom's large petrochemical company Sibur at a low price and bought a large share of the private gas producer Novatek, which not surprisingly received substantial gas licenses.[23]

To sum up, Nemtsov and Milov estimated that during the years 2004–2007, Gazprom transferred the stunning sum of $60 billion to Putin's cronies, or $15 billion a year.[24] Those were good years for Gazprom, but a fair assessment is that the cronies have continued to tap Gazprom of similar amounts, perhaps $10–$15 billion a year, because the same techniques of enrichment have continued—that is, privileged procurement of mainly pipelines to the Rotenberg brothers and Timchenko, and asset stripping to the benefit of all the cronies. As the Sberbank analysts Alex Fak and Anna Kotelnikova wrote in 2018: "Gazprom's investment program can best be understood as a way to employ the company's entrenched contractors at the expense of shareholders."[25] They were dismissed for this politically incorrect report. In addition, the cronies have extracted money from other government entities, notably the Rotenbergs from the Sochi Winter Olympics and road building.[26] It was obvious that they received these privileges because they were close to Putin, but it was not clear how money was transferred to Putin.

At the end of 2010, a greater scandal erupted that brought considerable clarity. Sergei Kolesnikov, a junior partner of Nikolai Shamalov, who was a less prominent Putin crony, fled Russia, fearing for his life. Kolesnikov revealed that $1 billion of public funding for medical equipment had been diverted to build a palace for

Putin in Gelendzhik, on the Black Sea coast near Sochi. Kolesnikov claimed that kickbacks were 35% for medical equipment.[27]

Kolesnikov gave many interviews describing in detail how they channeled diverted state funds through multiple offshore companies. Several layers of shell companies were used in multiple offshore havens. Kolesnikov's part of the business contained thirty-two offshore companies involving Shamalov and Putin. They were located in places such as the British Virgin Islands and Panama.[28] Kolesnikov clarified that Putin personally owned individual shares in each of these companies. Each person involved (including Kolesnikov) had a specific share that varied from company to company, but the general picture seems to be that the two principal partners together held the overwhelming majority, while the junior partners, who carried out the actual work, obtained a few percent. Presumably, Putin held half the ownership, but Kolesnikov stated that the specific shares varied between companies. An additional spice in Kolesnikov's story was that Putin and his cronies used nicknames, as is the custom among Russian gangsters.[29]

There were many other means of making illicit money:

- During Putin's first term in office, two oligarchs were called to the Kremlin and asked to put up $10 million or $20 million in "donations" either to Putin's re-election campaign or for some charitable purpose. Putin obtained $300 million in "donations" for the rebuilding of the Konstantinov Palace in St. Petersburg, which became his official residence there.[30]
- The Panama Papers contain several such donations to Putin's childhood friend, the cellist Sergei Roldugin. The biggest gift identified there was $259 million from the private businessmen Suleiman Kerimov, who was sanctioned by the United States in April 2018.[31]
- A big source of dubious income is forgiven loans from state banks. State banks currently account for about 70% of all banking assets, but banks other than the highly profitable Sberbank are hardly making any profits and are regularly being recapitalized by the state. One of the offshore companies connected with Roldugin received a credit line of $650 million from RCB Bank in Cyprus, the state-owned subsidiary of VTB Bank.[32] The loan was written off, and as if to cover the tracks, RCB was sold to VTB-related private bank Otkritie, which soon afterwards went under.
- Nemtsov and Milov mention various forms of stock manipulation as a common source of illicit enrichment. Specifically, Putin appears to have extracted 6% of the shares in Gazprom in 2006.[33]

- Another form of enrichment is at the expense of private enterprises, namely through hostile takeovers or corporate raiding with the help of various law enforcement bodies. Russia has opened more than 200,000 cases of "economic crimes" against businessmen, who are usually forced to sit in pretrial detention until they pay their tormentors the required extortion. The businessmen then tend to lose their enterprises.[34]

The Putin system of authoritarian kleptocracy is plain. First, his KGB generals guarantee his political power. In return, they can serve themselves through extortion and kickbacks. Second, he has appointed his assistants as chief executives of Russia's biggest state companies. Their duty is to provide Putin and his cronies with ample asset stripping and procurement gains. In return, they may enrich themselves as they care from the state-owned companies they mismanage. Third, Putin's cronies take out assets from the state companies in co-ownership with the boss. If any problem arises with real Russian businessmen, Putin's fourth circle of friends, which is made up of loyal oligarchs, can take care of it.

Ironically, Putin and his friends also transfer their funds abroad, as we know from the Panama Papers and Pandora Papers. If Putin were to lose power in Russia, he would also lose all of his property there; therefore, he tries to secure substantial property abroad. According to *Forbes*, his closest cronies have an official wealth of about $30 billion, but that reflects only their known assets in Russia. Their real wealth is probably many times greater because of the extraordinary secrecy of their offshore holdings. In addition, Putin has four childhood friends in St. Petersburg who hold $500 million to $2 billion of what is presumably Putin's money. He also has four cousins who hold about that much money. Putin is both greedy and paranoid.[35]

However, the personal wealth of Putin is a moot point. My assessment, based on Nemtsov and Milov, is that he and his four main cronies (Kovalchuk, the Rotenberg brothers, and Timchenko) made an average of about $15 billion net a year since 2005 and took all of it to offshore havens. That would give them about $250 billion of the total Russian offshore wealth. Presuming that half of that money belongs to Putin, in line with the Kolesnikov statements on the thirty-two offshore companies in which he and Putin had shares, Putin's wealth would be $125 billion.[36]

What We Know About Putin's Wealth

The question is naturally always raised: What do we actually know about Putin's wealth and how he makes it? The answer is that we have numerous alternative sources of information, and they all paint the same picture.

The starting point is Russian Central Bank statistics, which are amazingly exact and credible. From them, we can deduct that the total net capital outflow from 1990 to 2021 has been about $1 trillion.[37]

The big revelation of government corruption was in the book *Putin and Gazprom*, published in 2008, by the two opposition activists Boris Nemtsov and Vladimir Milov, who revealed how Putin and his cronies had looted Gazprom.[38] There was then a steady stream of minor revelations until the next big revelation, in 2010, by a minor partner of Putin, Sergei Kolesnikov, who revealed the existence of "Putin's palace" on the Black Sea.[39]

The next big blow was the publication of the Panama Papers in April 2016, which contained a lot about the Putin connections.[40] Two follow-ups were the Paradise Papers, with mainly legal information about Bermuda-based companies, and the Pandora Papers in the fall of 2021, which contained more illicit information. There are many other sources, such as the *Forbes* assessments of Putin, his friends, and his family. The palaces, superyachts, and private jets are all too conspicuous.

Why This Preoccupation with Palaces, Superyachts, and Private Jets?

A standard question of outsiders is this: Why do they want this wealth? They can never enjoy it. Well, that is not the point. Like the monarchs in the old days, US billionaires are not focused on their consumption. They have so many other values: How rich are they in comparison with others? Does their wealth reinforce their power and influence? Russian oligarchs and rulers are just the same. They try to keep up with the (very rich) Joneses. The seizure of the oligarchs' superyachts and palaces shines a light on how they use their extraordinary wealth.

Most conspicuous are the yachts. They fall into four categories, based on the wealth of their owner. The biggest yacht is, of course, one that allegedly belongs to Putin: the *Scheherazade*, which is worth $700 million, although it is frozen in Italy.[41] Next come two top oligarchs, Roman Abramovich and Alisher Usmanov, with yachts worth $600 million, followed by major oligarchs such as Timchenko, with a yacht of some $300 million. The run-of-the-mill Russian billionaires have yachts worth about $100 million. In total, Russians own 180–200 superyachts.[42]

56   Anders Åslund

Similarly, a serious oligarch needs a palace or two, although some call them humble mansions. The biggest palace is of course Putin's alleged one on the Black Sea, costing more than $1 billion. It would be rude to have a bigger palace. Major state enterprise managers, such as Miller and Sechin, allegedly have palaces outside of Moscow costing $300–$400 million, while many run-of-the-mill billionaires have mansions all over the world—in London, France, Italy, Switzerland, the United States, and sometimes even in Russia—for about $100 million.

The third insignia of an oligarch in Russia is a private jet. Abramovich used to have a Boeing 767, but he has now moved up to a Boeing 787. You also have to have a top watch.

This quick review offers three conclusions. Russian oligarchic society is extremely status-conscious. You have to have as big a yacht and as big a mansion as possible, while not overstepping your line. Otherwise, you are not serious, but you must not move beyond your rank. This sounds very much like the old tsarist Russia, and Russia's new aristocracy treats their children accordingly.

But conspicuous consumption is usually a sign of uncertain property rights: The wealthy want to enjoy their wealth while they still have it. Presumably, the freezing of assets did not come as a surprise to most of these people. Thorstein Veblen argued in his famous 1899 book, *The Theory of the Leisure Class: An Economic Study of Institutions*, that conspicuous consumption was characteristic of the newly arrived capitalists, or robber barons, who wanted to prove their status while not trusting their property rights.

What Can Be Done to Combat Russia's Authoritarian Kleptocracy?

According to Freedom House, democracy both in Russia and the world has steadily declined since 2005, and the deterioration continues.[43] The wealth of the Russian and other authoritarian kleptocrats seems to grow ever greater, hidden, anonymous, and untaxed. However, it is never as dark as just before dawn. The Achilles' heel of the Putin kleptocracy is that most of his and his cronies' wealth is held in the West because of the lack of real property rights in the former Soviet Union.

In the West, a new awareness has arisen about the hazards of anonymous companies. Gradually, and somewhat haphazardly, the United States has adopted a new policy attempting to punish both human rights violations and corruption through sanctions. The groundbreaking move was the adoption of the Sergei Magnitsky Rule of Law Accountability Act by US Congress in December 2012.[44] Its origin was the death of the honest auditor Sergei Magnitsky in a Moscow prison after he had revealed the theft of $230 million from the Russian tax authorities by dozens of Russian officials from all kinds of state financial institutions and law enforcement. The fund manager, Bill Browder, was the main promoter of the Sergei Magnitsky Rule of Law Accountability Act, and he found strong support from the Russian liberals Boris Nemtsov and Vladimir Kara-Murza.[45] The Magnitsky sanctions exposed the links between organized crime and various state financial authorities, notably the tax authorities, such as judges, prosecutors, and police. The sanctioned individuals were prohibited to enter the United States and had possible assets here frozen. While Nemtsov argued that these sanctions were aimed at people who didn't uphold the rule of law in Russia, the Kremlin reacted very negatively—obviously, because it exposed their misdeeds. Nemtsov was killed outside the Kremlin on February 27, 2015. The key suspect is Putin.[46]

The United States has continued with similar personal sanctions combining human rights and financial crimes, and the rest of the West has followed. In their reaction to Russia's annexation of Crimea in March 2014, the West, led by the United States, opted for sanctions against Putin's leading cronies—Kovalchuk, Timchenko, and the brothers Rotenberg. Putin got so upset that he complained about this as violation of "human rights" in public no less than five times in a year.[47] After Russia's further aggression in eastern Ukraine in the summer of 2014, the United States, the European Union, Canada, and a few other countries sanctioned the top security officials mentioned above and the main state company chief executives.

In August 2017, US Congress adopted the Combating America's Adversaries with Sanctions Act (CAATSA). It was supposed to reinforce US sanctions against Russia, Iran, and North Korea. Its main novelty was a section focusing on oligarchs close to the Kremlin. In April 2018, six major Russian oligarchs were sanctioned on the basis of this law, but otherwise little happened.

Since Russia's assault on Ukraine in 2022, however, all the floodgates have been opened. The collective West has sanctioned most of the relevant culprits, even if some holdouts and inconsistencies persist. Suddenly, most of the big Russian oligarchs found themselves sanctioned. A completely different basis for Western actions against Russian authoritarian kleptocrats had been created.

A New Western Drive for Transparency May Render Sanctions Effective

For years, the sanctions against Russian billionaires close to Putin hardly resulted in any assets being frozen. The Panama Papers publicized in April 2016 and the Pandora Papers in October 2021 revealed plenty of Russian offshore funds, but few law enforcement actions were taken. The sanctioned appeared to escape, as if the law did not apply to them. Worse, sanctioned individuals repeatedly sued investigative journalists for libel in the United Kingdom or United States and won. The British journalist Catherine Belton was sued in London by four oligarchs and Rosneft for her eminent book *Putin's People* in 2020.[48]

The big problem is the lack of corporate transparency. Often, journalists cannot prove their cases against the very well-paid lawyers of oligarchs. Fortunately, in recent years, all major jurisdictions have adopted major legal acts to promote transparency. Their main goal is to establish public registries of the ultimate beneficial owners of all companies.

The European Union took the lead. In June 2018, the European Parliament and the European Council adopted their fifth anti-money-laundering directive. This requires all enterprises and entities in the twenty-eight countries of the European Union and the European Economic Area (Iceland, Liechtenstein, Norway, and Switzerland) to reveal their ultimate beneficiary owners. They must be registered in a centrally held registry in each member state, and that registry must be public. This obligation also applies to business owners residing outside of the region in which they operate. A beneficiary owner is defined as the owner of 25% plus one share of an entity.[49] An EU directive has no direct legal impact but obliges all member states to adopt appropriate national legislation within two years. Most countries are usually delayed, but however slowly the EU acts, it does act. Most member countries have adopted legislation and are implementing it.

The United Kingdom has gone far in its anti-money-laundering legislation, but its transparency is actually less because implementation is weak. Furthermore, the many overseas British territories operate independently, and London is the dominant financial center in Europe. Needless to say, Britain's vast sector of anonymous companies has many well-paid legal and financial helpers.[50] On paper, the British legislation should lead to the revelation of all beneficiary owners, but so far it has not happened.

In January 2021, the United States finally joined in these transparency efforts when the US Congress adopted the Corporate Transparency Act of 2020. It requires certain legal entities, such as corporations and limited liability companies (LLCs), to provide information about their beneficial owners to make it more difficult to operate anonymous shell companies for criminal purposes. The beneficial ownership information must be submitted to the US Treasury Department's Financial Crimes Enforcement Network (FinCEN) and maintained in a centralized database. Slowly, too slowly, FinCEN is now elaborating the implementation rules, but eventually it is supposed to come about. Unfortunately, unlike the EU or British legislation, the US law does not require the register of beneficial owners to be public, although it should be open to all law enforcement agencies.

The implementation of all these transparency laws is taking time. Transparency NGOs, such as Transparency International, are complaining about lacking compliance in one country after the other, but these transparency laws have turned the tables. The NGOs no longer call for new laws but for the swift and effective implementation of already adopted laws.

Russia's war of aggression against Ukraine, which was launched by Putin on February 24, 2022, altered the relationship between the West and Russia. Until that moment, the Western perception was that Russia could be expected to behave with decency. After the beginning of the war, nobody believed that any longer. The collective West came together as never before after the end of the Cold War. The Western distinction between good and bad players in Russia disappeared. Anybody who supported the Russian state financially, whether a government official, big businessman, or significant enterprise, was recognized as a bad player. Therefore, the Western sanctions on Russia suddenly rose from relatively mild to Iran-like sanctions, and they appear to be spiraling toward the kind of sanctions applied to North Korea.

Until recently, the assets that Western governments froze were tiny, a few billion dollars. In 2022, that changed. At present, many countries have frozen substantial assets, and the numbers rise by the day. The public has been greatly enraged, most of all with the freezing of many Russian superyachts, while other oligarchs have fled to safer jurisdictions, such as the Maldives, Dubai, Turkey, and Montenegro. Governments have to serve their citizens and stand up against illegal oligarchs. The assets frozen by the EU are the biggest, but the Cayman Islands, Jersey, and Switzerland have each frozen some $7 billion of Russian assets. The total amount has reached a publicly declared $60 billion. The two main dark holes in the global economy are the Cayman Islands (with 60,000 inhabitants) and Dubai, which has been gray-listed by global police against money laundering and by the Financial Action Task Force, which has been attached to the Organization of Economic Co-operation and Development (OECD) since its founding in 1989. Such small jurisdictions can hardly hold their own for dubious aims.

Apart from oligarch property, the G7 also decided to freeze the international reserves of the Central Bank of Russia, which Gary Clyde Hufbauer and Jeffrey J. Schott have assessed at $316 billion.[51]

The freezing of these large assets raises many new queries that require legislation in each nation involved. Who should be responsible for the management of the frozen assets? How can they be protected and insured? Who will pay for the management costs? What can and should be confiscated, and to what should the revenues be devoted? At present, the obvious suggestion is that a substantial share of the oligarch wealth should be confiscated and allocated to Russian reparations to Ukraine, but all this needs to be specified in new national laws. Hopefully, each country concerned will soon adopt such laws.

The Russian Central Bank reserves should be expropriated and used for the compensation of damage Russia has caused in Ukraine, as Hufbauer and Schott have argued on the basis of the US International Emergency Economic Powers Act of 1977.[52] On April 28, 2022, President Joe Biden proposed that the United States should hold Russian oligarchs and elites accountable by seizing and forfeiting oligarch assets.[53] At the end of December 2022, US Congress adopted a law on the confiscation of the assets of sanctioned Russian oligarchs in the United States. In April 2024, Congress adopted the Rebuilding Economic Prosperity and Opportunity for Ukrainians Act (or the REPO for Ukrainians Act), which authorizes the president to seize Russian sovereign assets and transfer them to a Ukraine fund. So far, the European Union has not adopted any such law, and most of the Russian sovereign assets are in Europe.

Conclusion

Until recently, the collective West ignored most of the problems that Russia's kleptocracy raised. Gradually, however, the West became more concerned about money laundering, in which Russian capital flight played a major role, but the biggest US act against money laundering was the 2001 Patriot Act, which focused on terrorist financing in the wake of 9/11. The recent adoption of new anti-money-laundering and corporate transparency legislation by the EU, the United Kingdom and the United States has altered the legal preconditions for offshore wealth. Yet, so far these laws appear ineffective.

Since Russia's war of aggression against Ukraine, starting in February 2014, the collective West has imposed personal sanctions against many wealthy Russian officials and businessmen. After Russia started its full-scale war on February 24, 2022, the Western financial and personal sanctions have become far more severe. As is evident from the many tabloid articles about oligarchs, the sanctions on the oligarchs are popular, and both activists and the voters at large want them to be implemented. Canada and the United States have adopted laws on the confiscation of sanctioned oligarchs' frozen assets, but so far very little has been done.

The confiscation of oligarchs' assets is a fool's errand. In total, Western countries have announced only $60 billion in frozen assets of sanctioned oligarchs, while a fair guess would be that they hold well-hidden wealth amounting to something like $1 trillion in the West. But this money is held in layers of shell companies in anonymous companies in a dozen offshore jurisdictions. The oligarchs hire the best lawyers in the world and will fight tooth and nail for their wealth. They have some habit.

The Ukraine-related Western sanctions on Russia are bound to stay until all Russian troops have withdrawn from Ukraine, but that will hardly be enough. Russia has caused tremendous damage to Ukraine, and it should have to pay compensation or war reparations for all that damage. Unless Russia collapses, the only way of extracting significant war reparations from Russia for Ukraine will be to legislate the confiscation of the $316 billion of currency reserves of the Central Bank of Russia, approximately two-thirds of which is held in the Euroclear bank in Belgium.

Meanwhile, the Western sanctions are instigating a redistribution of property among the truly rich in Russia in the same fashion as in Iraq under Saddam Hussein and in Serbia under Slobodan Milošević. The basic principles are that property is being transferred from foreigners to Russians, to the state, to the most criminal, and to the oligarchs who stay in Russia and do not emigrate. The most favored are the top Putin cronies—the Rotenbergs, Timchenko, and Kovalchuk. The big state companies Rosneft, Gazprom, and Rostec are obvious beneficiaries, primarily from the foreign companies that leave the oil and gas sectors. Meanwhile, Russian Gazprom and Rosneft are losing their companies in Europe either for nationalization or forced sales because of looming sanctions.

The short-term consequences will be that the tight Putin circle will gain increased control of the Russian economy, but because of this political selection of owners, the Russian economy is likely to perform even worse. It is already impossible for Russian businessmen to operate both in the West and in Russia. They have to choose, and any such choice degrades the Russian economy.

NOTES

This chapter is a further elaboration on my book, *Russia's Crony Capitalism: The Path from Market Economy to Kleptocracy* (New Haven: Yale University Press, 2019).

1. Karen Dawisha, *Putin's Kleptocracy: Who Owns Russia?* (New York: Simon & Schuster, 2014); Catherine Belton, *Putin's People* (New York: Farrar, Straus and Giroux, 2020).

2. Vladimir V. Putin, *First Person: An Astonishingly Frank Self-Portrait by Russia's President* (New York: Public Affairs, 2000).

3. Peter Baker and Susan Glasser, *Kremlin Rising: Vladimir Putin's Russia and the End of Revolution* (New York: Scribner, 2005), 47.

4. Dawisha, *Putin's Kleptocracy*; Belton, *Putin's People.*

5. Åslund, *Russia's Crony Capitalism*, 40–41.

6. Walter Laqueur, *Putinism: Russia and Its Future in the West* (New York: St. Martin's Press, 2015), 181.

7. Anton Barbashin and Hannah Thoburn, "Putin's Philosopher: Ivan Ilyin and the Ideology of Moscow's Rule," *Foreign Affairs*, September 20, 2015, https://www .foreignaffairs.com/articles/ukraine/2015-09-20/putins-philosopher.

8. Charles Clover, *Black Wind, White Snow: The Rise of Russia's New Nationalism* (New Haven: Yale University Press, 2016).

9. Baker and Glasser, *Kremlin Rising.*

10. Åslund, *Russia's Crony Capitalism*; Fiona Hill and Clifford G. Gaddy, *Mr. Putin*, 2nd ed. (Washington: Brookings, 2015); Steven Lee Myers, *The New Tsar: The Rise and Reign of Vladimir Putin* (New York: Knopf, 2015).

11. Anders Åslund, *How Russia Became a Market Economy* (Washington, DC: Brookings Institution).

12. Dev Kar and Sarah Freitas, *Russia: Illicit Financial Flows and the Role of the Underground Economy*, Global Financial Integrity, February 13, 2013, https://gfintegrity .org/report/country-case-study-russia/.

13. Åslund, *Russia's Crony Capitalism*, 164–169.

14. Gabriel Zucman, *The Hidden Wealth of Nations* (Chicago: Chicago University Press, 2015), 23–29.

15. "Preliminary Report on Foreign Holdings of U.S. Securities at End-June 2021," *United States Department of the Treasury*, February 28, 2022, https://home.treasury.gov /news/press-releases/jy0613.

16. Sam Jones, "Swiss Lawyers and Bankers to the Russian Rich Have Not Been Idle," *Financial Times*, April 28, 2022, https://web.opendrive.com/api/v1/download/file .json/NjVfNjA2OTgwNTRf?inline=1.

17. Zucman, *The Hidden Wealth of Nations*, 23–29.

18. Dawisha, *Putin's Kleptocracy.*

19. Boris Nemtsov and Vladimir Milov, *Putin i Gazprom* (Moscow: Novaya Gazeta, 2008).

20. Boris Nemtsov and Leonid Martynyuk, *Winter Olympics in the Subtropics: Corruption and Abuse in Sochi*, the Institute of Modern Russia, Moscow, 2014, http:// www.putin-itogi.ru/cp/wp-content/uploads/2013/05/Report_ENG_SOCHI-2014 _preview.pdf.

21. Aleksandr Melnikov, "Gennady Timchenko, Biografiya," July 29, 2012, http:// vspro.info.

22. "Treasury Sanctions Russian Officials, Members of the Russian Leadership's Inner Circle, and an Entity for Involvement in the Situation in Ukraine," U.S. Department of the Treasury, March 20, 2014, https://home.treasury.gov/news/press-releases/jl23331.

23. Melnikov, "Gennady Timchenko"; and Dawisha, *Putin's Kleptocracy*, 111–112.

24. Dawisha, *Putin's Kleptocracy*, 32–33.

25. Alex Fak and Anna Kotelnikova, *Oil and Gas: Tickling Giants*, Moscow: Sberbank CIS, May 2018.

26. Nemtsov and Martynyuk. *Winter Olympics in the Subtropics.*

27. Roman Anin, "Tainy 'Proekta Yug'" [The Secrets of "Project South"], *Novaya Gazeta*, January 11, 2011.

28. Evgeniya Albats, "Chisto konkretny kandidat" [Simply a Concrete Candidate]. Interview with Sergei Kolesnikov, *Novoe Vremya*, February, 2012.

29. Albats, "Chisto konkretny kandidat"; Anin, "Tainy 'Proekta Yug'"; Åslund, *Russia's Crony Capitalism*, 145–146.

30. Anders Åslund, *Russia's Capitalist Revolution: Why Market Reform Succeeded and Democracy Failed* (Washington: Peterson Institute for International Economics, 2007), 228.

31. Roman Anin, Olesya Shmagun, and Dmitry Velikovskiy. "The Secret Caretaker," *Organized Crime and Corruption Reporting Project*, April 3, 2016.

32. Anin, Shmagun, and Velikovskiy, "The Secret Caretaker."

33. Nemtsov and Milov, *Putin i Gazprom*, 20–21.

34. Vladimir V. Putin, *Presidential Address to the Federal Assembly*, December 3, 2015, www.kremlin.ru.

35. Åslund, *Russia's Crony Capitalism*, 175–176.

36. Åslund, *Russia's Crony Capitalism*, 172–176.

37. Kar and Freitas, *Russia: Illicit Financial Flows*; Filip Novokmet, Thomas Piketty, and Gabriel Zucman, *From Soviets to Oligarchs: Inequality and Property in Russia, 1905–2016*, NBER Working Paper 23712 (Cambridge, MA: National Bureau of Economic Research, August 2017).

38. Nemtsov and Milov, *Putin i Gazprom.*

39. Albats, "Chisto konkretny kandidat."

40. Bastian Obermayer and Frederik Obermaier, *The Panama Papers* (One World: London, 2016).

41. Chico Harlan, "Italy Impounds $700 Million Megayacht Linked to Putin," *Washington Post*, May 6, 2022, https://www.washingtonpost.com/world/2022/05/06/yacht-putin-italy-scheherazade/.

42. Kate Duffy, Grace Dean, and Gabrielle Bienasz, "Oligarchs Don't just Love Their Superyachts—They Also Use Them to Cement Their Status among Russia's Elite," *Business Insider*, April 7, 2022, https://www.businessinsider.com/russian-oligarch-billionaires-love-superyachts-megayachts-status-luxury-elite-2022-3

43. Freedom House, *Freedom in the World 2021*, https://freedomhouse.org/report/freedom-world/2021/democracy-under-siege.

44. U.S. Congress, *Sergei Magnitsky Rule of Law Accountability Act*, December 2012, https://www.congress.gov/bill/112th-congress/senate-bill/1039.

45. Rosie Gray, "Bill Browder's Testimony to the Senate Judiciary Committee," *Atlantic*, July 25, 2017, https://www.theatlantic.com/politics/archive/2017/07/bill -browders-testimony-to-the-senate-judiciary-committee/534864/.

46. John Dunlop, *The February 2015 Assassination of Boris Nemtsov and the Flawed Trial of His Alleged Killers: An Exploration of Russia's "Crime of the 21st Century"* (Stuttgart: Ibidem Press, 2019).

47. Åslund, *Russia's Crony Capitalism*, 148–150.

48. Belton, *Putin's People*; Jane Croft, "Calls for Reform of England's Libel Laws to Prevent Abuse by Wealthy Litigants," *Financial Times*, March 15, 2022, https://www.ft .com/content/ae8512d3-663e-4039-ba3e-6de4f8ca5120.

49. European Commission, *Directive (EU) 2018/843 of the European Parliament and of the Council of 30 May 2018 amending Directive (EU) 2015/849 on the Prevention of the Use of the Financial System for the Purposes of Money Laundering or Terrorist Financing*, June 19, 2018, https://eur-lex.europa.eu/legal-content/EN/TXT/?uri=celex%3A32018L0843, and https://eur-lex.europa.eu/legal-content/EN/TXT/?uri=celex%3A32015L0849.

50. Transparency International UK, *Hiding in Plain Sight: How UK Companies Are Used to Launder Corrupt Wealth*, 2017, https://www.transparency.org.uk/sites/default /files/pdf/publications/HidingInPlainSight_WEB3.pdf.

51. Gary Clyde Hufbauer and Jeffrey J. Schott, "The United States Should Seize Russian Assets for Ukraine's Reconstruction," Peterson Institute for International Economics, April 21, 2022, https://www.piie.com/blogs/realtime-economic-issues-watch /united-states-should-seize-russian-assets-ukraines.

52. Hufbauer and Schott, "The United States Should Seize Russian Assets."

53. The White House, *FACT SHEET: President Biden's Comprehensive Proposal to Hold Russian Oligarchs and Elites Accountable*, April 28, 2022, https://www.whitehouse.gov /briefing-room/statements-releases/2022/04/28/fact-sheet-president-bidens-compre hensive-proposal-to-hold-russian-oligarchs-accountable/.

Chapter Three

Vladimir Putin and the Russian Military

Alexandra Chinchilla and Raymond C. Finch III

Before Russia's full-scale invasion of Ukraine, Western analysts and policymakers predicted that Kyiv would fall within days. In anticipation, Western embassies and military trainers were evacuated from Ukraine. However, these gloomy predictions—which the Kremlin likely shared—turned out to be wrong. The "special military operation" is now in its third year, and an estimated 300,000 to 500,000 Russians have been killed or wounded on the battlefield.[1] This miscalculation, along with Russia's military shortcomings, raises several questions. Why did the West underestimate Ukraine's capabilities and overestimate Russia's? Why did the Russian military struggle so much in the early months of the invasion? And most importantly, why didn't Russian leadership, with more information than the West, form a more realistic view of their own military's abilities?

Western intelligence and the Kremlin's confidence that Russia was heavily favored to win may have been reasonable, and a series of unlucky mishaps could have prevented Russia from quickly taking Kyiv. But, although the outcome may have been "highly contingent,"[2] the performance of both militaries demonstrates that the odds were more in Ukraine's favor than acknowledged beforehand. Another possibility is that new technologies and the terrain heavily favored the defense over the offense. This was true later in the conflict in the Donbas, but not in the war's early days, when Kyiv was caught by surprise and had little time to prepare its defenses. The most likely explanation is that both Russia and the West did not fully understand Ukraine and were too optimistic about Putin's military reforms. Putin's obsession with dominating Ukraine fueled confidence about the likelihood of success and led him to ignore clear evidence of Ukraine's growing military strength and its shift toward the West.

This chapter examines the development of the Russian military under Vladimir Putin, focusing on the reforms and modernization efforts after Russia's five-day war with Georgia in 2008. These reforms aimed to achieve two goals: first, to create a modern expeditionary force capable of extending Russia's influence in places like Syria, and second, to ensure the Russian military could perform better if it was needed in its neighborhood. Although these reforms were not initially designed for an invasion of Ukraine, they were intended to support a more assertive Russian foreign policy. We examine this shift in Russian foreign policy, the extent of Russian military reforms, and Russia's efforts to prepare for greater confrontation with the West.

We also explore how both Russia and the West overestimated the success of these reforms and underestimated Ukraine's progress in military modernization and reform between 2014 and 2022. As a result, Russia misjudged the cost of war. The authoritarian nature of the Putin regime led to overly ambitious goals for invading Ukraine and contributed to poor planning of the operation. But despite its initial failures in Ukraine, the Russian military adapted. Support from China, trade with third parties, and shifting to a war economy allowed the Russian military to rebuild. This reconstitution, along with delays in Western aid to Ukraine, has given Russia another opportunity. We conclude by discussing the implications for the war in Ukraine.

Vladimir Putin, a Stronger Russia, and an Increasingly Aggressive Foreign Policy

Vladimir Putin and the Russian elite currently share a sense of alienation from and antagonism with the West. Several other chapters in this book address how current events came to be. We underscore a few key facts here.

The collapse of the Soviet Union and the subsequent "disorder bordering on chaos" of the 1990s profoundly affected Vladimir Putin's outlook on international politics.[3] Putin served on the front lines during the Cold War as a KGB agent in Dresden, helping to defend the Soviet-communist order.[4] As it began to crumble, Putin had a front-row seat to the collapse of communism and Soviet influence in Eastern Europe. He observed how the Soviet Union collapsed not because it lost its military power, but because the Soviet leadership under Mikhail Gorbachev lost faith in the communist ideal.[5] When protests broke out against the ruling regime in East Germany and Putin turned to Moscow for guidance, the response was silence.[6] Putin once again encountered the weakness of the Russian state when participating in St. Petersburg politics during the 1990s. His position as deputy to Anatoly Sobchak, mayor of St. Petersburg, gave him an opportunity to observe and participate in the corruption and pilfering of state resources that took place.

After coming to power, Putin invested significant energy into strengthening the Russian state so that it would be more modern and efficient. He also brokered a series of deals with key elite constituencies as well as provided stability and economic benefits for the public—all of which made him a genuinely popular leader.[7] During Putin's first two terms as president (2000–2008), higher fossil fuel prices helped the Russian economy grow at an impressive rate, and incomes and the standard of living improved for most Russians. The state's capacity grew too: pensions were paid on time, and a portion of the country's resource wealth was spent on capital improvements (e.g., healthcare, roads, and education). Although not dramatic, there were also steady improvements within Russia's armed forces.

But at the same time as he was building more competent bureaucracies, Putin worked to ensure that the invigorated Russian state would be authoritarian and loyal to him. One such organization where Putin successfully pursued loyalty and competency was the state judiciary.[8] Another was the successor agency to the KGB, the FSB, which became more effective at the same time as it was reaping the financial benefits of access to power. Putin and his associates amassed huge fortunes while the state grew stronger. Although this initial process of authoritarianism was slow and stealthy, after the 2011 legislative election, when Putin's party United Russia only won 49% of the vote, repression became more visible.

As Russia was becoming more authoritarian under Putin's leadership, its relationship with the West was also deteriorating. Numerous factors worked together to push Russia and the West farther apart. The US invasion of Iraq in 2003 led to a collapse in the counterterrorism partnership that Putin and the Bush administration briefly pursued after 9/11.[9] After this point, despite attempts by the Obama administration to "reset" relations with Russia—showing an intense desire to accommodate Russia even after its war with Georgia—the relationship never recovered. Russian perceptions of Western infringement on their real and imagined security interests contributed to this decline.[10] But above all, the increasingly authoritarian nature of the Russian state made a productive relationship with the West more and more untenable.[11]

Upon his return as Russian president in May 2012, Putin made military modernization a top priority. Strengthening the Russian military became the key component in the larger Kremlin strategy of building a multipolar global order. Putin claimed that Russia remained a great power and enjoyed a certain sphere of influence. He viewed a multipolar global order, with Russia as a key axis of power, as more stable than a unipolar version led by the United States. He was willing to take potentially costly action to increase the status of Russia as a great power.[12]

In addition to allowing Russia to pursue its foreign policy goals, Putin recognized that greater military power would provide important domestic political benefits to his regime. Although Russians generally have much less positive views of the coercive institutions that they regularly interact with—like the police and prosecutors—they hold generally positive views of the military.[13] The military's role in legitimizing the regime is only strengthened by Kremlin rhetoric that now paints the West as a predator and defines patriotism as military prowess.

For the last decade or more, the Russian information space has become increasingly authoritarian. Those few Russian media sources that dared to present a perspective different from the Kremlin's have been closed or forced to leave the country.[14] As a result, public support for Putin's foreign policy priorities, including the current war in Ukraine, has remained high.[15] In the new Kremlin narrative, to defend against the threat of the West and restore Russia to its rightful status, Russia needs a strong leader and formidable military. The success of this narrative is reflected in Putin's increased public opinion ratings following aggressive actions like the annexation of Crimea.[16]

A key component of the Kremlin's messaging has been its rewriting of the narrative surrounding the collapse of the USSR. Instead of seeing the fall of the Soviet Union as a result of a failed political and economic model, the Kremlin now emphasizes the nefarious role that the West (and the United States in particular) played in its demise. In their rendition, the West conspired to bring down the USSR, and then continued to humiliate and exploit Russia during the painful decade of the 1990s. This sense of humiliation and resentment toward the United States forms the nucleus of the Kremlin's chronicle of recent history. Current Kremlin propaganda is built around the need to defend Russia from this same Western threat, serving as justification for an aggressive foreign policy.

Russia's authoritarian identity and its resurgence as a great power intensified the need for a stronger military. However, the Russian military's poor performance in the August 2008 Georgia war underscored that military reform was also a practical necessity. Although Russia won the five-day war, it revealed serious problems with communication, equipment, training, and command and control.[17] These failures provided the will to push long-planned, but always ignored and under-resourced, reforms through. Pressure came not just from the top, but also from the bottom; Mark Galeotti quotes a former defense attaché to Moscow noting in 2010 how "the majors and the colonels, they are sick and tired of 20 years of decay."[18] Reforms finally began under the leadership of Anatoly Serdyukov, who served as minister of defense from 2007 until he was fired in 2012 and replaced by Sergei Shoigu, who slowed down the reforms.

Russian Military Reform Before 2022

Military reform was necessary to create a military strong enough to underpin an increasingly aggressive Russian foreign policy. After years of underspending on defense, the military needed to be equipped with modernized and advanced equipment and weapons systems. It was intended to remain large enough to fight land warfare in Russia's neighborhood as well as engage in out-of-area expeditionary warfare. To meet these goals, Russia needed to continue the practice of conscription while simultaneously increasing the professionalism of the armed forces to attract and retain contract soldiers. Contract soldiers are volunteers who sign up for military service for a period of a few years or even make the military their career. The military also shrunk in size, to a pre-2022 ground force size of 360,000.[19] The ratio of conscripts to contract soldiers decreased, although conscripts still constituted about one-quarter to one-third of manpower even in elite or maneuver units.[20] Increased professionalism was also intended to improve public attitudes about the military as well as willingness to serve. Under President Putin, the image of the Russian soldier was transformed from a drunk incompetent into a proud and professional "polite man."[21] Behind this transformation were substantial improvements in the military's infrastructure and equipment, manpower, and overall organization.

Reforms improved the experience of serving in the military for both contract and conscript soldiers. The term of conscription was reduced to one year, and defense officials implemented a series of reforms to improve living conditions for soldiers and allow them to focus on military tasks. Officer and contractor pay became largely competitive with pay in other government agencies. Living conditions for one-year draftees (e.g., barracks, food, and uniforms) improved. The waiting list for adequate housing for military officers was reduced to manageable levels. Discipline within the ranks was tightened up, and there were far fewer reported cases of hazing.[22] The Kremlin enacted legislation that provided incentives for some young Russian men to fulfill their military obligation while enrolled in college. Select students gained credit for military service by working on projects related to the country's defense industry.[23] These reforms helped to improve the image of military service and reduce draft evasion. A 2019 poll from the Levada Center found that 60% of Russians agreed with the statement that every real man should experience military service.[24]

There were similar improvements to the military's human capital. One such improvement was investment in training and professional military education. According to government sources, Russia developed modern combined-arms training facilities where military personnel could test the latest tactics and equipment in a realistic training environment.[25] The military's education system recovered from the 2008 reform (which had closed or consolidated nearly 75% of the military schools), and the subsequent reorganization reportedly resulted in greater efficiency and less redundancy. These reforms were limited, however. Reports indicate that even after reforms, most of the professional military remained poorly trained.[26] One proposed reform that could have had a big impact if completed was a Western-style noncommissioned officer (NCO) corps to provide training expertise, discipline, and continuity within the contract and draftee ranks. These plans were eventually abandoned.[27]

Despite efforts to increase training across the military, the combat readiness and technical expertise of conscripts remained low. The one-year term that conscripts served was hardly long enough for them to become fully proficient in even the most basic soldier skills, and the constant turnover of personnel weakened combat readiness. Some have suggested that the one-year draft was primarily designed to raise patriotic awareness and to create a large mobilization reserve in the event of major hostilities.[28] Conscripts who had completed their mandatory service also served as the primary recruiting pool for contract soldiers.

Personnel management policies also needed significant reform to ensure that the right people were promoted, given the right assignments, and then supported in their jobs so they would stay in the military for a career. These reforms were only partially successful. The officer promotion and assignment system remained somewhat arbitrary, where the immediate commander held inordinate sway over the officers serving in his command.[29] Even though there were significant improvements in prestige, pay, and living conditions for those who served in the armed forces, defense officials still struggled with attracting young Russians to serve as contract soldiers in the military—and then with retaining them once they joined.[30] When the administrative promises sometimes did not correspond with reality, those who signed contracts often left the military when contract provisions were unmet.[31] The infrastructure to support contract personnel (e.g., family housing, medical care, and employment for spouses) proved insufficient. Questions also remained regarding long-term career progression for contract soldiers and retirement benefits.[32]

Another key reform from 2008 helped to streamline the command and control of the Russian armed forces. The previous six military districts were consolidated into four joint-like commands, oriented toward a specific threat.[33] In this new model, parochial interests of the former branches have theoretically been subordinated to an overall command structure, which also incorporated elements of other power ministries. Overall command and control was now exercised by a massive new national military control center in Moscow.[34] On paper at least (and on the virtual screens of the new control center in Moscow), there was much greater unity of effort among the various Russian security forces (e.g., Ministry of Defense, Ministry of Internal Affairs, FSB, and Emergency Ministry).

The force structure and readiness of the Russian military was also transformed. Initial reforms envisioned a modern expeditionary force organized into a smaller number of brigades instead of divisions or armies. These brigades could participate in a range of small-scale interventions in the post-Soviet space or out-of-area operations in places like Syria. To support this shift, some eighty-five combat-ready brigades were created, moving away from the old Soviet model of having units that were not combat ready until filled with mobilized soldiers. Part of the justification behind this change was the conviction that modern war—as the West had demonstrated quite effectively—had evolved to privilege "smaller, highly mobile and agile forces" rather than "the massing of force and resources and firepower."[35] A war might be over by the time mobilization was completed, so Russian forces needed to be prepared to fight at a moment's notice.

By 2022, the Russian military had assumed a posture of permanent readiness on paper, though given continuing manpower challenges, likely only a certain percentage of these brigades were truly combat ready.[36] Supporting the need for readiness, battalion tactical groups (BTGs) were introduced as battalion-sized combined-arms formations that were staffed with professional contract soldiers and could be constructed from existing brigades at lower levels of readiness. The BTGs were more easily deployable because they were composed of contract soldiers. Conscripts, in contrast, legally cannot be deployed outside Russia.[37] The BTGs, then, could be rapidly deployed as part of large-scale combat or for counterinsurgency and local combat.[38]

Despite this reform to create combat-ready BTGs, Russian military leaders continued to rely upon their airborne forces as their rapid reaction force. Within the military, Russia's airborne forces are a distinct force and are regarded as one of the most elite and powerful weapons in the Kremlin's arsenal. Airborne forces played a key role during both the conflict with Georgia in 2008 and the seizure of key installations in Crimea in 2014. During Russia's full-scale invasion of Ukraine in 2022, airborne forces were part of a risky effort to seize Hostomel Airport near Kyiv, which, had it succeeded, may have changed the outcome of the war.[39] As problems developed with manning and training sufficient draftees to maintain conventional combat-ready brigades, the Russian military continued to rely on airborne or special-forces-type units (e.g., naval infantry), which were primarily manned with contract or professional soldiers.

The transition to combat-ready brigades as originally conceived after 2008, and rolled out in the 2010–2012 period, was intended to prepare Russia to fight "small wars." However, Russia's war in the Donbas region of Ukraine, which began in 2014, marked a key inflection point that saw Russia enhance its capability to fight a regional, conventional war. Russian defense planners felt they may potentially need to organize larger amounts of combat power, so plans to shelve organizational components of the military (e.g., the division) were canceled.[40] Responding to Russia's increasingly threatening posture on NATO's eastern flank, US Army Europe underwent a similar reorientation from being organized to fight counterterrorism wars as brigades to planning to fight with its NATO allies as divisions.

Despite retaining the division, the Russian military was still organized optimally for relatively small-scale intervention, not for large-scale protracted war with a peer competitor like NATO. It could, at most, conduct a limited incursion in the Baltics if NATO lacked the resolve to respond. Instead, the Russian military was "intended and structured primarily for a rapid attack or to engage in a war in a non-NATO country within its perceived sphere of influence."[41] And even a smaller regional war would have to be "short and sharp"—or Russia would need to mobilize to keep fighting.[42]

Although Russia did not have enough infantry to fight a protracted large-scale conventional war, it invested in military equipment, weapons, and large stockpiles of ammunition to fight such a conflict.[43] Investment in arms is a good indicator of preparedness; additional manpower can be built comparatively quickly after a period of mobilization, but arms must be invested in well beforehand. Russia allocated significant funding, the peak of which was spent between 2010 and 2016, toward modernizing everything from the soldier's basic kit to existing weapons systems.[44] Pervasive corruption, however, meant that many units still lacked basic equipment and supplies despite money spent on acquiring them.

During the decade of 2010–2019, Russia spent nearly 40% of its total military expenditure on arms procurement—more than twice that spent by France, Germany, and the United Kingdom.[45] As some analysts have pointed out, moreover, Russia's increase in defense spending was larger than what the dollar value of that spending might indicate. Because Russia has a large domestic-defense industry, it can buy more at home than the dollar-to-ruble exchange rate indicates.[46] After accounting for purchasing power parity, Russia is the fourth-largest spender on its military; only the United States, China, and India spend more. Moreover, indicators show that the money was not merely earmarked for defense but actually resulted in new and modernized weapons systems being delivered to the armed forces.[47]

Russia largely invested in modernized versions of old weapons designs. An example is the ballistic and cruise missiles used in the opening hours of Russia's full-scale invasion of Ukraine to hit high-value military targets. They are now used to target Ukrainian energy infrastructure and cities. The Kh-32 supersonic air-launched cruise missile, a modernized version of the Soviet-era Kh-22, was adopted in 2016 after modernization efforts.[48] It has been effective because it flies too fast to be shot down with air defense systems (except for the Patriot, which is only deployed in a few places around Ukraine).[49] Russia also increased its ability to use sea-launched Kalibr cruise missiles at scale. Although the Kalibr line of missiles dates back to the 1990s, Russia demonstrated its use in Syria to communicate that it has an extensive strike capability after these modernization efforts.[50] Other areas of modernization included improved versions of older models of battle tanks for the ground forces and aircraft for the aerospace forces.[51]

Russia also invested in research and development of new capabilities. Investment improved Russian capabilities for electronic warfare, the use of unmanned platforms, as well as space technology and artificial intelligence.[52] But the showpiece was meant to be Russia's development of advanced weapons systems. In 2018, Putin announced the existence of five major weapons systems, dubbed *superoruzhie* (superweapons).[53] Four out of the five *superoruzhie* are part of continued developments and improvements within Russia's strategic nuclear forces. These weapons systems are capable of being used as strategic weapons because they can travel over 5,000 km, can be outfitted with a nuclear warhead, and are thought to be able to evade missile defense systems—ensuring a secure second-strike nuclear capability for Russia. The fifth system, Kinzhal Kh-47M2 air-launched ballistic missiles,[54] was thought to help Russia compensate for weaknesses compared to the West in conventional precision-strike capability.

The Kinzhal missiles have not held up as well as expected when used in Ukraine. Russian forces attempted to use them to take out a Patriot battery in a sustained attack but ultimately failed.[55]

After these reforms, the Russian military emerged as a "smaller, better equipped, and more offensively oriented force."[56] Russia put this new force to work in interventions in Ukraine, beginning in 2014, and Syria, beginning in 2015. Even today, Russian forces conduct air and ground operations in Syria while the Russian army fights a large-scale ground war in Ukraine. These conflicts served as important training grounds and opportunities for testing new capabilities.[57] The conflict in the Donbas demonstrated the importance of artillery and provided testing grounds for unmanned systems and electronic warfare. Syria has provided the military with the opportunity to employ and test advanced weapon systems, particularly air and naval assets. The Russian military's good performance in Ukraine and Syria increased optimism that the reforms were successful.

The conflicts in Ukraine and Syria also demonstrated Russia's increasing risk acceptance and ability to absorb the costs of intervention, such as sanctions or damage to its international reputation. One such risk was accidental escalation with NATO countries, which increased after Russia's intervention to support the Assad regime in Syria while a US-led coalition intervened against the Islamic State. For instance, in November 2015, Turkey and Russia almost came to blows when Turkish forces downed a Russian Su-24 military aircraft after it crossed into Turkish airspace. The Kremlin was incensed when an American navy fighter jet downed a Syrian Su-22 fighter in June 2017.[58] In a surprising turn of events, Wagner forces and US Special Operations Forces fought one another in an engagement that resulted in hundreds of dead Russian professional military contractors.[59] Although Russia and the United States used tools like a deconfliction hotline to successfully manage the risks of escalation from that incident and others, Russia's behavior showed an increasingly aggressive foreign policy and the willingness to put military force behind it.

Russia also prepared on multiple levels for the possibility of confrontation with the West. Even before the full-scale invasion of Ukraine, RAND analysts, writing in 2021 as Russian forces conducted exercises on the border with Ukraine, noted how Russia was taking "legal and practical steps . . . to shore up the mobilization system, which suggests a desire to be prepared for a large-scale war."[60] Other analysts noted with alarm Russia's policy of "technological solitude" adopted after Western sanctions in 2014, which was improving the self-sufficiency and resilience of its defense industrial base to allow for "continued confrontation with Western countries."[61] Russia also successfully overcame its dependence on food imports to make its economy resilient to future conflict.[62]

The Decision to Invade Ukraine

After a decade of reforms, the Russian military projected confidence in its ability to succeed in its invasion of Ukraine. Valery Gerasimov, chief of the General Staff of the Russian Armed Forces, told "international interlocutors on the outbreak of the war, 'I command the second most powerful Army in the world.'"[63] Western analysts were also optimistic about Russia's prospects, most arguing that the Russian military had successfully reformed and Ukraine would have little chance of fending off defeat.[64] For example, Michael Kofman and Jeffrey Edmonds wrote in a *Foreign Affairs* piece just days before the full-scale invasion that Russia would quickly overwhelm Ukrainian air defenses with "hundreds of bombers as well as ground launched ballistic and cruise missiles." They argued Russian forces had "far more—and far better—artillery, reconnaissance, and logistical capabilities than Ukraine does" and consequently would "have the advantage along every axis of attack."[65]

US intelligence analysts similarly predicted that in a matter of days, Russian troops would seize Kyiv and install a puppet government, leaving only a rump state in the west. US planners developed an interagency "Tiger Team" to plan for responses to Russia's invasion. Although this planning was crucial for organizing an immediate and effective US government response after February 24, 2022, it could have benefited from considering outcomes more favorable to Ukraine. In the words of the Tiger Team lead, Alexander Bick:

> The Tiger Team got the scale, geography, and timing of Russia's military operations almost exactly right. But we were wrong on almost everything else. We overestimated the Russian military, underestimated Ukraine's capabilities and resolve, and failed to anticipate the extent to which fear and public revulsion would reshape European politics in favor of tougher response options, some of which seemed out of reach only days before.[66]

Pessimistic predictions relied too heavily on assessing the military balance between Russia and Ukraine. On paper, the Russian military was vastly stronger: it had more manpower and more and better firepower. It had also performed well in limited conflict in Ukraine and Syria. What these predictions did not account for was everything else about the Russian military. As a result of corruption within the force, poor training and leadership, and limited motivation compared to

Ukraine, the Russian military failed to fight effectively. Military leadership made poor decisions about how to employ its force, did not plan sufficiently for the invasion, and then failed to adjust when resistance was stronger than anticipated. As RUSI analysts put it, assessments of Russia's performance suffered from an "overriding focus on the quantity of equipment, rather than the quality of personnel, their leadership, training and motivations."[67]

The Russian military, like Western analysts, clearly underestimated the improvements in Ukraine's military made between 2014 and 2022. The Ukrainian military in 2014 could barely muster 6,000 troops to face the Russian army. It was, in the words of then-Chief of Defense Viktor Muzhenko, "literally in ruins, [with] Russian generals at the head of the armed forces and security agencies . . ."[68] Ukraine's army in 2022 had combat experience and high morale and was psychologically prepared to fight. The Ukrainian army was smaller than Russia's but had a large reserve of people with military experience who could be mobilized. They were called up in the days before and immediately after Russia's invasion. Ukraine had the second-largest amount of artillery in Europe after Russia and had invested in enough ammunition for six weeks of high-intensity war fighting. It had also invested heavily in anti-tank guided weapons—not just Javelins provided by Western security assistance. Ukraine had more air defense than Western estimates gave them credit for: radar to find Russian missiles, anti-aircraft missile forces, man-portable air-defense systems (MANPADS), and aircraft.[69] The Ukrainian army and Special Operations Forces, who played a crucial role in the defense of Kyiv, met or exceeded the Russian army's capabilities in skill and will. They had extensive combat experience in the Donbas and had trained extensively with Western advisers before 2022.[70] Ukrainian soldiers were also more motivated. The Russian military's "culture of not valuing individuals" had weakened morale at the tactical level, while Ukrainians drew strength from what they were fighting for.[71]

Russian Military Performance in the Full-Scale Invasion of Ukraine

From the very start, the Russian military's performance during the first period of the special military operation against Ukraine (February 24 to March 25, 2022) was stymied by poor planning. Perhaps envisioning a repeat of the 2014 bloodless Crimean annexation, military planners developed a plan where Russian forces would massively attack Ukraine along multiple axes. The main thrust would remove Ukrainian leadership from Kyiv, and the Ukrainian "Nazis" would be swiftly shocked into submission. Largely stemming from faulty expectations derived from poor intelligence, political and military leaders did not plan on meeting stiff Ukrainian resistance. Ukrainian will to fight was judged to be low; surveys conducted by the FSB "painted a picture of a largely politically apathetic Ukrainian society that distrusted its leaders, was primarily concerned about the economy and thought an escalation of the war between Russia and Ukraine was unlikely."[72]

Although it was correct that the invasion caught Ukraine largely by surprise, Ukrainians did not view Russia favorably and were determined to put up fierce resistance for their country. Russia largely failed in its attempts at irregular warfare to suppress the level of resistance before the conventional invasion. Despite being caught by surprise, Ukrainian units were able to disperse before airstrikes could target them and rushed to meet Russian forces in the field.[73] Russian military planners were left unprepared because they had no plan for what to do if they were wrong in their initial decisions.[74]

Based on inaccurate assumptions about how much resistance Ukraine could offer, the whole operation to take control of Ukraine was intended to be completed within a week.[75] Indeed, some frontline units purportedly carried dress uniforms in anticipation of an early victory parade.[76] These specious planning assumptions also undermined adequate logistics.[77] Because Russian soldiers were to be welcomed with bread and salt by the grateful Ukrainians, there was little need to worry about extra fuel, ammunition, and food/water. The lack of planning meant that even though Russian forces did achieve the element of surprise and favorable force ratios on their main axes of approach, they were unable to exploit these advantages.[78] The reality of fighting without a plan against a determined enemy was painful.

These planning delusions were reinforced by President Putin, who, in July 2021, wrote an essay concluding that Ukrainian national identity is a myth and that the "true sovereignty of Ukraine is possible only in partnership with Russia."[79] These beliefs about the necessity of forced partnership between Russia and Ukraine set the ambitious goals of regime change for the war; Russia sought "not control of the Donbas, nor any other piece of Ukrainian territory, but control of the country in its totality."[80] Given these aims, an attack on Kyiv, regardless of how risky it might be, was essential. Authoritarian politics prevented dissension that could have avoided such foolhardy planning. The Kremlin yes-men either agreed with their boss or were fearful to question the leader's fallacious assumptions. Their abject subservience was on full display during the Security Council meeting televised on February 21, 2022, where each member stood before Putin pledging allegiance to his distorted vision.[81]

But the Russian military did not invade in the way it did simply because it was blinded by optimism about the political situation in Ukraine or eager to seize Kyiv. The decisions Russia had made about force structure during the previous decade constrained what kind of force could be generated for the full-scale invasion. Political decision makers chose not to mobilize and sent Russia to war as a peacetime force, likely to ensure high public support for the war by limiting its costs. Without mobilization, the Russian military was constrained by the smaller pool of manpower it had available in the easily deployable BTGs composed of contract troops. The invasion was composed of 136 BTGs, totaling probably around 80,000 troops.[82] As a result, Russia did not have the force size for a protracted war; it had to win quickly. Maintaining operational surprise therefore was key, and Russian forces were successful in achieving it.

But the imperative of achieving surprise ended up making the operation even more risky; there was no air campaign before Russian forces entered Ukraine because that would have given Ukraine time to prepare. Russian soldiers got their orders only twenty-four hours before the invasion (around the same time Ukrainian intelligence became convinced the invasion was imminent), leaving the force wholly unprepared.[83] Given the small force size, it would have been more prudent to invade with a plan consistent with Russian doctrine: a protracted air campaign before a ground invasion as well as a focus on a main axis of approach.[84] The highly risky operation designed to force Ukraine into quickly capitulating was likely the result of political priorities constraining military planning.

The unfolding of the plan also revealed significant issues with Russian military reform. The air campaign revealed that the Russian air force struggled not because of technical limitations but because of "the 'software' of the Russian military, which lacked the capacity and experience for conducting complex air operations of this type and therefore hinged its hopes on a successful initial set of attacks."[85] Russian operations officers also struggled with battle damage assessments to evaluate whether they had hit a target, which gave mobile targets time to disperse if they survived the initial attack. As a result, many Ukrainian air defense systems remained online. The Russian military found itself relying heavily on satellite data—much of it publicly available—which left it too slow to interdict moving targets.[86]

The "skill" aspects of military power were also not in Russia's favor. Despite all the highly publicized major training exercises over the last decade, it was clear that the Russian military still suffered in combined-arms operations. Attacking units demonstrated weak convoy discipline and an overall lack of command and control. Part of this could be the result of the BTGs' structure. Although the

BTGs were great on paper and for small military interventions, when used in a conventional ground invasion, they were less than the sum of their parts. They were composed of soldiers who had not worked together until shortly before the invasion, leaving them in need of more collective training and commanders unsure of their actual capabilities.[87] These problems were made worse by the decision to keep the invasion force for months on the border with Ukraine, where they did not have the opportunity for collective training to prepare for the invasion.[88]

Human capital also remained weak, and leadership at all levels was lacking. There was little evidence of Russian NCOs making a positive difference, and general officers were often dispatched to the front lines to sort out tactical-level problems (where a few ended up killed or injured).[89] Ukrainian junior leaders, in contrast, showed significant skill and initiative. Compared with their Russian counterparts, specialists like Ukrainian tankers and pilots were better trained.[90]

The invasion highlighted the persistent issue of corruption within the Russian military. A significant number of soldiers were without essential equipment, such as night vision goggles, radios, tactical unmanned aerial vehicles (UAVs), and cold-weather gear, as well as vital supplies like water and unexpired rations. Tactical-level medical care was glaringly inadequate, vehicle maintenance was substandard, and repair parts were frequently unavailable. Additionally, many units were hindered by missing or nonfunctional communications equipment. Admittedly, some of these logistical issues were the result of poor operational planning for a longer-than-expected conflict, but others showed the ongoing corruption in the Russian military. As a result of systemic corruption within the military, Russian military leaders failed to realize that the military was less prepared for a full-scale invasion than they had hoped. They also failed to provide accurate assessments of their preparedness to civilian leaders.

After a week or two of the Russians confronting fierce Ukrainian resistance, some analysts assumed that the Russian military would have revised its multi-axes plan and focused on a single objective. Such a revision, however, would have cast doubt upon the planning assumptions and wisdom of the ultimate decider. Moreover, the pliant, pro-Kremlin media in Russia was broadcasting a far different narrative to its audience, whereby the Russian military was easily liberating Ukrainian cities and crushing the enemy. The Russian audience was fed with stories of brave Russian soldiers handily defeating the Ukrainians, who were also the culprits behind any Ukrainian civilian casualties. Such reports nested safely within the Kremlin's narrative, especially after it enacted legislation that criminalized any negative reporting about the military.[91]

As the Ukrainian resistance stiffened and Russian losses increased, there was a corresponding increase in the bombing of a greater range of military targets (Russia had held off on hitting infrastructure initially) as well as of the Ukrainian civilian population. Reluctant to fly low to engage targets more accurately, Russian pilots dropped their ordnance from safe and inaccurate distances. Claiming that Ukrainian military units had quartered in civilian housing districts, Russian rocket and artillery leveled city blocks throughout the country. Some Russian soldiers plundered and committed wanton violence as the result of corruption, poor discipline, and weak leadership.[92] Other units committed horrendous war crimes, indiscriminately killing, looting, and violating the civilian population, most notably in the Kyiv suburb of Bucha.[93]

In the beginning of April 2022, Russia lost the Battle of Kyiv and reconcentrated its efforts on the Donbas region (Donetsk and Luhansk oblasts), as well as the regions north of the Sea of Azov and Black Sea, which provide a land bridge to Crimea (Zaporizhzhia and Kherson oblasts). The Russian military reverted to what it does best: build up forces along a specific objective and then saturate the target with massive rocket and artillery fire, combined with high-altitude air force bombing. The Russian seizure of Mariupol in mid-May 2022 provides a grim example of this brutal strategy. After surrounding the city in early March, the Russian military continually pounded the city with artillery, rocket, and air attacks for the next eight weeks. Russian forces cut access to food, water, electricity, and healthcare for civilians trapped inside.[94] The city was largely destroyed, and conservative estimates claimed that more than 20,000 civilians died in the fighting. Nevertheless, this "victory" was exalted by the Russian media, where many commentators suggested that Mariupol's destruction should serve as an example to other Ukrainian cities.[95]

By the end of the summer, Russian infantry were exhausted and had taken heavy losses. Ukrainian losses were likely quite high as well, but their morale was better, and Western aid was beginning to flow to partially make up for Ukrainian shortfalls in firepower and ammunition stockpiles.[96] In September 2022, Ukrainian forces counterattacked, retaking a large area of the Kharkiv region. That same month, the Kremlin announced a "partial mobilization" of 300,000 new troops to fight in Ukraine. This decision was made too late to prevent the Ukrainian military from liberating significant territory in the Kherson region, including the capital city. At the time, it appeared that Ukraine had gained the strategic initiative, but this would prove to be short lived.

Since December 2022, the fighting has continued to rage, not only along areas occupied by Russia but throughout all of Ukraine. Unable to break through Ukrainian defensive positions, the Kremlin has used long-range assets (air force, UAVs, and long-range artillery and missile fires) to weaken and destroy critical Ukrainian infrastructure. Ukraine has responded in kind, bombing Russian cities close to its border (e.g., Belgorod) and targeting key Russian energy assets.

The much-anticipated Ukrainian offensive planned for the summer of 2023 failed to gain traction, with the front line barely changing. Hopes were initially high—unrealistically high, in fact—for Ukraine's performance. Over a six-month period in early 2023, Western partners trained nine combat brigades, totaling 63,000 soldiers, for the summer counter-offensive and equipped them with a variety of advanced weapons systems, such as Bradley infantry fighting vehicles, Leopard 2 and Challenger 2 tanks, and a HIMARS (high-mobility artillery rocket system). They also dug deep into existing stocks to provide ammunition to narrow Russia's firepower advantage. At Security Assistance Group–Ukraine (SAG-U), which is responsible for coordinating Western aid to Ukraine from its headquarters at a US Army base in Germany, military planners walked Ukraine through a series of war games to prepare.

However, once up against a prepared Russian defense, Ukrainian forces struggled to conduct combined-arms maneuvers to mass forces and break through the Surovikin line. The Forty-Seventh Mechanized Brigade, for example, suffered substantial losses, with up to twenty-five tanks and fighting vehicles destroyed in Russian minefields near Mala Tokmachka.[97] According to some estimates, Ukraine may have lost up to 20% of the weapons and equipment sent by the United States and its European allies during the opening weeks of the counter-offensive alone.[98] After these setbacks, Kyiv shifted to an attritional strategy, attempting to make incremental gains along three axes of attack.

Some argued that the counter-offensive failed because Ukraine did not take Western advice to concentrate on a single axis of attack. Others argued that Western training and equipping ultimately did not prepare Ukrainian forces appropriately. But these arguments discount the great difficulty in making breakthroughs against a defense like the one the Russians had prepared in the Donbas. During this conflict, both Russia and Ukraine have managed to make gains against a hasty defense and have struggled against a prepared one.[99] Complicating matters, the technology held by both sides, like unmanned aerial systems and electronic sensors, has made the battlefield extremely transparent, which means that it is difficult for enough forces to mass for an assault without being detected and destroyed by artillery and drones.[100] New equipment—including that provided by the West—is hardly a game-changer given both sides' parity in technological innovation and ability to develop countermeasures. By November 2023, Ukraine's top general at the time, Valery Zaluzhny, placed the blame for the failed counteroffensive on these technological factors and admitted that there would be no "deep and beautiful breakthrough."[101]

After this period, the war settled into one of attrition. Unfortunately, because of its greater size and resources, Russia has benefited from this shift. Russia has been able to recover from the effects of Western sanctions and ramp up its defense industrial production by substituting consumer products for banned military-grade components like semiconductor chips, trading with third countries like China, and buying weapons and ammunition from countries like North Korea and Iran.[102] Russia's economy has transitioned to a full war footing,[103] whereas the West has delayed improving its defense industrial base. The six months between October 2023 and April 2024 without new aid packages from the United States further eroded Ukraine's ammunition stocks and permitted Russia to make smaller gains, most recently around Kharkiv. During this period, the Russian military was able to backfill its losses with new contract soldiers and then mobilize; it is actually larger now than it was in February 2022.[104] However, the quality of the Russian army is now much lower since it lost about 87% of its prewar personnel, 65% of its tanks, and 33% of its armored personnel carriers.[105] Replacements for equipment losses are primarily pulled from storage rather than newly manufactured.[106] Ukraine has not fully mobilized and is encountering its own losses. Russian forces now appear to have a window of opportunity that they will try to exploit on the battlefield. Whether they will be able to make larger gains remains to be seen; so far, Russia has not been able to do more than make limited territorial gains at a great cost in men and materiel.

Russian Military Learning and Adaptation Since 2022

The Russian military's poor performance in the opening weeks of the invasion led some to inaccurately portray it as weak, incompetent, and incapable of adaptation. The wave of public support in the West for Ukraine further magnified the narrative that Ukraine would easily win, morale in the Russian military would crumble, and Russia would face pressure at home to withdraw. These narratives were ultimately counterproductive because they set up unrealistic expectations for Ukraine and allowed the West to avoid preparing for a long war, despite attempts by analysts to warn otherwise.[107] The transition from a war of maneuver to one of attrition has merely allowed the Russian military to play to its strengths.

The Russian military has been able to learn, adapt, and retain its combat effectiveness despite losses and low morale. It has proved remarkably resilient by the Russian military's own definition: retaining the ability to "perform complex tasks in dangerous conditions."[108] Through a mix of coercion, increased financial benefits for soldiers, messaging about the patriotic nature of the war, and suppression of negative information, Russian military leaders have managed to hold the force together despite great stress. Although the Russian military has been slow to innovate, especially when compared with Ukraine, it has proven adaptable at multiple levels, improving its ability to use electronic warfare and target Ukrainian positions, as well as protect its own command posts.[109] Despite Ukraine's initial lead in drone warfare, the Russian military has begun to improve both the quality and quantity of its drones.[110]

The current Russian military has learned from its earlier failings, with one key exception: authoritarian politics continues to interfere with military effectiveness. One such example is the armed mutiny led by Yevgeny Prigozhin, the leader of the Wagner Group. Wagner forces played a key role in capturing Bakhmut in May 2023 with a combination of highly trained and efficient professional fighters and human-wave attacks by recruits from Russian prisons. Instead of repaying this sacrifice with more prestige for Prigozhin, Shoigu decided to place Wagner under the formal control of the Ministry of Defense. Ahead of the July 1, 2023, deadline for Wagner forces to sign contracts with the Russian military, Prigozhin marched his forces toward Moscow in protest against what he saw as mismanagement of the war by corrupt senior military leadership.[111] He was likely counting on Putin intervening on his behalf, but he grossly miscalculated. Prigozhin had embarrassed Putin and would suffer the consequences; he was later killed on August 23, 2023, in a suspicious plane crash.[112]

Although posing little immediate risk to the stability of the Putin regime, Prigozhin revealed that the Russian state was weaker than it appeared. It failed even to have a monopoly on legitimate violence, which Max Weber famously wrote was an essential criterion for a state. The Prigozhin rebellion also showed the ongoing negative consequences of authoritarian politics on military effectiveness. Coup-proofing strategies and rampant corruption in the military impacted Russia's military effectiveness ahead of the invasion, and these problems clearly remain.[113]

Personnel decisions within the Russian armed forces are also influenced by authoritarian politics. Respected Russian military commanders like Sergei Surovikin, who was appointed as operational commander of Russian forces in October 2022, were replaced based on political criteria. In Surovikin's case, he was replaced by Valery Gerasimov, who played a key role in the General Staff in designing the failed invasion plan. Surovikin was later fired altogether for his alleged support of the Prigozhin rebellion. But Putin has shown a willingness to make some personnel changes to increase military effectiveness, like removing his longtime ally Sergei Shoigu from the minister of defense post and replacing him with the economic technocrat Andrei Belousov. This reshuffling is likely an attempt for Putin to "show that he requires a more pragmatic, less corrupt, and more professional approach when it comes to the needs of the military."[114]

Because defeating Russia on the battlefield has proven difficult, one might hope that the Russian public would grow tired of the war. But there is little indication of collapsing support among either soldiers or civilians.[115] Some Western leaders had hoped that strong economic sanctions would lead to collapsing political support, but by circumventing sanctions and developing new trading partners, the Kremlin has been able to keep the Russian economy growing at a moderate pace. The Putin regime is skillful in its messaging about why the war is worth fighting. It draws on different themes for different audiences. For some audiences, it draws upon the historical memory of the Second World War (known as the Great Patriotic War in Russia), which casts Russia in the role of defender against fascism—an important legacy to many Russians.[116] The regime draws upon a variety of other narratives, from patriotic themes to the claim that Russia is fighting a defensive war against NATO in Ukraine.[117] Whether because the cost of war is low or because of successful messaging and selective repression, the Russian public's attitudes range from "complete apathy to frenzied enthusiasm for the war," allowing the Putin regime to keep fighting.[118]

Conclusion

The increasingly authoritarian Russian state and its aggressive foreign policy shaped the development of the Russian military over the last twenty years. After performing poorly in the brief war in Georgia in 2008, the Russian military was ripe for reform. Reformers made critical decisions to invest in new equipment and capabilities and make the military more professional while cutting its overall size. The modernization of the Russian military supported Russia's more aggressive foreign policy and participation in smaller wars in Ukraine and Syria throughout the 2010s. When Russia tried to translate this success into a full-scale invasion of Ukraine, it failed dramatically. The invasion failed because it was poorly planned and executed, as well as being under-resourced and lacking sufficient manpower and logistical preparations for a potentially lengthier-than-anticipated engagement. The success of the plan depended on everything going right: catching Ukraine by surprise, rapidly taking Kyiv, and removing Ukraine's political leadership. Russian forces invaded, contrary to their doctrine, without a prolonged air campaign and without massing decisive force against their adversary along a main axis of approach. In other words, Russian military planners did not have a plan to win that could adjust for failing to knock out key Ukrainian military targets at the first try and for meeting the Ukrainian forces and encountering strong resistance.

Authoritarian politics and Putin's increasing obsession with dominating Ukraine brought about these planning errors. They dictated the expansive war aims of regime change as well as removed opportunities for dissent that may have existed had Russian politics been less authoritarian. At the same time, the Putin regime was unwilling to properly provide the invading force with the resources needed to accomplish these ambitious goals. It probably preferred to rely on the winning formula it had used previously of keeping the public costs of war extremely low; mobilization before the war would have imposed immediate costs on the public before it was adequately prepared to make such sacrifices. As a result, the Russian military went to war with enough equipment and ammunition but not enough infantry—a direct result of a decade of military reforms. Its performance on the battlefield also revealed persistent issues with insufficient junior leadership and initiative as well as corruption. Despite attempts at reform, the Russian military was just as corrupt as the rest of the regime.

After its initial struggles, Russia made key decisions in the fall of 2022 that set it up for its current position on the battlefield. Putin reluctantly ordered 300,000 men mobilized. His economic team stabilized the economy and overcame the worst effects of the sanctions. Trade from third parties and the substitution of civilian for defense components allowed Russia to restart its defense industry and replace initial heavy losses. At the tactical level, the Russian military has remained resilient as well as capable of adaptation. Wavering Western support for Ukraine opened a window of opportunity on the battlefield.

Despite these adaptations, the Russian military is not unbeatable. It is in worse shape in every way than it was on the eve of the full-scale invasion in February 2022. Although the Russian military has not been sensitive to large losses of people because it clearly believes manpower can be easily reconstituted, it has proven vulnerable to a strategy of denial against its equipment because that cannot be replaced as easily.[119] Russia has struggled to replace its ammunition and equipment at the rate they are lost. If these losses continue, Russia's position will weaken. The West's ability to manufacture more ammunition will also increase by 2025. If Ukraine retains full support from its Western partners in training new soldiers and providing equipment and ammunition, it will be able to regenerate its combat power. In a protracted war, victory depends on regenerating combat power. Ukraine will struggle in this area without support, which is in the best interest of NATO countries to provide. Although the Russian military will not emerge from this conflict more capable in terms of soldier skills and high-tech equipment, it remains large and is led by risk-acceptant, authoritarian political leaders. The threat the Russian military poses to European security should not be underestimated.

NOTES

1. "France Estimates That 150,000 Russian Soldiers Have Been Killed in the Ukraine War," *France 24*, May 3, 2024, https://www.france24.com/en/europe /20240503-france-estimates-that-150-000-russian-soldiers-have-been-killed-in-the -ukraine-war.

2. Michael Kofman, "The Russia-Ukraine War: Military Operations and Battlefield Dynamics," chapter 6 in *War in Ukraine: Conflict, Strategy, and the Return of a Fractured World*, ed. Hal Brands (Hopkins Press, 2024), 99–120, https://muse.jhu.edu/pub/1/oa _edited_volume/chapter/3881920.

3. Fiona Hill and Clifford G. Gaddy, *Mr. Putin: Operative in the Kremlin* (Brookings Institution Press, 2015),

4. KGB stands for *Komitet gosudarstvennoy bezopasnosti* or Committee for State Security, and was the main security agency for the Soviet Union until its break-up in 1991.

5. Stephen Kotkin, *Armageddon Averted: The Soviet Collapse, 1970–2000* (Oxford University Press, 2008).

6. Chris Bowlby, "Vladimir Putin's Formative German Years," *BBC News*, March 27, 2015, http://www.bbc.com/news/magazine-32066222.

7. Timothy Frye, *Weak Strongman: The Limits of Power in Putin's Russia* (Princeton University Press, 2022), https://books.google.com/books?hl=en&lr=&id=bGxpEAAA QBAJ&oi=fnd&pg=PR7&dq=weak+strongman+frye&ots=jiPjJcnWae&sig=CN2r4F9K nwzIcIr35Hy_t8JnboU.

8. Evgenia Arkadyevna Olimpieva, "Putin's Prosecutors: Personnel Politics and Building Authoritarianism in Russia" (PhD Thesis, University of Chicago, 2023), https://search.proquest.com/openview/d1e69fae94b3291ab4001235e76874bc/1?pq -origsite=gscholar&cbl=18750&diss=y&casa_token=YooOU3oq7NkAAAAA:6irnVjE36S 38BQ4LpWzOJzFwu-5Hz04KHQujJhjT2vMX8xbRQQDXwtK5PEtS1EyUEyxVW6ZPNA.

9. Angela E. Stent, *The Limits of Partnership: U.S.-Russian Relations in the Twenty-First Century* (Princeton University Press, 2015).

10. Andrey A. Sushentsov and William C. Wohlforth, "The Tragedy of US–Russian Relations: NATO Centrality and the Revisionists' Spiral," *International Politics* 57 (2020): 427–450.

11. Michael McFaul, "Putin, Putinism, and the Domestic Determinants of Russian Foreign Policy," *International Security* 45, no. 2 (2020): 95–139, https://doi.org/10.1162/isec_a_00390.

12. Pål Røren, "The Belligerent Bear: Russia, Status Orders, and War," *International Security* 47, no. 4 (January 4, 2023): 7–49.

13. Kirill Shamiev, "The Imperfect Equilibrium of Russian Civil–Military Relations," RUSI, April 21, 2021, https://rusi.org.

14. "War in Ukraine Has Devastating Effect on Journalism, RSF Says in Releasing Press Freedom Index," *RFE/RL*, May 3, 2022, https://www.rferl.org/a/world-press-freedom-index-rsf-russia-ukraine/31831712.html.

15. Daniel Freeman, "How Do Regular Russians Feel About the War in Ukraine?," *Responsible Statecraft*, June 17, 2022, https://responsiblestatecraft.org/2022/06/17/how-do-regular-russians-feel-about-the-war-in-ukraine/.

16. Ella Paneyakh, "Why Russians Now Trust the Army More Than Putin (Op-Ed)," *Moscow Times*, October 19, 2018, https://www.themoscowtimes.com/2018/10/19/russians-now-trust-army-more-than-putin-opinion-a63246.

17. Mark Galeotti, *Armies of Russia's War in Ukraine*, 1st ed. (Osprey Publishing, 2019).

18. Galeotti, *Armies of Russia's War*, 143.

19. Mark Galeotti, *Putin's Wars: From Chechnya to Ukraine* (Bloomsbury, 2022), http://ebookcentral.proquest.com/lib/tamucs/detail.action?docID=7098293; Andrew S Bowen, "Russian Military Performance and Outlook" (Congressional Research Service, March 8, 2024), https://crsreports.congress.gov/product/pdf/IF/IF12606.

20. Bowen, "Russian Military Performance and Outlook"; Gil Barndollar, "The Best or Worst of Both Worlds? Russia's Mixed Manpower System," CSIS, September 23, 2020, https://www.csis.org/blogs/post-soviet-post/best-or-worst-both-worlds.

21. The term "polite men" or "green men" (вежливые люди; зелёные человечки) refers to the moniker adopted by the Russian media to describe the uniformed forces responsible for seizing key installations in Crimea in late February to early March 2014. Because the Kremlin denied that it had sent military forces, and because the annexation was professional and largely bloodless, the term stuck. Today, there are numerous Russian social media sites dedicated to this term. For example, see https://vk.com/veglevost.

22. The lower numbers may reflect an improvement in discipline; they might also reflect tighter media control among those reporting on military matters.

23. Marina Lemtukina, "Страну защитит инженерный спецназ" [The Country Will Be Defended by Engineer Special Forces], *Moskovskiy Komsomolets*, March 31, 2015, http://www.mk.ru/editions/daily/2015/03/31/stranu-zashhitit-inzhenernyy-specnaz.html.

24. Levada Center, "Рекордное число россиян назвали службу в армии обязанностью мужчины" [A Record Number of Russians Have Called Military Service a Man's Basic Duty], June 18, 2019, https://www.levada.ru/2019/06/18/rekordnoe-chislo-rossiyan-nazvali-sluzhbu-v-armii-obyazannostyu-muzhchiny/.

25. For additional background, see "Mulino Combat Training Center to Be Commissioned in 2nd Half of 2015," *Interfax*, December 13, 2014, http://www.interfax.com/newsinf.asp?id=559270.

26. Sarah A. Topol, "The Deserter," *New York Times Magazine*, September 22, 2024, https://www.nytimes.com/interactive/2024/09/20/magazine/ukraine-russia-war-deserter.html.

27. Andrew S Bowen, "Russian Armed Forces: Military Modernization and Reforms," (Congressional Research Service, n.d.).

28. "Russia Will Never Fully Abandon Military Draft—Defense Minister," *RT*, November 11, 2013, http://rt.com/politics/defense-draft-russia-shoigu-529/.

29. Lyubov Chizhova, "Ситуация патовая. Как офицеру уволиться из российской армии" [The Situation Is Stalemate. How Can an Officer Quit the Russian Army], *Severreal.org*, July 27, 2021, https://www.severreal.org/a/oficer-minoborony-uvol-nenie/31378918.html.

30. "Adding (and Subtracting) Contracts," *Russian Defense Policy*, April 4, 2015. See entry dated April 4, 2015, https://russiandefpolicy.wordpress.com/category/manpower/.

31. There are also concerns that some draftees have recently been forced to sign contracts, allegedly to help support combat operations in southeast Ukraine. See Maxim Solopov, "Involuntarily Military Service: How Russia Conscripts Imposed with a Contract and a Trip to Rostov," *InformNapalm*, February 14, 2015, https://en.informnapalm.org/involuntarily-military-service-russia-conscripts-imposed-contract-trip-rostov/.

32. Andrey Kalikh, "A Semi-Professional Military: Problems Facing the Russian Armed Forces in the Effort to Transition to a Contract Army," *DGAPkompakt*, No. 5, April 2015, https://dgap.org/en/article/getFullPDF/26625.

33. They have since added a fifth joint strategic command directed at protecting their Arctic interests. See Chuck Bartles, "Russia Plans to Create New Strategic Command for the Arctic," *FMSO OE Watch*, October 2014, http://fmso.leavenworth.army.mil/OEWatch/201410/Russia_03.html.

34. There had been considerable conjecture as to which power ministries will be coordinated from this new C2 center. As in other countries, bureaucratic coordination among similar agencies can prove difficult. For a brief snapshot of the new center, see "Russia Launches 'Wartime Government' HQ in Major Military Upgrade," *RT*, December 1, 2014, http://rt.com/news/210307-russia-national-defence-center/.

35. Mikhail Barabanov, Kostantin Makienko, and Ruslan Pukhov, "Military Reform: Toward the New Look of the Russian Army," Valdai Discussion Club, July 2012, http://vid1.rian.ru/ig/valdai/Military_reform_eng.pdf.

36. Officially, Russia had no military units involved in southeast Ukraine in 2014–2015. However, there was evidence that Russia deployed battalion-sized units from distant regions to the Ukrainian border. See, for instance Mark Urban, "How Many Russians Are Fighting in Ukraine?," *BBC News*, March 10, 2015, http://www.bbc.com/news/world-europe-31794523. Those Russian brigades situated close to the Ukrainian border were presumably in a higher state of combat-readiness.

37. "Putin Signs Decree on Spring Military Conscription | Reuters," *Reuters*, March 31, 2024, https://www.reuters.com/world/europe/russias-putin-signs-decree-spring-military-conscription-2024-03-31/.

38. Lester Grau and Charles Bartles, "Getting to Know the Russian Battalion Tactical Group," June 12, 2024, https://rusi.orghttps://rusi.org.

39. Liam Collins, Michael Kofman, and John Spencer, "The Battle of Hostomel Airport: A Key Moment in Russia's Defeat in Kyiv," War on the Rocks, August 10, 2023, https://warontherocks.com/2023/08/the-battle-of-hostomel-airport-a-key-moment-in -russias-defeat-in-kyiv/.

40. Galeotti, *Putin's Wars*, 193.

41. Clint Reach et al., "Competing with Russia Militarily: Implications of Conventional and Nuclear Conflicts" (RAND Corporation, June 22, 2021), https://www.rand .org/pubs/perspectives/PE330.html.

42. Michael Kofman and Rob Lee, "Not Built for Purpose: The Russian Military's Ill-Fated Force Design," War on the Rocks, June 2, 2022, https://warontherocks.com /2022/06/not-built-for-purpose-the-russian-militarys-ill-fated-force-design/.

43. Norbert Świętochowski, "Field Artillery in the Defensive War of Ukraine 2022–2023 Part I. Combat Potential, Tasks and Tactics," *Scientific Journal of the Military University of Land Forces* 210, no. 4 (December 31, 2023): 341–358, https://doi.org/10 .5604/01.3001.0054.1631.

44. Richard Connolly, *Russian Military Expenditure in Comparative Perspective: A Purchasing Power Parity Estimate* (CNA, 2019).

45. Siemon Wezeman, "Russia's Military Spending: Frequently Asked Questions," SIPRI, April 27, 2020, https://www.sipri.org/commentary/topical-backgrounder/2020 /russias-military-spending-frequently-asked-questions.

46. Connolly, *Russian Military Expenditure in Comparative Perspective*.

47. Tomas Malmlöf and Johan Engval, "6. Russian Armament Deliveries," *Russian Military Capability in a Ten-Year Perspective–2019* (Swedish Defence Research Agency, 2019): 122.

48. David Cenciotti, "Rare Video Shows A Russian Tu-22M3 Firing A Kh-32 Supersonic Air-Launched Cruise Missile," *The Aviationist* (blog), May 12, 2024, https://theaviationist.com/2024/05/12/tu-22m3-kh-32/.

49. "Russia's Kh-22—The Missile Ukraine Has Yet to Shoot Down," *Kyiv Post*, December 29, 2023, https://www.kyivpost.com/post/26102.

50. CSIS Missile Defense Project, "3M-14 Kalibr (SS-N-30A)," *Missile Threat*, April 23, 2024, https://missilethreat.csis.org/missile/ss-n-30a/.

51. "Russia's Armed Forces: More Capable by Far, but for How Long?" IISS, October 9, 2020, https://www.iiss.org/sv/online-analysis/military-balance/2020/10 /russia-armed-forces/.

52. Samuel Bendett et al., "Advanced Military Capabilities in Russia," Chatham House—International Affairs Think Tank, September 23, 2021, https://www .chathamhouse.org/2021/09/advanced-military-technology-russia/03-putins-super -weapons.

53. Chatham House, "03 Putin's 'Super Weapons,'" November 2, 2021, https://www .chathamhouse.org/2021/09/advanced-military-technology-russia/03-putins-super -weapons.

54. CSIS Missile Defense Project, "Kh-47M2 Kinzhal," *Missile Threat*, April 23, 2024, https://missilethreat.csis.org/missile/kinzhal/.

55. Peter Mitchell, "Hypersonic Hype? Russia's Kinzhal Missiles and the Lessons for Air Defense," Modern War Institute, May 23, 2023, https://mwi.westpoint.edu/hypersonic-hype-russias-kinzhal-missiles-and-the-lessons-for-air-defense/.

56. Maj. J. Alexander Ippoliti, ANG, "Book Review: Russia's New Ground Forces: Capabilities, Limitations and Implications for International Security, by Igor Sutyagin with Justin Bronk," Air University (AU), October 15, 2020, https://www.airuniversity.af.edu/SSQ/Book-Reviews/Article/2382918/russias-new-ground-forces-capabilities-limitations-and-implications-for-interna/https%3A%2F%2Fwww.airuniversity.af.edu%2FAether-ASOR%2FBook-Reviews%2FArticle-Display%2FArticle%2F2382918%2Frussias-new-ground-forces-capabilities-limitations-and-implications-for-interna%2F.

57. Keir Giles, "Assessing Russia's Reorganized and Rearmed Military," Carnegie Endowment for International Peace, May 3, 2017, https://carnegieendowment.org/posts/2017/05/assessing-russias-reorganized-and-rearmed-military?lang=en.

58. "Turkey's Downing of Russian Warplane—What We Know," *BBC News*, December 1, 2015, https://www.bbc.com/news/world-middle-east-34912581.

59. Kimberly Marten, "The Puzzle of Russian Behavior in Deir Al-Zour," War on the Rocks, July 5, 2018, https://warontherocks.com/2018/07/the-puzzle-of-russian-behavior-in-deir-al-zour/; Thomas Gibbons-Neff, "How a 4-Hour Battle Between Russian Mercenaries and U.S. Commandos Unfolded in Syria," *New York Times*, May 24, 2018, https://www.nytimes.com/2018/05/24/world/middleeast/american-commandos-russian-mercenaries-syria.html.

60. Reach et al., "Competing with Russia Militarily."

61. Malmlöf and Engval, "6. Russian Armament Deliveries," 127.

62. Janetta Azarieva, Yitzhak M. Brudny, and Eugene Finkel, *Bread and Autocracy: Food, Politics, and Security in Putin's Russia* (Oxford University Press, 2023).

63. Mykhaylor Zabrodskyi et al., *Preliminary Lessons in Conventional Warfighting from Russia's Invasion of Ukraine, February–July 2022*, Royal United Services Institute for Defence and Security Studies London, 2022, https://static.rusi.org/359-SR-Ukraine-Preliminary-Lessons-Feb-July-2022-web-final.pdf.

64. Eliot A. Cohen and Phillips Payson O'Brien, "How Defense Experts Got Ukraine Wrong," *The Atlantic*, September 27, 2024, https://www.theatlantic.com/ideas/archive/2024/09/how-defense-experts-got-ukraine-wrong/680045/.

65. Michael Kofman and Jeffrey Edmonds, "Russia's Shock and Awe," *Foreign Affairs*, February 21, 2022, https://www.foreignaffairs.com/articles/ukraine/2022-02-21/russias-shock-and-awe.

66. Alexander Bick, "Planning for the Worst: The Russia-Ukraine 'Tiger Team,'" chapter 8 in *War in Ukraine: Conflict, Strategy, and the Return of a Fractured World*, ed. Hal Brands (Hopkins Press, 2024), 150, https://muse.jhu.edu/pub/1/oa_edited_volume/chapter/3881922.

67. Zabrodskyi et al., *Preliminary Lessons*, 44.

68. Valeriy Akimenko, "Ukraine's Toughest Fight: The Challenge of Military Reform," Carnegie Endowment for International Peace, February 22, 2018, https://carnegieendowment.org/research/2018/02/ukraines-toughest-fight-the-challenge-of-military-reform?lang=en.

69. Zabrodskyi et al., *Preliminary Lessons*.

70. Alexandra Chinchilla, "Lessons from Ukraine for Security Force Assistance," *Lawfare*, September 10, 2023, https://www.lawfaremedia.org/article/lessons-from-ukraine-for-security-force-assistance.

71. Zabrodskyi et al., *Preliminary Lessons*, 52.

72. Zabrodskyi et al., *Preliminary Lessons*, 7.

73. Kofman, "The Russia-Ukraine War."

74. Zabrodskyi et al., *Preliminary Lessons*, 12.

75. Jeffrey Edmonds, "Start with the Political: Explaining Russia's Bungled Invasion of Ukraine," War on the Rocks, April 28, 2022, https://warontherocks.com/2022/04/start-with-the-political-explaining-russias-bungled-invasion-of-ukraine/.

76. Sinead Baker, "Ukraine Said Russian Troops Brought Parade Uniforms to Kyiv, Expecting a Quick Triumph That Never Came," *Business Insider*, April 7, 2022, https://www.businessinsider.com/ukraine-said-found-russian-parade-uniforms-left-behind-in-kyiv-2022-4.

77. Seth Jones, "Russia's Ill-Fated Invasion of Ukraine: Lessons in Modern Warfare," *CSIS*, June 1, 2022, https://www.csis.org/analysis/russias-ill-fated-invasion-ukraine-lessons-modern-warfare.

78. Zabrodskyi et al., *Preliminary Lessons*, 28.

79. Quoted in Maria Popova and Oxana Shevel, *Russia and Ukraine: Entangled Histories, Diverging States*, 1st ed. (Polity, 2024), 215.

80. Popova and Shevel, *Russia and Ukraine: Entangled Histories*, 216.

81. Mark Galeotti, "The Personal Politics of Putin's Security Council Meeting," *Moscow Times*, February 22, 2022, https://www.themoscowtimes.com/2022/02/22/the-personal-politics-of-putins-security-council-meeting-a76522.

82. Zabrodskyi et al., *Preliminary Lessons*, 37; Kofman and Lee, "Not Built for Purpose."

83. Zabrodskyi et al., *Preliminary Lessons*, 26.

84. Dara Massicot, "What Russia Got Wrong," *Foreign Affairs*, February 8, 2023, https://www.foreignaffairs.com/ukraine/what-russia-got-wrong-moscow-failures-in-ukraine-dara-massicot.

85. Kofman, "The Russia-Ukraine War."

86. Zabrodskyi et al., *Preliminary Lessons*.

87. Zabrodskyi et al., *Preliminary Lessons*, 30.

88. Massicot, "What Russia Got Wrong."

89. Matt Murphy, "Ukraine War: Another Russian General Killed by Ukrainian Forces—Reports," *BBC News*, June 6, 2022, https://www.bbc.com/news/world-europe-61702862.

90. Zabrodskyi et al., *Preliminary Lessons*.

91. "Putin Signs 'Harsh' Law Allowing Long Prison Terms For 'False News' about Army," *RFE\RL*, March 5, 2022, https://www.rferl.org/a/russia-military-false-news/31737627.html.

92. Robert Dalsjö, Michael Jonsson, and Johan Norberg, "A Brutal Examination: Russian Military Capability in Light of the Ukraine War," *Survival* 64, no. 3 (May 2022): 7–28.

93. Yousur Al-Hlou, Masha Froliak, Evan Hill, Malachy Browne, and David Botti, "New Evidence Shows How Russian Soldiers Executed Men in Bucha," *New York Times*, May 21, 2022, https://www.nytimes.com/2022/05/19/world/europe/russia-bucha-ukraine-executions.html.

94. Ewelina U. Ochab, "The Siege Of Mariupol: Death, Starvation and Destruction," *Forbes*, June 14, 2024, https://www.forbes.com/sites/ewelinaochab/2024/06/14/the-siege-of-mariupol-death-starvation-and-destruction/.

95. "Мариуполь: 80 дней в осаде. Как цветущий город был превращен российскими войсками в руины" [Mariupol: 80 Days Under Siege. How a Flourishing City Was Turned into Ruins by Russian Troops], *BBC News*, 19 May, 2022, https://www.bbc.com/russian/features-61482818.

96. Isobel Koshiw, "We're Almost Out of Ammunition and Relying on Western Arms, Says Ukraine," *The Guardian*, June 10, 2022, https://www.theguardian.com/world/2022/jun/10/were-almost-out-of-ammunition-and-relying-on-western-arms-says-ukraine.

97. David Axe, "25 Tanks and Fighting Vehicles, Gone in a Blink: The Ukrainian Defeat Near Mala Tokmachka Was Worse Than We Thought," *Forbes*, July 19, 2023, https://www.forbes.com/sites/davidaxe/2023/06/27/25-tanks-and-fighting-vehicles-gone-in-a-blink-the-ukrainian-defeat-near-mala-tokmachka-was-worst-than-we-thought/.

98. Lara Jakes, Andrew E. Kramer, and Eric Schmitt, "After Suffering Heavy Losses, Ukrainians Paused to Rethink Strategy," *New York Times*, July 15, 2023, https://www.nytimes.com/2023/07/15/us/politics/ukraine-leopards-bradleys-counteroffensive.html.

99. Stephen Biddle, "How Russia Stopped Ukraine's Momentum," *Foreign Affairs*, January 29, 2024, https://www.foreignaffairs.com/ukraine/how-russia-stopped-ukraines-momentum.

100. Jack Watling, *The Arms of the Future* (Bloomsbury, 2023), https://www.bloomsbury.com/us/arms-of-the-future-9781350352988/.

101. Andrew Buncombe and Joe Barnes, "There Will Be No 'Deep and Beautiful Breakthrough', Ukraine's Top General Admits," *The Telegraph*, November 2, 2023, https://www.telegraph.co.uk/world-news/2023/11/02/ukraine-russia-war-stalemate-top-general/.

102. Steven Feldstein and Fiona Brauer, "Why Russia Has Been So Resilient to Western Export Controls," Carnegie Endowment for International Peace, March 11, 2024, https://carnegieendowment.org/research/2024/03/why-russia-has-been-so-resilient-to-western-export-controls?lang=en.

103. "As Russia Completes Transition to a Full War Economy, Treasury Takes Sweeping Aim at Foundational Financial Infrastructure and Access to Third Country Support," U.S. Department of the Treasury, June 12, 2024, https://home.treasury.gov/news/press-releases/jy2404.

104. Brad Dress, "U.S. General Says Russian Army Has Grown by 15 Percent since Pre-Ukraine War," *The Hill* (blog), April 11, 2024, https://thehill.com/policy/defense/4589095-russian-army-grown-ukraine-war-us-general/.

105. Katie Bo Lillis, "Russia Has Lost 87% of Troops It Had Prior to Start of Ukraine War, According to U.S. Intelligence Assessment," *CNN*, December 12, 2023,

https://www.cnn.com/2023/12/12/politics/russia-troop-losses-us-intelligence
-assessment/index.html.

106. Dara Massicot, "Time Is Running Out in Ukraine," *Foreign Affairs*, March 8, 2024, https://www.foreignaffairs.com/ukraine/time-running-out-ukraine.

107. Thomas G. Mahnken and Joshua Baker, "Fallacies of Strategic Thinking in the Ukraine War," chapter 11 in *War in Ukraine: Conflict, Strategy, and the Return of a Fractured World*, ed. Hal Brands (Hopkins Press, 2024), 187–202, https://muse.jhu.edu /pub/1/oa_edited_volume/chapter/3881925; Michael Kofman and Rob Lee, "Beyond Ukraine's Offensive," *Foreign Affairs*, May 10, 2023, https://www.foreignaffairs.com /ukraine/russia-war-beyond-ukraines-offensive..

108. Dara Massicot, "Russian Military Resilience and Adaptation: Implications for the War in Ukraine and Beyond," chapter 7 in *War in Ukraine: Conflict, Strategy, and the Return of a Fractured World*, ed. Hal Brands (Hopkins Press, 2024), 121–38, https://muse .jhu.edu/pub/1/oa_edited_volume/chapter/3881921.

109. Margarita Konaev and Owen J. Daniels, "The Russians Are Getting Better," *Foreign Affairs*, September 6, 2023, https://www.foreignaffairs.com/ukraine/russians-are -getting-better-learning.

110. David Hambling, "Russian Drones Could Win This War, If Entrenched Bureaucracy Lets Them," *Forbes*, August 13, 2024, https://www.forbes.com/sites/david hambling/2024/08/13/russian-drones-could-win-this-war-if-entrenched-bureaucracy-lets -them/.

111. Joshua Yaffa, "Inside the Wagner Group's Armed Uprising," *New Yorker*, July 31, 2023, https://www.newyorker.com/magazine/2023/08/07/inside-the-wagner-uprising.

112. "A Month after Prigozhin's Suspicious Death, the Kremlin Is Silent on His Plane Crash and Legacy," *AP News*, September 23, 2023, https://apnews.com/article /russia-putin-prigozhin-mutiny-wagner-ukraine-africa -03a8797d0c923d3db3f1dd8f604e9a38.

113. Ivan Gomza, "Roger That: Russia's Coup-Proofed Army and Its Combat Effectiveness, 2022–2023," *Journal of Slavic Military Studies* 36, no. 4 (October 2, 2023): 435–473, https://doi.org/10.1080/13518046.2023.2293371.

114. Tatiana Stanovaya, "Putin's Reshuffle Is About Optimization, Not Change," *Carnegie Politika*, May 15, 2024, https://carnegieendowment.org/russia-eurasia/politika /2024/05/belousov-shoigu-russian-government-reshuffle?lang=en.

115. "Conflict with Ukraine: Assessments for March 2024," Levada Center, May 17, 2024, https://www.levada.ru/en/2024/05/17/conflict-with-ukraine-assesments-for-march -2024/.

116. Marlene Laruelle, *Is Russia Fascist?: Unraveling Propaganda East and West* (Cornell University Press, 2021).

117. Jade McGlynn, *Memory Makers: The Politics of the Past in Putin's Russia* (Bloomsbury, 2023).

118. Keir Giles, "Ukraine Isn't Putin's War—It's Russia's War," *Foreign Policy* (blog), June 13, 2024, https://foreignpolicy.com/2024/02/21/ukraine-putin-war-russia-public -opinion-history/.

119. Massicot, "Russian Military Resilience and Adaptation."

Chapter Four

Russian Cyber Warfare

Scott Jasper

Russian cyberattacks and influence operations before and during the war in Ukraine have vividly demonstrated the Russian doctrine for cyber warfare. The Russians employ information-related concepts to exert technical and psychological effects. Cyberattacks are used to "collect, disrupt, deny, degrade, or destroy information system resources or the information itself,"[1] whereas influence operations are intended to alter the beliefs and behavior of specific populations, mainly through propaganda and disinformation.[2] Western and Ukrainian intelligence officials feared for months that Russian state-sponsored cyber actors would launch crippling cyberattacks to accompany Russia's military invasion of Ukraine in February 2022. Because of aggressive activities and technical capability shown in previous cyber incidents in Ukraine and the West, they worried about the possibility of massive cyberattacks on civilian infrastructure. Instead, they witnessed a calculated barrage of distributed denial-of-service attacks, website defacements, and destruction of computers and files. Nevertheless, Tom Burt, vice president of customer security and trust at Microsoft, stated that based on the "frequency and severity of the attacks . . . [t]his is full-on, full-scale cyberwar."[3]

Russian cyber warfare began in Estonia in April 2007. Russian patriotic hackers launched distributed denial-of-service attacks on Estonian websites in protest over the movement of a Soviet-era monument. The commissar of the Kremlin-backed Russian youth group Nashi claimed responsibility for organizing the attack.[4] Then, a year later, in Georgia in August 2008, cyberattacks and influence operations were integrated into a kinetic battle. When Russian ground troops advanced into South Ossetia, distributed denial-of-service attacks commenced against Georgian websites, followed by defacements.[5] The attack campaign constrained the ability of the Georgian government to convey the narrative to the international community, while Russian disinformation attempted to justify the operation to protect their peacekeepers. The cyberattacks in Georgia were carried out by civilian volunteers recruited by social networking forums. However, the timing of the attacks indicates advance notice by the Russian government of intentions to invade and subsequent military operations.[6]

In the Ukraine war, attribution to Russian state-sponsored groups for cyberattacks is clearer. At least seven groups from Russian military, security, and intelligence agencies have conducted cyberattacks for espionage or disruptive and destructive purposes. They have attempted to use the cyber domain to gain military or political advantage. Meanwhile, a prolific disinformation ecosystem has spread egregious Russian war propaganda on multiple media channels, some groups backed by Russian state agencies. Russian influence operations also have sought to shape how Ukrainian and Western audiences perceive the events leading up to the invasion and occurring on the ground during the war.

Russian state-sponsored or state-affiliated cyber actors and the pro-Russia disinformation ecosystem have a long history of malicious activity targeting the United States, its allies, and its partners. This chapter will explain how Russian doctrine incorporates cyberattacks and influence operations compared with Western views on cyber warfare. It will then assess Russian doctrine for cyberattacks and influence operations in the Ukraine war by looking at Russian objectives, actors, and targets. Next, it will trace the various actors and their methods and means seen in the Ukraine war back to malign cyber incidents and disinformation campaigns previously targeting Western-aligned nations. Then it will look at projected activity for the war at the time this chapter was written.

Russian Doctrine

Cyber warfare was once defined in a US Joint Chiefs of Staff *Memorandum on Joint Terminology for Cyberspace Operations* as "an armed conflict conducted in whole or part by cyber means." Yet the terms "cyber warfare" and "cyber war" do not appear in the latest US Department of Defense *Dictionary of Military and Associated Terms*.[7] Nor do they appear in the most recent NATO *Glossary of Terms and Definitions*.[8] Rather, the terms are routinely used colloquially by Western think tanks, scholars, commentators, and companies. For instance, one notable think tank defines cyber warfare as "a conflict between states where precise and proportionate force is directed against military and industrial targets for the purposes of political, economic or territorial gain."[9] US military theorists define cyber warfare as "the use of the cyber instrument as a dimension of a larger military conflict."[10] More recently, the war in Ukraine has been characterized to be "the first major conflict involving large-scale cyber operations."[11] Similarly, cyber security reporters have referred to "Russia's New Cyberwarfare in Ukraine."[12] And prominent cyber security firms have broadly alluded to "the Cyber War" in Ukraine.[13] However, Russian military theorists usually do not use the terms cyber (*kiber*) or cyber warfare (*kibervoyna*) except when referring to Western writings on the topic. Instead, they conceptualize cyber operations under the broader rubric of information warfare (*informatsionnaya voyna*).[14]

Information Warfare

The Russian Ministry of Defense's *Concept on the Activities of the Armed Forces of the Russian Federation in the Information Space* defines information warfare as follows:

> Confrontation between two or more states in the information space with the purpose of inflicting damage to information systems, processes and resources, critical and other structures, undermining the political, economic and social systems, a massive psychological manipulation of the population to destabilize the state and society, as well as coercing the state to take decisions for the benefit of the opposing force.[15]

The document defines the information space as the "sphere of activity associated with the formation, creation, transformation, transmission, use and storage of information that affects individual and public consciousness, information infrastructure, and information itself."

Information technology is seen in Russia as "a weapon that can be used for political and military purposes to violate a state's sovereignty and territorial integrity."[16] In the Russian military, "offensive cyber capabilities fit within the concept of information warfare" because offensive capabilities blur the boundaries between peace and war. Cyber weapons endanger critical infrastructure and military systems. In addition to having technological effects, cyber weapons can "completely disorganize state and military administration, demoralize and disorient the population and create mass panic."[17] The most recent *Military Doctrine of the Russian Federation* affirms information technology is a weapon by listing "to enhance capacity and means of information warfare" as a task of equipping the armed forces, other troops, and bodies with weapons and military and special equipment.[18]

Another term that can be roughly translated as meaning information warfare in Russian military literature and doctrine is *informatsionnoye protivoborstvo* (IPb), or information confrontation. The *Military Encyclopedic Dictionary* of the Russian Ministry of Defense defines IPb as "a form of conflict between opposing sides, each of which seeks to defeat the enemy through informational effects in the information sphere, while resisting or reducing such effects on one's own side."[19] The US Defense Intelligence Agency states that IPb encompasses informational effects for influence and that these effects can be categorized as either technical or psychological.[20] It characterizes the technical effect as analogous to cyber defense, attack, or exploitation. And it describes the psychological effect as referring to attempts to change beliefs and behavior of target populations in favor of Russian governmental objectives.

The RAND Corporation has concluded from multiple Russian scholars that the IPb doctrine is not limited to peacetime and competition. Rather, researchers state that the doctrine plays an important role during wartime by "gain[ing] and maintain[ing] information superiority over the enemy's armed forces" while simultaneously "creat[ing] favorable conditions for preparation and use of [Russia's] armed forces."[21] The researchers state that the "essence of information confrontation lies in the mutual dependence (vulnerability) of potential adversaries on information and information systems."[22]

Influence operations that attempt to alter beliefs and behavior are central to Moscow's information-related doctrine. According to the US intelligence community, Russia is a "serious foreign influence threat" because it uses its "intelligence services, proxies and wide-ranging influence tools to try to divide Western alliances and increase its sway around the world."[23] Its influence tools include disinformation and propaganda. President Vladimir Putin has developed and implemented a comprehensive strategy to justify his brutal attack on Ukraine.[24] On the one-year anniversary of the invasion, the US Department of State published and discounted five of the most salient false narratives deployed by Russia's disinformation ecosystem to justify this unjustifiable war. The false narratives are as follows: (1) NATO and the West are the aggressor threatening Russia's security by encirclement; (2) Genocide is taking place in Donbas; (3) Russia is protecting people from genocide by denazification and demilitarization; (4) Russia is fighting Western Satanism, in addition to denazifying Ukraine; and (5) Russia is defending its sovereignty against the West. The last one alludes to international partnership and cooperation on biological threat reduction in Ukraine as a threat to Russia's sovereignty. The State Department has declared that "the Kremlin's disinformation machine has mounted a full-scale assault on truth in multilateral organizations attempting to portray peaceful research in Ukraine as biological weapons experiments that train migratory birds and diseased bats to threaten Russia."[25]

Hybrid War

After the Crimea annexation in March 2014, the concept of hybrid warfare "gained prominence as a concept that could help to explain the success of Russian military operations in this conflict."[26] This time, instead of using heavy-handed conventional forces as in previous campaigns in Chechnya and Georgia, Russia employed a combination of military and nonmilitary means in a covert manner in Crimea and eastern Ukraine. Russia appeared to have found a "new art of war" in its intervention in Ukraine.[27] The most lucid description of the new concept known as "hybrid war" appeared in an article by General Valery Gerasimov, the chief of the Russian General Staff, in a Russian defense journal in February 2013. In it, Gerasimov articulated for a Russian readership his views on current and future warfare. He emphasized that war is now conducted by "a roughly 4:1 ratio of non-military and military measures."[28] A diagram in the article shows the range of nonmilitary measures (including diplomatic pressure, economic sanctions, and political opposition) and military measures (including strategic deployment), all reinforced by information confrontation.

In the article, Gerasimov said he was describing "what he thought the West was doing as much as he was prescribing a strategy for Russia."[29] His article depicted a pattern of US-forced change of political regime, in particular in Afghanistan and Iraq, through an overt military invasion, which was supplanted by a new method of installation of political opposition.[30] The Russians had watched what they saw as the roles Western agencies played in fostering social-movement revolts against unfavorable regimes in the so-called color revolutions in Georgia, Serbia, and Ukraine and during the Arab Spring, especially in Libya.

During a televised ceremony, Putin reiterated this position by telling the new US ambassador to Moscow that Washington was to blame for the war in Ukraine. He said, "The use of the United States in its foreign policy of such tools as support for the so called color revolutions ultimately led to the Ukrainian crisis."[31] Russia claimed in its 2021 National Security Strategy that "unfriendly countries" were implementing "a deliberate policy to contain the Russian Federation" using "indirect methods aimed at provoking long-term instability."[32] When asked when the war in Ukraine would end, Dmitry Peskov, the press secretary of the president of the Russian Federation, replied that the "hybrid war of unfriendly countries against the Russian Federation" would last a long time.[33]

Ukraine War

Prior to Russia's full-scale invasion of Ukraine, Microsoft Threat Intelligence contends that many observers expected a "Russian-led hybrid war, like that observed when Russia invaded Donbas and illegally annexed Crimea" that would combine "cyber weapons, influence operations, and military force to swiftly overrun Ukrainian defenses."[34] Likewise, Ukrainian officials viewed early cyberattacks and influence operations as "part of what it calls Russia's 'hybrid war' against Ukraine and its allies."[35] However, military commanders' and academic experts' predictions of how the so-called cyber war would unfold in Ukraine did not play out. Shortly after the February 24, 2022, Russian invasion by large numbers of tanks and ground forces, the internet and other key aspects of Ukrainian infrastructure were still functioning, and Russian disinformation efforts had failed to persuade the Ukrainian population that resistance was futile. One research scholar remarked, "We imagined this orchestrated unleashing of violence in cyberspace," and a corporate director said, "I would have thought that by now Russia would have disabled a lot more infrastructure around communications, power and water."[36]

Nevertheless, the cyber component of the initial assault was destructive and relentless, serving as a central part of the large-scale hybrid war in Ukraine. Through cyber activity, Russia attempted to destroy, disrupt, or penetrate the networks of government agencies and civilian organizations. In the two months after the war began, Microsoft observed nearly forty discrete attacks, destroying files in hundreds of systems across dozens of entities in Ukraine. Russian cyber actors sought to degrade functions of targeted victims and limit citizens' access to reliable information and life services, while weakening confidence in the country's leaders. Meanwhile, Russian influence actors flooded social media with messages to dehumanize Ukrainians and shift blame to the United States. The messages of Russian cyber actors employed the denazification theme, described above in false narrative number three, and the messages of Russian influence actors utilized the alleged US biolaboratories theme in false narrative five. Microsoft surmised that based on Russian military goals for information warfare, these cyberattacks and influence operations were "aimed at undermining Ukraine's political will and ability to fight, while facilitating collection of intelligence that could provide tactical or strategic advantages to Russian forces."[37]

General Paul Nakasone, commander of US Cyber Command, testified to Congress in March 2023 that "Russia's military and intelligence cyber forces are skilled and persistent."[38] According to Microsoft, at least seven advanced persistent threat (APT) groups in or affiliated with Russian military, security, and intelligence agencies have conducted cyberattacks while Russian military forces were attacking Ukraine by land, air, and sea. Microsoft Threat Intelligence has observed the groups and identified them as being from the Russian Main Intelligence Directorate of the General Staff, *Glavnoye Razvedyvatel'noye Upravlenye* (GRU). Specifically, they have been identified as APT28, also known as Strontium or Fancy Bear; APT44, also known as Sandworm or Iridium; and a new group, DEV-0586, suspected of GRU affiliation. Also said to be involved, from the Russian Foreign Intelligence Service, *Sluzhba Vneshney Razvedki* (SVR), is APT29, also known as Nobelium or Cozy Bear. Lastly, from the Russian Federal Security Service, *Federal'naya Sluzhba Bezopasnosti* (FSB), are the groups Gamaredon, also known as Armageddon or Actinium; Energetic Bear, also known as Berserk Bear and Bromine; and Turla, also known as Krypton.[39]

These APT groups vary in their purposes, which include facilitating destructive attacks and collecting strategic and battlefield intelligence. The State Service of Special Communications and Information Protection (SSSCIP) of Ukraine states that with regard to aggressive operations and cyber espionage, the most heavily attacked sectors are Ukraine's government institutions, critical infrastructure, and various ministries.[40] More specifically, the SSSCIP has found that Russia targets defense organizations for plans, procurement, personnel, and platforms. Russia's targeting of the telecom sector is intended to interfere with cell phone and internet connectivity to cause panic or increase response times. The logistics and transportation sectors are targeted to monitor or interfere with ways that Western weapons enter Ukraine and places where they are stored. Attacks against the media sector, such as radio stations, newspapers, and news agencies, are intended to psychologically manipulate the public. Attacks on the energy sector are meant to cut the power supply. Finally, the banking sector is targeted to interrupt the financial system and spread panic or create economic downturn.

Overall, the SSSCIP has found that cyberattacks, both destructive and espionage-related, and influence operations are "clearly connected to support and enable more efficient on-the-ground operations during the planning and active phases of the invasion."[41] The SSSCIP has observed a tactical shift in cyber operations over the course of the war. The first half of 2022 was dominated by disruptive operations to suppress Ukrainian resilience. In contrast, in the second half of 2022, only two or three out of ten operations focused on destruction. The remaining seven or eight out of ten operations focused on data exfiltration and cyber espionage, mostly by groups such as Gamaredon, although Sandworm continued to be active with disruptive operations using wiper-type malware that destroys data and computers. The types of Russian cyberattacks during the Ukraine war, and their methods and means, resemble those of previous cyber incidents or disinformation campaigns targeting Western or aligned nations, as will be discussed in the next few sections.

Main Intelligence Directive

The Russian Main Intelligence Directorate (GRU) is a military intelligence agency of the General Staff of the Armed Forces. It is headquartered in Moscow and consists of multiple military units. Russian cyber actors affiliated with GRU Units 26165 and 74455, known as APT28, also Strontium or Fancy Bear, gained notoriety for the 2016 hack of the Democratic National Committee (DNC) during the presidential election. APT28 has been seen penetrating private groups in popular messaging applications used by the Ukrainian military. It uses phishing emails or compromised web resources to obtain passwords.[42] Another group of Russian hackers, publicly known as Sandworm or Iridium and classified as APT44, resides in GRU Unit 74455, in the Main Center for Special Technologies.[43] This unit was identified by name for the first time in the 2020 US indictment of six GRU officers. The hackers and co-conspirators were accused of engaging in computer intrusions and attacks intended to "support Russian government efforts to undermine, retaliate against, or otherwise destabilize" the countries of Ukraine, Georgia, and France, along with the 2018 PyeongChang Winter Olympic Games, with spillover effects in the United States.[44] Among all groups operating in Ukraine, Sandworm is the most active in conducting attacks intended to disrupt, degrade, or destroy information system resources or the information itself.

Disrupt (Websites)

The US indictment described the disruptive Sandworm cyber assault on the country of Georgia in October 2019. Sandworm targeted government and privately run websites, including those of courts, nongovernmental organizations, media, and businesses. The unit defaced approximately 15,000 websites and disrupted service to some of them.[45] The incident also interrupted the broadcasts of at least two national television stations. Sandworm accomplished the attack by compromising the computer systems of Georgian web-hosting providers. Many of the sites were defaced as follows: When visitors opened the site's home page, they were greeted with a full-screen photo of former Georgian president Mikheil Saakashvili and the caption "I'LL BE BACK" (a famous statement by actor Arnold Schwarzenegger in the action movie *Terminator*) superimposed over a Georgian flag. At the time, Saakashvili was wanted by the Georgian government on multiple criminal charges.[46] The United States and United Kingdom both condemned the cyberattacks, the latter stating that the operations aimed "to undermine Georgian sovereignty, to sow discord and disrupt the lives of ordinary Georgian people."[47]

Disruptive cyberattacks on Ukrainian websites also occurred weeks before the invasion by Russian ground forces. On February 15, 2022, distributed denial-of-service (DDoS) attacks (which typically overwhelm victims' servers by flooding them with queries) struck Ukrainian government organizations, including the Ministry of Defense, Ministry of Foreign Affairs, Armed Forces of Ukraine, and publicly funded Ukrainian Radio. In addition, the attacks struck the online services of two state-owned banks, PrivatBank and Oschadbank. PrivatBank lost services, including those of automated teller machines (ATMs), for several hours.[48] The DDoS attacks on the banks were preceded by fake SMS text messages. The Cyber Police of Ukraine reported that residents were receiving text messages, likely intended to cause alarm, that ATMs were malfunctioning.[49] Three days later, Anne Neuberger, who is a senior White House official and the deputy national security advisor for cyber and emerging technology, blamed the GRU for flooding the Ukrainian defense agency and bank websites with phony traffic. Neuberger said the United States had technical information linking the GRU to the DDoS attacks. Specifically, she told reporters that infrastructure run by the GRU "was seen transmitting high volumes of communication to Ukraine-based IP addresses and domains."[50] Neuberger noted that the attacks were consistent with what Russia would do to lay "the groundwork for more disruptive hacks accompanying an invasion" of Ukraine.

Degrade (Data)

The US indictment described a cyberattack by Sandworm using NotPetya malware. In June 2017, the Russian military unleashed NotPetya in Ukraine, and it spread automatically across much of the world. In what appeared to be a crypto ransomware attack, NotPetya was designed to degrade data. The White House declared that NotPetya was "part of the Kremlin's ongoing effort to destabilize Ukraine."[51] NotPetya leveraged multiple propagation methods, including use of the Eternal Blue penetration tool stolen and leaked from the US National Security Agency to spread inside an infected network.[52] A Cisco expert said that "to date, it was the fastest-propagating piece of malware we've ever seen."[53] In Ukraine, NotPetya struck four hospitals, six power companies, two airports, twenty-two banks, and at least three hundred other companies. It also hit the French construction materials company Saint-Gobain, the Russian steel and oil firms Evraz and Rosneft, and the Heritage Valley Health System in Pittsburgh, Pennsylvania.[54] Several global corporations also were infected by the software. Shipping giant Maersk "had to reinstall [its] entire infrastructure."[55] The company replaced 45,000 personal computers and 4,000 servers and loaded 2,500 applications. The pharmaceutical firm Merck was forced to shut down production of Gardasil, a vaccine used to prevent HPV (human papillomavirus) infection.[56] All told, the White House estimated damages at $10 billion.[57]

The wiper-type capability seen in NotPetya has been the GRU's weapon of choice in the Ukraine war. Several hours before the invasion on February 24, 2022, Sandworm installed a data wiper called HermeticWiper on hundreds of machines in Ukraine. The name was based on a digital certificate issued by the company Hermetica Digital Ltd.[58] Broadcom's cyber security unit Symantec found evidence that the wiper also attacked machines of Ukrainian government contractors in Lithuania and Latvia.[59] When the wiper runs, it damages the master boot record of the infected computer, preventing a restart. In several of the attacks, Symantec observed deployment of ransomware at the same time as the wiper. Symantec suspected that ransomware was used as a decoy or distraction from the wiper attack.[60] Yet the most impactful wiper attack by the GRU was by AcidRain, which, according to Sentinel Labs, was designed to remotely erase vulnerable modems and routers. The data-corrupting code targeted US satellite communications provider Viasat's KA-SAT network on the day of the invasion in an attempt to disrupt Ukrainian command and control. The wiper disabled very small aperture terminals (used to transmit and receive data, voice, and video signals over the satellite network) in Ukraine and across Europe in the tens of thousands.[61] By May and June 2022, Sandworm was repeatedly using the simple wiper tool CaddyWiper.[62]

In October 2022, Microsoft identified another pseudo-ransomware campaign, which targeted transportation and logistics organizations in Ukraine and Poland. The campaign used a never-before-seen ransomware payload labeling itself "Prestige ranusomeware (sic)" in its ransom note. The cyberattacks on all victims occurred within an hour of each other. Microsoft surmised that Iridium (Sandworm) had executed the Prestige attack. That determination was based on artifacts, tradecraft, and infrastructure associated with known Iridium activity.[63] Microsoft's Digital Threat Analysis Center noted "the recent attacks in Poland suggest that Russian state sponsored cyber-attacks may increasingly be used outside Ukraine in an effort to undermine foreign-based supply chains."[64] Another pseudo-ransomware-style attack did occur the next month in November 2022, but only in Ukraine: the Slovakia-based cyber security company ESET discovered a malware strain they called "RansomBoggs." On its Twitter page, ESET said the deployment was "similar to previous attacks attributed to #Sandworm."[65] ESET noticed the PowerShell language used to deploy the RansomBoggs payload had also been used to deliver CaddyWiper malware in March 2022. ESET discovered in January 2023 "a new data wiping malware deployed by Sandworm" on a victim in Ukraine. Its researchers dubbed the malware "SwiftSlicer" on their Twitter page.[66] Around the same time, Sandworm deployed the CaddyWiper malware in an attack on the National News Agency of Ukraine (Ukrinform). Sentinel Labs said, "The unit will likely continue developing new attacks as the war drags on."[67]

Destroy (Critical Infrastructure)

The US indictment also described computer intrusions by Sandworm targeting Ukraine's electric power grid. First, in December 2015, the group attacked three energy companies within thirty minutes of each other, resulting in power outages affecting approximately 225,000 customers. The attackers remotely controlled the distribution management system to disconnect over thirty electrical substations. The companies, however, manually restored power in several hours.[68] A year later, in December 2016, Sandworm infected computers in the electricity control center in Kyiv with Industroyer malware. The cyberattack removed 200 megawatts of capacity, about 20% of the city's nighttime power consumption.[69] Industroyer was capable of directly controlling switches and circuit breakers in substations. The sophisticated malware contained a framework of multiple modules and payloads for four industrial control protocols. It even had an activation time stamp, set for the specific date and time for the outage, to launch the Industroyer payload.[70] Yet the outage lasted only an hour. Researchers believed the attack might well have been a test bed for further cyber assaults.[71]

That suspicion was realized in April 2022, when Ukrainian government officials said an attempt by Russian military hackers to knock out power to millions of residents was foiled. Sandworm had penetrated and disrupted an industrial control system at a high-voltage power station.[72] At the Black Hat 2022 cyber security conference in Las Vegas, Ukrainian cyber official Victor Zhora said, "The attack was thwarted thanks to a prompt response by the defenders at the targeted energy company and the work of CERT-UA [Computer Emergency Response Team of Ukraine] and our [SSSCIP's] assistance."[73] CERT-UA had discovered malware that looked like a new version of Industroyer. The malware, dubbed Industroyer2, was to execute at a designated time, followed by deployment of CaddyWiper. The additional wiper malware was intended to hamper response and recovery and to erase traces of Industroyer2.

Six months later, in October 2022, Sandworm caused an unexpected power outage in an undisclosed Ukrainian city during a barrage of missile and drone strikes across the country.[74] This time, however, Sandworm did not use complex modular malware like Industroyer2. Instead, the threat group employed a new class of cyber-physical attack on Ukraine's energy grid. They abused MicroSCADA, a common software used in critical infrastructure systems. By injecting malicious commands directly into the MicroSCADA software, the attackers were able to manipulate controls for multiple substations and disrupt power. The incorporation of an operational paradigm called "living off the land" (LotL), which relies on the misuse of built-in tools and protocols already present on the target system, is a fundamental shift in Sandworm tactics.[75] The cyber security firm Mandiant has observed Sandworm using LotL tactics across its operations to "increase the speed and scale at which it can operate while minimizing the odds of detection."[76]

Foreign Intelligence Service

The Russian Foreign Intelligence Service (SVR) is responsible for conducting intelligence activities, espionage, and electronic surveillance outside Russia's borders. The SVR group known as APT29 (Cozy Bear or Nobelium) targets political parties, governments, international organizations, think tanks, and nongovernmental organizations. APT29 also participated in the 2016 hack of the DNC during the presidential election. A few years later, researchers at the security firm ESET uncovered a stealthy cyber espionage campaign named Operation Ghost. The SVR was busy compromising three European ministries of foreign affairs and the embassy of an EU country in Washington, DC. The group had avoided drawing attention to its activities by using new malware families and steganography (conceal information within objects) to hide command and control communications.[77] Yet the most consequential cyber intrusion by the SVR occurred in the

United States in 2020, when the SolarWinds campaign infected thousands of customers. The hack was determined by the US government to be an intelligence-gathering effort. Likewise, in the Ukraine war, APT29 has focused mostly on cyber espionage in the political sphere to collect information.

Collect (Information)

In December 2020, the cyber security firm FireEye revealed a cyber intrusion campaign by a highly evasive attacker. The campaign was described as widespread, impacting public and private organizations around the globe. The attacker had leveraged the supply chain of SolarWinds business software to compromise its customers by using malware called SUNBURST.[78] Of the 18,000 customers that downloaded the backdoor, the attackers selected a smaller number for secondary cyber activity. Anne Neuberger has reported that nine federal agencies and about 100 private-sector companies, including many in the technology sector, were compromised.[79] The US Department of Energy confirmed that its computers had been compromised but said the malware did not affect "mission essential national security functions."[80] The US Department of Homeland Security reported that the hackers had gained access to email accounts of the acting secretary and staff.[81] Likewise, the hackers breached the email accounts of US prosecutors and associated employees working primarily in New York offices.[82] Fortunately, the Pentagon observed no indications of compromise of Department of Defense systems.[83] In March 2021, in a package of sanctions against the Russian Federation, the Biden administration formally accused the SVR of being responsible for the SolarWinds exploitation campaign.[84]

Microsoft Threat Intelligence perceived that Nobelium was preparing for conflict in Ukraine in early 2021, when Russian troops started moving toward the border. Nobelium launched a massive phishing campaign against Ukrainian organizations that were trying to rally international support against Russian intentions. By mid-2021, Nobelium was attempting to break into IT companies serving government customers in NATO member states. In some incidents, the SVR gained access to and leveraged accounts to compromise Western foreign policy organizations in order to steal data. Microsoft suspected that the goal was to obtain consistent access to glean insights on Western responses to Russian actions. Later in 2021, Nobelium shifted focus to Ukrainian organizations that could provide intelligence on military, diplomatic, or humanitarian responses.[85] For the war itself, SSSCIP reports that CERT-UA is working to attribute some cases to APT29, but with low confidence because of difficulty in attribution.[86]

Likewise, the CyberPeace Institute's quarterly analysis reports do not attribute activity to the SVR, which is no surprise given SVR technical proficiency in evading detection.[87]

Russian Federal Security Service

The Russian FSB is the main successor to the KGB, the intelligence agency that conducted operations beyond the borders of Russia for most of the Soviet period. The FSB reports directly to the president of the Russian Federation, and its chief sits on the Russian security council. In 2003, the FSB acquired the Federal Agency of Government Communication and Information (FAPSI) to increase its offensive cyber capabilities.[88] In the FSB, the main unit for cyber operations is Unit 71330, in the Center for Electronic Communications Surveillance (TsRRSS), also known as Dragonfly, Energetic Bear, and Berserk Bear. Other FSB units are Gamaredon, also known as Armageddon or Actinium, and Turla, also known as Krypton. Although the FSB focuses mainly on domestic intelligence, it also conducts foreign intelligence. Energetic Bear is blamed for hacking US energy companies in 2018 and German energy and water companies in 2020. Gamaredon has been the most active of the Russian APTs in the Ukraine war.

Deny (Implants)

In March 2018, the US Computer Emergency Readiness Team (US-CERT) released an alert titled "Russian Government Cyber Activity Targeting Energy and Other Critical Infrastructure Sectors."[89] The other sectors included nuclear facilities, water, aviation, and manufacturing. The alert said Russian government cyber actors first compromised staging targets and then later intended targets. It referred to a report by Symantec on Dragonfly for further information. In its report, Symantec had blamed the Dragonfly group for targeting the energy sectors in Europe and North America. Symantec warned that besides gaining access to operational systems, the group "now potentially has the ability to sabotage or gain control of these systems should it decide to do so."[90] This fear was confirmed by the US Department of Homeland Security when it announced that Dragonfly, or Energetic Bear, had entered into "control rooms of US electric utilities where they could have caused blackouts" during the campaign described in the US-CERT alert.[91] US officials went on to say that "they got to the point where they could have thrown switches" and interrupted power flows. Roughly two years later, in May 2020, the hacking group Berserk Bear, on behalf of the FSB, targeted German companies in the energy, water, and power sectors.[92]

SSSCIP has said that of all the actors that CERT-UA monitors, the FSB group Gamaredon carried out the most cyberattacks in Ukraine in the second half of 2022. Each week, CERT-UA observed a new mass phishing email attack by Gamaredon. The phishing emails were well crafted, with believable topics, and they often were sent from compromised accounts that seem genuine.[93] The SSS-CIP released in January 2023 a full report on Gamaredon, describing its techniques for access, execution, persistence, and command and control, along with malicious payload variants.[94] The Cisco Talos Intelligence Group has agreed that Gamaredon is a major player in the Ukraine war. It asserts that Gamaredon has "predominately focused on cyberespionage against Ukrainian entities."[95] Talos Intelligence has described an attack in September 2022 in which Gamaredon distributed malicious Microsoft Office documents as email attachments. The deceptive documents contained lures related to the Russian invasion of Ukraine. They also contained a custom-made information-stealer implant that would steal data from specific file types from Ukrainian victims' machines and deploy additional software payloads as directed by the attackers.[96]

Disinformation Ecosystem

The pro-Russia disinformation ecosystem consists of Russian intelligence-agency-linked fronts, Russian messaging amplifiers, Russian-sourced troll farms, and sponsored overt media. Pro-Russian media were especially active in promulgating disinformation during the COVID-19 pandemic. The campaign started with asserting that the United States was the origin of the coronavirus. In early 2020, tvzvezda.ru, a state-owned outlet operated by the Russian Ministry of Defense, claimed that COVID-19 was a US-made biological weapon. That conspiracy theory was repeated on multiple forums for months.[97] The outrageous assertion was later elaborated on, saying the US-made biological weapon was for use against China and would replace nuclear bombs.[98] The conspiracy further evolved to contend that the United States had created the coronavirus in Ukrainian laboratories.[99] That claim expanded when a Russian foreign ministry spokesperson blamed "Pentagon-controlled US laboratories in the former Soviet republics for the severe outbreak of the COVID-19 coronavirus in Russia."[100] The spokesperson implied that the US-backed Lugar Center in Georgia was working to develop dangerous pathogenic agents.

The disinformation campaign shifted after Russia registered the world's first COVID-19 vaccine, named Sputnik V, amid safety concerns over accelerated clinical evaluations.[101] In 2021, Russia sought to undermine confidence in Western vaccines, such as those from Pfizer and BioNTech, through misleading claims on Russian state media, Russian government Twitter accounts, and false-front websites.[102] Russian sources expressed concerns about efficacy and side effects in an effort to promote the sale of the rival Sputnik V vaccine.

For the war in Ukraine, the disinformation ecosystem expanded beyond legacy elements. In addition to established media and war correspondents in the Donbas region, localized news websites and newly launched media outlets have pushed Kremlin-aligned narratives in Ukraine.[103] The self-declared Donetsk and Luhansk People's Republics have used their centralized information environments to spread Russian war propaganda, and the Crimea-based *NewsFront* website has pushed virulently anti-Ukrainian content under the guidance of the FSB. On Telegram (an encrypted messaging service), accounts focused on local news and managed by the GRU have aimed to influence people living in cities that have been critical of the war effort. In addition, Russian television channels attempted to influence Western audiences before the war and in its early days, although their ability to do so was constrained when the Russian state-backed media outlet RT America, with offices in New York, Miami, and Los Angeles, was shut down.[104] More recently, local propaganda outlets such as Radio Tavria and Za! TV have promoted Kremlin talking points in occupied and annexed territory. In the disinformation ecosystem online, websites that claim to provide local Ukrainian news pull content from Russian state-affiliated sources and display Russian war symbols in digital brand symbols, and pro-Russian social media groups, such as the Digital Army of Russia, spam Ukrainian social media communities with war propaganda.[105]

Projected Activity

In March 2023, President Putin signed a foreign policy document that casts the West as fundamentally hostile. It plays down Russia's aggression against Ukraine, referring to the fighting on the ground only indirectly. This document also blames the United States and Europe for initiating a "new type of hybrid war."[106] Putin, however, is using every hybrid playbook technique to achieve his goals.[107] To discourage Western support for Ukraine, Putin has threatened to use nuclear weapons and generated energy and food crises. While concentrations of ground troops and heavy firepower have been using "scorched earth" tactics, his elite hacking units have employed cyberattacks and influence operations.[108] Meanwhile, missile and drone attacks continue to target Ukrainian civilian housing and infrastructure far from the front lines.[109] It seems that "Russia's earlier cyberwar in the country" foreshadowed its full-scale physical attacks.[110] The goal of the NotPetya campaign released by GRU hackers is paralleled by that of the ongoing bombardment of the Ukraine's power grid: to demoralize and punish civilians. Russian cyberattacks on civilian infrastructure follow the Russian doctrine of information confrontation to exert technical effects on systems and psychological effects on the population. Ukrainian cyber official Victor Zhora notes that cyberattacks on civilians have not stopped; they have "only fallen off the radar as vastly more destructive, lethal physical attacks have eclipsed them."[111]

As the "hybrid war" in Ukraine continues, Microsoft Threat Intelligence has attempted to forecast what types of cyberattacks and influence operations will persist. It opines that if Russian forces suffer setbacks on the battlefield, Russian cyber actors may pursue destructive attacks on supply chains beyond Ukraine and Poland. The Russians also are predicted to conduct cyber espionage to understand nations' deliberations regarding military and political support of Ukraine. Cyber-enabled influence operations may also interfere in European politics to undermine NATO and EU support for Ukraine. Those operations could include hack and leak operations targeting key figures and elections.[112] The cyber security firm Check Point has already identified a notable increase in the average number of weekly cyberattacks against certain NATO countries, such as the United Kingdom, the United States, Estonia, and Denmark.[113] Russian cyber actors and pro-Russian operatives have adapted their hacking techniques and influence operations to support the war effort and show no signs of slowing down.[114] For instance, while Sandworm, classified as APT44, presents "one of the widest and highest severity cyber threats globally," Mandiant anticipates "Ukraine will remain the principal focus of APT44 operations."[115]

Conclusion

The Ukraine war has confirmed that Russia under Putin is attempting to undermine the rule-based international order with asymmetrical instruments of power that are disruptive but not powerful enough to collapse the order. The rules that guide international order are defined by laws and conventions ratified by alliances and institutions. An example is the Charter of the United Nations, first signed by member states in 1945 and since amended three times. The charter codifies fundamental legal principles of international relations. The secretary general of the United Nations argued that "Russia's invasion of Ukraine is a violation of its territorial integrity and of the Charter of the United Nations."[116] The invasion specifically violates Article 2(4) of the charter, which requires members to refrain from the "use of force against the territorial integrity or political independence of any state."[117] Russian attempts to justify the use of force in collective self-defense under Article 51 of the charter have no support in fact or law. Instead, international law and institutions have been used to condemn Russia's illegal war.[118]

In the use of force, Russia has violated international humanitarian law (IHL), also known as the law of armed conflict. IHL seeks to limit the effects of armed conflict, whereas the Charter of the United Nations regulates the lawful resort to force.[119] One IHL tenet is the principle of distinction, which provides that parties to an armed conflict must "distinguish between the civilian population and combatants and between civilian objects and military objectives."[120] Russian leaders have nonetheless ordered missile and bombing attacks against nonmilitary objectives, such as hospitals, medical facilities, drama theaters, and shopping centers. Another IHL tenet is the principle of proportionality, which prohibits attacks expected to cause civilian injury or damage excessive to anticipated concrete military advantage. The Russian propaganda machine constantly denies the targeting of civilians. Yet, for example, Russia bombarded Kyiv in May 2023 with seventeen aerial attacks on the capital. One predawn missile assault did cause superficial damage to the headquarters of Ukraine's military intelligence directorate, but this hardly justified the death of innocent civilians.[121]

The *Tallinn Manual 2.0 on the International Law Applicable to Cyber Operations* delineates that cyber operations "executed in the context of an armed conflict are subject to the law of armed conflict."[122] The manual was written by an international group of experts from mostly Western institutions at the invitation of the NATO Cooperative Cyber Defence Centre of Excellence. Although the *Tallinn Manual 2.0* is not legally binding, the legal experts determined this rule applies to any cyber activity undertaken in the furtherance of the hostilities. The manual also states that the principle of distinction and the principle of proportionality apply to cyberattacks. One rule on distinction reiterates that the civilian population must not be the object of a cyberattack, and a rule on proportionality declares cyberattacks on civilians or civilian objects to be prohibited if excessive to concrete and direct military advantage. The operation of the rule does allow a cyberattack on a dual system, such as GPS, considered to be a lawful target. Yet consequential harm to civilians must not be excessive to real and quantifiable benefits. The rule does not include cyberattacks that cause "inconvenience, irritation, stress, or fear" because they do not amount to loss of life, injury to civilians, or damage to civilian objects.[123]

Russia has apparently violated the law of armed conflict with relentless cyberattacks on civilians and civilian objects to cause effects excessive to military benefit. Lawyers would have to make legal determinations by incident for each sector under cyberattack. For instance, lawyers would have to consider whether Russia deployed destructive CaddyWiper malware in the network of a bank to cause panic; however, disruptive distributed denial-of service attacks on banks to cause a minor inconvenience would not apply. Lawyers would have to evaluate cyberattacks on dual-use systems, such as the attack on Viasat communications and telecom networks. They would also need to consider whether serious violations of the law of armed conflict by cyber means actually qualify as war crimes; for instance, if Sandworm accesses the industrial control system of the power grid and causes civilian deaths, can this cyberattack be considered a war crime when neither are valid military objectives?[124] Regardless of legal determinations, Russian cyberattacks have undoubtedly caused extensive financial damage to Ukraine's and to some extent Europe's economy in the case of the Viasat outage. Putin's war of aggression, conducted by kinetic strikes and cyberattacks on the civilian population and objects, accompanied by influence operations, threatens the very fabric of international laws.[125] Russia's leaders have to be held to account in order to sustain the rules-based international order.

NOTES

1. "Cyber Attack" Online Glossary, *NIST*, https://csrc.nist.gov/glossary/term/cyber_attack.

2. Jon Bateman et. al., "Measuring the Effects of Influence Operations: Key Findings and Gaps from Empirical Research," Carnegie Endowment for International Peace, June 28, 2021.

3. Dustin Volz and Robert McMillan, "In Ukraine, a 'Full-Scale Cyberwar' Emerges," *Wall Street Journal*, April 12, 2022.

4. Charles Clover, "Kremlin-Backed Group behind Estonia Cyber Blitz," *Financial Times*, March 11, 2009.

5. Eneken Tikk, Kadri Kaska, and Liis Vihul, *International Cyber Incidents: Legal Considerations* (NATO CCD COE Publications, 2010): 69–71.

6. John Bumgarner, "Overview by the US-CCU of the Cyber Campaign against Georgia in August of 2008," U.S. Cyber Consequences Unit, August 2009: 3.

7. U.S. Department of Defense, "DoD Dictionary of Military and Associated Terms," April 2023.

8. NATO Standardization Office, "NATO Glossary of Terms and Definitions," AAP-06, Edition 2021.

9. Paul Cornish et. al., *On Cyber Warfare* (Chatham House, November 2010): 3.

10. Thomas G. Mahnken, "Cyberwar and Cyber Warfare," in *America's Cyber Future: Security and Prosperity in the Information Age*, eds. Kristin M. Lord and Travis Sharp (Center for a New American Security, 2011): 58.

11. James A. Lewis, "Cyber War and Ukraine," Center for Strategic and International Studies, June 2022.

12. Andy Greenberg, "Russia's New Cyberwarfare in Ukraine is Fast, Dirty, and Relentless," *Wired*, November 10, 2022, https://www.wired.com/story/russia-ukraine-cyberattacks-mandiant/.

13. Microsoft, "Defending Ukraine: Early Lesson from the Cyber War," June 22, 2022.

14. Michael Connell and Sarah Vogler, *Russia's Approach to Cyber Warfare* (Center for Naval Analysis, March 2017): 3, https://www.cna.org/archive/CNA_Files/pdf/dop-2016-u-014231-1rev.pdf.

15. Russian Ministry of Defense, "Concept on the Activities of the Armed Forces of the Russian Federation in the Information Space," 2011.

16. Bilyana Lilly and Joe Cheravitch, *The Past, Present, and Future of Russia's Cyber Strategy and Forces* (NATO CCDCOE Publications, 2020): 135–138.

17. Bilyana and Cheravitch, *The Past, Present, and Future of Russia's Cyber Strategy*, 138.

18. President of the Russian Federation, "The Military Doctrine of the Russian Federation," December 25, 2014: 8–9.

19. Ministry of Defense of the Russian Federation, *Military Encyclopedic Dictionary*, 2011.

20. Defense Intelligence Agency, "Russia Military Power," 2017: 38.

21. Michelle Grise et. al., "Rivalry in the Information Sphere," *RAND Corporation*, RRA198–8, 2022: 10.

22. Grise et. al., "Rivalry in the Information Sphere."

23. Office of the Director of National Intelligence, "Annual Threat Assessment of the U.S. Intelligence Community," February 6, 2023: 15.

24. William Danvers, "Disinformation May Be One of Russia and China's Greatest Weapons," *The Hill*, April 5, 2023, https://thehill.com/opinion/national-security/3932031-disinformation-may-be-one-of-russia-and-chinas-greatest-weapons/.

25. U.S. Department of State, "Disinformation Roulette: The Kremlin's Year of Lies to Justify an Unjustifiable War," Global Engagement Center, February 23, 2023.

26. Bettina Renz, "Russia and 'Hybrid Warfare'," *Contemporary Politics* 22.3 (2016): 283.

27. Sam Jones, "Ukraine: Russia's New Art of War," *Financial Times*, August 28, 2014.

28. Charles K. Bartles, "Getting Gerasimov Right," *Military Review*, January–February 2016: 34.

29. Sydney J. Freedberg Jr., "U.S. Needs New Strategy to Combat Russian, Chinese Political Warfare: CSBA," *Breaking Defense*, May 31, 2018.

30. Bartles, "Getting Gerasimov Right."

31. Ann M. Simmons, "Putin Tells Envoy U.S. Is to Blame for War," *Wall Street Journal*, April 6, 2023.

32. Vladimir Putin, president of the Russian Federation, "On the National Security Strategy of the Russian Federation," (Moscow: Kremlin, July 2, 2021).

33. Ukrainska Pravda, "Kremlin Predicts Long Hybrid War, so Russians Should 'Unite Around Putin,'" *Yahoo News*, March 29, 2023, https://www.yahoo.com/lifestyle/kremlin-predicts-long-hybrid-war-102239260.html.

34. Microsoft Threat Intelligence, "A Year of Russian Hybrid Warfare in Ukraine," March 15, 2023: 3, https://nsarchive.gwu.edu/document/31752-20-year-russian-hybrid-warfare-ukraine.

35. Pavel Polityuk, "Massive Cyberattack Hits Ukrainian Government Websites as West Warns on Russia Conflict," *Reuters*, January 14, 2022, https://www.reuters.com/technology/massive-cyberattack-hits-ukrainian-government-websites-amid-russia-tensions-2022-01-14/.

36. Joseph Menn and Craig Timberg, "The Dire Predictions About a Russian Cyber Onslaught Haven't Come True in Ukraine. At Least Not Yet," *Washington Post*, February 28, 2022, https://www.washingtonpost.com/technology/2022/02/28/internet-war-cyber-russia-ukraine/.

37. Microsoft Digital Security Unit, "An Overview of Russia's Cyberattack Activity in Ukraine, *Special Report: Ukraine*, April 27, 2022: 2, https://query.prod.cms.rt.microsoft.com/cms/api/am/binary/RE4Vwwd.

38. General Paul M. Nakasone, Commander, United State Cyber Command, *Posture Statement Before the 118th Congress, Senate Committee on Armed Services*, March 7, 2023: 2.

39. Microsoft Digital Security Unit, "An Overview of Russia's Cyberattack Activity," 4.

40. State Service of Special Communications and Information Protection of Ukraine, "Russia's Cyber Tactics: Lessons Learned 2022," March 2023: 16–23.

41. State Service of Special Communications and Information Protection of Ukraine, "Russia's Cyber Tactics," 24.

42. State Service of Special Communications and Information Protection of Ukraine, "Russia's Cyber Tactics," 28.

43. National Security Agency, "Sandworm Actors Exploiting Vulnerability in Exim Mail Transfer Agent," *Cybersecurity Advisory*, May 28, 2020.

44. Department of Justice, "Six Russian GRU Officers Charged in Connection with Worldwide Deployment of Destructive Malware and Other Disruptive Actions in Cyberspace," October 19, 2020.

45. Department of State, "The United States Condemns Russian Cyber Attack Against the Country of Georgia," Global Public Affairs, February 21, 2020.

46. DFRLab, "Cyber-Attack Knocks Out Georgian Websites, Comes with a Surprise," Blog post, November 19, 2019, https://medium.com/dfrlab/cyber-attack-knocks-out-georgian-websites-comes-with-a-surprise-93aade6e6179.

47. Foreign Secretary Dominic Raab, "UK Condemns Russia's GRU over Georgia Cyber-Attacks," February 20, 2020, https://www.gov.uk/government/news/uk-condemns-russias-gru-over-georgia-cyber-attacks.

48. David Uberti, "Ukrainian Defense Ministry, Banks Hit by Suspected Cyberattacks, Officials Say," *Wall Street Journal*, February 15, 2022.

49. Palo Alto Networks, "DDoS Attacks Impacting Ukrainian Government and Banking Institutions," Unit 42 blog post, February 15, 2022, https://unit42.paloaltonetworks.com/preparing-for-cyber-impact-russia-ukraine-crisis/.

50. Martin Matishak, "White House Blames Russia for Latest Digital Attacks on Ukraine," *The Record*, February 18, 2022, https://therecord.media/white-house-blames-russia-for-latest-digital-attacks-on-ukraine.

51. Sean Gallagher, "In Terse Statement, White House Blames Russia for NotPetya Worm," *ArsTechnica*, February 15, 2018, https://arstechnica.com/tech-policy/2018/02/white-house-uk-blame-russian-military-for-notpetya-wiper-worm/.

52. US-CERT, "Petya Ransomware," Alert (TA17–181A), July 28, 2017.

53. Andy Greenberg, "The Untold Story of NotPetya, the Most Devastating Cyberattack in History," *Wired*, August 22, 2018, https://www.wired.com/story/notpetya-cyberattack-ukraine-russia-code-crashed-the-world.

54. Jon Henley, "Petya Ransomware Attack Strikes Companies Across Europe and US," *The Guardian*, June 27, 2017, https://www.theguardian.com/world/2017/jun/27/petya-ransomware-attack-strikes-companies-across-europe.

55. Doug Olenick, "NotPetya Attack Totally Destroyed Maersk's Computer Network: Chairman," *SC Magazine*, January 29, 2018, https://www.scmagazine.com/news/malware/notpetya-attack-totally-destroyed-maersks-computer-network-chairman.

56. Paul Roberts, "NotPetya Infection Left Merck Short of Key HPV Vaccine," *Security Ledger*, November 1, 2027.

57. Greenberg, "The Untold Story of NotPetya."

58. Cybereason Security Research Team, "Cybereason vs. HermeticWiper and IsaacWiper," Blog Post, March 3, 2022, https://www.cybereason.com/blog/cybereason-vs.-hermeticwiper-and-isaacwiper

59. Sean Lyngaas, "U.S. Firms Should Be Wary of Destructive Malware Unleashed on Ukraine, FBI and CISA Warn," *CNN World*, February 26, 2022, https://www.cnn.com/2022/02/26/politics/ukraine-malware-warning-cybersecurity-fbi-cisa/index.html.

60. Symantec Threat Intelligence, "Ukraine: Disk-Wiping Attacks Precede Russian Invasion," Blog post, February 24, 2022, https://www.security.com/threat-intelligence/ukraine-wiper-malware-russia

61. Antony J. Blinken, "Attribution of Russia's Malicious Cyber Activity Against Ukraine," United States Department of State, Press Statement, May 10, 2022.

62. Andy Greenberg, "Ukraine Suffered More Data-Wiping Malware Last Year Than Anywhere, Ever," *Wired*, February 22, 2023, https://www.wired.com/story/ukraine-russia-wiper-malware/.

63. Microsoft Security Threat Intelligence, "New 'Prestige' Ransomware Impacts Organizations in Ukraine and Poland," Blog post, October 14, 2022, https://www.microsoft.com/en-us/security/blog/2022/10/14/new-prestige-ransomware-impacts-organizations-in-ukraine-and-poland/

64. Phil Muncaster, "Microsoft: Beware Russian Winter Cyber-Offensive," *Infosecurity Magazine*, December 5, 2022.

65. Daryna Antoniuk, "Sandworm Hacking Group Linked to New Ransomware Deployed in Ukraine," *The Record*, November 29, 2022, https://therecord.media/sandworm-hacking-group-linked-to-new-ransomware-deployed-in-ukraine.

66. A. J. Vicens, "Russia's Sandworm Hackers Blamed in Fresh Ukraine Malware Attack," *Cyberscoop*, January 27, 2023, https://cyberscoop.com/sandworm-wiper-ukraine-russia-military-intel/.

67. Vicens, "Russia's Sandworm Hackers Blamed."

68. E-ISAC and SANS ICS, "Analysis of the Cyberattack on the Ukrainian Power Grid," Defense Use Case, March 18, 2016: iv–v.

69. Jamie Condliffe, "Ukraine's Power Grid Gets Hacked Again, a Worrying Sign for Infrastructure Attacks," *MIT Technology Review*, December 22, 2016.

70. Anton Cherepanov, "WIN32/INDUSTROYER: A New Threat for Industrial Control Systems," *ESET Report*, June 12, 2017.

71. Charlie Osborne, "Industroyer: An In-Depth Look at the Culprit Behind Ukraine's Power Grid Blackout," *ZDNet*, April 30, 2018, https://www.zdnet.com/article/industroyer-an-in-depth-look-at-the-culprit-behind-ukraines-power-grid-blackout/.

72. Frank Bajak, "Ukraine Says Potent Russian Hack Against Power Grid Thwarted," *ABC News*, April 12, 2022, https://abcnews4.com/news/nation-world/ukraine-says-potent-russian-hack-against-power-grid-thwarted-russian-invasion-industrial-control-system-cybersecurity-us-cybercommand.

73. Rob Wright, "Industroyer2: How Ukraine Avoided Another Blackout Attack," *Tech Target*, August 10. 2022, https://www.techtarget.com/searchsecurity/news/252523694/Industroyer2-How-Ukraine-avoided-another-blackout-attack.

74. Nate Nelson, "Sandworm Cyberattackers Down Ukrainian Power Grid During Missile Strikes," *Dark Reading*, November 9, 2023.

75. Dan Black, "Russia Ushers in a New Era of Cyber-Physical Attack," *Binding Hook*, November 14, 2023.

76. Ken Proska, et. al, "Sandworm Disrupts Power in Ukraine Using a Novel Attack Against Operational Technology," *Mandiant Blog*, November 9, 2023, https://cloud.google.com/blog/topics/threat-intelligence/sandworm-disrupts-power-ukraine-operational-technology/.

77. Mandiant, "APT44: Unearthing Sandworm," April 2024: 14.

78. Matthieu Faou et. al., "Operation Ghost: The Dukes Aren't Back—They Never Left," *ESET Research White Paper*, October 2019.

79. FireEye Threat Research, "Highly Evasive Attacker Leverages SolarWinds Supply Chain to Compromise Multiple Global Victims with SUNBURST Backdoor," Blog post, December 13, 2020, https://cloud.google.com/blog/topics/threat-intelligence/evasive-attacker-leverages-solarwinds-supply-chain-compromises-with-sunburst-backdoor.

80. White House, Press Briefing by Press Secretary Jen Psaki and Deputy National Security Advisor for Cyber and Emerging Technology Anne Neuberger, February 17, 2021.

81. Robert Walton, "DOE Confirms Its Systems Were Compromised by SolarWinds Hack," *Utility Dive*, December 18, 2020, https://www.utilitydive.com/news/doe-confirms-its-systems-were-compromised-by-solarwinds-hack/592441/.

82. Alan Suderman, "SolarWinds Hack Got Emails of Top DHS Officials," *AP*, March 29, 2021, https://apnews.com/article/solarwinds-hack-email-top-dhs-officials-8bcd4a4eb3be1f8f98244766bae70395.

83. Liam Tung, "SolarWinds Attackers Breached Email of U.S. Prosecutors, Says Department of Justice," *ZDNet*, August 2, 2021, https://www.zdnet.com/article/solarwinds-attackers-breached-email-of-us-prosecutors-says-department-of-justice/.

84. Mariam Baksh, "Pentagon Not Compromised by SolarWinds, Microsoft Exchange Hacks, Official Says," *Nextgov*, April 14, 2021, https://www.nextgov.com

/cybersecurity/2021/04/pentagon-not-compromised-solarwinds-microsoft-exchange-hacks-official-says/173377/.

85. U.S. Department of the Treasury, "Treasury Sanctions Russia with Sweeping New Sanctions Authority," Press Release, April 15, 2021.

86. Microsoft Digital Security Unit, "An Overview of Russia's Cyberattack Activity in Ukraine," 5.

87. State Service, "Russia's Cyber Tactics," 29.

88. CyberPeace Institute, "Cyber Dimensions of the Armed Conflict in Ukraine," Quarterly Analysis Report Q4 October to December 2022.

89. Bilyana Lilly, *Russian Information Warfare* (Naval Institute Press, 2022): 27–28.

90. US-CERT, "Russian Government Cyber Activity Targeting Energy and Other Critical Infrastructure Sectors," Alert (TA18–074A), March 15, 2018.

91. Symantec Security Response, "Dragonfly: Western Energy Sector Targeted by Sophisticated Attack Group," Blog post, September 6, 2017, https://www.security.com/threat-intelligence/dragonfly-energy-sector-cyber-attacks,

92. Rebecca Smith, "Russian Hackers Reach U.S. Utility Control Rooms, Homeland Security Officials Say," *Wall Street Journal*, July 23, 2018.

93. Sean Lyngaas, "German Intelligence Agencies Warn of Russian Hacking Threats to Critical Infrastructure," *Cyberscoop*, May 26, 2020, https://cyberscoop.com/german-intelligence-memo-berserk-bear-critical-infrastructure.

94. State Service, "Russia's Cyber Tactics," 26.

95. State Cyber Protection Center, State Service of Special Communications and Information Protection of Ukraine, "Another UAC-0010 Story," January 2023.

96. Cisco Talos, "Gamaredon Remains a Major Player in Ukrainian Conflict," Blog post, 2022.

97. Asheer Malhotra and Guilherme Venere, "Gamaredon APT Targets Ukrainian Government Agencies in New Campaign," *Talos Intelligence*, Blog post, September 15, 2022, https://blog.talosintelligence.com/gamaredon-apt-targets-ukrainian-agencies/,

98. EUvsDisinfo, "Capitalizing on the Coronavirus Conspiracist Frenzy," *EUvsDisinfo* 196: 14 May, 2020, https://euvsdisinfo.eu/capitalising-on-the-coronavirus-onspiracist-frenzy/.

99. EUvsDisinfo, "Coronavirus Is a U.S. Biological Weapon Against China, It Replaces a Nuclear Bomb," *EUvsDisinfo* 195, April 20, 2020, https://euvsdisinfo.eu/report/coronavirus-is-the-uss-biological-weapon-against-china-it-replaces-a-nuclear-bomb.

100. EUvsDisinfo, "Coronavirus Was Created by Americans in Ukrainian Laboratories," *EUvsDisinfo* 196, April 26, 2020, https://euvsdisinfo.eu/report/coronavirus-created-by-americans-in-ukrainian-laboratories/.

101. Zaal Anjaparidze, "Russia Dusts Off Conspiracy Theories About Georgia's Lugar Center Laboratory in Midst of COVID-19 Crisis," *Eurasia Daily Monitor*, May 5, 2020, https://jamestown.org/program/russia-dusts-off-conspiracy-theories-about-georgias-lugar-center-laboratory-in-midst-of-covid-19-crisis/.

102. Thomas Grove, "Russia Registers World's First Covid-19 Vaccine Despite Safety Concerns," *Wall Street Journal*, August 11, 2020.

103. Michael R. Gordon and Dustin Volz, "Russian Disinformation Campaign Aims to Undermine Confidence in Pfizer, Other Covid-19 Vaccines, U.S. Officials Say," *Wall Street Journal*, March 7, 2021.

104. Microsoft Security Threat Intelligence, "A Year of Russian Hybrid Warfare in Ukraine," March 15, 2023: 6, https://nsarchive.gwu.edu/document/31752-20-year-russian-hybrid-warfare-ukraine.

105. Tali Arbel, "Russia-Backed RT America to Cease Production, Internal Memo Says," *Los Angeles Times*, March 4, 2022, https://www.latimes.com/entertainment-arts/tv/story/2022-03-04/russia-backed-rt-america-to-cease-production.

106. Microsoft Security Threat Intelligence, "A Year of Russian Hybrid Warfare in Ukraine" March 15, 2023: 9, https://nsarchive.gwu.edu/document/31752-20-year-russian-hybrid-warfare-ukraine.

107. Maksym Skrypchenko, "Russia's New Foreign Policy Looks Old and Soviet," *Wall Street Journal*, April 14, 2023.

108. Scott Jasper, "Can Russian Hybrid Warfare Win the Day in Ukraine?", *National Interest*, October 7, 2022, https://nationalinterest.org/blog/techland-when-great-power-competition-meets-digital-world/can-russian-hybrid-warfare-win-day.

109. Matthew Luxmoore and Ann M. Simmons, "Ukraine Says Russia Is Decimating Bakhmut," *Wall Street Journal*, April 11, 2023.

110. Marcus Walker, "Russian Drones Target Odessa as Ukraine Seeks More Air Defense," *Wall Street Journal*, April 29, 2023.

111. Andy Greenberg, "Russia's Cyberwar Foreshadowed Deadly Attacks on Civilians," *Wired*, December 28, 2022, https://www.wired.com/story/russia-cyberwar-ukraine-target-civilians/.

112. Greenberg, "Russia's Cyberwar Foreshadowed."

113. Microsoft Security Threat Intelligence, "A Year of Russian Hybrid Warfare in Ukraine," March 15, 2023: 17, https://nsarchive.gwu.edu/document/31752-20-year-russian-hybrid-warfare-ukraine.

114. Check Point Research, "The Russian-Ukrainian War, One Year Later," Blog post, February 20, 2023.

115. A. J. Vicens, "Russia's Digital Warriors Adapt to Support the War Effort in Ukraine, Google Threat Researchers Say," *Cyberscoop*, April 19, 2023, https://cyberscoop.com/russia-sandworm-ukraine-wagner-youtube.

116. UN Sustainable Development Group, "Russia's Invasion of Ukraine Is a Violation of the UN Charter, UN Chief Tells Security Council," Announcement, May 5, 2022.

117. John B. Bellinger III, "How Russia's Invasion of Ukraine Violates International Law," Council on Foreign Relations, February 28, 2022, https://www.cfr.org/article/how-russias-invasion-ukraine-violates-international-law.

118. Oona A. Hathaway, "How Russia's Invasion of Ukraine Tested the International Legal Order," Brookings, April 3, 2023, https://www.brookings.edu/on-the-record/how-russias-invasion-of-ukraine-tested-the-international-legal-order/.

119. International Committee of the Red Cross, "What Is International Humanitarian Law?", *ICRC*, April 6, 2022, https://www.icrc.org/en/document/what-international-humanitarian-law.

120. Milena Sterio, "The Russian Invasion of Ukraine: Violations of International Law," *JURIST*, Legal News & Commentary, July 12, 2022, https://www.jurist.org/commentary/2022/07/milena-sterio-russia-war-crimes-ukraine/.

121. Ian Lovett and Laurance Norman, "Missiles Kill Three in Kyiv as Russia Claims to Thwart New Border Incursion," *Wall Street Journal*, June 1, 2023.

122. Michael N. Schmitt, *Tallinn Manual on the International Law Applicable to Cyber Warfare* (UK: Cambridge University Press, 2013): 375.

123. Schmitt, *Tallinn Manual*: 420–423 and 470–473.

124. Schmitt, *Tallinn Manual*: 391–393.

125. Lise Morje Howard, "A Look at the Laws of War—and How Russia Is Violating Them," United States Institute of Peace, September 29, 2022, https://www.usip.org/publications/2022/09/look-laws-war-and-how-russia-violating-them.

Chapter Five

Putin's Economy

On the Road to Ukraine and Empire?

Paul Gregory

Vladimir Putin ascended to the presidency of Russia in the last days of the twentieth century. He promised economic stability, prosperity, and an enhanced standing in the world community. His was an appealing message considering the turmoil and chaos of the "wild capitalist" Boris Yeltsin years. The Russian people had had enough of unpaid pensions and wages, criminal bands and oligarchs running the economy and government, and no rule of law. They were ready for stability and growth under the then-unknown Putin.

A decade and a half later, Putin would tap into another promise—namely, to restore Russia's imperial greatness to citizens who had grown up in a Soviet empire that extended from the borders of Western Europe to Central Asia. His promise of a return to empire would be opposed by the West. Therefore, Putin would have to realign Russia with new partners such as China, Iran, and North Korea. As this restructuring of alliances occurs, the world has taken on a new shape.

Has Putin delivered on his promises?

Under Putin's rule, Russia has engaged in three military operations in Europe and Eurasia: Georgia (2008), Crimea and the Donbas (2014–2022), and Ukraine (starting February 2022), plus ongoing engagements in Syria and Africa carried out by mercenary troops. The Ukrainian conflict is of such magnitude and duration (entering its third year) that it qualifies as the first European war of the twenty-first century. Let us hope it will be the last.

As 2024 grinds toward its midpoint and the Ukraine war ravages on, the Russian people are experiencing declines in their living standards, unpaid wages, unstocked shelves, soaring inflation, and a country run by a kleptocratic Kremlin band that increasingly tolerates no opposition. Opposition politicians have been excised from the marketplace of ideas. Street protests are dangerous to attend, and a massive propaganda campaign of "All is well, and if not, it is due to foreign enemies" dominates the Russian press, social media, and airwaves. Moreover, Russia has become a pariah nation as a consequence of its unprovoked attack on Ukraine. Even its "allies" afford it uncertain support.

As Putin was amassing troops on the Ukrainian border in February of 2022 the United States and its NATO allies threatened Putin with what it promised to be debilitating sanctions. So far, the Russian economy has avoided the most extreme economic disasters predicted by the West. Russia's allies have stepped in as buyers and suppliers. Its former Central Asian republics have engaged in intermediary trade between Europe and Russia. There is massive evasion as the West moves to close loopholes.

What is clear is that inflation will continue to plague the Russian economy, and living standards will stagnate as resources are diverted from civilian to military uses as Russia moves to an all-out war economy. But so far, the Putin regime seems to have the resources for its war machine. How long this will hold remains to be seen.

Putin can no longer scapegoat the Yeltsin years, which now lie a quarter century back. Nor can he blame the policy recommendation of his "liberal" advisers. They have been expunged, and most live abroad. He has without provocation entered Russia into a war with no end in sight, generating casualties in the hundreds of thousands and a stagnant (at best) civilian economy. The Russian people are told to sacrifice while Putin builds his war economy.

Putin has been elected president of Russia five times: in 2000, 2004, 2012, 2018, and 2024. Due to an amendment in the constitution, Putin is now president for life, barring some unforeseen event.[1] Putin had to sit out the 2008 election for constitutional reasons in favor of his stooge, Dmitry Medvedev. His imperious decision to return to the presidency in November 2011 sent tens of thousands of protesters onto the streets.

The November 2011 to March 2012 protests constituted the greatest threat to date to Putin's hold on power. They were a combination of Putin fatigue, disappointment over the slow economic recovery, and a sense of morass. The protesters'

"Anyone but Putin" slogan captured the mood.[2] Putin's response was to crack down on the opposition, the most visible being the Navalny team, jailing even ordinary protesters, use his "electoral commission" to disqualify opposition candidates, and crack down brutally on the independent press, the internet, and television. With these fraudulent assists, Putin was easily "re-elected" for his third term in March of 2012. He has not been subjected to such a serious challenge since then, with the exception of the short-lived, abortive Prigozhin march on Moscow in June 2023.

Upon re-election in March 2012, Putin faced a momentous choice: Should he restructure and reform the economy by reining in the inner-circle kleptocrats, so ably described in Karen Dawisha's book?[3] That is, should he return to offering the people growth and prosperity as an integral member of the world order? Or should he stick with the isolated kleptocratic state he created to ensure loyalty through fear? The status quo sees the economy not as an engine of long-term growth and prosperity but as an ATM machine to pay for military ventures, reward Putin and his circle, and pay bills denominated in dollars. The Russian people get the limited money left over, but they are told they should be grateful to Putin for protecting them from the mighty NATO armies poised for the invasion of Russia.

With Putin and his Kremlin associates stripping assets from "national champions" like Gazprom and Rosneft, and with the Kremlin following populist policies at home, there has been little chance of improved economic performance. Putin rejected the advice of his few remaining liberal advisers to break up crony monopolies and have them create value rather than serve as private piggy banks for the elite. Prosperity also requires a Russia integrated into world markets and observing international rules as a member in good standing with the world community.

Figure 5.1 shows the anemic and sporadic growth associated with the span of Putin's Ukraine operation, from Crimea to all-out war. The goal of prosperity, productivity, and stability has been tossed by the wayside. Putin's 2000 promise is long forgotten.

Had Putin moved toward free markets in 2012, Russia likely would not be engaged in a hot war in Ukraine, not be threatening its neighbors, not be facing crippling sanctions, and not be viewed as a rogue state. With luck, Putin would be in jail or on the dock at the International Criminal Court.

Economic Performance During the Putin Years

During Putin's first two terms, the economy was growing at a rapid rate as it recovered from the Yeltsin depression of the 1990s and benefited from Putin's most liberal period as an economic reformer (figure 5.1). His election to a second term

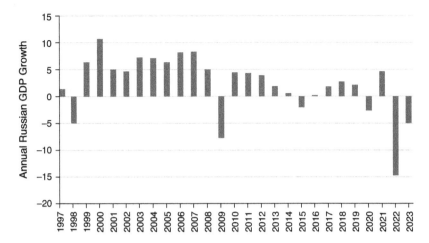

Figure 5.1 Annual Russian GDP Growth, 1997–2013. *Source*: Russian State Federal Statistics, https://eng.rosstat.gov.ru/folder/11335.

was more or less a sure thing. He stood against divided opponents and was easily re-elected.

At this point, Putin could have easily won a fair election on the basis of the performance of the economy. His strict control of the election process was not even necessary. Russia was growing. It was included in the ranks of the fast-growing emerging markets in the BRICS countries, among Brazil, India, China, and South Africa. Pensions and wages were paid on time. Optimism was in the air. Whatever the real reasons for Russian growth, the Russian people did not care.

As Kathryn Stoner and Michael McFaul put it: "Putin got the credit [for growth]. He was in the right place at the right time."[4]

If we condense Putin's narrative for Russia into one phrase, it would be "I saved the Russian economy from ruin. If I go, chaos will return. Our enemies are waiting."

This narrative actually does not hold much water. Russia's economic recovery began before Putin became Russia's "elected Czar"—as some fawning followers call him.[5] Since Putin's assumption of power in the last days of the twentieth century, Russia's economic growth has been lower than that of two-thirds of its former Soviet neighbors (see figure 5.2). Growth resumed throughout the former Soviet Union at about the same time. This suggests that the other former Soviet republics would have each had to have national saviors like Putin, or they were simply part of a recovery that happened in the former USSR for organic reasons.

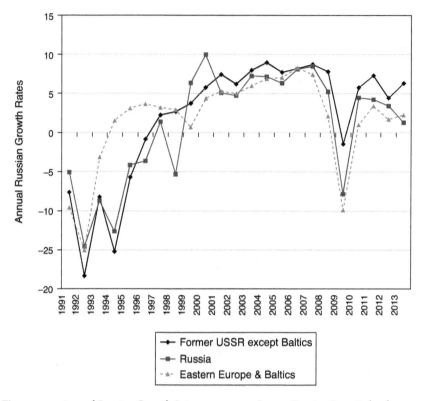

Figure 5.2 Annual Russian Growth Rates, 1991–2013. *Source*: Russian State Federal Statistics, https://eng.rosstat.gov.ru/folder/11335.

Putin's rise to power could not have been better timed for him. Russia, like the other slow reformers, had reached bottom and had started to recover after 1998. Russian economic growth between Putin's accession in 2000 and the global economic crisis of 2008 ranked in the bottom third of the twelve (non-Baltic) former republics of the USSR.

The rapid economic growth of this first period masked a number of failures. First, Putin did not deliver his promise of a diversified modern economy. Russia remains today a petro-state. The Russian Federation still gets half its revenues from oil and gas. If we include raw materials, it gets two-thirds. The Putin dream of a Russian Silicon Valley in Skolkovo outside of Moscow remains unfulfilled. Russia remains at the mercy of fluctuating oil and gas prices in a world of high-tech fracking.

Second, although Putin promised to turn the state-owned "national champions" into models of efficiency and value, his brand of state capitalism proved to be a model for corruption, inefficiency, and waste.[6] In 2007, Putin set the goal to make Gazprom the world's first trillion-dollar corporation.[7] At the time, Gazprom was valued at $360 billion and was the world's third most valuable company. Today, Gazprom does not even show in the top 100 despite its 15% share of world gas reserves and what is left of its lucrative European energy market. Instead of creating value, Gazprom funnels clandestine income to Putin's inner circle and funds Putin's favorite projects, such as the corporation's $3 billion "social obligation" for the Sochi Winter Olympics.[8] Funds diverted from state companies serve to promote Russia's policy interests abroad. At this point, we cannot calculate the degree to which state enterprises, rather than the military budget, have financed the Ukraine war.

Some two-thirds of listed Russian companies are state owned—theoretically owned by the Russian people, not by Putin and his inner circle, who have proven to be poor shepherds of citizen property.[9] Their corruption, mismanagement, and misuse of assets have proven immensely costly. If Russia's largest companies operated like Chinese state companies[10] (which themselves have low valuations), as of 2015, they would double in value or even more.

Third, Putin's disregard for rule of law and his foreign misadventures were increasingly isolating Russia from the world economy. His cavalier treatment of international energy concerns discouraged further investment in unlocking Russia's mammoth but difficult reserves.[11] Putin's expropriation of Yukos shareholders[12] has come home to roost with a $50 billion international arbitration judgment against Russia.

Fourth, Putin appears to have set aside voices of reason in favor of the claims of quacks that autarchy and isolation are actually good for Russia. Stalin listened to the pseudoscience of Trofim Lysenko and ruined agriculture. Putin is learning from the pseudoeconomics[13] of his favored economic adviser,[14] Sergei Glazyev, who advises that Russia go back to the good old Soviet days of economic planning and autarchy. Russia can prosper on the basis of its own resources and brain power, or so assured his economic advisers.

There is not one example of a successful economy cut off from globalization. The old import-substitution models promoted by Putin's advisers are thoroughly discredited. The success stories of the last half century—China, the Four Tigers, India, and Brazil—have succeeded by opening, not closing their economies. One of Russia's most prominent economists (now in exile) put it this way: "It is a pure fantasy that something good can come of isolation."[15]

The point is that Putin had decided by 2008 that he was not going to focus on making Russia into a modern, prosperous country that could become part of the affluent West. Other goals, he had decided, were more important.

The second period starts with the 2008 hand-off to proxy president, Dmitry Medvedev. Medvedev became the titular head of state; most understood that Putin, who took the job of prime minister, was actually in charge.

As the world financial crisis began to unfold in 2008, Russia's growth started its decline. The drop accelerated, and real GDP collapsed by almost 10% before starting a recovery in mid-2010. Among the BRICS (Brazil, Russia, India, China, and South Africa)—the then rapidly growing emerging market economies—Russia suffered the deepest blow and the deepest loss of image during the world financial crisis.

Russia's military siding with Georgia's Abkhazian rebels in 2008 did not help on the growth side, but compared with the sanctions to come, the impact of Russia's Georgian incursion was not significant. Rather, it was the waiting for the world financial crisis to work its way out that dominated Russian policy.

The Russian economy resumed healthy growth for a brief period, but then stagnated between 2012 and 2014, barely eking out positive growth.

During this period, Putin offered no new economic reform ideas to reinvigorate the economy. In his annual 2015 address to the Russian people, Putin could only promise that the world economy would get better soon and would restore growth to Russia. He offered no ideas as to what Russia itself could do to pull itself out of stagnation.[16]

From 2008 to 2014, Russian growth was minuscule. At the start of 2014, Russia was producing an output level only slightly above that of 2008.[17] This anemic recovery was made more ominous by the fact that oil prices had more than doubled between 2008 and 2014 and the credit freeze associated with Georgia had ended.[18] Russian growth had not improved even under favorable conditions.

By the beginning of 2014, the Russian economy appeared to have run out of steam. Putin could advance no reform ideas (other than to hope that world economic performance improves[19]), and his reputation as a leader who could produce strong economic results was at risk.

Putin's popularity was also at risk. His "rating" (as the only political name Russians would recognize other than nonentities such as Sergei Shoigu) fell to the sixties down from highs of the eighties.

It was in this context that Putin began his Crimean and eastern Ukrainian adventures against the backdrop of the Euromaidan revolution in Kyiv. Putin's massive propaganda campaign against Ukraine plus his popular annexation of Crimea, which remains unrecognized by international organizations, was to give Putin a substantial popularity boost according to Russia's flawed political ratings.

If we go back in time, Putin faced in 2014 the prospect of what his Soviet predecessors termed the "period of stagnation."[20] Even high oil prices were not enough to generate reasonable growth. Moreover, he had notably failed to deliver on his promise of diversification away from an energy-dependent economy. Russia's dependence on oil and gas revenues had increased under Putin.[21] Russia had become even more of a Latin American or African style "one crop" economy, dependent on the vagaries of raw material markets. This is not what Putin had promised.

War in Ukraine as Bread and Circuses

It is a trope of political science and political economy that a totalitarian regime stays in power by offering its people, as did the Roman emperors, "bread and circuses." By 2014, Putin realized that he could not offer "bread" in the form of a growing economy, but he could offer "circuses" in the form of a foreign enemy threatening Mother Russia's very existence. During the 2008 economic crisis, Putin diverted the Russian people's attention with his attack on Georgia. In 2014, he could offer them an even bigger circus with the return of Crimea to the bosom of Mother Russia, and he could also protect the Russian-speaking innocents of the "Russian world," especially those threatened by the neo-Nazi "junta" that he claimed took over Ukraine in early 2014.

This basic message was imparted by a non-stop propaganda campaign to convince the Russian people that the United States was intent on stealing Siberian resources, splitting off Russian regions, and preparing an attack on Mother Russia, and that the United States and its NATO puppets were behind the Ukrainian Maidan color revolution. Putin's cronies (such as Yevgeny Prigozhin) employed armies of trolls to flood normal communications on the internet with Russian propaganda. The Russian campaign began with the appearance of Russian special forces (dressed in generic green) in the Crimean parliament building in the early morning hours of February 21, 2014. Putin subsequently admitted that he began planning this action weeks earlier, thus dispelling the myth of a popular Crimean uprising against Ukrainian authorities.

The goal was not to strengthen Russia, or to restore it to greatness, but to ensure the survival of the regime. As Stoner and McFaul put it: "Putin needed a new argument in order to achieve re-election as President of Russia for a third time, in 2012. To counter this new wave of social mobilization, Putin revived an old Soviet-era argument as his new source of legitimacy—defense of the motherland against the evil West, and especially the imperial, conniving, threatening United States. In particular, Putin argued that the United States was seeking to topple his regime."[22]

Putin's campaign in eastern Ukraine and Crimea began in February 2014. One and a half years later, in June 2015, Russia's GDP was below its level in February 2014.[23] Meanwhile, Russia's EU neighbors registered "normal" growth. Although official Russian statistics tried to put a favorable spin on the decline, Russian GDP continued to decline throughout the rest of 2015 and remained stuck at zero in 2016.[24] Even the most optimistic forecasters at that time did not see a return to robust growth any time in the near future.[25]

It is difficult to divide Russia's economic problems into those directly related to Ukraine and those related to other factors. Energy prices were largely unrelated to the Ukraine war, but the collapse of earnings from gas sales to Ukraine and Europe was a consequence of Russian pipeline politics, which bully, bluster, and scare (away) customers. Russia's key gas export earnings from the European market fell by 27% in 2015 alone, and they were a vital source of state revenue.[26] Ukraine's purchases from Russia fell from 75% to below 10% as Ukraine weaned itself off Russian gas.[27]

The Role of Sanctions and the War Against Ukraine

In his military ventures in Georgia, Syria, and Ukraine, Putin steered clear of a direct conflict with the United States and NATO. Although Kremlin propaganda warned of an imminent attack from the West, there was no danger of such an action from the defensive NATO alliance.

In February of 2022 Russian troops began what they claimed was a massive military exercise on the borders to Ukraine from Russia and Belarus. Mistaken as a bluff, Russia began a multipronged invasion of Ukraine on February 24. Putin's war plan was to capture Kyiv, eliminate the Ukrainian leadership, and install a puppet government. Against all odds, Ukrainian forces were able to repulse the invasion, driving Russian forces out of captured territory.

Now entering its third year, the Russian war on Ukraine has proven costly to both sides. On the Russian side, there have been up to 200,000 casualties and serious loss of equipment.[28] The Putin regime, at the beginning, promised the people this would be a limited engagement. It was to be called a "special military operation." To call it a "war" was punishable by prison.[29] The internal crackdown reached such proportions as to drive any opposition into exile or prison, the most notable event being the murder of Alexei Navalny in February 2024 in a Siberian penal camp after he had survived Novichok poisoning while on the campaign trail.

With respect to Ukraine, the West had two ways to punish Russia's unprovoked attack on a sovereign nation: First, it could impose sanctions on Russia as a threat to the Kremlin's ability to finance its military. Second, it could provide military assistance to Ukraine to allow Ukrainian forces to repel the Russian invasion without any NATO boots on the ground.

When Putin began staging forces for a general attack on Ukraine, including its capital, Kyiv, the United States and NATO countries warned that an invasion would require the West to impose sanctions of unprecedented proportions. Based on his experience in 2014–2021, Putin wagered that the United States and NATO could not find common ground on biting sanctions and that the sanctions would fall apart when the costs of imposing them became apparent to the West. Moreover, the Kremlin had built a considerable war chest in the form of central bank reserves and reserve funds.

As Putin unleashed his invasion on Ukraine on February 24, 2022, the shocked Western world reached a quick consensus on the toughest possible sanctions, which were unleashed in tranches depending on Russian behavior. These sanctions were issued on oligarchs, government officials, and members of parliament, and on Russian companies and banks, including Russia's largest, Sberbank. The most shocking sanctions were the freezing of central bank assets stored in Western financial capitals and the removal of Russia from the SWIFT international transactions system. The assets of oligarchs were subjected to seizure, including their yachts and villas.

Contrary to Putin's usual stance of belittling Western sanctions as ineffective, Putin began to emphasize that tough times lay ahead, that the Russian people must make sacrifices as they did when facing down the Nazis, and that the sanctions will be dropped when the West sees the cost of sanctions to its own people. Putin reminded the Russian people of their victory in the Great Patriotic War and began to praise the murderous Stalin regime as a positive feature of Russian heroism.

It is too early to gauge the effects of the sanctions on the Russian economy, the Russian military, and the mood of the Russian people. It is obvious that substitutions for foreign imports and new customers for Russian energy exports will play a major role in limiting their effect. Russia has established deeper trade relation with its new allies—China, North Korea, and Iran. So far, economic factors do not seem to have profoundly harmed Russia's war machine. Harm seems to be coming from another direction—namely, from shortages of soldiers and workers. To dampen domestic concerns, Russia has recruited largely from remote areas and from prisons in order to avoid the reaction of the public to a general mobilization.

In such unsettled times, it is difficult to predict the future. What is clear is that virtually no one is projecting strong growth of output and productivity in the face of labor shortages, diversion of resources to defense, and double-digit inflation.

A major source of uncertainty is the durability and workability of the sanctions regime. Do they get stronger or weaker with the passage of time? Another source of potential trouble has to do with the military aid the West is supplying to Ukraine. Some argue that military assistance should be of such magnitude as to deliver a decisive victory to Ukrainian forces. Others fear that the delivery of certain weapons would cross Putin's "red line" and raise the threat of a World War III. Complicating matters is the US Congress's hesitation to continue the flow of money and arms. Will increased EU aid compensate for any hesitation on the US side?

Tough sanctions are only part of the story. As a consequence of the mortal threat to Ukraine, NATO has admitted two new members, Sweden and Finland. Putin's goal in beginning what he first called the "special operation" against Ukraine was to weaken NATO. With the admission of two significant new members, Putin's calculation proves to be palpably wrong.

Russia's incursions into Crimea and eastern Ukraine have constituted a learning curve for both Russia and the West. The West had to learn how to impose sanctions—on individuals, companies, and state actions—and Russia had to learn to live with sanctions. The first set of economic sanctions associated with Crimea and eastern Ukraine deprived Russian companies of access to world credit markets at a time of massive debt repayments by Russia's highly leveraged companies, the most prominent being the state oil company Rosneft. By freezing out Russia from credit, sanctions depressed investment finance. The West has continued to increase the pressure of sanctions as they extend to more Russian companies and individual persons and are applied to third-party transactions.

By strict budget stringency, robbing funds from Russia's social security system, and building up reserve funds and central bank reserves, Russia has been able to maintain its international reserves after recovery from the first shock of sanctions. With its own weak capital market, Russia's lack of access to Western capital strikes a severe blow both in terms of new investment and new technology.

With the decline in state revenues and the loss of foreign borrowing, the Kremlin has had to plug gaps with "extraordinary measures" that burn reserves. Russia's 2015 budget was scheduled to draw down the oil-revenue-funded reserve fund by $53 billion.[30] Some $52 billion in social security pension funds will henceforth be redirected annually from funded social security accounts.[31] Russia has little choice but to draw down reserves. As a finance ministry official confessed: "Besides non-state pension funds, we don't have anybody who will bring long-term investment in the economy."[32]

One thing has become clear: Russia's natural resources remain highly valued in world markets. They can find ready customers in China and India, albeit at lower prices. The West can erect obstacles such as maximum prices for Russian oil, but so far, Russian state revenues from sales of natural resources have been sufficient to fuel the Russian military machine. But for how long?

It appears that Putin has decided to place the burden on the Russian people while convincing them that he is not to blame. It is he who is protecting the Russian people and the Great Russia from outside evil forces, but the prize—a renewed Russian empire that protects the world from the Nazi forces of the West—will be worth it, assures Putin. Russia's defeat of the United States and NATO will stand out in Russian history as an achievement on par with Mother Russia's defeat of Hitler, promises Putin.

We cannot look inside Russia to take the pulse of the Russian people. We do not know how much longer the Russian people will swallow this fable.

Favorability Ratings as the Source of Legitimacy

The "election theater" practiced in autocratic regimes, including Russia, is only one link in Putin's claim to legitimacy. Elections can be controlled, but as long as Putin can show the Russian people support him, he can argue that he is as much the true leader of Russia as any democratically elected world leader. In fact, he may be more legitimate insofar as Western politicians can only dream of favorability ratings like his. His rating, he claims, proves that he is doing what is good for Russia. How else to explain his "atmospheric" and "Teflon" approval amid double-digit inflation, declining living standards, and international pariah status—with no end in sight?[33] Outsiders ask: How can we counter a ruthless leader who violates international norms and represses domestic opposition when he has his people solidly behind him? Our own people are divided but his are not, is Putin's claim.

132   *Paul Gregory*

We must note that the rating of a dictator like Putin is a strange animal. In Putin's world, people will not know much, if anything, about public figures other than Putin. Putin will not allow for ratings of public figures who oppose his policies, such as anti-war candidates. Instead, citizens are allowed to rate only Putin cronies. Reliance on approval ratings for legitimacy is a double-edged sword. As long as they are high, the leader is on solid ground, but if they fall, his claim to legitimacy vanishes. Hence, Putin must be in a position to control his approval ratings. Otherwise, the future of his regime is left to the whims of the Russian people.

An analysis by the semi-independent Levada Center[34] (which conducts the above-mentioned surveys[35]) points to Putin's "amazing ingenuity in adapting to changing conditions, and a strong desire to stay in power at any cost." I would like to underscore the "at any cost" part of the conclusion. Western leaders have been accused of policymaking with an eye to their effect on popularity, but none have taken it as far as Putin, who has started three wars and used apartment bombings of his own citizens for the express purposes of boosting his ratings.

Approval ratings mean different things in different types of regimes. Putin's vast propaganda and law enforcement machines (which cost only 15% less than the bloated defense budget)[36] punish dissent and overwhelm the internet with Putin's narrative. Putin appoints virtually all officials, national and regional, ensuring that he has no viable rivals. The leaders of the three opposition parties in parliament at one time ranked among the ten most untrustworthy figures, as rated by the Russian people.[37]

In this setting, the absolute values of approval ratings are not comparable. For Putin, a 60% approval rating is dangerously low—close to regime collapse. In the United States, a presidential approval rating of the same magnitude would be considered quite good.

Putin was riding a wave of approval in 2000 and 2004. Only in the 2012 election was Putin's approval rating in the low sixties as Muscovites demonstrated in the tens of thousands with the slogans "Russia without Putin" and "Putin is a crook." For Putin, the lesson was the urgent need to maintain an approval rating above eighty.

The following tribute to Vladimir Putin, posted on the aptly named blog *Heralding the Rise of Russia*, illustrates the standard Putin claim to legitimacy based upon his economic and foreign policy achievements:[38] "Mr. Putin has restored Russian pride and enhanced Russia's power. The economy has not only recovered all the ground it lost in the 1990s . . . Mr. Putin has rebuilt an authoritative state . . . Russia is stable; living standards are soaring. It is once again feared and respected abroad. No wonder Mr. Putin is wildly popular among Russians, who now look to the future with greater optimism and confidence than ever over the past two decades."[39]

In other countries, citizens approve or disapprove of their leader based upon the performance of the economy, foreign policy, and other issues, such as social policy or appeals to nationalism. Putin can therefore hope to raise his approval and oversee a growing and prosperous economy by achieving foreign policy successes for the Russian people or by pursuing themes of national pride or the Russian world that may appeal to his citizens.

The Roman emperors kept the support of Roman citizens by offering them bread and circuses. With a worsening economy, Putin cannot offer his people more bread. Therefore, he must offer them circuses. If Putin's ratings depended on the economy alone, they would be in the sixties or below, which, as the experience of 2011–2012 showed, resulted in the near death of the Putin regime.

Putin pumps up his approval ratings using "extraordinary measures," such as wars and external threats, when fundamentals, such as the economy, threaten to drive them down. He also uses spectacles, such as the 2014 Sochi Winter Olympics, the 2018 FIFA World Cup, or the heroic victory in the Great Patriotic War, to distract attention from economic woes and repression and to whip up national sentiment (see figure 5.3).

A first such extraordinary measure brought Putin to power. In August 1999, as the newly appointed prime minister, Putin had an approval rating of 31%; meanwhile, 37% of Russians did not know who he was.[40] Less than a year later, Putin's approval had risen to 84% after a series of mysterious apartment bombings,[41] which Putin blamed on Chechen terrorists, although they were most likely carried out by his own FSB. When the active military phase ended in April 2002 in Chechnya, thousands of civilians and soldiers had been killed and wounded and more than 200,000 persons displaced, not counting the more than 300 civilians[42] who died in the apartment bombings. Putin was the big winner, having been easily elected as Yeltsin's successor in 2000 after starting out at the bottom of the polls.

Putin's August 2008 war against Georgia, which separated South Ossetia and Abkhazia from Georgia, raised his favorability rating to 88% during active hostilities, despite coinciding with the beginning of Russia's severe hit from the world financial crisis. The five-day war resulted in more than 800 killed[43] on both sides—a seemingly small price to pay for a five-point increase in approval ratings.

Lacking a new foreign policy diversion and confronted with a stagnating economy, Putin's favorability ratings had fallen to the mid-sixties by the end of 2011.

In the days following the disputed Russia parliamentary election of December 2011, Putin's rating stood at sixty-six. Hundreds of thousands of Russian demonstrators[44] went out on the streets, shouting "Russia without Putin."[45] Putin's ratings collapse continued throughout the period of his crackdown on domestic opposition and muzzling of the press. In January 2014, his favorability rating bottomed out at sixty-one; only 29% of Russians expressed a willingness to vote for Putin's re-election.

At the start of 2014, Putin did not look anything like a "Teflon president." With a weakening economy, he could not offer growth and prosperity. He had to resort to draconian measures to keep demonstrators off the streets. Putin desperately needed a new and more sweeping extraordinary measure to reverse the 20% collapse in his approval rating since the Georgian war.

Putin rolled the dice again, launching his third and boldest extraordinary measure—namely, his hybrid warfare campaign that annexed Crimea and then expanded into eastern Ukraine.[46] His propaganda machine worked overtime from its St. Petersburg headquarters[47] to explain that Russia was protecting "the Russian world" from the Nazi extremists who had overthrown the legitimate government of Ukraine, backed by NATO, the United States, and the CIA as part of their plot to destroy Russia.[48] Putin's propaganda trolls warned their fellow citizens that Russia was the last bulwark against the decadent West's agenda of homosexual marriage and atheism.

Putin's adventures in Crimea and Ukraine raised his popularity rating by some twenty points at the cost of some 60,000 killed (according to conservative estimates by the United Nations[49]) and several million displaced persons.

Figure 3 details how Putin used extraordinary measures to manipulate his approval ratings. He extracted his biggest bang per propaganda buck from the Crimean annexation and Ukraine campaign, during which Putin's approval rating soared despite economic stagnation and malaise. The Georgian campaign had a lesser effect, but it did blunt some of the drag of the 2008–2009 economic crisis.

Figure 3 shows the treadmill Putin is on. His approval ratings slumped by a third in the six years between the invasions of Georgia and Crimea. With no prospect of reform of Putin's kleptocracy[50] and an expected long-term decline in energy prices, Putin cannot boost his popularity by offering prosperity to the general public.

Indeed, Putin rolled the dice again in February of 2022 with his wholesale invasion of Ukraine. With a multipronged invasion, Putin's war plan counted on a blitzkrieg victory and the removal of Ukraine's democratically elected government of Volodymyr Zelensky. The initial attack was blunted by an unprepared Ukrainian army, and the fighting has settled down to a war of attrition.

Importantly for Putin, the Ukrainian war again produced the hoped-for bump in Putin's rating (back up above eighty). Although Ukraine did allow Putin to restore his popularity, it clearly shows the treadmill he is on. With his resource base shrinking, Putin cannot buy off his supporters. An expert on Russian public opinion polling writing in 2015 suggests there are limits to diversions: "The rallying of the people around the president by peaceful means has been exhausted." No Olympic Games or World Cup can raise his approval rating "more than three to four percent." Putin will require "new extraordinary measures: massive propaganda and distortion of the image of the enemy, and the effectiveness of these measures in a prolonged economic crisis is difficult to assess because there is no basis for comparison."[51]

Yevgeny Primakov, a Russian establishment figure and former prime minister, warned that if Vladimir Putin continues his Ukraine policies, Russia will become a pariah and a third-world petro-state fully dependent on oil in a fickle market.[52]

The fundamentals of the Russian economy suggest that Russia is fulfilling Primakov's prophecy. Russia's fate depends on economic factors beyond its control (energy prices and gas markets) and on Putin's continued international adventurism, which he is loath to abandon for fear of regime change. He can no longer keep his promise to the Russian people of prosperity and stability. No wonder his propagandists are fighting full-time to convince the West to drop its sanctions.

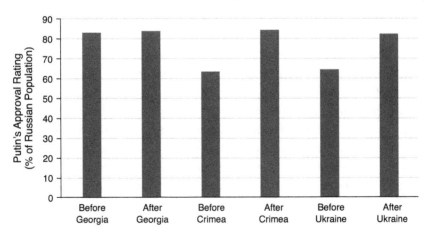

Figure 5.3 Putin's Job Approval. *Source*: Data taken from https://www.levada.ru/en/ratings/approval-of-the-authorities/.

Who Will Win?

Early in its third year, the Ukraine war has settled into a stalemate along a long line of contact. If anything, Russian forces may have the momentum due to political delays in arms deliveries from the United States. Things should change as the West resupplies Ukraine's military.

A tally of relative manpower and resources gives the advantage to Russia. With almost four times the population, Putin can field a much larger army. Russia's GDP is more than ten times Ukraine's. With such basic disadvantages, the fight should be "no contest." However, we must ask whether the war is truly a battle between Russia and the West, as Putin has claimed. With a combined GDP twenty-five times that of Russia, NATO has an industrial economy that could outlast any Russian wartime economy. For example, NATO has six times the number of Russian aircraft and four times the number of helicopters, despite the fact that NATO has been underspending on defense for a very long time.[53]

These figures do not address Ukraine's manpower disadvantage, unless Russia directly attacks a NATO country, drawing NATO "boots on the ground" into the fight. With boots on the ground unlikely, the question would be whether NATO can deliver advanced equipment to more than compensate for Ukraine's manpower disadvantage.

There is also the question of how long Putin can endure the huge manpower losses that they have experienced so far. Are there limits to which Putin can empty his prisons of convict-recruits or attract soldiers via generous pay? With his domestic repression maneuvers, Putin is seeking to keep a restive population under control. He counts on his personal army to fend off domestic threats. But he cannot continue indefinitely to choose "guns" over "butter" when supplies of both are scarce. He cannot change his economic and political system without increasing his risk of being removed.

At some point, and we do not know when, Putin will leave the scene, most likely because of the many weaknesses discussed above. When he does go, we will say that only fools should have missed the signs, but among those "fools" will be the brightest minds that the West and Russia have at their disposal. Putin's goal has not been to strengthen Russia or to restore it to greatness, but to ensure the survival of his regime.

NOTES

1. A revision of the Constitution under Medvedev raised the presidential term to six years.

2. Paul Gregory, "Russian Voters Have Spoken: Anyone but Putin," *Forbes*, December 5, 2011. http://www.forbes.com/sites/paulroderickgregory/2011/12/05/russias-voters-have-spoken-anybody-but-putin/.

3. Karen Dawisha, *Putin's Kleptocracy* (New York: Simon and Schuster, 2014).

4. Kathryn Stoner and Michael McFaul, "Who Lost Russia (This Time)?", *Washington Quarterly*, July 30, 2015, http://www.tandfonline.com/loi/rwaq20.

5. "Who Is Putin? | Return of the Czar," *FRONTLINE*, PBS, November 18, 2015, http://www.pbs.org/wgbh/pages/frontline/shows/yeltsin/putin/putin.html.

6. Anders Åslund, "Putin's Conservative State Capitalism," *Moscow Times*, December 17, 2013, https://www.themoscowtimes.com/2013/12/17/putins-conservative-state-capitalism-a30594.

7. Vladimir Soldatkin, "How Gazprom's $1 Trillion Dream Has Fallen Apart," *Reuters*, June 28, 2013, https://www.reuters.com/article/business/how-gazproms-1-trillion-dream-has-fallen-apart-idUSBRE95R0XW/.

8. Nataliya Vasilyeva, "Russian Oligarchs Foot Most of 2014 Sochi Olympics," *AP*, May 30, 2013, https://apnews.com/general-news-20a70c981bf84784ab1b39d339ac796f.

9. Anders Åslund, "The Role of State Corporations in the Russian Economy," Wilson Center, October 12, 2012.

10. Jason Karaian, "Russian Stocks Are Incredibly Cheap—for a Reason," *Quartz*, July 21, 2022, https://qz.com/243663/russian-stocks-are-incredibly-cheap-for-a-reason.

11. Paul Gregory, "BP, Putin, and Russian Oil: Will They Never Learn?", *What Paul Gregory Is Writing About*, January 16, 2011, https://paulgregorysblog.blogspot.com/2011/01/bp-putin-and-russian-oil-will-they.html.

12. Lukas I. Alpert, "Russia Must Compensate Yukos Shareholders, European Court Rules," *Wall Street Journal*, July 28, 2014, https://www.wsj.com/articles/russia-must-compensate-former-yukos-shareholders-court-rules-1406536768.

13. "Нужно опираться на собственные силы," *Нужно опираться на собственные силы*, accessed July 26, 2015.

14. Anders Åslund, "Putin's State Capitalism Means Falling Growth | Opinion," *Moscow Times*, May 21, 2013, https://www.themoscowtimes.com/2013/05/21/putins-state-capitalism-means-falling-growth-a24217.

15. "Экономист, проректор ВШЭ Константин Сонин: "От изоляции может что-то улучшиться—это чистая фантазия," *Экономист, проректор ВШЭ Константин Сонин: "От изоляции может что-то улучшиться—это чистая фантазия*, accessed July 27, 2015.

16. *Direct Line with Vladimir Putin* was broadcast live on Channel One, Rossiya-1, and Rossiya-24 TV channels, and Mayak, Vesti FM, and Radio Rossii radio stations. *Direct Line with Vladimir Putin*, April 16, 2105, http://en.kremlin.ru/events/president/transcripts/49261.

17. ИНДЕКСЫ ИНТЕНСИВНОСТИ ВЫПУСКА ТОВАРОВ И УСЛУГ ПО БАЗОВЫМ ВИДАМ ЭКОНОМИЧЕСКОЙ ДЕЯТЕЛЬНОСТИ ЯНВАРЬ 2005—МАЙ 2015, p. 5, http://www.hse.ru/data/2015/07/06/1083111261/indbas_15-05.pdf.

18. Paul Roderick Gregory, "A Russian Crisis With No End in Sight, Thanks to Low Oil Prices and Sanctions," *Forbes*, May 14, 2015, http://www.forbes.com/sites/paulrode rickgregory/2015/05/14/a-russian-crisis-with-no-end-in-sight-thanks-to-low-oil-prices -and-sanctions.

19. *Direct Line with Vladimir Putin.*

20. Paul Gregory and Robert Stuart, *Russian and Soviet Economic Structure and Performance*, 7th ed. (New York: Harper Collins, 1994).

21. Paul Gregory, Hoover Institution, and University of Houston, "Do Sanctions and Low Energy Prices Constrain Russia's Foreign Policy?", April 16, 2015, Scowcroft Institute.

22. Stoner and McFaul, "Who Lost Russia?", 177.

23. Higher School of Economics Development Center, "Indexes of Output of Goods and Services."

24. Higher School of Economics Development Center, "Consensus-Forecast of the Development Center," http://dcenter.hse.ru/prog2/.

25. Higher School of Economics, "Indexes of Output of Goods and Services."

26. Anastasia Bazenkova, "Russia's Gazprom Sees Gas Output Fall to Record Lows as Demand Slumps," *Moscow Times*, July 22, 2015, https://themoscowtimes.com/articles /russias-gazprom-sees-gas-output-fall-to-record-lows-as-demand-slumps-48462.

27. Leonid Bershidsky, "How Ukraine Weaned Itself from Russian Gas," *Bloomberg*, January 12, 2016, https://www.bloomberg.com/view/articles/2016-01-12/how-ukraine -weaned-itself-off-russian-gas.

28. Ann M. Simmons and Nancy A. Youssef, "Russia's Casualties in Ukraine Near 200,000," *Wall Street Journal*, February 24, 2023, https://www.wsj.com/articles/russias -casualties-in-ukraine-near-200-000-11675509981.

29. "Kremlin Says Goals of Russia's 'Special Military Operation' in Ukraine Remain Unchanged," *Reuters*, February 7, 2024, https://www.reuters.com/world/europe/kremlin -says-goals-russias-special-military-operation-ukraine-remain-unchanged-2024-02-07/.

30. "New Russian Budget Based on $50 Oil Passes First Hurdle in Parliament," *Moscow Times*, March 27, 2015, http://www.themoscowtimes.com/business/article/new -russian-budget-based-on-50-oil-passes-first-hurdle-in-parliament/518152.html.

31. Alexei Lossan, "Russia to Raid Pension Funds to Finance Infrastructure Project," *Russia Beyond the Headlines*, May 7, 2015, http://rbth.com/business/2015/05/07/russia_to _raid_pension_funds_to_finance_infrastructure_projects_45841.html.

32. "Russia Seen Favoring Longer Pension Freeze over $52 Billion Grab," *Bloomberg*, March 29, 2015, http://www.bloomberg.com/news/articles/2015-03-29/russia-seen -favoring-longer-pension-freeze-over-52-billion-grab.

33. "Рейтинг Путина: аномалия или закономерность?", *Институт современной России*, December 22, 2014. The translation is the author's.

34. Levada Center, "Indexes," accessed July 25, 2015.

35. "Archives." *Crossing Wall Street RSS*, accessed July 25, 2015.

36. *Consolidated Budget of the Russian Federation*, accessed July 25, 2015.

37. Levada Center, "April Ratings," accessed July 25, 2015.

38. Arevordi, "My Tribute to President Vladimir Putin, the Great Czar of Eurasia," *Heralding the Rise of Russia*, May 2012, http://theriseofrussia.blogspot.com/p/tribute-to -vladimir-putin.html.

39. Levada Center, "Indexes."

40. Levada Center, "Indexes."

41. John Dunlop, *The Moscow Bombings of September 1999: Examinations of Russian Terrorist Attacks at the Onset of Vladimir Putin's Rule* (New York: Columbia University Press, 2014).

42. Dunlop, *Moscow Bombings.*

43. "2008 Georgia Russia Conflict Fast Facts," *CNN*, March 13, 2014, updated 2015, http://www.cnn.com/2014/03/13/world/europe/2008-georgia-russia-conflict/index.html.

44. Paul Gregory, "Russia's Voters Have Spoken: Anybody but Putin," *Forbes*, December 5, 2011, https://www.forbes.com/sites/paulroderickgregory/2011/12/05 /russias-voters-have-spoken-anybody-but-putin/#75b3e6605795.

45. Gregory, "Russia's Voters Have Spoken."

46. "2008 Georgia Russia Conflict Fast Facts."

47. Associated Press, "Ex-Kremlin Internet 'Troll' Sues to End Putin Propaganda," *NBC News*, June 2, 2015, http://www.nbcnews.com/tech/internet/ex-kremlin-internet -troll-sues-end-putin-propaganda-n368311.

48. "Putin's Russian World," *Moscow Times*, May 6, 2014, https://themoscowtimes .com/articles/putins-russian-world-35150.

49. "Ukraine Death Toll Hits 6,000 Amid Ongoing Fighting," *UN News Centre*, March 2, 2015. http://www.un.org/apps/news/story.asp?NewsID=50215#.VcuOTPlVhBc.

50. Dawisha, *Putin's Kleptocracy.*

51. "Левада-Центр," *Рейтинг Путина: аномалия или закономерность?* | *Левада-Центр*, accessed July 27, 2015.

52. Paul Gregory, "Putin Shrugs Off Oligarch Opposition to His 'Holy War' and Policies," *Forbes*, February 3, 2015, https://www.forbes.com/sites/paulroderickgregory /2015/02/03/putin-shrugs-off-oligarch-opposition-to-his-holy-war-and-policies /#e7907ae3bd0a.

53. "NATO—Statistics & Facts," https://www.statista.com/topics/9079/nato /#statisticChapter.

PART II / The Mythology of the Putin State

Chapter Six

Russian Power in Decline

A Demographic and Human Resource Perspective

Nicholas Eberstadt

The 2022 Russian invasion of Ukraine may have marked the end of one era and the beginning of another—but it was only one step (albeit a fateful one) along a strategic path the Kremlin has marked out, and methodically pursued, for over a decade and a half. It revealed the classic modus operandi of a "revisionist power." From President Vladimir Putin's 2005 declaration that "the demise of the Soviet Union was the greatest geopolitical catastrophe of the [twentieth] century,"[1] to his famous 2007 Munich Security Conference speech denouncing the "pernicious" "unipolar" (US-dominated) order,[2] to the 2008 war against neighboring Georgia, to the 2014 annexation of the Crimea, to the "special military operation" now underway in Ukraine, contemporary Russia's strategic logic and behavior will be altogether familiar to students of history's previous "revisionist" kingdoms, empires, and governments.

But there is an interesting wrinkle in the current Russian case. History is full of instances where a rising power, aggrieved and dissatisfied, acts aggressively to obtain new borders or other international concessions. In Russia today, we see a much more unusual situation, for here the increasingly menacing and ambitious geopolitical actor may actually be a state whose power is *in decline*.

Notwithstanding its nuclear arsenal and its vast territories, a striking feature—arguably, the distinguishing feature—of contemporary Russia is its underdevelopment and relative economic weakness.

144   *Nicholas Eberstadt*

For all its vaunted oil and gas, Russia's international sales of goods and services in 2021, the latest year for which we have figures, fell short of Belgium's (at roughly $550 billion versus Belgium's nearly $680 billion, according to the World Trade Organization).[3] That same year, Russian exports were positively dwarfed by the Netherlands' (at nearly $1.2 *trillion*, more than double Russia's earnings).[4] Russia's international economic standing was likewise overshadowed by the little Benelux countries even in the earlier boom times for global energy markets.

In the modern era, the ultimate source of national wealth and power is not natural resources; rather, it is human resources. And unfortunately, Russia's human resource situation is peculiarly dismal—with worse quite possibly in store for the years directly ahead.

In this chapter, we will examine Russia's demographic and human resource conditions: recent, current, and prospective. Some of the facts and figures in this chapter will be more or less familiar to both area specialists and students of international affairs. Other facets of this assessment, although in our view highly consequential, are likely to be much less familiar—even though these same realities are in effect "hiding in plain sight."

There are three major virtues to examining Russia through the prism of demographics and its allied disciplines.

First, among all of the social sciences, it is arguably demography whose empirical depictions of reality are the most intrinsically accurate and intuitively comprehensible. It is after all easier to count heads than to determine, say, income levels or purchasing power. Furthermore, demographic change is an inherently "closed system" and a fairly simple one, and thus is relatively easy to track and to check for inconsistencies. In principle, next year's population should equal today's population, netted for deaths, births, and migration. In addition, basic metrics for demography (such as births per woman for fertility or life expectancy at birth for mortality) are more readily understood than such constructs as gross domestic product (GDP), gross national product (GNP), or gross national income (GNI).

Second, demography permits us to look farther into the future—in appreciable detail and with tolerable reliability—than any of the other social sciences. Quite simply, this is because—absent catastrophe of Biblical proportion or perhaps total state breakdown—the overwhelming majority of a low-birth-rate society's population some fifteen or twenty years hence, including virtually all working-age manpower and absolutely all pensioners-to-be, is already alive today. Consequently, we know much more today about a modern country's demographic outlook for the next two decades than we do about its economic or political outlook.

Third, demographic trends matter. They afford a direct and meaningful reading on a society's well-being and cast light on a country's economic potential. Demographic trends also provide information about a country's capabilities on the international chessboard. None of this is to assert, per the famous dictum, that "demography is destiny." A less sweeping and ethereal claim would be that demographics slowly but inexorably alter the realm of the possible in human affairs. We shall attempt to demonstrate in accordance with this more modest dictum just how demographic constraints currently limit the realm of the possible for Russia and the Russian state—and how those demographic constraints may be growing even tighter in the years immediately ahead.

Most of the research in this chapter is presented in the accompanying figures, which are referred to in our text. Those figures also contain the footnotes for the sources from which our charts and calculations are derived.

Basic Demographic Trends in Twenty-First-Century Russia

Let us start with the basic "head count" facts about Russia's post-Soviet demography: population totals, births, and deaths.

Since the collapse of the USSR, Russia has been a country depopulating (see figure 6.1).

To be clear here: population decline may not intrinsically matter so much for personal living standards in our modern era—prosperous Japan, after all, has been a "shrinking society" for over a decade at this writing, and dynamic Germany has been on the verge of depopulation for years—but population totals do happen to bear directly on the human resources the Kremlin can command.

For a period of time, Russia's post-Soviet population decline not only halted but marked out a modest recovery. Between the 2009 nadir and the start of 2014, thanks to modest immigration inflows, the Russian Federation's total population increased by nearly 1 million, according to official estimates of the Russian Federal State Statistics Service (also known as both Rosstat and Goskomstat).

In 2014, the Kremlin apparently came upon a new means of reversing population decline: territorial annexation. By wresting the Crimea from Ukraine and incorporating it into the Russian Federation, total Russian population instantly increased by 2.3 million persons. Forcible incorporation of external land has to date done considerably more to raise the Russian Federation's head count than the Kremlin's own initiatives in pronatal population policy, which were launched in 2007.[5]

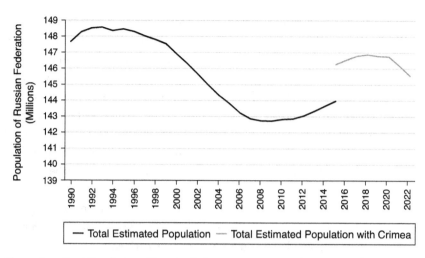

Figure 6.1 Total Population of Russian Federation, 1990–2022 (Beginning of the Year, in Millions). *Sources:* 1990–2018: Russian Federation Federal Statistical Service (Goskomstat), *Demographic Yearbook of Russia 2019*, http://www.gks.ru/bgd/reg/B17_19/Main.htm, accessed March 2, 2022; 2019–2022: Federal State Statistics Service, "Population of Russia as of January 1," https://rosstat.gov.ru/, accessed February 16, 2023; 2019–2021: Federal State Statistics Service, "De jure population of Russia as of January 1," https://eng.rosstat.gov.ru/ accessed March 16, 2022; 2022: "Why the Population Decline in Russia Has Hit Its Highest in History," *TRTWorld*, https://www.trtworld.com/magazine/why-the-population-decline-in-russia-has-hit-its-highest-in-history-54327, accessed March 16, 2022.

The Russian Federation's reprieve from depopulation, however, was only temporary. In 2018—that is to say, before the grim demographic shocks from the COVID-19 pandemic—population decline had already resumed, and marginal but symbolically significant decreases were tallied for both calendar years 2018 and 2019.

With the COVID calamity, however, depopulation picked up terrible momentum. Whereas the officially estimated population decline for 2018 and 2019 together amounted to less than 150,000, the drop in 2020 and 2021 came to almost 1.3 million. (By way of comparison, Russia's aggregate population drop between the beginning of 1993 and the start of 2009 amounted to about 5.8 million.)

As COVID-19 evolves from a pandemic to an endemic contagion, it will exert less pressure for depopulation in Russia. The demographic shock from the coronavirus, in other words, should probably be regarded as a one-off (at least until such a presumption is proved wrong). But other factors pressing for continued, and perhaps accelerating, depopulation are gaining force. As we shall see, these factors will make even another temporary stabilization of Russia's population totals an increasingly challenging proposition.

The size and composition of the Russian population are shaped predominantly by vital events—births and deaths. These intrinsically important trends deserve examination in their own right (see figure 6.2).

Until the COVID-19 shock, Russia's birth totals had been rebounding from their post-Soviet collapse (hitting a low point in 1999), and death totals had been heading downward since 2003. In 2013—for the first time since the end of the communist era—yearly births ever so slightly exceeded yearly deaths (by about 24,000).

In 2014, births ever so slightly outnumbered deaths for the second time in Russia's post-communist history (by about 39,000 under pre-annexation boundaries, or about 34,000 including Crimea). The year 2015 marked a "three-peat" with a

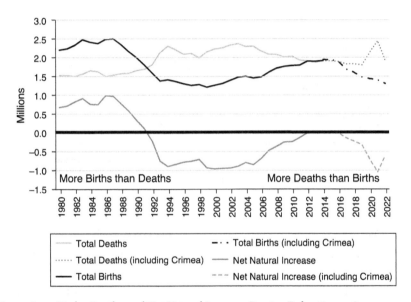

Figure 6.2 Births, Deaths, and Net Natural Increase: Russian Federation, 1980–2022. *Sources*: 1980–2018 data from "1980 General Population Replacement Indices," *Demographic Yearbook of Russia 2019*, http://www.gks.ru/bgd/reg/B17_19/Main.htm, accessed March 2, 2022; 2019 data from Rosstat, "Vital Movement of the Population Conditions of the Russian Federation—2020 (archive)," edn12_2020k.xlsx, Table 1, https://rosstat.gov.ru/storage/mediabank/wxWlqMlx/edn2020.rar, accessed March 16, 2022; 2020–2021 data from Rosstat, "General Results of the Natural Movement of the Population of the Russian Federation," https://rosstat.gov.ru/storage/mediabank/2021-edn12.htm, accessed March 16, 2022; 2022 data from Rosstat, "Rosstat Presents Vital Statistics for December 2022," https://rosstat.gov.ru/folder/313/document/197667.

reported net surfeit of births over deaths of about 32,000 (this time including Crimea). But that achievement was fleeting. It was an apogee. In 2016, Russia once again reported (fractionally) fewer births than deaths. Thereafter, the gap between deaths and births began again to widen steadily.

By the year 2019—that is, before COVID-19—Russian "negative natural increase" (the infelicitous demographic formulation for an excess of deaths over births) exceeded 300,000. Under the deadly shadow of the coronavirus, 2020 and 2021 brought a cumulative total of over 1.7 million more deaths than births to Russia—with net mortality of more than a million in 2021 alone.

During the COVID-19 pandemic, Russia suffered a bout of excess mortality in which actual causes of death were not necessarily diagnosed and recorded accurately in official Rosstat/Goskomstat numbers. Russian losses from COVID and pandemic-associated causes were severe. Two independent assessments both estimated Russia's combined 2020–2021 excess mortality at over 1 million deaths. One of these studies placed total excess mortality for Russia above corresponding absolute totals for the United States during those same years.[6] When one considers how poorly the United States coped with limiting mortality during the pandemic and bears in mind that Russia's total population is well under half as large as that of the United States, one begins to get a sense of the scale of excess mortality in Russia during those years. According to these studies, only India (and possibly the United States) lost more people as a consequence of the pandemic. Russian age-standardized excess mortality over the course of those two pandemic years is estimated to have been among the world's highest, over three times the global average.

In the post-Soviet era, Russia became a net-mortality society during peacetime. Over the three decades of the 1992–2021 period—the years before the Ukraine invasion—mortality in Russia surpassed natality by a cumulative total of 15.7 million, according to Rosstat. In absolute terms, the only postwar country to register a larger bout of "negative natural increase" was Maoist China in the immediate aftermath of the catastrophic Great Leap Forward. Nevertheless, in relation to each country's preexisting total population, Russia's prolonged cumulative surfeit of deaths over births thus far has been proportionately much larger than China's much briefer and more extreme episode.

The peacetime emergence of "negative natural increase" in Russia over the past generation is by no means unique (see table 6.1).

A number of other countries also reported more deaths than births over those same decades. Further, Russia was not the most exceptional outlier, at least

Table 6.1 Greatest Global Surfeits of Deaths over Births,
1992–2022 (US Census Bureau Estimates)

Russia	–17.6	Bulgaria	–1.22
Ukraine	–7.58	Hungary	–1.13
Germany	–4.52	Belarus	–1.05
Italy	–2.37	Serbia	–0.95
Romania	–1.57	Japan	–0.72

Source: United States Census Bureau, "Components of Population Growth 1992–2022," International Database, www.census.gov /population/international/data/idb/region.php (accessed February 15, 2023).

in proportional terms—although all of its close company in this regard did happen to come from post-communist states. By the reckoning of the US Census Bureau, several post-communist states more or less matched Russia proportionally in cumulative net mortality for 1992–2022, including Hungary and Belarus, whereas ratios of net mortality to total population actually exceeded Russia's in Bulgaria, Ukraine, Latvia, and Serbia.[7]

Over the three decades of 1992–2022, Russia reported an average ratio of deaths to births of 138:100 (see table 6.2).

This was extraordinary for an urban and literate society during peacetime—although again not unparalleled, given the situation in some other post-communist countries.

Eventually, high ratios of deaths to births may become characteristic of affluent societies under conditions of orderly progress as their populations age and shrink. In the years since 2012, the twenty-seven countries in the European Union (EU-27) as a whole has slipped into "net mortality."[8] For the time being, however, an extreme and persistent excess of deaths over births is still more likely to be an indicator of social shocks and dysfunctions—much as in days of old, when it was a warning sign of war, famine, pestilence, and disastrous upheavals.

Fertility and Family Formation in Contemporary Russia

Between 1999 and 2012, Russia witnessed a "birth surge" of sorts, with annual births jumping from 1.2 million to 1.9 million. (Qualification is required because this jump was actually a recovery from the slump that followed the end of Soviet Communism, not a boom in its own right.) But the "surge" was a passing event, not a "new normal." By 2015, birth totals had again begun to decline, and by 2019—before the pandemic shock—birth levels had dropped by almost a fourth

Table 6.2 Ratio of Deaths to Births: Top 10 Net Mortality Countries, 1992–2022 (US Census Bureau)

Bulgaria	1.59	Hungary	1.38
Ukraine	1.53	Belarus	1.34
Latvia	1.53	Lithuania	1.29
Serbia	1.42	Estonia	1.28
Russia	1.38	Romania	1.23

Source: United States Census Bureau, "Components of Population Growth 1992–2012," International Data Base, www.census.gov /population/international/data/idb/region.php (accessed February 15, 2022).

from their 2014 levels, down roughly 450,000. Birth levels dropped further during the COVID-19 years of 2020 and 2021. (In 2022, the first year of the "special military operation" in Ukraine, birth totals dropped again, reaching the lowest level in twenty years.)

The rise of births in Russia between 2008 and 2014 coincided with the Kremlin's pronatal birth benefits program, leading the Kremlin (and some foreign observers) to call that effort a success. But the program continued beyond 2014—it was in force during the birth downswing of 2014–2019 and beyond. By 2018–2019, Russian fertility levels (by the metrics of total fertility rates, or TFRs—births per woman per lifetime) did not look appreciably different from some erstwhile Soviet Bloc European states *without* big expensive pronatal policies, such as the Baltic countries, Poland, and Romania.[9] In fact, some of these places were reporting higher fertility than the Russian Federation. Fertility change is always taking place everywhere, and it is exceedingly difficult to explain the factors accounting for it unambiguously. Just how much (if at all) those Kremlin population policies impacted and altered Russia's fertility patterns will probably remain a matter of conjecture and unsettled debate.

That said, it is possible to offer a few confident observations about fertility and family formation patterns in contemporary Russia.

First, notwithstanding its passing baby surge, which temporarily took Russia's fertility level from below to above the European average, births in Russia, as in the rest of Europe, remain below the replacement level. According to official Rosstat calculations, the high-water mark for the Russian Federation's net reproduction rate (NRR) in the post-Soviet era was in 2015, when the rate hit 0.85—this by an index where 1.00 is the number for long-term population stability without in-migration (see figure 6.3).

Russian Power in Decline 151

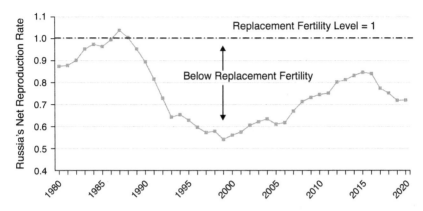

Figure 6.3 Russia's Net Reproduction Rate, 1980–2020. *Sources:* "Net Reproduction Rate," *Demographic Yearbook of Russia 2019*, Table 2.08, https://www.gsk.ru/regl/B19–16/Main.htm, accessed March 2, 2022; "Net Reproduction Rate," *Demographic Yearbook of Russia 2006*, Table 2.08, https://www.gsk.ru/bgd/regl/B06–16/Main.htm, accessed April 26, 2014; *Demographic Yearbook of Russia 2021*, https://rosstat.gov.ru/storage/mediabank/dem21.pdf, accessed February 15, 2023.

To be sure, that reading was up very substantially from the low-water mark of 1999, when the NRR was 0.54. Even so, by this metric, contemporary Russia never came close to reaching childbearing patterns that could have assured the country of intrinsic long-term population stability. By 2018—the most recent date for which Russia has calculated an official NRR—the rate was back to roughly 0.75, a trajectory on which the country's population would still be set to shrink by a quarter from one generation to the next, absent in-migration. The 2019 birth drop pushed Russia almost 30% below the replacement level in 2019 and 2020, and Rosstat reported Russia's NRR to be 0.72. NRRs have likely declined further during the COVID-19 period, given the birth drops reported in 2021 and 2022—they may have dropped close to 0.65 during the first year of the Ukraine invasion. But it is difficult to tell what exactly this will portend for post-pandemic trends.

Second, Russia's nationwide NRR is an arithmetic average of fertility levels that differ considerably from one region to another. We can show this for the year 2018, the most recent year for which Rosstat has published such data.

Whereas national NRR in 2018 averaged 0.75, it was as low as 0.54 in the Leningrad oblast surrounding the city of St. Petersburg. On the other extreme, the 2018 estimated NRR for Chechnya was 1.24—and almost 1.4 for Tuva.

Given those fertility differentials, population composition within the Russian Federation would be shifting. Very few places within Russia, however, were on a course for naturally generated population stability, much less population growth. Of the eighty-five regions for which Rosstat provided NRR estimates for 2018, just three registered at or above net replacement. These three regions together accounted for under 2% of Russia's total population in 2018.

Third, Russia's pronounced and geographically pervasive sub-replacement fertility must be borne in mind when one hears claims about the country's supposedly prolific "Muslim" population.

Like the United States and a number of European countries, the Russian Federation does not collect information on the religious profession of its population—so there is an inescapable measure of uncertainly in any discussion of the country's religious demography. Nevertheless, some careful international efforts have attempted to estimate the size of Russia's Muslim population by drawing inferences from enumerated totals for identified nationalities and ethnicities with historical/cultural Islamic traditions.

The Pew Research Center, for example, estimates Russia's 2020 Muslim population at about 16 million, or roughly 11% of the total population. To go by those figures, Russia would include far more Muslims than any other European country, though some European countries (areas once under Ottoman rule) would have much higher Muslim proportions of their national populations (see table 6.3).

But Russia's "Muslim" groups are mainly characterized by sub-replacement fertility. We can see hints of this from regional fertility patterns—of all the historically/culturally Muslim-majority areas in Russia, only Chechnya's fertility levels are persistently above replacement.[10] Although Russians of Muslim heritage may on average have higher fertility than the rest of the country—and thereby stand to account for a somewhat larger share of the national population

Table 6.3 Estimated Muslim Population for Select European Countries, 2020 (% of total population)

Russia	11.40	Kosovo	94.30
Germany	6.90	Bosnia Herzegovina	46.50
France	8.30	Spain	3.30
United Kingdom	6.10	Netherlands	6.90
Italy	4.90	Bulgaria	14.20
Albania	82.10		

Note: Russia's Muslim population is defined as groups with historical or traditional affinity for Islam.
Source: "Religious Composition by Country, 2010–2050," April, 2, 2015, Pew Research Center, http://www.pewforum.org/2015/04/02/religious -projection-table/2010/number/Europe/# (accessed March 2022).

in the years ahead than they do today—Russia's "Muslims" are also on a trajectory of overall population decline unless their current childbearing patterns dramatically change.

Finally, it is worth emphasizing that childbearing and family formation patterns in the Russian Federation look characteristically European. We can see this by creating a scatterplot showing TFRs against the proportion of births outside marriage for 2018–2019 for the Russian Federation and the twenty-seven European Union countries plus the United Kingdom (see figure 6.4).

In 2018, at 1.58 births per woman, Russia's TFR was almost identical to the European Union's levels in 2018 (1.54 for the EU-27, 1.56 if the United Kingdom were still included). Its percentage of births outside marriage was lower than in most EU societies, although several European populations did have distinctly lower out-of-wedlock birth ratios.

All in all, as a society with below replacement fertility and a bit less than one in four births occurring outside marriage, Russia's childbearing patterns in 2018 may be regarded as "typically European," considering contemporary EU fertility patterns. The "second demographic transition"[11] that European demographers first noted in Western Europe in the 1980s—characterized by an evolution toward

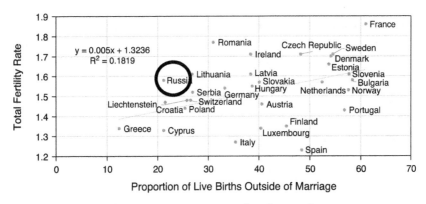

Figure 6.4 Total Fertility Rate versus Percentage of Births Outside Marriage: Russia (2018) and Select European Nations (2019). *Sources:* EU data from Eurostat, "Total Fertility Rate," TPS00199, https://ec.europa.eu/eurostat/databrowser/view/tps00199/default/table?lang=en, accessed March 2, 2022; Eurostat, "Live Births Outside Marriage," TPS00018, http://ec.europa.eu/web/products-datasets/-/tps00018, accessed March 2, 2022; Russian data from World Bank, "Russia Data: Fertility Rate, Total (Births per Woman)," https://data.worldbank.org/indicator/SP.DYN.TFRT.IN?locations=RU, accessed March 2, 2022; Rosstat, "Fertility, Live Births by Mothers Marital Status," Table 4.5, *Demographic Yearbook of Russia 2017*, http://www.gks.ru/bgd/regl/B17_16/Main.htm, accessed February 23, 2018.

Nicholas Eberstadt

higher rates of cohabitation and divorce, rising out-of-marriage childbearing, and a shift to indefinite sub-replacement fertility—appears to be very much underway in Russia nowadays as well.

Russia's Disastrous Survival Profile

Although Russia's childbearing patterns today look entirely European, its mortality patterns look Third World—actually worse than Third World in important respects. The most recent life tables—actuarial calculations tracking a population's survival trajectories—available at this writing for Russia and the rest of the world from the World Health Organization (WHO) Global Health Observatory are for the year 2019.[12] The year 2019 was a good one for life expectancy in Russia—indeed, higher than ever previously recorded. (As we shall see in a moment, it was higher than in either 2020 or 2021, when levels plummeted during the deadly COVID-19 pandemic.) Thus, 2019 seems particularly apposite for international comparisons, as it may be the most favorable possible benchmark from the Russian standpoint.

According to WHO estimates, life expectancy in 2019 for a fifteen-year-old male was all but indistinguishable in Russia and Haiti (see table 6.4).

No, that is not some typographical error in the WHO tables. By the WHO's reckoning, male life expectancy in 2019 in both Haiti and Russia stood at 53.7 years (rounding to the nearest decimal). That same year, a fifteen-year-old youth stood worse estimated survival chances in Russia than in at least twenty-three of the forty-eight places the UN categorizes as "least-developed countries (LDCs)"—including such impoverished locales as Mali, Yemen, and even Afghanistan.[13] (We say "at least twenty-three" because the WHO does not estimate life tables for all the LDCs.) By way of comparison, the corresponding 2019 figure for France was 65.2 years.

According to these same WHO data, the Russian Federation's mortality schedule for adult men in 2019 was strikingly similar to that for African males that same year (see figure 6.5). (The Africa data are continent-wide and thus include North Africa, not just the sub-Sahara.)

On 2019 survival trajectories, over one in four of both Russia's and Africa's twenty-year-old males would have died before their sixtieth birthday. The corresponding risk of death in the WHO's Europe region is only half that high—and those Europe numbers, remember, are seriously distorted by including Russia. (Spain's risk was just a fourth of Russia's, for example.) Further: after age sixty, survival odds actually appear to be slightly better for African men than for Russian men. When one considers the tremendous socioeconomic advantages

Table 6.4 Male Life Expectancy at Age Fifteen: Russia versus All Least Developed Countries, 2019 (WHO Estimates)

Bangladesh	60.95	Laos	55.13	Russia	53.74	Angola	52.02
Bhutan	59.74	Rwanda	55.11	Haiti	53.65	Burundi	51.94
Mauritania	59.31	Tanzania	54.81	Sierra Leone	53.6	Malawi	51.1
Sudan	57.6	Niger	54.66	Gambia	52.84	Eritrea	49.66
East Timor	56.71	Cambodia	54.65	Afghanistan	52.76	Solomon Islands	49.51
Sao Tome and Principe	56.58	Myanmar	54.6	Uganda	52.44	Zambia	49.46
Nepal	56.56	Yemen	54.45	Chad	52.39	Guinea-Bissau	48.53
Ethiopia	56.54	Djibouti	54.06	DR Congo	52.35	Somalia	47.79
Comoros	56.47	South Sudan	53.93	Guinea	52.33	Kiribati	45.03
Senegal	55.91	Madagascar	53.88	Burkina Faso	52.13	Mozambique	44.85
Mali	55.4	Benin	53.88	Togo	52.07	Central African Republic	42.6
Liberia	55.33						

Source: World Health Organization, Global Health Observatory Data Repository, "Life Expectancy: Life Tables by Country," https://apps.who.int/gho/data/node.main.LIFECOUNTRY (accessed March 9, 2022).

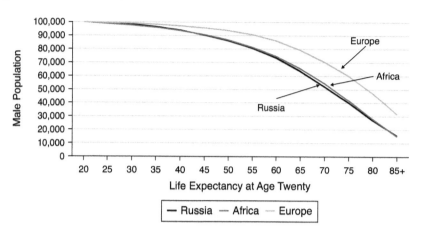

Figure 6.5 Survival Schedule for Male Population at Age Twenty: Russia versus Africa and Europe, 2019 Estimates. *Source*: World Health Organization, *Health Statistics and Health Information Systems*, http://apps.who.int/gho/data/node.main.687?lang=en/, accessed March 11, 2022.

that Russians enjoy over Africans vis-à-vis income, education, housing, and other factors, these estimated Russian male mortality patterns are—there is no diplomatic word for it—shocking.

Although survival prospects are distinctly better for women than for men in Russia, the WHO estimated life expectancy for fifteen-year-old Russian females in 2019 was comparable with that of Bangladesh, the healthiest of the UN's least-developed countries (see table 6.5).

No less significantly, the overall (male plus female) risk of dying between fifteen and sixty years of age was appreciably higher in 2019 for Russia than Bangladesh: roughly 19% versus roughly 12%. Even more striking: combined male and female life expectancy at age fifteen in 2019 was estimated to be over three years higher in Bangladesh than in Russia: 62.0 years versus 58.8 years. (In Switzerland, the corresponding national risk of dying between the ages of twenty and sixty was roughly 4%, and life expectancy at fifteen was almost sixty-nine.[14])

The Russian Paradox: High Levels of Education, Low Levels of "Human Capital"

Unlike Bangladesh, Russia is an urbanized and literate society—seemingly, a highly educated society. By UNESCO estimates, the Russian Federation population aged twenty-five and older may have one of the very highest shares of men and

Table 6.5 Female Life Expectancy at Age Fifteen: Russia versus All Least Developed Countries, 2019 (WHO Estimates)

Russia	63.52	Rwanda	59.05	Burkina Faso	57.07	Zambia	54.91
Bangladesh	63.24	Uganda	58.8	Niger	56.69	Eritrea	54.88
Bhutan	61.68	Comoros	58.74	Gambia	56.54	Guinea	54.51
Myanmar	60.45	Senegal	58.73	DR Congo	56.52	Solomon Islands	54.33
Sudan	60.2	Yemen	58.6	Liberia	56.34	Haiti	54.3
Nepal	60.19	Tanzania	58.3	Angola	56.25	Guinea-Bissau	53.72
Cambodia	59.79	Benin	57.87	Burundi	56	Somalia	52.78
East Timor	59.69	South Sudan	57.64	Mali	55.77	Afghanistan	52.1
Ethiopia	59.42	Togo	57.33	Madagascar	55.76	Mozambique	52.04
Sao Tome and Principe	59.35	Malawi	57.31	Sierra Leone	55.13	Kiribati	51.34
Laos	59.33	Djibouti	57.25	Chad	55.09	Central African Republic	48.53
Mauritania	59.07						

Source: World Health Organization, Global Health Observatory Data Repository, "Life Expectancy: Life Tables by Country," http://apps.who
.int/gho/data/view.main.60600?lang=en (accessed March 9, 2022).

women with some postsecondary or tertiary education in the contemporary world (see figure 6.6).

Of course, Russian higher education may be "diploma happy"—the educational systems of the Russian Federation and its precursor the Soviet Union may have granted higher degrees at lower levels of educational attainment than was routine in many counterpart countries. That apparent systemic bias notwithstanding, overall years of schooling in Russia nevertheless look to be quite comparable to those of societies belonging to the Organization for Economic Co-operation and Development (OECD).

We can see as much by comparing mean years of schooling (MYS) in the year 2010 for the population fifteen years of age and older in the Russian Federation and the OECD country grouping, thanks to the Barro–Lee dataset,[15] a project on global educational attainment directed by Professors Robert Barro of Harvard and Jong-Wha Lee of Korea University[16] (see figure 6.7).

According to the Barro–Lee estimates, Russia's MYS for the fifteen-plus population in 2010 averaged 11.5 years. Such a rating would have placed the Russian Federation squarely in the middle of the OECD's corresponding rankings. Russia's MYS would have been lower than those of the United States or Switzerland

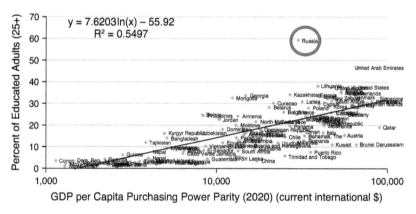

Figure 6.6 Percentage of Adult Population with Bachelor Degree or Higher (Latest Available 2009–2021) versus GDP per Capita PPP: Russia and Selected Other Countries, 2020. *Sources*: World Bank, "GDP per Capita, PPP (Current International, $)," *World Development Indicators*, http://data.worldbank.org/indicator/NY.GDP.PCAP.PP.CD, accessed March 3, 2022; United Nations UNESCO Institute for Statistics, Sustainable Development Goals, "Educational Attainment Rate, Completed Bachelor's or Equivalent Education or Higher, Population +25 Years, Both Sexes (%)," http://stats.uis.unesco.org/unesco/Report Folders/ReportFolders.aspx, accessed March 3, 2022.

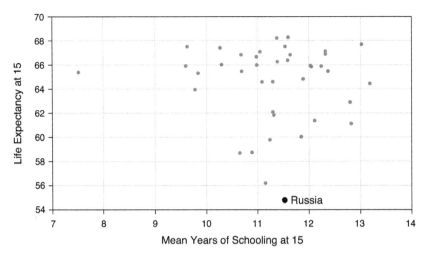

Figure 6.7 Barro–Lee Estimates of Mean Years of Schooling at Age Fifteen versus Human Mobility Database (HMD) Estimated Life Expectancy at Fifteen for All Forty-One Countries in the HMD Database. *Sources*: University of California, Berkeley, and Max Planck Institute for Demographic Research, *Human Mortality Database*, www.mortality.org and www.humanmortality.de, accessed April 25, 2022; R. Barro and J.-W. Lee, "A New Set of Educational Attainment in the World, 1950–2010," *Journal of Development Economics* 104 (2013), 184–198, https://doi.org/10.1016/j.jdeveco.2012.10.001.

(both over thirteen)—but it would have been higher than the MYS for either France or Belgium (both 10.7) and more or less equivalent to those of Australia (11.5) or Japan (11.6).

Herein lies a terrible Russian paradox and mystery: in one and the same country, internationally high levels of educational attainment seem to coincide with strikingly low levels of human capital. Despite Russia's nearly twelve estimated mean years of schooling for the fifteen-plus population, life expectancy at age fifteen is reportedly lower for Russian males than for their counterparts in Yemen or South Sudan—and lower for Russian adults of both sexes than for adults in Bangladesh or Sudan. Yet Barro–Lee estimates place the MYS in 2010 for the fifteen-plus population of Bangladesh at less than six years—and at just over three years for Sudan!

How does a country with the educational profile of a developed country end up with a least-developed county's survival profile? "Attaining" such profiles—and during peacetime—is not that easy: in effect, it requires the development of extraordinary, anomalous new causes of premature mortality. Alas: this is something Russia has "succeeded" at for decades.

The Mystery of Russia's Mortality Structure

According to the Human Mortality Database (HMD)[17]—a project launched by demographers at the Max Planck Institute for Demographic Research in Germany and the University of California at Berkeley with the aim of examining international mortality data for internal inconsistencies, reconstructing long-term mortality trends, and presenting these in fully comparable fashion for over three dozen countries from the OECD, Asia, Oceania, and the Newly Independent States (NIS) area—life expectancy at birth in the Russian Federation for both sexes was no higher in 2010 than it had been in 1961 (in the Russian Federation's predecessor republic within the USSR), half a century earlier (see figure 6.8).

Although life expectancy at birth for females was a bit higher in 2010 than it had been in 1961, male life expectancy was actually nearly a year lower in 2010 than it had been in 1961—half a century earlier. According to the estimates of the Human Mortality Database, as of the year 2010, combined male and female life expectancy at birth in Russia had not yet broken the seventy-year threshold.

The HMD project's most recent update of its Russian Federation trends at this writing (April 2022) are from 2016, offering life tables for the country through to 2014. But Rosstat reports on Russian life expectancy at birth are very close to HMD reconstructions for the many decades both series cover—so

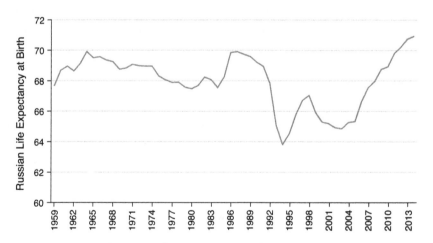

Figure 6.8 Estimated Russian Life Expectancy at Birth According to the Human Mortality Database. *Source*: University of California, Berkeley, and Max Planck Institute for Demographic Research, *Human Mortality Database*, www.mortality.org and www.human mortality.de, accessed April 25, 2022.

we can probably take official Russian estimates since 2014 as reasonably reliable indicators.

By these numbers, Russia enjoyed a steady improvement in life expectancy at birth for its entire population between 2005 and 2019, with a jump in overall life expectancy of nearly eight years overall and of nearly a decade for men. This was the most sustained improvement in Russian life chances since the death of Stalin—and also the most significant in absolute terms (see figure 6.9).

Exhibiting mortality trends of a "normal country" is a new development in modern Russia, one to be welcomed. Two qualifications here are nevertheless necessary here.

First, because steady health improvements are the norm rather than the exception in the rest of the world, Russia's recent improvements still leave the country well behind its peers with comparable income levels. Russia's officially reported 2019 overall life expectancy at birth of seventy-three years was roughly similar to

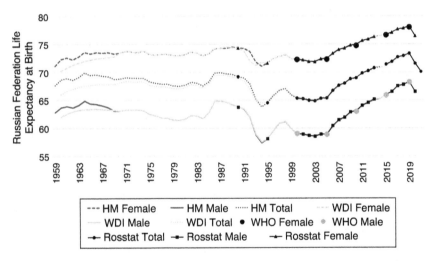

Figure 6.9 Russian Federation Life Expectancy at Birth, 1959–2021: Comparison of Human Mortality Database, Rosstat, WHO, and WDI Data. *Sources*: University of California, Berkeley, and Max Planck Institute for Demographic Research, *Human Mortality Database*, www.mortality.org and www.humanmortality.de, accessed April 25, 2022; World Health Organization, *Life Tables*, https://who.int/data/gho/data/indicators/indicator-details/GHO/gho-ghe-life-tables-by-country; World Bank, *World Development Indicators*, https://databank.worldbank.org/source/world-development-indicators; Russian 1990–2020 data from Rosstat, *Life Expectancy at Birth in the Russian Federation*, https://rosstat.gov.ru/folder/12781; Russian 2021 data from Institute of Demography, *Demoscope Weekly*, http://www.demoscope.ru/weekly/2022/0939/rossia01.php.

162   *Nicholas Eberstadt*

the UN Population Division (UNPD) estimate for *global* life expectancy[18]—a decade and a half of (for Russia) exceptional health progress only brought the country up to the world average. Even at its 2019 peak, life expectancy in Russia was still about three years lower than the average for the countries in the World Bank's upper-middle-income grouping, and almost eight years below the designated high-income countries.[19]

Second, as noted, Russia suffered a harsh upswing in death rates during COVID-19—and thus a marked drop in life expectancy. According to Rosstat, life expectancy in the Russian Federation fell by 1.6 years in 2020.[20] Russia's life expectancy setback in 2020, according to one international study, was the largest in absolute terms of the thirty-seven high-income and upper-middle-income countries for which corresponding data were available.[21] Rosstat has recently also announced that life expectancy in the Russian Federation dropped in 2021 by an additional 1.6 years.[22] By that report, Russian life expectancy would be back to about seventy years again. How quickly it recovers as the pandemic attenuates will remain to be seen.

How could it be that a country whose overall life expectancy at birth was average in global terms (as Russia's was in 2019) should also suffer from the woeful survival patterns we already highlighted? The contradiction is explained by Russia's mysterious mortality structure. Although death rates for Russian infants and children are close to First World levels, death rates for Russia's working-age population are Fourth World. And generating Fourth World death rates in a literate urban society during peacetime requires very different causes of death from those that impose brutal survival trajectories on Fourth World populations today.

One way of examining this mystery is through age-standardized mortality rates, which are adjusted national death rates aggregating a country's various age-specific death rates against a fixed and unchanging notional population structure. Using age-standardized mortality rates can help us avoid the misleading inferences that might be drawn if one society had an unusually youthful population (biasing calculated mortality levels downward) and another had an unusually "gray" population (biasing results upward) (see figure 6.10).

Figure 6.10 shows estimates from the WHO-Europe Health for All database[23] for age-standardized mortality using a "European" model age structure for the Russian Federation (and its predecessor republic within the USSR), the "old EU" (the fifteen original EU countries that make up all of Western Europe, apart from Norway and Switzerland—now fourteen countries, given Brexit), and the "new EU" (the states

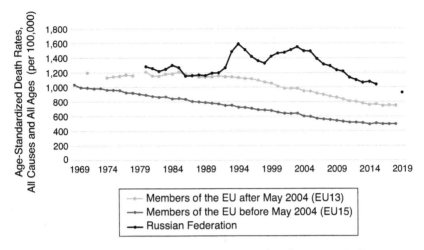

Figure 6.10 WHO-HFA Age-Standardized Death Rates for All Causes and All Ages: Russia versus Old and New European Union Members, 1969–2019. *Source*: World Health Organization-European Health, *Health for All Database*, https://gatewau.euro.who.int/en/hfa-explorer.

that joined in 2004 or later—all of them former members of the Soviet bloc or of communist Yugoslavia, excepting only tiny Malta and Cyprus).

Over the decades under consideration, Western Europe's mortality levels have undergone a smooth and continuing decline. The same is true for the postcommunist societies represented in the "new EU" grouping—at least since the end of communism. But Russia is a gruesome exception to these European tendencies. Its mortality level—both under communism and since—has been erratic and unstable, with improvements in one period tending to be erased by mortality upswings in the next.

As is well known, communist Europe had much poorer public health performance than non-communist Europe in the last decades of the Cold War era. In 1990, mortality levels for what are now the "new EU" countries were on average 46% above those of the "old EU" countries; mortality levels in the Russian Federation were about 53% higher. This means mortality levels in Russia and much of the rest of communist Europe were fairly similar at the end of the Soviet era. After that, however, the mortality gap between Russia and those former Soviet states widened. Evidently, whatever ails Russian public health cannot be attributed to a legacy of Soviet-type communism per se.

Just as Russia's life expectancy headed into a phase of sustained (albeit now interrupted) improvement after 2005, so too age-standardized mortality for the Russian Federation reached a turning point in 2005, dropping sharply thereafter. Consequently, the differential between Russia on the one hand and both "old" and "new" EU countries on the other has narrowed—but only to a degree. By 2015 (the most recent year for which the WHO Health for All dataset has numbers for all three places in question) age-standardized mortality was still 35% higher than in the "new" EU countries, and a bit over twice as high as in the "old" EU countries—though those differentials narrowed further, through 2019, before splaying out again.

The relative improvements in overall Russian mortality from 2005 up to 2019 can be seen in figure 6.11, which draws on estimates from the University of Washington's Institute for Health Metrics and Evaluation (IHME) and compares age-standardized mortality in Russia with that of the OECD countries since 1990 (remember that the OECD now includes a number of countries that were members of the Soviet bloc) (see figure 6.11).

By these estimates, age-standardized mortality dropped more dramatically between 2005 and 2019 in Russia than in the OECD—but because mortality trends in the Russian Federation over the previous decade and a half had been so awful, the mortality gap separating Russia and the OECD was actually wider in 2019 than it had been in 1990, in the last days of communism. In 1990, Russian age-standardized

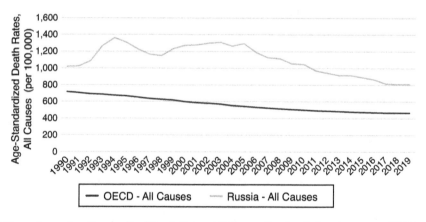

Figure 6.11 Age-Standardized Death Rates, All Causes: Russian Federation versus OECD, 1990–2019. *Source*: Institute for Health Metrics Evaluation, "Explore Tool," *Results from the 2021 Global Burden of Disease (GBD) Study*, https://ghdx.healthdata.org/gbd-results-tool.

death rates were around two-fifths higher than those of today's OECD members. Nearly three decades later in 2019, they were almost three-fourths above OECD levels. According to the IHME, the EU–Russia mortality differential doubled between 1990 and 2019—from a 37% surfeit for Russia in 1990 to 74% in 2019.[24] Those Russian differentials with the OECD and EU would be even wider today, in the wake of COVID-19, if we had more up-to-date numbers.

In least-developed countries, foreshortened life is typically due to the collision of malnutrition and communicable disease (tuberculosis, malaria, cholera, and other "diseases of poverty"). Although Russia's tuberculosis and HIV problems are very real, estimates from WHO-Europe and the IHME nevertheless suggest that differences in death rates from infectious and parasitic diseases account for only a tiny share—around one-fiftieth—of the vast chasm separating all-cause age-standardized mortality levels in Russia and the EU. Russia's terrible new killers are instead cardiovascular disease (or CVD—heart attacks, strokes, and the like) on the one hand, and injuries (homicides, suicides, traffic fatalities, deadly accidents) on the other. For decades—year-in, year-out—Russia's death rates from CVD were higher than the highest levels ever recorded in any Western country (i.e., Finland, circa 1970). As late as 2008, according to WHO estimates, working-age Russian men had the worst CVD death levels of any country covered by the WHO.[25] Indeed, male CVD mortality levels for the Russian Federation that year were about three and a half times higher than would have been predicted on the basis of the country's income.[26]

Age-standardized Russian CVD mortality fell by two-fifths between 2005 and 2019, in the IHME's reckoning. Even so, 2019 CVD mortality was two and a half times higher in Russia than in Finland—with similar disparities for both males and females. According to the IHME, progress since 2005 notwithstanding, 2019 Russian CVD rates were still 2.7 times higher than EU levels and 3.2 times higher than overall levels for the OECD—this despite the roughly equivalent levels of educational attainment in Russia, the EU, and the OECD (see figure 6.12).

As for injuries and poisonings, the WHO estimated death rates in 2008 for working-age Russian men were four times higher than would have been predicted by their income levels—with absolute levels of violent death exceeded only in a handful of places: civil war–riven Iraq and Sri Lanka among them.[27] Violent death, of course, is overwhelmingly a male problem more or less everywhere, but in Russia the general levels are so shockingly high that for a time the country managed to achieve a dubious "crossover." For much of the first decade

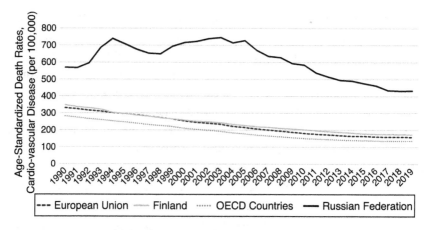

Figure 6.12 Age-Standardized Death Rates from Cardiovascular Disease: Russian Federation versus OECD, European Union, and Finland, 1990–2019. *Source*: Institute for Health Metrics Evaluation, "Explore Tool," *Results from the 2021 Global Burden of Disease (GBD) Study*, https://ghdx.healthdata.org/gbd-results-tool.

of the twenty-first century, according to the IHME, age-standardized death rates from injuries and poisonings were higher for Russian *women* than for EU or OECD *men* (see figure 6.13).

Between 2005 and 2019, Russia reportedly managed to cut its injury and poisonings death rate by more than half—a meaningful achievement. Even so, in 2019 injury and poisoning death levels in Russia remained over twice as high as in the OECD and over two and a half times higher than in the European Union.

Although the mortality gap between Russia and the West (whether we mean the European Union or the broader OECD grouping) narrowed between 2005 and 2019, it remained imposing in scale—and its basic structure was unchanged. In 2019, as earlier, almost all of Russia's excess mortality was attributable to its much higher level of adult mortality and its much higher rates of death from noncommunicable disease—specifically, cardiovascular disease and injuries/poisonings. These two killers accounted for 94% of the overall difference in death rates in Russia and the EU in 2019 and for 98% of the death gap separating Russia and the OECD. And as figure 6.14 demonstrates, even in the "peak health" year of 2019, Russia remained an outlier in its cause-of-death structure (see figure 6.14).

We have identified the mystery of Russia's mortality structure for the reader here—but explaining that mystery stands as a major task, one far beyond the scope of this chapter.[28]

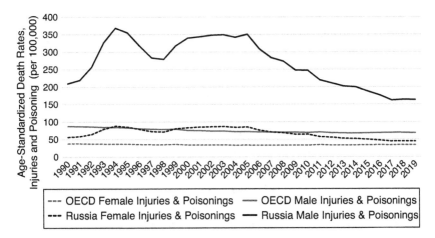

Figure 6.13 Age-Standardized Death Rates from Injuries and Poisoning: Russian Federation versus OECD, 1990–2019. *Source*: Institute for Health Metrics Evaluation, "Explore Tool," *Results from the 2021 Global Burden of Disease (GBD) Study*, https://ghdx.healthdata.org/gbd-results-tool.

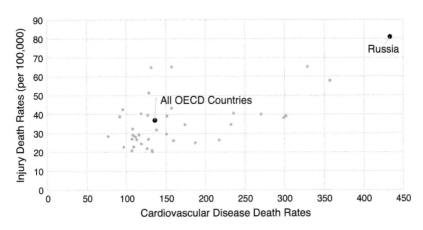

Figure 6.14 Age-Standardized Death Rates from Cardiovascular Disease and Injuries: Russia versus OECD Countries, 2019. *Source*: Institute for Health Metrics Evaluation, "Explore Tool," *Results from the 2021 Global Burden of Disease (GBD) Study*, https://ghdx.healthdata.org/gbd-results-tool.

Russia's "Knowledge Production" and "Knowledge Economy" Problems

Russia's "high education, low human capital" paradox does not end with health: it shows up acutely as well in the country's deep "knowledge production" and "knowledge economy" deficits. In our era, long-term economic progress depends critically on improving productivity through knowledge—but this is something Russia appears oddly ill-equipped to do. The United States Patent Office (now known as the US Patent and Trademark Office, or USPTO) was established in the 1830s, but nearly half of its total patent awards and well over half of its awards to foreign inventers have been granted just since the year 2000. Of the 2.5 million such overseas patents awarded between 2000 and 2020, applicants from Russia took home fewer than 6,600—a mere 0.3% of the overseas total, and in fact a smaller fraction of total international patents than Washington had earlier awarded to the USSR during the Soviet era. In the 2002–2020 period, the USPTO award tally saw Russia ranked twenty-fifth, behind places like tiny Norway and Finland and only just ahead of New Zealand (see table 6.6).

In the US domestic mirror, the Russian Federation's total annual USPTO awards, although gradually increasing, are currently only on par with those of the state of Alabama (see figure 6.15).

Alabama's population is just 5 million, whereas Russia's is over 140 million, very nearly thirty times larger. And although it boasts of some fine research facilities, Alabama is not one of America's "knowledge production" hubs. The contrast between Russia and California is also telling. Russia's population is over three and a half times larger, but in 2020 California produced over eighty times more patents—meaning that on a per capita basis, Californians generated 300 times more US patents than Russians did.

Table 6.6 International Patent Awards by USPTO 2000–2020 (% by country)

Japan	35	India	2
Germany	11	Australia	1
South Korea	10	Finland	1
Taiwan	7	Belgium	1
China	5	Austria	1
Canada	4	Denmark	1
United Kingdom	4	Hong Kong	1
France	4	Singapore	1
Italy	2	Spain	0
Israel	2	Norway	0
Netherlands	2	Ireland	0
Sweden	2	Russia	0
Switzerland	2		

Source: USPTO, "Patent Counts, Single Year Reports—Total," https://www.uspto.gov/web/offices/ac/ido/oeip/taf/reports_stco.htm (accessed May 2, 2022).

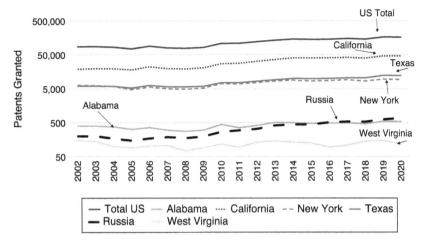

Figure 6.15 Annual USPTO Patents Awarded 2001–2019: Select US States and Russia. *Sources:* Data for 2002–2015 from USPTO, *Patents by Country, State, and Year—Utility Patents*, December 2015, https://www.uspto.gov/web/offices/ac/ido/oeip/taf/cst_ult.html, accessed October 17, 2016; data for 2016–2020 from USPTO, *Calendar Year Patent Statistics*, https://www.uspto.gov/web/offices/ac/ido/oeip/taf/reports_stco.htm, accessed March 17, 2020.

Some might perhaps harbor suspicions that the US patent regime is somehow biased against Russia (although such an argument would also raise the question of how the old Soviet system managed to fare better than the new Russian Federation in USPTO grants). So another take on the Russian knowledge creation problem comes from the international Patent Cooperation Treaty, the global system for tracking these out-of-country applications. Once again, Russia's performance is extremely poor. In 2019, according to the UN World Intellectual Property Organization, Russia came in number twenty-two—after Belgium—racking up less than 0.5% of the world's total (see table 6.7).

Russia's record here is worse than this initial Belgium–Russia comparison implies. Russia has over twelve times Belgium's population—but the share of adults with university or tertiary education is higher in Russia than in Belgium, as we saw in figure 6.7. This means Russia's yield of international patent applications per university-educated working-age adult would be all the lower.

We can get a sense of the magnitude of Russia's global underperformance in international patent applications by drawing upon the estimates of the Wittgenstein Centre for Demography and Global Human Capital in Austria, with its educational attainment dataset akin to the aforementioned Barro–Lee dataset.[29] On the basis

Table 6.7   International Patent Applications under Patent Cooperation Treaty by Country of Origin, 2021

China	69,604	Israel	2,119
USA	59,405	India	2,087
Japan	50,275	Finland	1,894
South Korea	20,723	Australia	1,763
Germany	17,267	Turkey	1,739
France	7,333	Singapore	1,653
United Kingdom	5,843	Austria	1,583
Switzerland	5,461	Spain	1,561
Sweden	4,441	Denmark	1,553
Netherlands	4,116	Belgium	1,389
Italy	3,568	Russian Federation	981
Canada	2,596		

Source: WIPO Statistics Database, "International Applications by Origin," https://www.wipo.int/export/sites/www/pressroom/en/documents/pr_2020_848_annexes.pdf (accessed February 15, 2023).

of those Wittgenstein Centre estimates, and using 2020 as the benchmark year for national totals of working-age people with university or tertiary education, Belgium's 2020 yield of international patent applications would have been fifteen times higher than Russia's (see table 6.8).

Over fifty countries in 2020—not just Western countries and China, but also places like Saudi Arabia and South Africa—registered higher patent application yields per million working-age persons with higher education than Russia did.

By the same token, Russia performs like a knowledge-poor economy in the international economy. As of 2019, the Russian Federation accounted for about 2% of the world's population, according to the US Census Bureau's International Database.[30] By the estimations of the World Bank, in 2019 Russia's share of global economic output when adjusted for purchasing power parity was half again as large (3.1%).[31] Yet in that same year, according to the World Trade Organization, Russia generated only 1% of total global service-sector exports (see figure 6.16).

International service exports are a trade in human skills—unlike merchandise trade, which is a commerce in commodities or natural resources and thus intrinsically less "skills intensive." Curiously, given Russia's well-known expertise in this particular realm, the Russian Federation fares poorly even with information technology service exports, where its 2019 share of the global market was only slightly ahead of the Philippines (see figure 6.17).

Table 6.8 PCT Applications per 1 Million Post-Secondary Education of Working Age (2020)

Antigua and Barbuda	4,592.6	USA	761.2	Slovenia	231.6	Belize	100.3
Switzerland	2,610.8	Iceland	619.5	New Zealand	226.8	Bahamas	78.1
Luxembourg	2,299.4	Belgium	561.7	Mauritius	199.1	South Africa	77.4
Sweden	1,761.3	Singapore	542.7	Canada	175.8	Latvia	76.4
Japan	1,378.5	France	537.7	Seychelles	173.9	Hungary	72.9
Denmark	1,285	Norway	504.1	Portugal	159.3	Malaysia	56.6
Finland	1,265.9	Malta	497.4	Estonia	156.7	Slovakia	52.7
Israel	1,209.9	Ireland	484	Turkey	148.2	Qatar	48.8
Republic of Korea	1,128.7	China	472.8	Cyprus	137.8	Poland	43.5
Barbados	1,082.6	Italy	462.2	Czech Republic	134.1	UAE	42.8
Netherlands	1,060.8	United Kingdom	369.8	Spain	132.8	Bulgaria	40.7
Germany	971.1	Australia	255.9	Saudi Arabia	130	Lithuania	39.2
Austria	886.3	Samoa	243.9	Chile	110.6	Russia	37.8

Note: Working age is defined as fifteen to sixty-four years old.
Source: WIPO Statistics Database, "1—PCT Applications by filing date" (Total PCT Applications selected for shown countries), March 2022, http://www.wipo.int/ipstats/en/statistics/pct/ (accessed: March 15, 2022); Education Data: Wittgenstein Centre for Demography and Global Human Capital, *Wittgenstein Centre Data Explorer Version 2.0*, http://www.wittgensteincentre.org/dataexplorer (accessed: March 15, 2022).

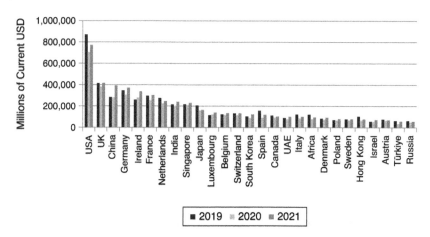

Figure 6.16 Top Global Commercial Service Exporters, 2019–2021 (Current $US Millions). *Source*: World Trade Organization, "Trade in Commercial Export Services—Commercial Services Exports by Main Sector—BOP6 SOX," *Statistics Database—Time Series of International Trade*, https://stats.wto.org, accessed February 15, 2023.

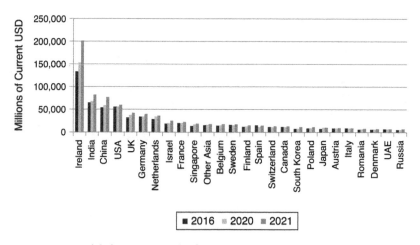

Figure 6.17 Top Global Computer and Information Service Exporters, 2019–2021 (Current US$ Millions). *Source*: World Trade Organization, "Telecommunications, Computer and Information Services–BOP6 SI," *Statistics Database—Time Series of International Trade*, https://stats.wto.org, accessed February 15, 2023.

Russia's talent base for its knowledge economy at this writing is being affected by the Ukraine invasion—and adversely. Russia's military action appears to have triggered a brain drain—not in Ukraine, but in Russia. In the initial weeks of the war, by some estimates, up to 200,000 high-skilled Russians fled their country[32]—

many of them IT specialists.[33] According to another early assessment, as much as 10% of Russia's IT manpower might have left the country in just the first three months of the war.[34] Depending on the coming course of that war, and on the consequent Russian domestic outlook, the bleeding of talent out of Russia may be faster or slower in the months and years ahead—but it is difficult at the moment to envision a plausible scenario that stanches the outflow altogether. Thus, the newly precipitated decline in manpower for Russian knowledge production and the Russian knowledge economy could, all else being equal, further diminish the performance of the Russian Federation in those realms.

Russia's Demographic/Human Resource Outlook

Compromised as Russia's current demographic and human resource situation may appear, the outlook for the years ahead promises to be still less favorable—at least in relative terms, the metric arguably most important to would-be practitioners of power politics in the Kremlin.

Consider first the matter of "head counts"—total population and its composition. Given the birth slump of the last two decades, Russia's labor force, which is already shrinking, is set to be still smaller in 2030 and 2040 than it is today. There is not too much conjecture in these projections, given that all, or almost all, of Russia's prospective working-age 2040 manpower has already been born as of 2022 (depending upon which ages groups we use to define working-age manpower).

According to US Census Bureau estimates and projections, Russia's age twenty to sixty-four cohort peaked in 2011 and is on a path of steady shrinkage through to at least 2040 (see figure 6.18).

Very similar prognoses are offered by the UNPD (for ages fifteen to sixty-four) (see figure 6.19), the Wittgenstein Centre (ages twenty to sixty-four) (see figure 6.20), and—not so incidentally—by Rosstat.

Early 2020 projections from Rosstat extend only to 2036, but all three variants—high, medium, and low—envision a smaller age fifteen to sixty-four population for Russia in 2036 than in 2021 (see figure 6.21).

In light of the continuing prospective growth of the global population over the decades immediately ahead, the absolute drop in Russian manpower can only mean that Russia's share of global manpower is set for continuing decline.

Then there is the issue of Russia's total future population—a somewhat more conjectural matter that raises the question of births and deaths in the years ahead.[35] But there is reason to think that Russian deaths will continue to outnumber Russian births. One of the principal reasons for this conjecture is that Russia's

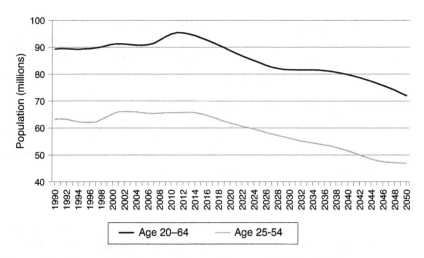

Figure 6.18 Estimated and Projected Russian Manpower by Selected Measures, 1990–2050. *Source*: US Census Bureau, *International Database*, https://www.census.gov/data-tools/demo/idb/, accessed March 17, 2022.

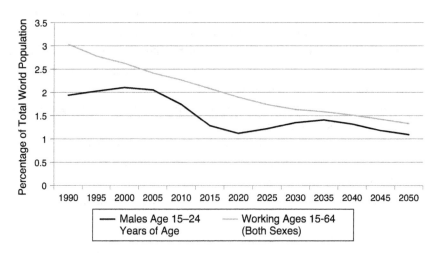

Figure 6.19 Key Russian Federation Population Groups as Percentage of Total World Population: 1990–2050 United Nations Population Division Medium Variant Projections. *Source*: United Nations Department of Economic and Social Affairs, Population Division, *World Population Prospects 2019*; United Nations Department of Economic and Social Affairs, Population Division, "Population Aged 15–64," *World Population Prospects: The 2017 Revision*, https://esa.un.org.undp/wpp/DataQuery/, accessed March 17, 2022.

Russian Power in Decline   175

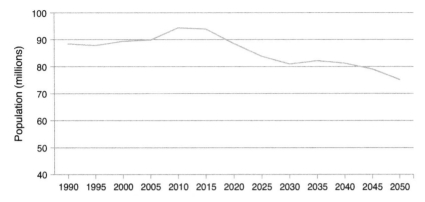

Figure 6.20 Actual and Projected Russian Manpower Aged Twenty to Sixty-Four: 1990–2050. *Source*: Wittgenstein Centre for Demography and Global Human Capital, *Wittgenstein Centre Data Explorer Version 2.0* (2018), http://wittgensteincentre.org/data explorer, accessed May 4, 2022.

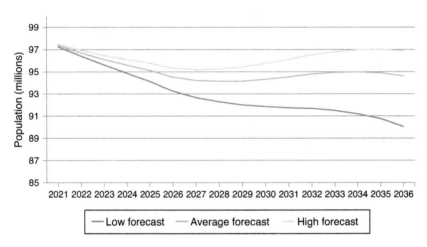

Figure 6.21 Actual and Projected Russian Working-Age Population: 2021–2036. *Note*: Working age is considered to be ages fifteen to sixty-four. *Source*: Rosstat, "Demographic Forecast up to 2036—Population by Individual Age Groups," https://rosstat.gov.ru/storage/mediabank/progn3a.xls, accessed May 4, 2022.

population structure is creating long-term pressure for higher death totals and lower birth totals (see figure 6.22).

Due to the post-Soviet baby crash of the 1990s and the early 2000s, the pool of Russian women entering their twenties is set to stagnate or shrink for the next decade and more. At the same time, the overall Russian population is

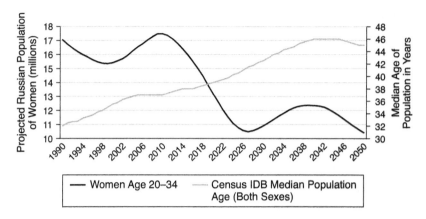

Figure 6.22 Projected Russian Female Population Ages Twenty to Thirty-Four and Overall Median Population Age, 1990–2050. *Sources:* US Census Bureau, *International Database,* https://census.gov/data-tools/demo/idb/, accessed March 14, 2022; United Nations Department of Economic and Social Affairs, Population Division, *World Population Prospects 2019, Online Edition, Rev. 1, Medium Variant,* https://population.un.org/wpp/Download/Files/1_Indicators%20(Standard)EXCEL_FILES/1_Population/WPP2019_POP_F05_MEDIAN_AGE.xlsx, accessed March 17, 2022; Wittgenstein Centre for Demography and Human Global Capital, *Wittgenstein Centre Data Explorer Version 2.0,* http://wittgensteincentre.org/dataexplorer, accessed March 17, 2022.

simultaneously getting grayer. Again, there is little to surmise here, as most of the people under consideration are already alive and living in Russia. All other things being equal, these two trends create pressure for increasing "negative natural increase"—even if fertility does not fall below current levels and Russia does not experience further health setbacks.

Russian fertility prospects will depend in large measure on the outlook for desired family size on the part of prospective parents in the country: barring a revolution in attitudes, the continuation of sub-replacement childbearing is the most likely trend in store for the decades ahead. The prospects for long-term improvements in mortality, for their part, could be somewhat more constrained than one might first assume. The reason is that mortality trends are "cohort-dependent," following the life course of the men and women in question. Russia's current cohorts have a significant measure of "negative health momentum" in their population structure, as may be seen by comparison with counterparts in Japan (see figures 6.23 and 6.24).

This matter of "negative momentum" is one reason the UNPD's projections for Russia's life expectancy are so cautious for the decades immediately ahead (see figure 6.25).

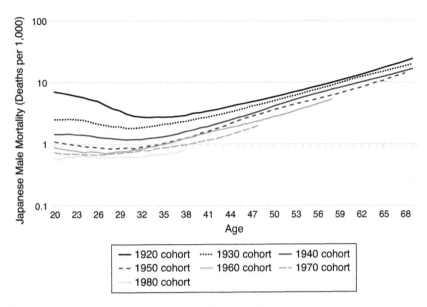

Figure 6.23 Japanese Male Mortality Ages Twenty to Sixty-Nine for Selected 1920–1980 Birth Cohorts. *Source*: University of California, Berkley, and Max Planck Institute for Demographic Research, *Human Mortality Database*, http://mortality.org, accessed March 16, 2022.

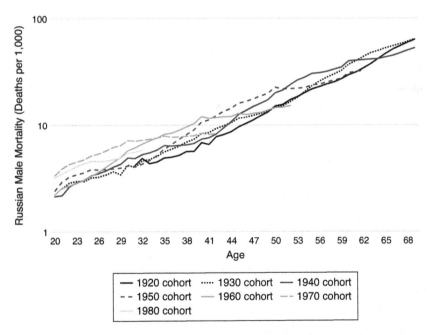

Figure 6.24 Russian Male Mortality Ages Twenty to Sixty-Nine for Selected 1920–1980 Birth Cohorts. *Note*: 1980 cohort is from 1980 to 1984; all other cohorts include ten years. *Source*: University of California, Berkley, and Max Planck Institute for Demographic Research, *Human Mortality Database*, http://mortality.org, accessed March 16, 2022.

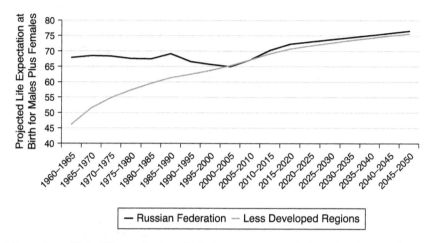

Figure 6.25 United Nations Projected Life Expectation at Birth for Males Plus Females: Russia versus Less Developed Regions, 1960–2050. *Source:* United Nations Department of Economic and Social Affairs, Population Division, "Life Expectancy at Age 0," *World Population Prospects 2019*; United Nations Department of Economic and Social Affairs, Population Division, *World Population Prospects: The 2017 Revision*, https://esa.un.org.undp/wpp/DataQuery/, accessed March 17, 2022.

Where Russia's combined male and female life expectancy at birth, by the UNPD's reckoning, was over twenty years higher than that for the world's developing regions in the early 1960s, Russian levels were indistinguishable from those of the less developed regions (a.k.a. Third World countries) by the early twenty-first century—and UNPD projections envision that symmetry to continue for the next several decades.

This background helps explain why all of the demographic authorities offering projections for Russia's future population see Russia as a net-mortality society in the years ahead (see figure 6.26).

Strikingly, this vision is shared by Russia's official statistical service, Rosstat, in all its projections—including its "high variant" for Russia.

Given such portents, continuing depopulation in Russia would only be prevented by substantially increased immigration. Immigration is an imponderable for demographers because it is so dependent upon non-demographic factors. But with that important caveat in mind, we may note that population decline is regarded as the plausible outlook for Russia for the next several decades under all scenarios contemplated by the UNPD, the US Census Bureau's International

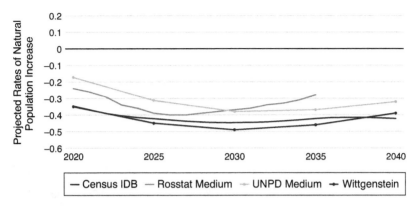

Figure 6.26 Comparison of Projected Rates of Natural Population Increase in Russia. *Sources:* US Census Bureau, *International Database*, https://census.gov/data-tools/demo/idb/, accessed March 14, 2022; United Nations Department of Economic and Social Affairs, Population Division, *World Population Prospects 2019, Online Edition, Rev. 1, Medium Variant*, (https://population.un.org/wpp/Download/Files/1_Indicators%20(Standard)EXCEL_FILES/1_Population/WPP2019_POP_F05_MEDIAN_AGE.xlsx, accessed March 17, 2022; Rosstat, "Births, Deaths, and Natural Population Growth," March 26, 2020, https://rosstat.gov.ru/storage/mediabank/progn5.xls; Wittgenstein Centre for Demography and Human Global Capital, *Wittgenstein Centre Data Explorer Version 2.0*, (http://wittgensteincentre.org/dataexplorer, accessed March 17, 2022.

Database, and the Wittgenstein Centre—as well as by Russia's own official Rosstat "medium variant" projection (see figure 6.27).

Note, however, that the Rosstat projections—like all of the other series in figure 6.27—were devised *before* the onset of the COVID-19 pandemic. Projections undertaken today would undoubtedly envision even steeper trajectories of depopulation for Russia in the years ahead. Either way, Russia's share of total world population is expected to shrink through to at least the year 2040.

If all this were not bad enough for Moscow, Russia's geopolitical potential is being squeezed further by the rapid worldwide growth of skilled manpower pools. Russia's global share of working-age manpower with secondary and postsecondary education is on track to decline even more rapidly over the coming decades than its "head count" share of global working-age manpower (see figure 6.28).

Projections from the Wittgenstein Centre envision Russia as accounting for barely a fortieth of the world's highly educated working-age manpower by 2040—not only trailing distantly behind the United States, China, and India, but also lagging behind Japan, Indonesia, and Nigeria by 2050 (see figure 6.29).

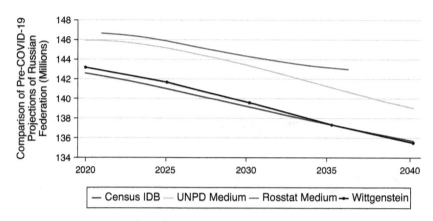

Figure 6.27 Comparison of Pre-COVID-19 Projections of Russian Federation Population, 2020–2040. *Sources:* US Census Bureau, *International Database*, https://census.gov/data-tools/demo/idb/, accessed March 14, 2022; United Nations Department of Economic and Social Affairs, Population Division, *World Population Prospects 2019, Online Edition, Rev. 1, Medium Variant*, (https://population.un.org/wpp/Download/Files/1_Indicators%20(Standard)EXCEL_FILES/1_Population/WPP2019_POP_F05_MEDIAN_AGE.xlsx, accessed March 17, 2022; Rosstat, "Population Change by Forecast Options," March 26, 2020, https://rosstat.gov.ru/storage/mediabank/progn1.xls; Wittgenstein Centre for Demography and Human Global Capital, *Wittgenstein Centre Data Explorer Version 2.0*, http://wittgensteincentre.org/dataexplorer, accessed March 17, 2022.

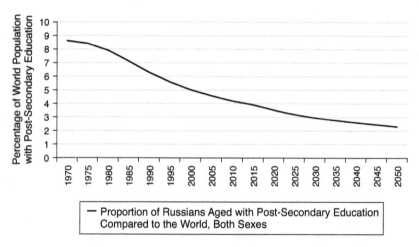

Figure 6.28 Population with Post-Secondary Education: Russia as Percentage of World Population, 1990–2050. *Source:* Wittgenstein Centre for Demography and Human Global Capital, *Wittgenstein Centre Data Explorer Version 2.0*, http://wittgensteincentre.org/dataexplorer, accessed March 17, 2022.

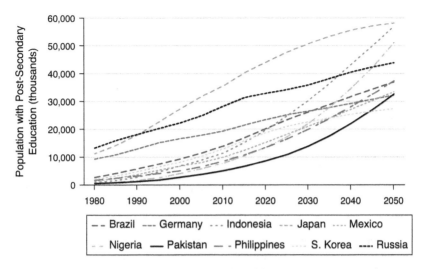

Figure 6.29 Post-Secondary Education in Select Middle-Size Countries: Estimates and Projections for Total Population, 1980–2050. *Source*: Wittgenstein Centre for Demography and Human Global Capital, *Wittgenstein Centre Data Explorer Version 2.0*, http://wittgenstein centre.org/dataexplorer, accessed March 16, 2022.

In addition, the economic potential of Russian human resources stands to be constrained by continuing health problems because Russian life expectancy is projected to remain below the world average through at least 2040 (see figure 6.30).

Concluding Observations

Russia's demographic and human resource problems are daunting. It is a country already in the midst of a prolonged if still gradual population decline driven by a continuing surfeit of deaths over births. Russia has also been experiencing a long-term decline in working-age population. In addition, Russia's working-age manpower is beset by an extraordinary and continuing health crisis, which is generating Fourth World mortality rates for a country with First World educational attainment.

Although education is widely observed to confer health benefits in the modern world, Russia is in many respects an ominous exception to this global rule. Further, despite an adult education profile (in terms of mean years of schooling) that is comparable to those of the affluent European members of the OECD, Russia appears to be strangely incapable of competing in knowledge production. Russia's performance in the global trade in services—a highly skills-intensive sector of the

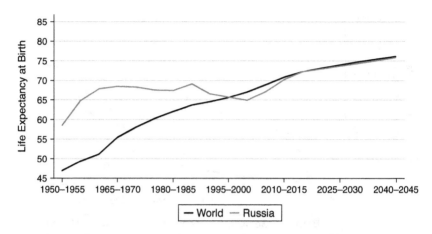

Figure 6.30 Life Expectancy at Birth: Russian Federation versus World Average, 1950–2045. *Source*: United Nations Department of Economic and Social Affairs, Population Division, "Life Expectancy at Age 0," *World Population Prospects 2019*, https://esa.un.org.undp/wpp/DataQuery/, accessed March 17, 2022.

world economy—is likewise drastically smaller than one would expect for a country with such an ostensibly high level of schooling.

Surveying these various fundamentals, we may appreciate how imposing the demographic and human resource constraints on Russian potential promise to be in the years ahead. These trends place considerable downward pressure on Russia's relative potential in the world in the decades immediately ahead. Demographic change slowly but inexorably alters the realm of the possible in human affairs. From the standpoint of ambitious leadership in Moscow, demography has been relentlessly reducing options.

There is a striking contrast between Russia's negative human resource trends on the one hand and the Kremlin's assertive, indeed revisionist, international policies on the other. Witness the dictator's proclivity for ever-greater risk-taking internationally, from Georgia to Crimea and now Ukraine, and likewise, the steady rise in implicit and explicit nuclear saber-rattling.

But given the demographic foundations of Russian power, these gambles are ultimately unsustainable. The only question is how Russian ambitions can eventually come back into conformity with Russian human resource realities—that is to say, the nature of the ultimate adjustment bringing these in line with the capabilities of a declining middle power.

Given the long-term difficulties highlighted in this chapter, a deliberate Kremlin stratagem of brinkmanship for maintaining the Kremlin's global reach would appear to be unsustainable on its very face. A variety of circumstances could be envisioned that might bring this state of affairs to an end. Few of them are pleasant to contemplate.

NOTES

The author wishes to thank Alex Coblin for his superb research assistance on this study. Thanks also to Professor Sarah M. Misemer of Texas A&M University for her valuable comments, constructive criticisms, and helpful queries, and to Peter Van Ness of the American Enterprise Institute for valuable help in updating the data analysis in this chapter. Any remaining errors are the author's own. This study is a substantially expanded and revised version of an essay that originally appeared in the *Wall Street Journal*.

1. "Putin: Soviet Collapse a 'Genuine Tragedy,'" *NBC News*, April 25, 2005, https://www.nbcnews.com/id/wbna7632057.

2. "TRANSCRIPT: 2007 Putin Speech and the Following Discussion at the Munich Conference on Security Policy," *Johnson's Russia List*, March 27, 2014, https://russialist.org/transcript-putin-speech-and-the-following-discussion-at-the-munich-conference-on-security-policy/.

3. Derived from World Trade Organization, "WTO Stats," 2021 export data for merchandise and commercial services combined, accessed April 23, 2022, https://stats.wto.org.

4. World Trade Organization, "WTO Stats."

5. Tomas Frejka and Sergei Zakharov, "The Apparent Failure of Russia's Pronatalist Family Policies," *Population and Development Review* 39, no. 4 (December 2013): 635–647, https://doi.org/10.1111/j.1728-4457.2013.00631.x.

6. David Adam, "The Pandemic's True Death Toll: Millions More than Official Counts," *Nature*, January 18, 2022, https://www.nature.com/articles/d41586-022-00104-8.

7. Serbia's totals in table 6.1 would imply it would have been in the same proportional league as Russia—but it is excluded from comparison because it was not a peacetime society for the entirety of the period under consideration. Note as well the discrepancy between official Russian estimates of cumulative net mortality totals for Russia 1992–2021 and those of the US Census Bureau's International Data Base: 15.7 million versus 17.1 million. We do not attempt to reconcile those discrepancies here.

8. Eurostat, "Population Change - Demographic Balance and Crude Rates at National Level," January 6, 2022, https://appsso.eurostat.ec.europa.eu/nui/show.do?dataset=demo_gind&lang=en.

9. Eurostat, "Population Change."

10. Russian Federation demographic data allow us to estimate fertility by region and by ethnicity/nationality, but not directly by self-reported religion. Researchers have

therefore used nationality as a marker for religiosity in estimating Russia's "Muslim" population—identifying and aggregating groups with historical or traditional affinity for Islam. See for example Timothy Heleniak, "Regional Distribution of the Muslim Population of Russia," *Eurasian Geography and Economics* 47, no. 4 (May 2013): 426–448, https://www.tandfonline.com/doi/abs/10.2747/1538-7216.47.4.426; Timothy Heleniak, "Census Atlas of Russia: Fertility," National Council for Eurasian and East European Research, August 29, 2014, https://www.ucis.pitt.edu/nceeer/2014_828-06_Heleniak.pdf; and Forum on Religion and Public Life, "The Future of the Global Muslim Population," Pew Research Center, January 2011, https://www.pewresearch.org/religion/2011/01/27/future-of-the-global-muslim-population-regional-europe/. Details concerning fertility levels by nationality in Russia today will be available when the returns from the RF 2021 census are made available; its release is currently scheduled for December 2022. "When Was the Census?", All-Russian Population Census, https://www.strana2020.ru/faq/v-kakie-sroki-proshla-perepis/.

11. Cf. D. J. Van De Kaa, "Europe's Second Demographic Transition," *Population Bulletin*, 42, no. 1 (1987): 1–59, https://pubmed.ncbi.nlm.nih.gov/12268395.

12. The WHO estimates life tables for 194 countries and territories. World Health Organization, "Global Health Observatory Data Repository," https://apps.who.int/gho/data/node.main.LIFECOUNTRY.

13. The United Nations' officially designated "Least Developed Countries" are "defined as low-income countries suffering from structural impediments to sustainable development." United Nations Development Policy and Analysis Division, "2021 Country Snapshots," May 5, 2021.

14. Combined survival schedules for the countries and regions in question for 2019 derived from World Health Organization, Global Health Observatory Data Repository, "Life Expectancy: Life Tables by Country," accessed April 24, 2022, https://apps.who.int/gho/data/node.main.LIFECOUNTRY.

15. Robert Barro and Jong-Wha Lee, "A New Data Set of Educational Attainment in the World, 1950–2010," *Journal of Development Economics* 104 (2013): 184–198, https://doi.org/10.1016/j.jdeveco.2012.10.001.

16. MYS profiles for the twenty-five-plus populations are unlikely to have changed greatly over the past decade, given the gradual nature of population-wide changes in educational attainment.

17. Human Mortality Database, University of California, Berkeley), and Max Planck Institute for Demographic Research, accessed May 1, 2022.

18. Department of Economic and Social Affairs Population Dynamics, "World Population Prospects 2019," United Nations, https://population.un.org/wpp/.

19. World Bank, "World Development Indicators," https://databank.worldbank.org/reports.aspx?source=world-development-indicators.

20. "Study Shows COVID-19 Slashed Russia's Life Expectancy by Over Two Years," *Radio Free Europe*, November 5, 2021, https://www.rferl.org/a/russia-covid-life-expectancy/31547862.html.

21. Nazrul Islam, Dmitri Jdanov, Vladimir Shkolnikov, Kamlesh Khunti, Ichiro Kawachi, Martin White, Sarah Lewington, and Ben Lacey, "Effects of COVID-19

Pandemic on Life Expectancy and Premature Mortality in 2020: Time Series Analysis in 37 Countries," *BMJ* 375 (2021), e066768, https://doi.org/10.1136/bmj-2021-066768.

22. "Life Expectancy Has Fallen Sharply in Russia—The Moscow Times," *Hindustan News Hub*, March 24, 2022, https://hindustannewshub.com/russia-ukraine-news/life-expectancy-has-fallen-sharply-in-russia-the-moscow-times.

23. WHO-Europe, "European Health for All Database," accessed April 28, 2022, https://gateway.euro.who.int/en/hfa-explorer/.

24. The IMHE and WHO-HFA standardization "models" are slightly different, so figures from the two databases are not directly comparable.

25. Derived from World Bank, "World Development Indicators," available at http://databank.worldbank.org/data/views/variableselection/selectvariables.aspx?source=world-development-indicators; and World Health Organization Global Health Observatory Data Repository, "Disease and Injury Country Estimates, 2008: By Sex and Age, Data by Country," http://apps.who.int/gho/data/node.main.1006?lang=en.

26. World Bank, "World Development Indicators"; and World Health Organization Global Health Observatory Data Repository, "Disease and Injury Country Estimates, 2008."

27. World Bank, "World Development Indicators"; and World Health Organization, Global Health Observatory Data Repository, "Disease and Injury Country Estimates, 2008."

28. For an initial foray, see "The Mystery of Russian Mortality," chapter 4, in Nicholas Eberstadt, *Russia's Peacetime Demographic Crisis: Dimensions, Causes, Implications* (Seattle, WA: National Bureau of Asian Research, 2010).

29. For more detail, consult the Wittgenstein Centre Data Explorer, accessed December 26, 2016, http://dataexplorer.wittgensteincentre.org/wcde-v2/.

30. United States Census Bureau, "International Database," accessed December 26, 2016, https://www.census.gov/programs-surveys/international-programs/about/idb.html.

31. World Bank, "World Development Indicators," https://databank.worldbank.org/reports.aspx?source=world-development-indicators.

32. Leonid Bershidsky, "Russia's Brain Drain Becomes a Stampede for the Exits," *Bloomberg*, March 16, 2022, https://www.bqprime.com/businessweek/russia-emigration-up-after-putin-s-ukraine-invasion.

33. Cade Metz and Adam Satariano, "Russian Tech Industry Faces 'Brain Drain' as Workers Flee," *New York Times*, April 13, 2022, https://www.nytimes.com/2022/04/13/technology/russia-tech-workers.html.

34. Anthony Faiola, "Mass Flight of Tech Workers Turns Russian IT into Another Casualty of War," *Washington Post*, May 1, 2022, https://www.washingtonpost.com/world/2022/05/01/russia-tech-exodus-ukraine-war/.

35. We leave aside immigration—not because it is irrelevant here, but because demographers have no tools by which to offer accurate forecasts for this quantity.

Chapter Seven

The End of Glory?

Putin's Use and Abuse of the Legacy of the Second World War

Roger R. Reese

In 2012, the historian Roger Markwick wrote, "The Second World War has never ended for the citizens of the former Soviet Union." He believes that, despite the challenges to the legacy from outside Russia, "it continues to strike a real resonance with the individual life and death experiences and memories of millions of former Soviet citizens."[1] This chapter questions that assessment and suggests that after more than seventy-five years, the war has only an abstract meaning for the majority of Russians, and Russian President Vladimir Putin's attempt to use it as an instrument to compel action has failed. The memory of the war lost most of its utility for the government with the demise of communism and the breakup of the Soviet Union and the birth of a generation that never knew communism or experienced the Soviet Union. The negative, anti-Russian connotation for the citizens of the now independent states of the former USSR is not lost on younger Russians. Evidence from more than two years of war against Ukraine suggests that Putin's attempt to use the legacy of the war to rally a racially diverse and politically fragmented Russian people behind his authoritarian domestic policies and belligerent foreign policies in the name of patriotism and anti-fascism has been a failed use of history for political purposes that has sharpened divisions rather than promoted unity in the country.

What do we mean by "legacy," and why is it worth talking about? Common dictionaries give two definitions of "legacy." The first is a noun: "a thing handed down by a predecessor;" the second, in the jargon of the computer world, is an adjective "denoting software or hardware that has been superseded but is difficult to replace because of its wide use." Both of these definitions have meaning when analyzing the legacy of the Second World War for Putin's Russia. Following the disintegration of the USSR, some things handed down from the war have disappeared; foremost among them are great power status and the political and economic domination of Eastern Europe. Other things such as collective trauma and an acute gender imbalance of the war generation have mercifully passed. What remains is a landscape cluttered with thousands of monuments to the war scattered across the former USSR and Eastern Europe, the dwindling remnants of the war generation who feel entitled to public subsidies and are simultaneously idealized and neglected by the state, expatriate communities of Russians in the former Soviet republics, and a contest over what meanings should be taken from the war nearly eighty years after its end. It is the contest over the meaning of the war that fits the computer scientist's adjective "legacy": "software or hardware that has been superseded but is difficult to replace because of its wide use."

Before the disintegration of the USSR, the meaning the state assigned to the war passed through several distinct interpretive phases, depending on who was in power in the Kremlin. Two ideas were constant across the phases: that the USSR bore the greatest burden of defeating Hitler's Germany in cost of lives and destruction of property, and that because the USSR liberated Eastern Europe from fascism, it was therefore entitled to exert hegemony over it.[2] Until 1992, the victory was used to validate the rule of the Communist Party and the Soviet social system despite their failures.

Before there was a public meaning given to the war, every family created a private one. There were no public commemorations for the first twenty years after the war. Instead, people marked both June 22 (the day the Germans invaded) and May 9 (Victory Day) privately as days of remembrance and mourning. The general tone of family and small group gatherings was somber. The war was remembered for the sacrifices of the people, not the glory of the state.[3]

Leonid Brezhnev, in the mid-1960s, promoted a heroic, top-down legacy of the war to validate his regime despite its failures, to the disgust of many of the war generation. Eventually, his focus on the party and state led to cynicism and then finally to the war's first critical reevaluation under Mikhail Gorbachev.[4] Then, after more than a decade in power, Putin, like his Soviet predecessors, took an active role in pushing a reinterpretation of the legacy that supports his domestic political agenda and foreign policy, but, unlike during the Soviet era, the reinterpretation has been publicly contested. Putin's version has had to contend with competing narratives from within and without, has served as the basis for attacks on his governance and foreign policy, and has generated international tensions.

Putin's interpretation of the meaning and legacy of the so-called Great Patriotic War of the Soviet Union takes further the Stalinist version that Russia (seldom mentioning the USSR) bore the major share of the load in defeating Nazi Germany to claim that Russia won the war and "saved the world from Nazi Domination."[5] For Putin, the legacy of the war focuses exclusively on Russia's victory. Following from this, the world—specifically the European Union, the former states of the USSR, and the United States—should be more respectful of Russia and especially defer to its hegemonic foreign policy agenda in the near abroad (the former Soviet Union). In 2014, Putin began to use the legacy of the war to justify the attacks on Ukraine by labeling its government "fascist."

It is apparent that the Putin government's agenda regarding how it portrays the legacy of the war to the nation, now three generations past the "great victory," is quite deliberate. The memory of the war is used as a tool to promote patriotism and national pride in a Russia that has yet to produce contemporary heroes, heroic events, or any noteworthy domestic achievements—especially among the post-Soviet generation.[6] Putin has gradually shifted credit for the victory from Stalin and the Communist Party and assigned it to the Russian people. He has attempted to use the memory of the war and its enormous sacrifice to build unity among the people. He has attempted to use the legacy of shared suffering to create a wedge between the Russian people and the West by portraying the European Union, NATO, the former East European satellite states, the Baltic states, and Ukraine as ungrateful and even fascist.

Since Putin was first elected to office in 2000, nearly every national holiday has been manipulated to celebrate or commemorate the Great Patriotic War. He redefined the anniversary of the October Revolution on November 7 as National Unity Day in 2004 to celebrate the war. In 2011, he had soldiers clad in period uniforms, armed and equipped with period weapons and vehicles, recreate the famous 1941 parade in which soldiers marched through the capital directly to the front during the Battle of Moscow. To heighten the emotional quality of the event, he had a handful of aged veterans who had marched in 1941 participate in the parade.[7] By appropriating the day in this manner, Putin offended Russia's communists and many of the older generation who feel nostalgia for the communist ideals of the Soviet period.[8]

Putin's record on communicating his Russo-centric message is mixed. For the generation that came of age during the 1960s, when Brezhnev's propaganda ma-

The End of Glory?   189

chine pressed on youth an over-organized, ritualized memory through the veneration of eternal flames and visits to schools by veterans (all who told their stories from the same script), the war took on a generic quality in which the individual was lost. The uniformity of it irritated and bored school children. For the younger generations born after the disintegration of the USSR, the war is communicated through the stories that come secondhand from people whose connection to the war was as youths away from the fighting. This generation, too, is weary of being belabored by war stories and by the revelations of the true cost of the war and the repression of innocent people at the hands of the Stalinist state.

Although the history of the war is part of the national school curriculum, students are evidently not paying close attention to their lessons. On June 21, 2002, the day before the celebration of the Day of Memory and Sorrow, which commemorates the German invasion in 1941, a public opinion poll revealed that only 18% of the respondents knew the significance of the next day's date.[9] This lack of knowledge may be in part due to the fact that under Yeltsin, the national school curriculum reduced the number of lessons on World War II in high school from twenty to eight.[10]

In 1993, 98% of Russians polled named victory in the Great Patriotic War as the greatest moment in the twentieth century, and in 2020, 95% polled still agreed. In 2003, 87% of respondents named the Great Patriotic War as the proudest moment in Russian history, but in 2020, it had fallen to 69%. In 2011, Moscow Humanitarian University published the results of a poll of 800 students from various universities it conducted about the feelings of Russian youth regarding the heroism of Soviet soldiers in the Great Patriotic War. Only 14% of them correctly identified Joseph Stalin as the supreme commander of the Red Army during the war. When asked to name other prominent figures of the war, many students named Hitler and Roosevelt, but nearly 37% could not name even one important person. Nearly half (47%) could not think of a single hero of World War II. Despite their lack of factual historical knowledge, 96% of those polled believed that they should be proud of Russia's role in the Great Patriotic War, and 82% believed it was necessary to continue to hold Victory Day parades.[11] The support for Victory Day celebrations does not mean that people necessarily accord them reverence. Alcohol was banned from the St. Petersburg celebrations in 2014 because the annual festivities frequently turned into drunken melees during the evening fireworks.[12]

As for major battles or campaigns, a quarter of respondents claimed no knowledge of the battles of Moscow, Stalingrad, and Kursk. Just over half (54%) had heard of the Siege of Leningrad, and only one-third (35%) of students knew of the

Battle of Berlin. Fully 25% of the students polled equated the Great Patriotic War with the First World War and thought Napoleon's invasion in 1812 was so far in the past as to be irrelevant to contemporary life.[13] In sum, the survey shows that the Great Patriotic War is well on the way to becoming legendary to young people and the commemorations hollow rituals.

It is far from clear whether Putin understands or appreciates how the generation gap has affected the level of reverence for the war in contemporary Russian society. Putin may be blinded by his own emotional attachment to the legacy of the war, which is shared by many of his and the older generation. His father served in the Red Army for the duration of the war, and his mother was a survivor of the Siege of Leningrad. On January 1, 2014, to commemorate the Siege of Leningrad, Putin led a procession of siege survivors to the Piskarëvskoe cemetery, where he laid a wreath in honor of his brother, who was buried there.[14] There can be no doubt that the shadow of the war shaded his childhood and perhaps closes his mind to alternative narratives. His inner circle of military, security, and foreign policy advisers are all members of his generation, born in the 1950s, and thus share his outlook.

Putin and his generation's attachment to the war and their sense of patriotism is separated by a wide gap from that of Russia's younger post-Soviet generation, as illustrated by the minor uproar caused by twenty-four-year-old Natalia Pereverzeva, Russia's candidate for Miss Earth, crowned in November 2012. When asked what made her proud of Russia, she answered as follows:

> My Russia is a beautiful and majestic lady, full-blooded, red-cheeked, wearing an embroidered sundress and a long, thick braid, with multi-colored ribbons in it. She is a fabulous girl. My Russia is a cow with huge eyes and funny horns that always chews something. Oh, and how sweet its milk is! But my Russia is also a poor, huge and suffering country that has been ruthlessly torn by greedy, dishonest atheists. My Russia is a big artery, from which a few people take away her wealth. My Russia is a beggar. My Russia cannot help the elderly and orphans. It is bleeding and sinking like a ship, and engineers, doctors, and teachers escape from this ship because they have nothing to live on. My Russia is an endless war in the Caucasus. These embittered brotherly nations that previously spoke the same language, which is now forbidden to teach in schools. My Russia is the winner that destroyed fascism and bought the victory at the expense of millions of lives.[15]

This was not the unqualified expression of national pride that Putin and the conservative element in Russia wanted to hear.

The End of Glory?   191

Linking the legacy of the war and patriotism to his leadership was Putin's goal from the beginning. Putin chose May 9, Victory Day, for his first inauguration. A Levada Center poll taken in November 2013 revealed that the proportion of Russians who consider themselves patriots had dropped 8% since Putin first took office in 2000. That year, 77% of respondents identified themselves as patriotic; in 2013, that number fell to 69%. How one defined "patriotism" determined how one responded to the poll. Those who interpreted patriotism as "working or acting for the good of the country" dropped from 35% in 2000 to 21% in 2013. Russians who understood the concept as "loving your country" remained consistent at just under 60%. Those who thought that patriotism meant "considering one's own nation better than other countries" increased only marginally from 17% in 2000 to 21% in 2013.[16]

For all of Putin's use of the war's legacy to promote patriotism, the poll results must have been disappointing. In a Levada Center poll of 1,603 Russians conducted in February 2014, shortly after the Winter Olympic Games in Sochi, the number of people who agreed that "a patriot should defend the country from any kind of insults and criticism" dropped to 18%, down from 24% in 2000. However, over the same time period, the number of respondents who interpreted patriotism as "the personal feeling of love for one's homeland" increased from 58% to 68%. More troubling was the disparity in numbers between those who agreed and those who did not agree with the statement that "a patriot should support the authorities no matter what": 23.3% agreed, but 65.3% did not.[17]

How relevant the emotional legacy of the Great Patriotic War is for Russian patriotism today is impossible to quantify, but if willingness to serve in the armed forces is an indicator, then the war's legacy surely has become irrelevant to draft-age men. Draft evasion has been a problem since the waning days of the USSR. Rates of evasion remain extremely high despite all efforts to promote patriotism. The Ministry of Defense estimated in 2012 that 200,000 men had evaded the draft and a further 244,000 in 2013.[18] The examples of sacrifice and heroism of the Great Patriotic War veterans held out as models for youth to emulate have apparently not made the desired impression. What has motivated patriotism and improved the military in the eyes of the Russian population is Putin's aggressive foreign policy, beginning with the invasion of Georgia in 2008. In annual Levada Center polls conducted between 1997 and 2007, no more than 35% of respondents supported conscription. After the successful five-day war with Georgia, support for conscription rose above 40%. In 2017, after three years of Russian-supported conflict in the Donbas, 61% of respondents agreed that they would support a family

192   *Roger R. Reese*

member obeying their draft summons. Only 23% acknowledged support for draft evasion, down from a high of 53% in 2006. The same poll reported that 84% of respondents claimed they would enlist if Russia were attacked. Five years later and nine months into the war with Ukraine, another Levada Center poll reported that the percentage of Russians who believed that "every real man should serve in the army" had dropped to 49%, and 13% considered military service to be meaningless and dangerous and thought it should be avoided. Interestingly, and worrisome for the army, support for service was strongest among people over age fifty-five (57%) but weakest among draft-age men (19%).[19]

Veterans as Instruments of Patriotism

Veterans, as living legacies of the war, have proved to be both a blessing and a curse to the Putin administration in its artless attempts to glorify the war in the name of national pride. Only since Putin has been in power has the Russian government publicly held up veterans as living role models for Russia. Speaking in Volgograd in 2003, on the sixtieth anniversary of the conclusion of the Battle of Stalingrad, Putin said of the war generation: "The experience of the unity that was demonstrated during the Great Patriotic War is especially valuable at present, when extremism and terrorism are rearing their heads in the world."[20] Three months later on Victory Day, Putin said:

> May 9th will always remain a glorious historic date: it reminds us of the prowess of the fighters who defeated fascism and saved humanity from slavery. The glorious memory of the feat of arms and labor of our compatriots for the sake of freedom and the happiness of future generations is still fresh in the hearts of all peoples. I'm convinced that the power and unity that our peoples demonstrated during the war years will be a good example for future generations to follow.[21]

Newspapers regularly publish a plethora of interviews of veterans around all the milestone dates associated with the war or national holidays. During the rest of the year, however, there is little mention of them.[22]

Unfortunately for the veterans, although Putin swore to fulfill the promises of social support that these men failed to receive under the Soviet regime, he has been as unable—or, some argue, as unwilling—to deliver as the Soviets had been. In the process, Putin validated the expectations of veterans yet discredited his government, whose critics point out that his actions do not correspond to his words.[23] Even as he raised their expectations, Putin, as if to minimize the import of their complaints and deflate their expectations, told veterans that the main reward for their suffering was the victory itself, and that whatever difficulties they still endure, it is minor compared to the war experience.[24]

Rather than simply basking in the glory of the victory and the praise showered on them three or four times a year, the dwindling number of veterans vent their anger at the continuing failure of the government to deliver benefits to which they feel entitled. Newspapers and broadcasters and internet news sources typically report veterans' claims of neglect around every holiday associated with the war.[25] Veterans have been known to sue local, regional, or the national government, citing the various legal statutes guaranteeing them apartments and pensions, in hopes that their suits will result in concrete action.[26] In 2011, one veteran sent his medals back to Moscow to protest the government's failure to provide him adequate housing.[27]

Further diminishing the status of veterans is a perceived lack of respect for elderly people in Russia. A poll taken in December 2013 revealed that 75% of respondents felt that the elderly—the war generation—were not respected in Russia.[28] The glorification of the war and veterans and the public complaints of the veterans about their unfulfilled entitlements have gotten to the point where people, especially the young, have become cynical. Veterans' voices fill the media with lament after lament of the dwindling respect among youth for veterans and for their absence of knowledge about and gratitude for the victory.[29] When a new memorial veterans' cemetery was opened in Moscow on June 22, 2013, a young journalist described it sarcastically as a "pet cemetery," resulting in a predictable wave of indignant protest from veterans.[30] This calls into question the efficacy of Putin's attempts to use the war to bring the younger generation to his side.

Other Complications to the Legacy: Popular Culture, Other Wars, and Stalin

Since the collapse of communism, films made for popular consumption have not always supported the heroic version of the legacy Putin wants to convey. Some movies are predictable action thrillers in which the Red Army is clearly in the right and the Nazis are pure evil. But for the last thirty years or so, more often than not, screenwriters and directors have portrayed the war in far more complex terms with myriad characters that do not fit neatly into the former narrative that treated all soldiers as heroes and the population as long-suffering and unfailingly patriotic. Issues of collaboration and the moral dilemmas faced by Soviet citizens under occupation, the continuing repression by the Soviet secret police during the war, and an ambivalent appreciation of what constitutes patriotism or cowardice and the true nature of the enemy leave the viewer uncertain as to who or what was right or wrong. These issues inhibit popular acceptance of the Great Patriotic War as an absolute anchor of identity for the contemporary Russian.[31]

Putin's attempt to highlight Russia's unity, suffering, and glory in World War II has to compete not only with all the distractions of popular culture but also with calls to honor veterans and the memory of other wars. Veterans of the Soviet-Afghan War who want to be acknowledged as patriots who did their duty, formed the Organization of Afghan War Veterans to represent their interests. Their efforts were rewarded in 2014 on the twenty-fifth anniversary of the withdrawal of Soviet troops from Afghanistan with an official ceremony at the Poklonnaia Gora war memorial in Moscow. Simultaneously, a special exhibition dedicated to the Afghan war was established at the Central Museum of the Great Patriotic War.[32] It is worth noting that the ceremony and exhibit to honor Afghan war veterans were at sites of commemoration of the Great Patriotic War. The thirtieth anniversary commemoration of the withdrawal from Afghanistan was also held at Poklonnaia Gora. As part of the ceremony, an aged World War II veteran was honored with a plaque.[33] Veterans of the Chechen Wars have formed an organization called Soldat to lobby for similar social guarantees allotted to veterans of the Great Patriotic War.[34]

Another complicating factor for Putin is how to place Stalin in the legacy of the war. Stalin's crimes against the people make it problematic to use him—the victorious war leader and Georgian—as a symbolic rallying point to create a new Russian national identity. Putin, reflecting an uncertain national sentiment, proved to be inconsistent in his stance on whether or how to credit Stalin for his contribution. At times, Putin has been soft on Stalin, portraying him as a unifying figure for the nation, but in the 2010s, after denouncing Stalin for the Katyn massacre, Putin started mentioning Stalin, the Communist Party, and the USSR far less when speaking of the war.[35] This omission caused a backlash from the Communist Party, which still insists on crediting all three for the victory. Others, particularly victims of Stalinist repression, whose stories are collected, publicized, commemorated, and archived by the organization Memorial, object to sanitizing Soviet history and want to claim that the victory was won despite Stalin and his mistakes.[36]

It is also a problem that a considerable number of people still see Stalin in a positive light regarding his role as commander in chief. A poll conducted in 2005 revealed that only 11% of respondents viewed Stalin's role in the war negatively, whereas 58% believed he made a major contribution to the victory.[37] What we see, then, is that Putin feels the need to co-opt Stalin's positives somehow without being tarred by the negatives. For a few years, he avoided highlighting Stalin's wartime role yet simultaneously did not deny that Stalin played an important part in the victory. By 2020, it became evident that Putin had shifted to an overtly pro-Stalin stance, not only because Stalin represents a successful authoritarian wartime leader but also because he presided over a unified body politic.

Competing Interpretations of the Legacy

Putin has had to contend with competing interpretations of the legacy of World War II. The Russian Orthodox Church gives God, the faith of the Russian people, and itself credit for the victory. Inferring that the enemies of the church were both Nazis and communists, a newspaper article proclaimed in 2006 that "Russia obtained the victory by prayers. And the lives that the country sacrificed during fighting and in the rear areas were necessary for establishing the Truth [of God] in the country and for the regeneration of people's souls."[38] The church's interpretation fully rejects the claims that the Communist Party saved the nation. The church challenges the line pushed by the Russian right and supported by Putin, which praises Russian patriotism and loyalty to the state above all else, and the church instead directs attention to the Russians' faith in the divine.

Also troublesome for Putin and his image of the war are Russia's monarchists, who have their own political party, For Faith and Fatherland. They launched a failed campaign to formally rehabilitate General Andrey Vlasov, who had been recruited out of a German prisoner of war camp in 1943 to form the anti-Soviet Russian Army of Liberation with volunteers from among Russian POWs. He was convicted of treason and hanged in 1946.[39] Making heroes of Russians who fought for Germany against the Red Army and communism challenged the image that Putin is trying to create of Russian national unity under the leadership of a strong state.

Then there is outright rejection of the anti-fascist legacy of the war by the radical right in Russian society. Russia has had various national socialist parties that use Nazi-like insignia as their symbols. The fringe right parties espouse racist, nationalist policies. Until they were suppressed in 2015, skinheads wearing Nazi regalia and emblems marched through the streets, brutalizing national minorities and foreigners with relative impunity.[40] They embraced the very values that the Russian people defeated and discredited in the Great Patriotic War. Putin outlawed all such neo-Nazi parties in the 2010s.

Some Russians combined their protests against Putin's annexation of the Crimea and sponsorship of the insurgency in the Donbas and Luhansk, and later the war in Ukraine, with a rejection of his patriotic spin on the memory of the Great Patriotic War. On September 2, 2014, a protester in St. Petersburg dressed in the colors of the Russian flag and tied her wrists with St. George's ribbons—a popular symbol of the victory.[41] A combat veteran of the war in Ukraine told a journalist in May 2023, "I don't understand when they compare the war in Ukraine and the Great Patriotic War. Then we defended our country and won, but now it's generally unclear what's happening." In contrast to Putin's intent, the veteran exclaimed, "What is happening now in Ukraine has nothing to do with May 9." Other veterans associated victory in 1945 with a rejection of war and the tragic human cost.[42]

One other problem is that since the Gorbachev era, many ugly truths about the war have been presented to the Russian people through solid, objective historical work. Thousands of scholarly books and memoirs have been published giving perspectives on the war previously suppressed. From the late 1980s until 2015, scholars and veterans told of the many failings and abuses of the army, party, and government that cost millions of people their lives. Scholars challenged cherished heroic myths, such as those of Zoe Kosmodemianskaia and the Panfilov Twenty-Eight.[43] Heroic suffering became unnecessary sacrifice. The sheen of the great victory lost some of its luster.

Contesting the Russian Memory of the War

Also vexing for Putin and Russia's nationalist right is the rejection of the Russian version of the legacy of the war by the now independent states of the former USSR. The legacy of the war, the Russians' attempt to impose their interpretation of it on others, and Putin's intent to destabilize Eastern Europe have created international tensions with the former Soviet republics of Estonia, Latvia, Lithuania, and Ukraine, all of which use their own interpretations to create anti-Russian national identities. In these states, pro-German veterans of the war, who fought against the Soviets, are celebrated at the grassroots. In accepting the Kremlin's invitation to attend the 2005 Victory Day celebration in Moscow, Latvia's president, Vaira Vike-Freiberga, said: "May 9 is not only the day of victory over fascism . . . it also represents the loss of independence for all three Baltic states. We have to show the world the other side of the date."[44]

As part of creating new national identities, the Baltic states joined the European Union and rejected the Soviet and Russian narratives of the Second World War,

The End of Glory? 197

earning their governments the distinction of being the first to be labeled fascist by Putin. High on their lists was the removal of Soviet monuments to World War II, which had been erected to remind the Baltics of their indebtedness for the sacrifices the USSR made to "liberate" them. Estonia removed the Bronze Soldier of Tallinn from Liberation Square in April 2007, which led to three days of rioting by of Russians living in Estonia and a massive cyberattack by Russia.[45] In 2023, the Latvian government decreed that all Soviet monuments be dismantled.

When former Soviet republics rewrite their histories, citizens who resisted the Soviets are now made heroes, even if they collaborated with the Nazis. Baltic veterans of the war who fought for the Germans against the Russians have begun to organize and seek public recognition for their anti-communist, anti-Soviet sacrifices. In many cases, these veterans are given positive acknowledgment by their governments. This has heightened tension with Putin's Russia. In 2009, the Russian foreign ministry protested the Estonian government's tacit support for a reunion of former Estonian SS veterans in the town of Sinimäe, a site of fierce World War II battles between the Red Army and German forces that included large numbers of Estonian volunteers. The SS veterans referred to themselves as fighters for freedom, which Russia described as blasphemous.[46]

Also to Russia's dismay, in March 2009, Latvians, without official endorsement, proudly celebrated the anniversary of the forming of the Fifteenth and Nineteenth Latvian Waffen-SS divisions. Although the Latvian government banned the veterans of these divisions from holding parades, they do so anyway without interference. Russian-speaking anti-fascist organizations in Latvia regularly protest these marches to no avail. Then, in 2010, the Latvian government successfully prosecuted Vasily Kononov, leader of a pro-Soviet commando unit in Latvia in 1944, for murdering nine civilians. To Russia's consternation, the European Court of Human Rights upheld the ruling.[47] Latvians also hold annual commemorations of their anti-Soviet partisans who fought Soviet reoccupation for several years after the war. The Russian government objects to Latvian and Estonian claims that the Soviet occupation of their countries was worse than that of the Germans.[48] Russia's protests fell on deaf ears. In 2012, the Latvian town of Bauska defiantly erected a monument to the Latvian Legion of the Waffen-SS, which bore an inscription dedicating it to "Bauska's defenders against the second Soviet occupation."[49]

In 2010, Ukraine named Stepan Bandera, the most well-known leader of the Organization of Ukrainian Nationalists (OUN), a hero of Ukraine and erected a statue of him in his hometown of Lviv. Ukrainians who collaborated with the Germans or served in their armed forces during World War II to fight the Soviet

Army are celebrated as anti-Russian heroes. Marches to celebrate the anniversary of the founding of the Ukrainian-manned Fourteenth Waffen-SS Division "Galicia" have been held annually in April in Lviv since the early 2010s and in Kyiv in 2021 (to the disapproval of President Volodymyr Zelensky). The public largely ignored the marches until the 2014 invasion of Crimea sparked wider interest.[50]

Similarly, Georgia and Uzbekistan have gradually de-Sovietized themselves. They have renamed towns and removed Soviet-era monuments, including those memorializing the Great Patriotic War. Those that the government has yet to remove have been subjected to vandalism.[51] All of these counternarratives to the Soviet/Russian version of the war were dutifully reported in the Russian media.

Both galling and irksome for Putin is that Europe in general has rejected the aspect of the legacy that justified Soviet occupation of Eastern Europe, a challenge to the idea that contemporary Russia has any right to dominate those areas. On July 3, 2009, the Parliamentary Assembly of the Organization for Security and Co-operation in Europe (OSCE) approved the Vilnius Declaration, which states that Nazi Germany and the Soviet Union, on the basis of the Molotov–Ribbentrop Pact, were equally guilty of unleashing the Second World War. It further endorsed designating August 23 (the day the pact was signed) as a day of remembrance for the victims of Nazism and Stalinism, which the Baltic states had already been observing. Lithuania subsequently adopted a law in 2008 to ban both Nazi and Soviet insignia as symbols of oppression.[52] By equating Nazism with communism, the Red Army with the German army, and Nazi conquest with Soviet "liberation," Estonia and Latvia, along with the rest of Eastern Europe as supported by the OSCE, have dismissed the claim that the Great Patriotic War freed them from totalitarian rule. They therefore feel no debt to Russia today, an attitude with which the younger generation of Russians feels some sympathy but Putin and Russian nationalists deplore.[53]

Legislative Attempts to Defend the Legacy

Between 2009 and 2024, more than half a dozen legislative measures have been introduced into Russia's State Duma to criminalize defaming the Putin administration's heroic version of the war. Suggested punishments ranged from fines, deportation, and up to five years in prison. Only in 2022 did these measures pass into law. Until then, every attempt to pass such laws erupted into a storm of protest that highlighted opposing viewpoints, exactly what Putin did not want.[54] In May 2009, as a reaction to the events in the Baltic states, President Medvedev set up a commission to investigate and analyze attempts to "falsify history against the interests of Russia." Simultaneously, the State Duma drafted a bill that would enable the state to punish people for "distorting the verdicts of the Nuremburg Trials," or rehabilitating the Nazis or "calling the actions of the Allied countries a crime."[55] Well before the legislative proposals became law, publishers, educators, and archivists felt pressured to not challenge the state's evolving interpretation of the legacy of World War II.

Nevertheless, Russian civic groups such as Memorial continued to publicize—until being shut down in February 2022—ugly and complicated truths about the war that challenged Putin's version and indeed gave strength to the views of the victims repressed by Stalin at home and abroad. For example, Memorial published an article on the seventy-fifth anniversary of the Molotov–Ribbentrop Pact in which it labeled the pact criminal and immoral for enabling the arrest and deportation of massive numbers of people from the Baltic states.[56] Russian liberals insist on seeing the magnitude of the USSR's wartime losses not as making the victory more glorious but as making Stalin's government guiltier. Rather than celebrating soldiers and civilians as heroes, they cast them as victims. In 2022, as Putin was putting the finishing touches on his authoritarian rule, the State Duma made defamation of the armed forces, including criticism of it in past wars, illegal. By October 2023, Russian courts had handled more than 8,000 charges of "discrediting the armed forces."[57]

In 2009, the Duma proposed a law that sought to defend the legacy beyond Russia's borders. If a country was found to promote or tolerate the denigration of the Soviet victory or comment favorably on the Nazis or German occupation, its ambassador could be expelled and diplomatic relations severed. Russians living abroad would be held accountable, as would foreign citizens, who would be declared persona non grata. Russians and foreigners alike, if convicted in Russia, were to be subject to serving from three to five years in prison. Public reaction to the proposed legislation was mixed. When polled, younger and more highly educated Russians expressed opposition to the law, but older and less educated Russians favored it.[58] Although the legislation was not approved, an air of self-censorship began to pervade Russian publishing houses. Another law was proposed to punish the "rehabilitation of Nazism," with fines of varying weight depending on the extent to which the perpetrator went to propagate the pro-Nazi views or defamation of the actions of the "anti-Hitler coalition." As expected, journalists and anti-Stalin civic groups protested this proposal.[59]

In another, although rather delayed, response to the Baltic states' revisionist interpretation of the legacy of World War II, Russia's State Duma, in September 2013, drafted a law to begin payment of allowances to the approximately 12,000 former Red Army veterans who had fought in World War II and now resided in the Baltic states. Latvia protested the wording of the preface to the draft law, which read, "Through the will of the political elite of the focus countries [the Baltic states], the defenders of the homeland [veterans] were suddenly turned into 'occupiers,' who would often be subject to prosecution. This happens amid the glorification of former Waffen-SS units, as well as local Nazi collaborators by the authorities of Vilnius, Riga and Tallinn."[60] Such language could be construed as a threat by Russia to intervene to defend the interests of Russians in the near abroad as they have done in Ukraine. Undeterred, as soon as the Russian draft law became known, several monuments to Soviet soldiers in Lithuania were vandalized, being spray-painted in the colors of the Lithuanian flag—yellow, red, and green.[61]

Like the Baltic states, Ukraine in the 2010s began the process of revising the Russian version of World War II by issuing new textbooks that eliminated the term "Great Patriotic War" and replaced it with "Second World War." The war is cast in the context of Ukrainian rather than Soviet history. Displays in schools honoring local World War II heroes are now framed in the blue and yellow of Ukraine's flag, no longer with Soviet red. Schoolbooks include positive coverage of the OUN. It describes them as fighters for Ukrainian freedom against the Soviet Union.[62] In 2024, Ukraine changed their celebration of Victory Day from May 9 to May 8, adopting the date the Germans first surrendered to the Western Allies. Putin abjectly failed to coerce these former Soviet republics into accepting the Russian version of the war and with it, Russia's right to dictate policy to them. Instead, they embraced Western Europe and continue to contradict Putin's version and defy his foreign policy.

The Acid Test: Using the Legacy of World War II to Justify the Invasion of Ukraine and Gain Popular Support

Using the labels fascist, Nazi, and neo-Nazi explicitly refers to World War II and the evils of Nazi Germany. Since the 1930s, the USSR labeled its enemies fascist to excuse all forms of repression. Under Stalin, the Soviets labeled the native political opposition in Soviet-occupied Eastern Europe fascist after the war as justification to disband their parties, arrest their leaders, and take power for the communists. Any group, regardless of its politics, was in danger of being called fascist and shut down. Putin has followed Stalin's precedent, labeling both foreign and domestic opponents to his regime fascist. The defamation of Ukraine as fascist began in 2008, when Ukraine disapproved of Russia's invasion of Georgia.

The End of Glory? 201

Putin's subsequent accusations of Ukraine being Nazi were meant to prepare the Russian people for aggression, which manifested in the annexation of Crimea in 2014. To signal that he did not accept as legitimate the ouster of their corrupt president, Viktor Yanukovych, by popular Ukrainian opposition, Putin called the Maidan revolt of 2013–2014 a fascist coup supported by NATO. His propaganda campaign may have helped reduce opposition to action against Ukraine. In 2013, polls showed that 75% of Russians were against using armed force against Ukraine, but by 2016, with the proxy war in the Donbas in progress, opposition fell to 57%–60% of respondents. Still, the majority of those polled saw no justification for military action.[63]

Russia's seizure of Crimea in 2014, Putin announced, was to defeat the "fascist revolutionaries" there. This, along with false claims of oppression of Russians, was an integral part of justifying the attack. Putin claimed that Russia's support of the insurgency in the Donbas, also in 2014, was to save the Russians there from pending genocide—another allusion to the Second World War—at the hands of Ukrainian fascists. Putin justified the all-out invasion of Ukraine in February 2022 as a "special military operation" against fascism. In his speech announcing the start of the invasion, he said the "goal is to protect the [Russian] people who are subjected to abuse, genocide from the Kyiv regime," which was supposedly a government of Nazis supported by NATO: "To this end, we will seek to demilitarize and de-nazify Ukraine and put to justice those that committed numerous bloody crimes against civilians, including Russian nationals."[64]

Putin's use of the word "fascism" and characterization of the Ukrainian government as variously neo-Nazi and Nazi were completely cynical and aimed primarily at Russians to justify aggression and mobilize popular support. That the West (and the rest of the world) would predictably reject his justification was inconsequential. The Nazi label is a way not only to stigmatize Ukrainian society by suggesting that it is permeated by anti-Semitic, racist members of the alt right, but also to efface the record of Ukrainians in the defeat of the Nazis. (Ukraine was one of the main theaters of war on the Eastern Front and suffered devastating destruction and loss of life.) Putin frames Ukraine's claim to sovereignty as disloyalty to his ideal of a Russian-dominated Greater Russia, but his rhetoric that the Ukrainians are not a separate people led many Russians to question the attack.

Indications of Russians' Attitudes to the War Based on Polling

It is impossible to tell how accurate poll results are because, since the suppression of anti-war protests, self-censorship may play a role in people's willingness to express their opinion. But the variety of different polling operations, both by state-owned and private organizations, provide parameters that lead to a general appreciation of national sentiment, particularly among different age groups. If any opinion is affected by social pressure and state sanctions, it has been the anti-war voice. Some people who are against the war refuse to participate in polling out of fear of retribution. The sociologist Lev Gudkov of the Levada Center estimates that between 13% and 15% of people called on the telephone for polls refuse to participate. Alexey Minyaylo, founder of the Chronicles polling agency, puts refusals of his polls at 10%. They and Vladimir Zvonsovsky of ExtremeScan polling believe this refusal rate has been constant since before the war. According to Gudkov, elderly women loyal to the authorities and young people "indifferent to everything except themselves" are most likely to decline to answer surveys, whereas Minyaylo thinks that with the onset of mobilization, reservists are unlikely to answer the phone and thus be polled.[65]

It is not clear how many Russians truly believe that Ukraine is a fascist state—especially because its president, Volodymyr Zelensky, is a Russian-speaking Ukrainian Jew whose grandfather fought against the Nazis in World War II and great-grandfather and great-uncles were murdered in the Holocaust. A large segment of the Russian population slavishly and unconditionally accepts whatever the pro-Putin media pumps out, ignoring or dismissing all contradictory evidence. A Levada Center poll of April 2022 revealed that, among the respondents aged eighteen to thirty-nine, 73% supported the "special military operation" to one degree or another. Simultaneously, those under forty had the highest proportion (about 20%) of those who definitely did not support "the actions of the Armed Forces of the Russian Federation on the territory of Ukraine," as the poll asked. Over half (56%) of those aged forty to fifty-four professed support for the actions in Ukraine, while 86% of those aged fifty-five and up supported the war.

Among respondents who identified themselves as Putin supporters, the level of support for the "special military operation," was 89%. Among respondents who supported the war, the dominant opinion (43%) was that Russia had launched a "special military operation" to "protect the Russian population, civilians of the LPR/DPR [Luhansk/Donetsk People's Republics]," followed by 25% who believed it was necessary to "prevent an attack on Russia," and 21% who agreed with the government that war was required to "get rid of nationalists, eradicate fascism, restore order." Of those who disapproved of Putin's policies in general, only 32% supported military action while 57% opposed it. When asked why they did not support the conflict in Ukraine, 43% of respondents said they were "against the war, people are dying, civilians are suffering," and 19% agreed that "this is another state, you cannot climb into another country, let them figure it out themselves."[66]

Two months after the Levada Center poll, the Chronicles polling agency conducted a telephone survey of 1,800 respondents in all regions of the Russian Federation. Its results showed that since April, the level of support for war in society had decreased by 9%, from 64% to 55%. One in seven of those who had supported the "special military operation" either became an opponent, doubted the need for the war, or refused to answer the question. When asked about the effects of the war on their lives, one in four (25.7%) reported that they had stopped communicating with close friends or relatives, and 43% experienced anxiety or bouts of depression (a 10% increase over May). When asked if they were prepared to sacrifice for the war, only 8.4% of those surveyed said they were ready to give more than a tenth of their income to the army, and almost two-thirds (63.4%) responded that they would not give anything. When asked what it would mean to them if Putin's stated goals were achieved, 55% said they could not conceive of any personal benefit; 28.5% thought that victory in the war would bring them peace, give them moral satisfaction, enable trips to relatives in Ukraine and the Commonwealth of Independent States (CIS), ensure security, normalize the economy, and end economic sanctions. Only 3.3% felt that victory would increase their pride, give Russia territory, strengthen Russia's international military and diplomatic positions, and equate to victory over Nazis.[67]

The Moscow Times revealed that a confidential poll conducted in July by the state-owned, all-Russian Public Opinion Research Center (*Vserossiiskii tsentr izucheniia obshchestvennogo mneniia*, VTsIOM) on behalf of the Kremlin delivered less positive findings: 30% of the polled population wanted the war to stop immediately. In the age group of eighteen to twenty-four years—the age group liable to conscription—56% were in favor of ending the war, whereas only 19% favored continued military action. Among Russians aged twenty-five to thirty-four—the age group with the most army reservists—43% supported an early end to the war, whereas 41% supported the continuation of hostilities.[68]

One month later, as casualties mounted, Putin ramped up his maximalist claims of intending to de-Nazify Ukraine in the interest of Russian security, yet support for the war steadily eroded. In August, the Russian Field Sociological Service conducted a survey which revealed that almost two-thirds of Russian men (62%) of military age wanted to avoid participating in the hostilities in Ukraine, if possible, while 29% did express a desire to fight. The group that had the largest contingent (37%) of people who expressed a willingness to fight were those least likely to be called upon—men aged forty-five to fifty-nine years. The number of people who would refuse to financially aid the war effort rose to 67%. The poll reported, on one hand, that nearly two-thirds of Russians would approve if Putin decided to stop the war in Ukraine and sign a peace deal without de-Nazifying the Ukrainian government. On the other hand, if Putin decided to launch a new offensive against Kyiv, 60% said they would support that. These respondents thought Putin knew best, and they would support whatever he decided to do. The Russian sociologist Lev Gudkov interpreted this seemingly contradictory response as follows: "This consensus was imposed on them, they agree with the authorities, but they are not going to pay for it: neither to participate in the military operation themselves, nor to sacrifice something for its sake."[69]

Elena Koneva, founder of the ExtremeScan polling agency, concluded that "real, conscious support" for the war in October 2022 was around 40%—not the oft-cited figure of 70%. Koneva's group arrived at the figure of 40% after six waves of polling showed 55% of respondents answered yes when directly asked if they back the war. However, when asked the questions "Are you willing to contribute financially to the Russian army? Do you think a Russian victory would personally benefit you? Are you ready to mobilize?" only 38% answered in the affirmative. Alexey Minyaylo's independent Chronicles polling agency settled on the figure of 41.9% support, also in October 2022.[70] "These polls" according to Yekaterina Schulmann, a political scientist and researcher at the Robert Bosch Academy in Berlin, "reflect Russian society as inert and frightened; a country with a broken back," and not a united mass of patriots inspired by the legacy of the Second World War. Two years into the war, a survey conducted by Russian field sociologists in February 2024 showed that Russian citizens increasingly regret Putin's invasion of Ukraine: 38% of citizens said they would reverse the decision to launch a "military operation" if it were possible. In March 2022, only 28% of those polled would have undone the attack. In that same time frame, the pro-war segment of the population shrank from 57% to 49%.[71]

Polling evidence thus suggests that after two decades of Putin's nationalist, anti-fascist propaganda, the believers are concentrated in the older generation, whose members are closer to the Second World War through direct memory or their parents, in the nationalist Russian extreme right of all ages, and in the less educated and economically disadvantaged. In July 2022, only 9%–10% of pensioners were anti-war.[72] Among Russians that do believe the propaganda, an insignificant few have thought it sufficiently important to volunteer to fight—in contrast to their great-grandparent's generation, who volunteered by the millions to fight Nazi Germany.

If the majority of Russians do believe Putin, their passivity in the face of the supposed Nazi threat at their doorstep is telling. By their failure to volunteer for military service to fight in 2014 or 2022, the younger generation has demonstrated that the legacy of German fascism and the Nazi invasion of the USSR resonates only superficially, if at all. There is a pronounced generation gap between believers and non-believers in Putin's propaganda. The younger generation is far more skeptical. They assign the pejorative nickname "*vatnik*" to those—including their parents—whom they see as being emotionally trapped in the past and willfully ignorant of the true nature of Putin's domestic and foreign policies. Their elders primarily receive their information from state-controlled media and trust this official information. Putin's reference to the war and xenophobic rhetoric have succeeded in convincing those parents that their children and others who are against the war should be considered traitors.[73]

Confidence in Russia's victory and anticipation of a rapid end to the "special military operation" is vital to pro-war Russians' outlook. The war's protraction has reduced faith in victory and willingness to support the special military operation. The conclusions of ExtremeScan's researchers align with the opinions of other independent and even state-funded polling outlets: among all respondents, negative changes in their lives—such as anxiety disorders or a drop in material well-being—greatly reduce their support for the war. The most significant factor in declining support for the war among those polled is the anticipation that their quality of life will deteriorate further. The most significant and stable sociodemographic factor is that of age: middle-aged respondents are less inclined to support the war, and young people are radically less supportive of the war than older respondents.[74]

To be sure, millions of Russians support the war against Ukraine, but it is unclear whether Putin's linking it to World War II is an important factor. Evidence gathered from journalists' interviews and social media in the first nine months of the war indicated that Russian nationalism and Putin's narrative of Russian victimization by the West influences people's outlook the most. A woman who spearheaded a donation drive to buy soldiers gear criticized those who refused to contribute, saying, "I think when a NATO tank arrives . . . you won't be able to stop them." She was angry that, in her estimation, 85% of Russians did not care about the war or the soldiers: "I clearly understand that there is not just a small, small-town war going on, but a world war with the West, and we must endure."[75]

As indicated in polling, interviewees who were fifty years or older were most often ardent supporters of the "special military operation." They would repeat almost verbatim the very phrases they heard on propaganda TV: "Do you want NATO missiles under our noses?" When asked if they accepted the government's claim that it was a preventive war, they gave a textbook answer: "Where have you been for eight years? 14,000 civilians died in Donbas." A young man told a journalist, "My mother served in the military, and she talks to me in phrases from the TV." When the journalist asked, "Like what?" the young man said, "Do you want NATO to come and attack our house?" and "You support Nazis."[76] Pollsters credit the regime's claim that Russia is now fighting NATO as having prevented a more drastic fall in support for continuing the war.

Co-Opting Important Dates to Link the Great Patriotic War to the Current War

To clearly link the legacy of World War II with the ongoing Ukraine war, Putin co-opted Victory Day in 2022. Until 2015, Victory Day was not observed as a monumental event. Before Putin appropriated Victory Day by introducing the ribbon of St. George and other symbols into the decorations and monopolizing public ceremonies, the day had been, from the 1960s until 1991, not a day for parades, but a time for people, veterans, and their families to gather and reflect on their personal part in the collective effort of the Soviet people. After the collapse of the USSR, it became a day of family remembrance. Putin also appropriated Victory Day's march of the so-called Immortal Regiment. This march began spontaneously as a grassroots movement in 2012, when people paraded locally while carrying photos of their families' veterans of the Second World War. The march was meant to publicly honor their family members as individuals with names and faces and who had endured the war in millions of different ways. Participation was voluntary and genuine, and turnout was large. In 2021, 88% of Russians polled claimed to have had a relative serve in the war. In 2022, local governments provided special mass-produced frames for families to carry their veterans' photos in, complete with St. George's ribbon décor and Za motifs (where "Za" stands for peace, for Putin, for victory). The parades became officially sponsored by various organizations, which are provided with portraits and require their members or employees to march.

Putin's use—or abuse—of Victory Day did not please everyone, indicating that not all Russians have a knee-jerk patriotic response to Putin's waving the bloody shirt. According to Victor Vakhshtayn, dean of the Faculty of Social Sciences at

The End of Glory? 207

Moscow School of Social and Economic Sciences, many people were offended by Putin's efforts to monopolize the celebrations and to define a new state-centered narrative of the meaning of the victory:

> [From that moment] some people began to perceive what is happening as a defilement, an attempt by the state to "put its paw" on their own memory of the war, the memory of their families. A serious moral conflict appears between those people for whom May 9 is the last thing that reconciles them with the Russian state, becomes a source of patriotic unity, and those for whom May 9 is still the memory of the family that the state is trying to take away and say: "This is not your grandfather, this is a great people, whose heirs are now sitting in the Kremlin." After 2015, Victory Day became a much more ambivalent holiday than it was even in the 1990s.[77]

Vakhshtayn believes that Putin's propaganda effort to draw a direct parallel between the events of the Second World War and the war in Ukraine, "when everything is called 'de-Nazification,' was an almost farcical attempt to present it as a second crusade, an attempt to 'repeat.'" He thought this began the desacralization of May 9, that the day has been cheapened and ceases to be significant for some families and is instead seen as a tool of manipulation. Some began to equate the celebration of victory in World War II with Russian aggression.[78]

Irena Shcherbakova, a historian who worked for Memorial before Putin closed it down at the start of the war, agreed with Vakhshtayn. She states that many people, especially of the generation whose parents had lived through the war, became dismayed when Putin changed the narrative of the war from a complex one of human courage, suffering, and sacrifice, with its attendant crimes, atrocities, and mistakes, to a simple one of a heroic people led to victory by a powerful state headed by great men. Roman Guliaev, professor of political philosophy, observed a disjuncture in the popular treatment of the Second World War and the war in Ukraine. Since 2000, Russians have been given a generalized image of the war: from the difficulties of the first years and defeats, through a turning point, to victory. Presented in general terms and cleansed of everything inconvenient, it is a redemptive narrative. But the reality of the war in Ukraine has proven to be anything but redemptive. Guliaev, Vakhshtayn, and Shcherbakova all considered this problematic for Putin's messaging.[79]

Alexey Minyaylo expressed his take on the legacy of the war thus: "Both my grandfathers fought in World War II, and they defeated Hitler, they didn't run from him, they actually ran towards him. So now my duty is to defeat Putin, who is

Hitler's spiritual successor."[80] Interestingly, on Victory Day in 2022, the news source *Meduza* interviewed five survivors of the war, aged seventy-eight to ninety-four. All accepted that the war in Ukraine was necessary if Putin said so, but without exception, they regretted that it had come to war. None repeated any heroic platitudes about the Great Patriotic War. Others who had relatives who had served in the war were disgusted by Putin's co-opting of Victory Day. Anastasia, a Muscovite, interviewed in 2023, said, "My attitude towards Victory Day hasn't changed since the start of the war, but my attitude towards the authorities has. They're clumsily trying to manipulate people by interweaving the achievements of the USSR in the Second World War [with narratives about contemporary Russia]." Tatiana, interviewed in Ekaterinburg, said: "[My attitude toward May 9] has changed dramatically. I feel that the people behind this war have destroyed one of the topics that was most sacred to me. I always considered this holiday one of the most important ones of the year; the songs and films about war always touched me and brought tears to my eyes. Now we've betrayed the memory of our ancestors."[81]

Not only did Putin co-opt Victory Day, but in November 2022, he used Mother's Day to stage a meeting with women said to be the wives and mothers of soldiers killed in Ukraine. During his meeting with this handpicked group, Putin reiterated his de-Nazification message to equate the deaths of their husbands and sons with the deaths of soldiers in World War II, deaths for which no mother dared condemn the government. He told the women that their sons and husbands were fighting Nazis. He blamed the West for the war, saying, "We are not at war with the Ukrainians, but with those who pay them." The men who died, died heroically for a purpose. Putin used the occasion to suggest that anti-war people were unpatriotic, saying, "Today's events are the path to purification. The key to our success is unity."[82] The kind of unity that the Great Patriotic War supposedly had generated.

Actions Speak Louder than Words

Alexei Astashov, a veterinarian from Khabarovsk, felt compelled to volunteer for the "special military operation," in February 2022 after watching Putin's televised speech announcing the start of the invasion. He enlisted on a short-term contract "to beat the Nazis and defend the Russian world," thinking he would be helping to liberate the Donetsk and Luhansk People's Republics (DPR and LPR). However, when he found himself in the battle for Kharkiv, he began to have doubts. "There was confusion in my soul. I understood about imperial ambitions, I realized that I was a participant, in fact, in a civil war." His doubts mounted about

The End of Glory? 209

the justification of the war over the next few weeks, and eventually he went home and refused to go back to the army, arguing that he had been misled into volunteering.[83] Astashov was not alone; thousands of other Russian soldiers went to war with the same motivation as he, but on seeing the situation for themselves, turned against the war. One soldier, who was punished for merely asking to be sent home, told a journalist in July 2022:

> I had a friend who really wanted to go [to war], as I did. At that moment we were thinking the same thing. And the realization [when we arrived in Ukraine] hit us at the same time, give or take an hour. I said to him, "You do realize we're the fascists?" He said, "I was afraid of saying the same thing to you. I thought you'd shoot me. Yes, we're the fascists, I'm aware of that. I'm ashamed that I've been blind to it this whole time. And that I needed to see it for myself before I realized."[84]

Public displays of support for the war are almost exclusively related to Putin's *Za* campaign (for peace, for Putin, for victory), awash in the white, red, and blue of the Russian flag and the orange and black of the ribbon of St. George; they are always sponsored by local governments and state institutions. Counterprotesters in October 2022 pushed back, marching with placards reading "Security! Employment! Wages!" which in Russian all start with "Za."[85] Nonetheless, Putin chose to rely more and more on the legacy of the Great Patriotic War to promote support for the Ukraine war as the conflict dragged on longer than he had anticipated. He added to the narrative of the invasion of Ukraine that it was a preemptive strike to prevent a 1941-like attack on Russia, portraying it as an existential threat.

A smattering of soldiers involved in the invasion of Ukraine visibly embraced the legacy of World War II. During the first weeks of the war, a handful of Russian troops flew the old Soviet flag from their vehicles, recalling Russia's last great military victory. By May, however, the Russian flag had become the soldiers' banner of choice. Others used the de-Nazifying rhetoric to justify terrorizing the Ukrainian population and to assert Russian domination through both random and targeted looting, rape, and mass murder.[86]

Many Russians do not believe the claims that Ukraine is fascist and that there is a Nazi threat to Russia, and they instead see that Putin adopted these claims to cement his authoritarian power. This is evidenced by the flight from the country of an estimated 500,000 or more educated, middle-class Russian men, including army reservists and men eligible for the draft in 2022. These men, some with their families, joined an estimated 1.1 million Russians who had emigrated since Russia's seizure of Crimea. The prosperous, educated, liberal middle class, which stands to suffer from Western sanctions, largely does not believe the propaganda, and it is they who openly protest the war, risking beatings, arrest, and termination from their jobs. Several hundred thousand more young men fled Russia when mobilization was announced because they did not want to be sent to fight an unjust war. They rejected the claims that Russia was in danger of fascist attack and that Ukraine is a Nazi state, and they dismissed Putin's claims of genocide. They admire the West.[87]

The anti-war movement, which manifested immediately at the announcement of Russia's 2022 invasion of Ukraine and has resulted in more than 20,000 arrests by 2024, is further evidence that many Russians reject the state's narrative. Mass demonstrations were held in Moscow and St. Petersburg in February and March 2022 before being suppressed by riot police. Social media was rife with anti-war sentiments. Draft-age men fire-bombed several score recruitment centers across Russia to disrupt the draft and mobilization. A nationwide anti-war feminist movement was founded on the internet within hours of the invasion.[88] Suspicious fires at government and military installations and lone-wolf attacks on police suggested the existence of an underground resistance.

To counter the anti-war challenge to its narrative, the Putin regime outlawed all criticism of the "special military operation" and criminalized calling it a war. Threats of expulsion from university were used to keep a lid on youth opposition; anti-war faculty were dismissed. A second wave of anti-war protests erupted in October 2022, when the Ministry of Defense announced a partial mobilization of reservists. Hundreds of thousands more men fled the country. The Path Home, an anti-war movement among wives of mobilized reservists, arose in 2023, when it was announced that mobilized reservists were to serve for the duration of the war, as during the Second World War.

The Kremlin's attempt to dehumanize Ukrainians by labeling them Nazis received a mixed reaction from the people it was most necessary to persuade—Russian soldiers and their mothers. Many soldiers in the first wave of the invasion experienced cognitive dissonance due to the stiff resistance not only of the Ukrainian army but also from ordinary Ukrainians, who did not welcome the soldiers as liberators but took up arms against them. The Russian soldiers reacted by not pressing the attack, deserting, surrendering to the Ukrainian army, or wrecking their vehicles to prevent further action. Some soldiers' morale fell so low they murdered their own officers, unconvinced of the necessity or justice of the war. Hundreds of Russian National Guardsmen (Rosgvardiia) refused to be trans-

The End of Glory? 211

ferred to fight in Ukraine. Some army officers resigned their commissions in disgust, while others flatly refused to participate in the invasion. Thousands of reservists ignored instructions to report to their local military commissions to update their files. Hundreds of active-duty soldiers refused orders to deploy to Ukraine.

In September 2022, the Ukrainian army set up a telephone hotline for Russian soldiers to call to arrange their surrender. By the end of January 2023, 6,543 soldiers had called it. Hundreds of anti-Putin Russians went so far as to create a detachment within the Ukrainian army.[89] Hundreds of serving soldiers petitioned to have their contracts canceled, and hundreds of conscripts petitioned to do alternative service. Others have refused to renew their contracts after having fought the "fascists" in Ukraine. The Putin regime resorted to offering fantastically high enlistment bonuses to get volunteers to sign up to fight in Ukraine for as few as three months; it also started recruiting from prisons. Financial inducements proved to be more effective at generating volunteers (tens of thousands more people "volunteered") than did the appeal to the legacy of the Great Patriotic War. Overall, motivation on the part of soldiers and junior officers to "de-Nazify" Ukraine was and remains low. By the end of 2023, nearly 5,000 soldiers had deserted. The press reports trials of deserters weekly, hoping to deter further desertions.[90]

Conclusion

Putin's regime defined the legacy of the Great Patriotic War as supportive of unity under an authoritarian state through shared sacrifice and patriotic valor, and it exploited this legacy to mobilize support for aggression against Ukraine and rejection of the West. But this attempt has been undermined by generational change, widespread ignorance of the history of the war, freedom of speech and the press (until 2022), and the availability of alternative and conflicting interpretations of the legacy. In the age of global social media and interconnectedness, when people have many options for information, and given Russians' freedom to travel, alternative views are widely accessible. The variety of different political outlooks inhibits a single interpretation of the Great Patriotic War from satisfying everyone, perhaps not even a majority. In some ways, the attempt to keep the legacy alive is a handicap, especially regarding public confidence in the state's ability or willingness to fulfill its promises to veterans and the prospect of long-term sacrifice.

The Great Patriotic War once stood unchallenged as the greatest accomplishment for the good of the Russian-led Soviet Union, and its legacy formed the basis of a positive common Soviet identity. But since the disintegration of the Soviet Union, this interpretation has been widely contested. On the political right, it was contested by the national socialist political movement, as well as by skinheads who adopted Nazi clothing, symbols, and slogans, and espoused overtly anti-Semitic and anti-Muslim sentiments with Nazi racial undertones. The Russian Orthodox Church had its own take on the legacy that challenges the supremacy of the state in the victory. On the political left, meanwhile, the legacy has been challenged by pro-democracy, anti-communist, anti-Stalinist, anti-Putin liberals. Human rights organizations have highlighted the dirty deeds of the Stalin era, and the history profession has reevaluated many myths of the war tarnishing its glory. Further to the left, communists want to fully rehabilitate Stalin as a great wartime leader and savior of the nation, which alienates progressive Russians. In the middle are Russians whose family memories contradict Putin's state-centered heroic narrative.

The legacy is also disputed from abroad, with Europe, Ukraine, and the Baltic states pairing the Nazis and Soviets as equals in oppression. Eastern Europeans responded to Putin's war against Ukraine by accelerating the pace at which they removed monuments to their Red Army "liberators." Polish protesters doused the Russian ambassador with blood-red paint when he tried to lay a wreath at the foot of a monument in the cemetery of Soviet World War II dead in Warsaw. Of all the former Soviet republics, only Tajikistan held a Victory Day parade in 2022. The French have not invited representatives from Russia to observe their annual Victory in Europe Day festivities since 2022. Kazakhstan, Azerbaijan, and Uzbekistan, participants in the victory over Germany as Soviet Republics, spoke out against Russia's invasion of Ukraine. Nearly all the former Soviet republics banned the use of the letter Z in the manner used in Za propaganda.

If Putin's Z for the Za propaganda campaign was meant to unite the Russian people behind him and mobilize them to participate in the war, it has failed. However, if it was intended to be a wedge to divide the population to identify those who support him as patriots and to marginalize those who oppose him by marking them as traitors, then it has been a success. A large part of the post-Soviet generation of Russians is simply not invested in the legacy of the war to the degree that would compel them to support Putin's belligerent foreign policy. Many Russians reject Putin's attempt to manipulate them with a distorted memory of World War II. Although public dissent is brutally suppressed and the orchestrated displays of support for Putin and the war give the impression of societal support, passive resistance is evident, and in private, opinion of the war remains divided. Protests against the war in Ukraine and the active and passive resistance shown

The End of Glory?   213

by hundreds of thousands of Russians at home and abroad challenge the Kremlin's claim of fascism on the border as a *casus belli*. New anti-war graffiti appears every day. Green anti-war ribbons are tied on objects in public places. And in January 2023, flowers, teddy bears, and children's toys amassed at the foot of monuments to victims of political oppression and monuments to the Ukrainian poets Larysa Kosach-Kvitka in Moscow and Taras Shevchenko in St. Petersburg and other Russian cities after a missile strike on an apartment building killed dozens of Ukrainian civilians. All these signs of resistance highlight the fact that Putin failed to make the legacy of the Great Patriotic War a mobilizing and unifying shibboleth for twenty-first-century Russia.[91]

NOTES

1. Roger Markwick, "The Great Patriotic War in the Soviet and Post-Soviet Collective Memory," in Dan Stone, ed., *The Oxford Handbook of Postwar European History* (Oxford University Press, 2012), 692, 693.

2. Markwick, "The Great Patriotic War," 694–707; Jonathan Brunstedt, *The Soviet Myth of World War II: Patriotic Memory and the Russian Question in the USSR* (Cambridge University Press, 2021).

3. "Kak meniaetsia otnoshenie rossiian k Velikoi Otechestvennoi voine iz-za voiny v Ukraine? Otvechaiut istoriki, sotsiolog i filosof," *Meduza.io*, May 8, 2022.

4. Nina Tumarkin, *The Living and the Dead: The Rise and Fall of the Cult of World War II in Russia* (Harper Collins, 1994).

5. Anna Arutunyan, "Sacred Beliefs," *Moscow News*, May 13, 2013. A note on translations is appropriate here. I assume responsibility for all of my translations. The reader can tell if a translation is mine by the endnote. If the note source is in Russian, then I have translated the quote; however, if the note is in English, though it be a Russian source, then I have used the provided translation.

6. Olga Kucherenko, "That'll Teach'em to Love Their Motherland! Russian Youth Revisit the Battles of World War II," *Journal of Power Institutions in Post-Soviet Societies*, no. 12 (2011), https://doi.org/10.4000/pipss.3866.

7. "Red Square Hosts Historic Parade," *Moscow News*, November 7, 2011.

8. Vadim Telitsyn, "Preodolenie smuty," *Kareliia*, no. 123 (1401), November 3, 2005; *Literaturnaia gazeta*, no. 45 (6197), November 6, 2008.

9. Oleg Artiukov, "Mournful Day for Russia: 61 Years Ago, Great Patriotic War Started," *Pravda.ru*, June 22, 2002.

10. Olga Kalashnikova, "Impact of War Losing Its Effect on Youth," *St. Petersburg Times*, 1809 (17), May 7, 2014.

11. Sergei Vasilenkov, "'Creative Class' Has Its Heroes," *Pravda.ru*, August 8, 2013; Levada Centre, "Russians are Most Proud of Victory in Great Patriotic War and Accession of Crimea," JAM News, https://jam-news.net/levada-center-russians-are-most-proud-of

-victory-in-great-patriotic-war-and-accession-of-crimea/; "Great Victory: The Key Event of the 20th Century in the Russian History," WCIOM, https://wciom.com/press-release/great-victory-the-key-event-of-the-20th-century-in-the-russian-history, June 23, 2020.

12. "Glass Bottles, Cars Banned for Victory Day," *St. Petersburg Times*, 1809 (17), May 8, 2014.

13. Vasilenkov, "'Creative Class' Has Its Heroes."

14. *Moscow News*, January 1, 2014.

15. Igor Bukker, "Should Russians Be Ashamed of Their Patriotism?", *Pravda.ru*, November 30, 2012.

16. "Russian Patriotism Has Fallen during Putin's Rule—Poll," *RIA Novosti*, November 19, 2013. The Levada Center is a scholarly Russian polling organization that also does sociological research. It is completely independent of the government and is known for its integrity and resistance to political influence.

17. Victor Davidoff, "Putin Shifts Focus of Patriotism," *St. Petersburg Times*, 1810 (18), May 14, 2014.

18. "Army 20 Percent Understaffed," *Moscow News.ru*, June 9, 2012; Aleksandras Budrys, "Over 240,000 Russian Men Dodged Draft Last Year," *Moscow News.ru*, March 13, 2013.

19. Matthew Bodnar, "Russians Learn to Love the Army," *Moscow Times.com*, February 20, 2017; "Levada: Half of Russians Believe that 'Every Real Man Should Serve in the Army,'" *Novaya gazeta Evropa.eu*, December 9, 2022.

20. "Russia Remembers Stalingrad," *Russia Journal*, February 2, 2003.

21. "Vladimir Putin Congratulates CIS Leaders and WWII Veterans on Victory," *Pravda.ru*, May 9, 2003.

22. *Argumenty i Fakty* (aif.ru), September 13, 2014, is representative of national government owned and pro-Putin news sources in its coverage of veterans. The entire run of *Kareliia* in 2010 conforms to the pattern of coverage asserted above.

23. Aleksandr Golts, "For Whom the Drum Rolls," *St. Petersburg Times*, 34, (1068), May 10, 2005.

24. "Reception for Veterans on Victory Day in the Kremlin," *Pravda.ru*, May 9, 2003.

25. "Veterany protestuiut," *Kareliia*, no. 38 (1316), April 12, 2005; Tat'iana Romanenko, "Trudnaia pobeda v dolgoi voine," *Arsen'skie vesti*, no. 9 (1093), January 29, 2014.

26. Tat'iana Romanenko, "My pobedili i my pobedim!", *Arsen'skie vesti*, no. 19 (1051), May 8, 2013.

27. Ksenia Obraztsova, "World War II Veterans Only Remembered on Victory Day," *Pravda.ru*, May 17, 2011.

28. "Russians Do Not Trust Each Other—Report," *RIA Novosti*, December 12, 2013.

29. Olga Savka, "The Truth About WWII Gets Perverted in Today's World," *Kommuna.ru*, May 7, 2003.

30. Vasilenkov, "'Creative Class' has its heroes."

31. Mark H. Teeter, "Training an Eye on Russia's Post-War Chaos," *Moscow News*, December 20, 2010; L. Morozova, film review of "Svoi," *Karelia*, no. 11 (1289), February 3, 2005; Anna Arutunyan, "'Stalingrad:' Saving Katya, or saving Russia?" *Moscow News*, October 25, 2013.

The End of Glory?   215

32. "Afghan Veterans Ask to Revise Negative Assessment of War," *Pravda.ru*, February 11, 2014.

33. Elisabeth Sieca-Kozlowski, "Photo-Gallery - 30th Anniversary of the Withdrawal of the Soviet Troops from Afghanistan, Moscow, 14th and 15th February 2019," *Journal of Power Institutions of Post-Soviet Societies*, no. 20/21 (2019).

34. "Piket protesta vo Vladivostoke," *Arsen'evski vesti*, no. 38 (1122), September 17, 2014.

35. Alexandra Odynova, "A Sharp Ideological Turn Against Stalin," *St. Petersburg Times*, 1575 (36), May 21, 2010.

36. Alina Lobzina, "Russian History - Glory or Shame?" *Moscow News*, July 26, 2011; Iurii Trifonov, "Delo voennykh," *Arsensk'ie vesti*, February 19, 2014.

37. Vladimir Griaznevich, "A System Dedicated to Preserving Power Is Prone to External Threats," *St. Petersburg Times*, 1742 (1), January 16, 2013.

38. Dmitrii Sudakov, "Hitler's Invasion of USSR Revived Russian Orthodox Church," *Pravda.ru*, September 13, 2006. The rear area is the area behind the front lines. It refers to the logistical and civilian support for the front lines.

39. Valeria Korchagina and Andrei Zolotov, "It's Too Early to Forgive Vlasov," *St. Petersburg Times*, 719 (86), November 6, 2001.

40. Otto Lasis, "Russian Fascism Worse than German," *Russia Journal*, no. 439, October 3, 2002.

41. The Order of St. George, from which comes the George Ribbon, dates back to the tsarist era. It was awarded in four grades, the first being Russia's highest award for military valor. The medal was suspended on a ribbon of alternating black and orange stripes.

42. "Nikakikh, 'na Berlin' i 'mozhem povtorit' v tvoei kartine mira net," *Verstka*, May 9, 2023.

43. Stephen M. Norris, "War, Cinema, and the Politics of Memory in Putin 2.0 Culture," in Anton Weiss-Wendt and Nanci Adler, eds., *The Future of the Soviet Past: The Politics of History in Putin's Russia* (Indiana University Press, 2021), 170–190.

44. "Victory Day Irks Baltics," *St. Petersburg Times*, 1035 (1), January 14, 2005.

45. Steven Lee Myers, "Russia Rebukes Estonia for Moving Soviet Statue," *New York Times*, April 27, 2007. The original "Bronze Soldier" was blown up in May 1946 as an act of resistance by a handful of Estonian youths.

46. Dmitrii Sudakov, "Russia Begins to Lose Temper as Estonia Continues to Glorify Nazism," *Pravda.ru*, July 7, 2009.

47. Iulia Latynina, "The Red Partisans," *St. Petersburg Times*, 42 (1581), June 11, 2010, 15.

48. Vadim Trukhachev, "Fascism in Europe Acceptable as Long as It Angers Russia," *Pravda.ru*, March 16, 2010.

49. "Latvia Unveils Monument to Nazi Butchers," *Pravda.ru*, September 18, 2012.

50. Cnaan Lipshsiz, *Times of Israel*, May 4, 2021; *Russian Times*, April 28, 2014.

51. "Georgia Bans Soviet Orders Along with Nazi Award Pins," *Pravda.ru*, December 6, 2013; *Pravda*, November 11, 2010; "V Gruzii snesli poamiatnik Stalinu," *Lenta.ru*, January 1, 2014.

52. "Lithuania Equates Soviet Symbols with Nazism," *Pravda.ru*, June 17, 2008.

53. "Duma Outraged by Estonian Parliament's Statement Equalizing Nazi and Soviet Regimes," *Pravda.ru*, June 19, 2002; "Europe Loses Its Mind Equating Stalinism to Nazism," July 6, 2009; "Georgia Bans Soviet Orders Along with Nazi Award Pins."

216   Roger R. Reese

54. Anna Arutunian, "Commission to Defend Russia's View of History," *Moscow News*, May 21, 2009; Dmitrii Sudakov, "Russia to Introduce Criminal Punishment for Rehabilitating Nazism in Former USSR," *Pravda.ru*, April 23, 2009; Sergei Balashov, "War Thought-Crimes," *Russiaprofile.org*, May 15, 2009; "Rejection of USSR's Victory in WWII Should Be Punishable, Russian Minister Says," *Pravda.ru*, February 26, 2009.

55. Arutunian, "Commission to Defend Russia's View of History."

56. "K 75-letiiu pakta Ribbentropa-Molotova," *Arsen'skie vesti*, no. 35 (1119), August 27, 2014.

57. "Russian Liberals See Nothing Holy in Great Patriotic War," *Politonline*, January 30, 2014; "V rossiiskie sudy postupilo bol'she 8 tysiach administrativnykh del o 'discreditatsii' armii," *Mediazona*, October 10, 2023.

58. Sudakov, "Russia to Introduce Criminal Punishment;" Balashov, "War Thought-Crimes"; "Rejection of USSR's Victory in WWII Should Be Punishable, Russian Minister Says."

59. "Russia's Upper House Proposes Outlawing 'Rehabilitation' of Nazism," *Moscownews.ru*, June 27, 2013.

60. "Baltic States Opposed to Russia's Moves against Glorification of Nazism," *Pravda.ru*, September 30, 2013.

61. "Russia Sends Note to Lithuania over Desecrated WWII Memorial," *Russia Today*, September 18, 2014.

62. Vadim Trukhachev, "Ukraine Glorifies Nazism and Defames Great Patriotic War in New History Books," *Pravda.ru*, June 16, 2009.

63. Elena Vladimirova, "'Eto passivnaia forma privychnogo souchastiia v prestupleniiakh gosudarstva' Sotsiolog Lev Gudkov—o tom, pochemu mnogie rossiiane smirilis' s voinoi i prodolzhaiut podderzhivat' vlast'", *Meduza.io*, July 18, 2022.

64. TASS, March 14, 2022.

65. Nadia Evangelian and Andrei Tkchenko, "The First Phase of a Special Military Operation in the Minds of Russians," https://www.extremescan.eu/post/6-respondents -cooperation-in-surveys-on-military-operations; "Bednost' protiv televizora," https:// www.chronicles.report/; https://www.levada.ru/2017/05/04/natsionalnaya-gordost-2.

66. "The Conflict with Ukraine." https://www.levada.ru/en/2022/04/11/the-conflict -with-ukraine.

67. *Moscow Times.ru*, July 13, 2022.

68. Farida Rustanmova and Maxim Tovkaylo, "What Secret Russian State Polling Tells Us about Support for the War," *Moscow Times.com*, December 6, 2022.

69. Vladimirova, "'Eto passivnaia forma privychnogo souchastiia v prestupleniiakh gosudarstva' Sotsiolog Lev Gudkov . . ."

70. Svetlana Shkolnikova, "Startup Pollsters Challenge Accepted Wisdom on Russians' War Support," *Moscow Times.com*, October 11, 2022.

71. Rustanmova and Tovkaylo, "What Secret Russian State Polling Tells Us"; "Dolia rossiian, schitaiushchikh voinu oshibkoi, dostigla pochti 40%," *Moscow Times.ru*, February 26, 2024.

72. Vladimirova, "'Eto passivnaia forma privychnogo souchastiia v prestupleniiakh gosudarstva' Sotsiolog Lev Gudkov."

The End of Glory?   217

73. Uliana Pavlova, "Putin Is the Only Leader They've Known. And They're Done with Him," *Politico*, April 7, 2022; James Beardsworth, "'My Father Said I'm a Traitor Who Should be Shot First': War in Ukraine Splits Russian Families," *Moscow Times.com*, March 15, 2022; "Russian Actress Criticizes Famous Father's Support for Ukraine War," *Moscow Times.com*, March 22, 2022; Nadezhda Svetlova, translated by Eilish Hart, "'When the Blitzkrieg Failed, He Started to Have Doubts': The Kremlin's Invasion of Ukraine Put Some Russians at Odds with Their Loved Ones. For Others, It Brought Them Together," *Meduza.io*, March 10, 2022; Sasha Sivtsova, trans. by Sam Breazeale, "'Nobody Understood What Was Happening': Meduza Tells the Story of Albert Sakhibgareyev—a Russian Contract Soldier Who Deserted from the War in Ukraine," *Meduza.io*, March 25, 2022.

74. Shkolnikova, "Startup Pollsters Challenge Accepted Wisdom," *Moscow Times.com*, October 11, 2022.

75. "Kak 'mamochki' obespechivaiut rossiiskuiu armiu vmesto Minoborony. Chto tolkaet rossiian za svoi schet zatykat' dyry v osnatschenii armii i vliiaet li ikh pomoshch' khot' na chto-to," *Vazhnye istorii* (istories.media), July 4, 2022.

76. Yevgenia Albats, "Banderovskaia shavka," *Moscow Times.com*, May 5, 2022.

77. "Kak meniaetsia otnoshenie rossiian k Velikoi Otechestvennoi voine iz-za voiny v Ukraine? Otvechaiut istoriki, sotiolog i filosof," *Meduza.io*, May 8, 2022.

78. "Kak meniaetsia otnoshenie rossiian k Velikoi Otechestvennoi voine iz-za voiny . . ."

79. "Kak meniaetsia otnoshenie rossiian k Velikoi Otechestvennoi voine iz-za voiny . . ."

80. Shkolnikova, "Startup Pollsters Challenge Accepted Wisdom."

81. "Televizor ne mogu smotret'. Vse vremia plachy.' Rossiskie vlasti delaiut vid, chto vtorzhenie v Ukrainu—eto prodolzhenie velikoi Otechestvennoi. My uznali chto ob etom dumaiut te, kto videl tu voinu svoimi glazami," *Meduza.io*, May 9, 2022; "'We Shouldn't Celebrate Until We've Repented.' *Meduza*'s Readers on How Their Views of Victory Day Have Changed Since the War Began," *Meduza.io*, May 9, 2023.

82. "'Your Son Didn't Die in Vain, He Had a Purpose.' Watch How Putin Talked to the Mothers of the War Veterans in Ukraine," *Meduza.io*, November 25, 2022.

83. "Veterinar i zhivodery: Medik s Dal'nego Vostoka otpravilsia zashchishchat' 'russkii mir' v Ukranu i okazalsia v 64-i brigade, sredu ubiits, Buchi. Vot ego svidetel'stva," *Novaya gazeta Evropa.eu*, August 25, 2022.

84. Irina Dolinina, "'You Do Realize We're the Fascists?' Why Russian Servicemen Are Refusing to Fight in Ukraine and How Russia Is Trying to Send Them Back to the Front," *Vazhnye istorii* (istories.media) August 18, 2022.

85. Dar'ia Kozlova, "(Ne)svobodnye liudi Sibiri: Kak zhiteli Novosibirska i ego Akademgorodka vstretili 'spetsoperatsiiu' v Ukraine," *Novaya gazeta Evropa.eu*, March 26, 2022; "Dozens Detained on May Day in Russia," *Moscow Times.com*, May 3, 2022. In Russian, *Zashchita! Zaniatost'! Zarplata!*; Ian Shenkman, "Mozhem povtorit'— eto zamena roekta budushchego: Osnovatel' 'bessmertnogo polka'—o reiderskom zakhvate patriotizma," *Novaya gazeta Evropa.eu*, October 19, 2022.

86. Yaroslav Trofimov, "In Ukrainian Villages, Fears Grow for Men taken to Russia," *Wall Street Journal*, April 26, 2022; Brett Forrest and James Marson, "Horrors of Ukraine's Bucha Laid Bare on Yablunska Street," *Wall Street Journal*, April 7, 2022.

87. Georgi Kantchev, Evan Gershkovich, and Yulia Chernova, "Fleeing Putin, Thousands of Educated Russians Are Moving Abroad," *Wall Street Journal*, April 10, 2022; Kristina Safonova, "Skol'ko liudei uekhalo iz Rossii iz-za voiny? Oni uzhe nikogda ne vernutsia? Mozhno li eto schitat' ocherednoi volnoi emgratsii? Ob'iasniaiut demography Mikhail Denisenko i Iuliia Florinskaia," *Meduza.io*, May 7, 2022.

88. Anna Fillipova, "Putinskai Rossiia—Zhivoi Zakoldovannyi Trup" Odnoi iz Samykh Zametnykh antivoennykh Organizatsii v Rossii Stalo 'Feministskoe soprotivlenie,'" *Meduza.io* March 22, 2022; "5 Russian Recruitment Offices Hit by Arson Attacks," *Moscow Times.com*, April 22, 2022; "20 tysych zaderzhanii. 900 ugolovnykh del. 267 chelovek za reshetkoi. Chetyre s polovinoi goda—srednii srok lisheniia svobody. Dva goda repressii protiv antivoenno nastroennykh rossiian—v podschetakh 'OVD-Info,'" *Meduza.io*, February 22, 2024.

89. Vladimir Sevrinovsky, "'Refusing to Kill People Isn't a Crime': The Russian National Guard Is Firing Officers Who Refuse to Join the War in Ukraine," *Meduza.io*, March 29, 2022; "60 Russian Paratroopers Refuse to Fight in Ukraine—Reports," *Moscow Times.com*, April 7, 2022; Isabel Coles and Yaroslav Trofimov, "Belarussians, Russians Join Ukraine Forces," *Wall Street Journal*, April 8, 2022; Sophia Ankel, "Former Russian Officer Describes Quitting the Army from Guilt and Shame After Being Deployed to Invade Ukraine," *Business Insider*, May 23, 2022; "Bolee 6500 rossiiskikh soldat zakhoteli sdat'sia s pomoshchiu ukrainskogo proekta 'Khochu zhit,'" *Moscow Times.ru*, January 26, 2023.

90. Andrei Ianitskii, "Rossiiskie Ofitsery Govorili: 'Ne Znaem, chto tut delaem. Chuvstvuem Sebia Fashistami," *Meduza.io*, April 22, 2022; Olga Romanov, "A Group of Armed Russian Soldiers Fled from Kherson to Ukraine," *Meduza.io*, October 6, 2022; "Russia's Sakhalin Court Gives Three-Year Sentence to Soldier Who Fled His Military Unit Due to Not Wanting to Fight in Ukraine War," *Novaya gazeta Evropa.eu*, December 30, 2022.

91. "V Volgograde nakanune 80-letiia pobedy SSSR v Stalingradskoi bitve otkryli pamiatnik Stalinu. V. 120 metrakh ot memoriala zhertvam politicheskiky repressii," *Meduza.io*, February 1, 2023.

PART III / The Russian Revisionist
Foreign Policy

Chapter Eight

Project Russia

The Bestselling Book Series of Putin's Kremlin

Lynn Corum

This work will split the world into two divided camps.
The one that is right wins.[1]

Project Russia is one of the most widely read Russian book series. The five-volume series may remain a bestseller in Russia, but because it has yet to be published in any other language but Russian or released in any other country but Russia, it remains largely undiscovered in the West. The series is perhaps the most candid source of Putin's outlook on Russia's present state of affairs, its relations with the West, and, most alarmingly, his stated plans for the future—plans that it appears he is now putting into effect. This chapter will provide original translations of key passages from *Project Russia* as an introduction to the current ideas circulating within Putin's Kremlin. It will examine these key elements of the Russian national ideology under the Putin regime: the limitations of democracy; the decadence of the West; the West as the enemy; the coming world collapse; and Russia's future role in world leadership, including Putin's color revolution theory and its development from the Kremlin's study of Ukraine's Orange Revolution. It will also compare the major strategic propositions in the text to the actual behavior of the Russian government since its publication, thus showing the policy influence of *Project Russia*.

Before we move into the text, we must first put *Project Russia* in the context of other scholarship on Putinist ideology. In many ways, *Project Russia* represents a long tradition of Russian thinking dating back to the nineteenth century. Walter Laqueur in his book *Putinism*, which was published in 2015, argues that state ideology under Putin is based on three foundational ideas: a messianic Russian Orthodox Church, a Russian version of (US) Manifest Destiny doctrine called

222   *Lynn Corum*

Eurasianism, and a "grossly exaggerated fear of foreign enemies" out to destroy Russia. Laqueur writes that comparisons of Putin's ideology to that of Nazi Germany are "not helpful," and he instead compares Russia to clerical fascism in Franco's Spain in the 1930s.[2] Philip Short and Steven Lee Myers in their biographies of Putin, although recognizing his increasing authoritarianism, suppression of civil liberties, and crushing of political opposition, see him fundamentally as a pragmatist (although Short takes a more ominous view of Putin in the final two chapters of his book, which appears to have been written just after the second invasion of Ukraine).[3]

Stephen Kotkin, the preeminent biographer of Stalin and historian of the Soviet Union and Russia, argues that Russia under Putin, particularly since the invasions of Ukraine, is a reactionary throwback to nineteenth-century tsarist autocracy, imperial expansionism, ultra-nationalism, militarism, and Russian Orthodox theology.[4]

Putin himself has become devoted to one particular early twentieth-century Russian intellectual, Ivan Ilyin, who was militantly hostile to communism and went into exile in the 1920s, first to Germany, where he worked in Joseph Goebbels's Ministry of Propaganda in the Third Reich. Ilyin was sympathetic to Hitler, hostile to democracy, supportive of religion, and virulently anti-Semitic. (Putin himself is no anti-Semite, unlike much of the Siloviki elite.) Ilyin only distanced himself from Hitler after the Nazi regime began claiming the Slavs were a subhuman race. He then moved to Switzerland, where he wrote prolifically until his death in 1954. Putin had the remains of Ilyin and his wife exhumed and brought to a monastery outside Moscow, arranged to have an Orthodox bishop preside over this reburial, and laid flowers at his grave. Putin has repeatedly quoted him publicly on talk shows and in public addresses and sent a copy of one of Ilyin's books to all of the state governors to read. In many ways, *Project Russia* reflects Ivan Ilyin's philosophy and world view, although he is hardly mentioned in the books (which contain no anti-Semitic commentary).

Background

The Kremlin's original first volume of *Project Russia* was distributed in early fall 2005 by the State Courier Service of the Russian Federation (GFS Rossii) via the special overnight courier mail reserved for the highest level of documents to all the executive offices of the Kremlin; no author was identified.[5] Copies were also delivered to a few selected Russian public figures, including the film director

Nikita Mikhalkov.[6] Although not yet on sale commercially, the book nevertheless became one of the most discussed works in Russian political circles and was included in the register of publications recommended for reading by government officials, as well as by public and political figures, by the Office of the President of Russia.[7] As such, from the very first, the book was accepted as an official ideology. A censored edition of the work was published a full year later, in 2006,[8] soon followed by three additional volumes[9] and more recently by an omnibus edition, *Proekt Rossiya: Polnoye Sobraniye* (*Project Russia: The Complete Collection*) in 2014.[10] These books continue to be sold in large numbers by Russia's largest publisher, Eksmo. According to Moskva Books, they have now been read by more than 3 million people (for comparison, the average run of Russian books, according to Walter Laqueur in *Putinism*, is 2,000 copies).[11]

It was only with the publication of the declassified fourth volume that any author of *Project Russia* was identified: well-connected Russian billionaire Yuri Shalyganov. He was identified in the Russian press as its author in an article by Larisa Kaftan based on her interview with Shalyganov on October 10, 2010, for *Komsomolskaya Pravda* (*Communist Truth*).[12] In the article, Shalyganov reminds his audience that "all the possible authors among notable Russian political scientists and politicians have denied authorship." He adds, "Many came to conclude that its source must be the Kremlin." Of course, there is also the fact that this statement appears in an official, Kremlin-generated journal, *Komsomolskaya Pravda* (*Communist Truth*), which happens to be the official journal of Russia's Communist Youth Organization.

According to Shalyganov, this opinion was reinforced with the second volume, *Proekt Rossiya: Vtoraya Kniga: Vybor Puti* (*Project Russia Volume 2: Path Selection*), its release timed to coincide with Putin's bid for a third term so that it includes reflections on the need for "constant power at the top."[13] In Part V of *Vybor Puti*, the ideal power for a "great country" is said to be a "huge state mechanism" that "revolves around a powerful axis," with everyone under a "single command."[14] Throughout the interview, Shalyganov uses "we," not "I," to speak as the author and admits, "Only one of the authors has been revealed, and the other—and perhaps major—creators of the 'Project' still prefer to remain anonymous."[15] Thus, Shalyganov himself seems to be just one of several authors. Indeed, throughout the above-mentioned second volume of *Project Russia*, the series is discussed in terms of being the product of an inner circle of unnamed, influential "elites": "A higher elite [i.e., the 'thinkers'], capable of grasping the situation intellectually, will express

The Limitations of Democracy

meaningful information in a more expressive form, making it available to the elite of the second level [i.e., the 'intelligentsia' and elite classes], who will then communicate this information [i.e., using mass media] to the masses."[16]

The Limitations of Democracy

The main thrust of *Project Russia* is its general disdain for democracy and its advocacy for a state led by a strong ruler, a new kind of czar. Shalyganov began his interview with, "If you take a poll today and ask what democracy is, many will say it is deception and delusion. Five years ago, we had the illusion that democracy is possible: Achieve it, and all would be well. Now many people understand democracy—it is a utopia, a myth."[17] In *Project Russia*, democracy is dismissed as a form of government that is possible only at the local level and impossible for states. According to Shalyganov, "In Germany, Russia, and the United States there is no democracy. The myth of democratic elections in these countries is a deliberate lie."[18]

Part IV, chapter 1 of *Project Russia* disparages "novaya forma gosudarstva—demokratiya" (the new form of government: democracy).[19] According to *Project Russia*, US democracy is a sham: "Centuries have passed, but the world is not one iota closer to realization of this dream."[20] The United States is discussed as a country in which the real power is concentrated in the hands of an enduring elite class[21]—exactly like the USSR—selected via what is disparagingly referred to as an "electoral extravaganza."[22] This point is reiterated throughout the book. *Project Russia* insists that it does not really matter which party wins the US presidential elections because "The candidates from both American parties do not differ from each other. All differences are first, of secondary importance, and second, laughable . . . If you call this choice, I am jealous of the power of your imagination."[23]

Indeed, Russian hackers worked during the 2016 US presidential election to actively interfere with the electoral process and destroy US voter confidence. In all, at least twenty-one states were targeted, although no votes were actually changed.[24] For instance, voting databases in Illinois and Arizona are known to have been hacked.[25] According to Ken Menzel, general counsel for the Illinois State Board of Elections, hackers accessed as many as 200,000 personal voter records in late June 2016; it was discovered a month later. According to Matthew Roberts, director of communications for the Arizona Secretary of State, in late May 2016 the FBI alerted the Arizona Department of Administration that there was a credible cyber threat to their voter registration system. The Arizona Secretary of State's office learned of possible Russian involvement through internal IT and cyber security staff, who recognized the credentials and username posted online as from a known Russian hacker.

The hack did erode public confidence in the reliability of US voting machines, despite the fact that they are not connected with the internet in any state. This is significant because five states—Delaware, Georgia, Louisiana, New Jersey, and South Carolina—conduct their voting exclusively by machine, leaving no paper record. Other states, including Virginia, Texas, Florida, and Pennsylvania, use paperless machines in many of their counties.[26]

Project Russia insists it is impossible to provide people with sufficient knowledge to select their leaders. Not all are capable of learning, nor is it possible to gain the vast experience needed to understand the issues, for "much of the needed knowledge would constitute a state secret."[27] According to *Project Russia*, this knowledge is not enough, for each voter will select candidates based upon a personal agenda.[28] Thus, "National elections are reduced to outright stupidity because the people, like children, always prefer the candy wrappers, not the contents."[29]

To encourage this approach, Russians also appear to have exploited social divisions within the United States to influence US voters. According to a blog post from September 6, 2017, by Alex Stamos, Facebook's chief information security officer, between June 2015 and May 2017, some 470 "inauthentic" Facebook accounts and pages were used to purchase $100,000 worth of Facebook advertisements. The bogus accounts appear to have been operated out of Russia and were affiliated with one another. The ads did not specifically discuss the elections; rather, according to Stamos, they focused on "amplifying divisive social and political messages across the ideological spectrum—touching on topics from LGBT matters to race issues to immigration to gun rights."[30]

The social media strategy of the Kremlin-backed Internet Research Agency to interfere in the 2016 US presidential election was so successful that it was back in place for the 2020 election. Beginning in early 2019, social media profiles originating in Russia built a network of accounts, fifty on Instagram and one on Facebook, designed to appear to belong to interest groups in swing states. These included accounts with usernames like @black.queen.chloe and @michigan_black_community_, meant to appear like Black Lives Matter activists. Other account names included @stop.trump2020, @bernie.2020_, @iowa.patriot, and @feminist_agenda_. Others posed as LGBTQ rights activists and environmentalists. Liberal-looking accounts attacked Trump while conservative-looking accounts attacked Kamala Harris, Elizabeth Warren, and Alexandria Ocasio-Cortez. Accounts pitched to college students championed student debt forgiveness; to parents of school-age children, education reform. Before Facebook removed the accounts, a combined 250,000 followers were claimed, which of course would include fake or bot accounts to lend legitimacy.[31]

Throughout *Project Russia*, ordinary people are cast in the role of preschoolers, too selfish and ignorant to be entrusted with political power: "If the children are in charge of the kindergarten, in the end, they will destroy it without ever understanding, because their thoughts are fixed on other things."[32] Democratic leaders fare no better at the hands of *Project Russia*. They too are depicted like selfish children, seeing elections as "an opportunity, according to their concept of society, to buy a new 'toy.'"[33] *Project Russia* also scorns the tripartite system of government and the balance of powers found in Western democracies. As *Project Russia* mocks, "Montesquieu split political power into three pieces: the executive, legislative, and judicial branches. Now power passes from the hands of a man into the hands of the law. The world is ruled by this new 'ruler act.' The high-sounding phrase 'rule of law' in practice means the power of lawyers."[34]

This is not to say that bad leaders are held responsible for the "failure" of democracy. In *Project Russia*, the democratic *system* itself is held responsible:

> Democratic [leaders] stubbornly insist that all the troubles are due to bad elements in the state mechanism, i.e., due to bad officials and embezzlers. If the bad officials are exchanged for good, and the embezzlers eliminated, the situation will be corrected. People happily pick up on this "valuable advice" and again seek to choose the honest. But the situation does not improve, but rather deteriorates. After each election there is growing corruption and immorality. It's time to hang a price list for a bribe at public institutions. But people have become so totally stupid, they cannot link the relationship between elections and their misfortunes into a single chain.[35]

The Decadence of the West

Project Russia insists that Western thought is evil, leading to all manner of decadence. But *Project Russia* does not simply portray the West as decadent. It goes so far as to equate Western democratic ideals with Nazism. According to *Project Russia*, problems such as falling birth rates, declining morality, increasing drug abuse, and other vices are endemic in democratic systems of government ("democratic" being defined in *Project Russia* as any political system in which people have the right to vote): "It seems obvious that the cause must be sought, not in the official but in the basic [democratic] structure."[36] In fact, Western thought is equated with the extremes of Nazi ideology repeatedly in *Project Russia*:

The apotheosis of Western thought is realized in Hitler. It turns out that babies can be tortured because there is no God, and you are superman, for which there are no restrictions or obstacles in the implementation of the will and desires. Do you want to? Do it! Realize your will or die. Sounds cool? Cool. Especially dangerous. Some Satanic energy is behind this, attractive in its denial of any limitations, with credibility and legitimacy.[37]

Project Russia betrays a preference for Nikita Khrushchev's USSR, prior to Mikhail Gorbachev's perestroika and glasnost modernization programs. As Shalyganov comments during his interview:

The Soviet people believed in communism . . . And while they believed, the Soviet Union was strong . . . In the late Soviet Union, the idea of communism was emasculated . . . Already in the 70s, the Soviet people tried not to build communism, and to have a lot of carpets, crystal, [and] other household valuables [instead]. But the idea of personal good is too small and does not provide motivation for achievement. Construction began to fall apart. . . . Today . . . in the absence of ideas, the trend "get rich by any means" has spawned total corruption.[38]

The West as the Enemy

According to *Project Russia*, the idealized communist state did not fail but was sabotaged. It was corrupted by the West through a sinister propaganda campaign:

The first step in the destruction of the planet's vast empire was the split of the USSR. Emphasis was no longer placed on industrial and strategic targets, as in traditional warfare . . . the world view of the Soviet citizen was replaced by [that of] the consumer. There occurred deep ideological rifts. . . . Soon after the Soviet Union collapsed. Our enemies are personally convinced of the effectiveness of these monstrous new offensive technologies. The Velvet Revolution rocked the world louder than the blasts at Hiroshima and Nagasaki . . . "Democratic" elections completed the process . . . As a consequence, the state has changed to a commercial mindset. The destruction of industry, education, science, the military, etc., has occurred—not because Russia is suddenly filled with bad people, but because the commercial approach killed the nonprofit institutions.[39]

US propaganda agencies did indeed direct major secret psychological warfare campaigns against the USSR—President Dwight D. Eisenhower's "total cold war"—through such innocuous initiatives as Atoms for Peace, People-to-People, the US Information Agency's propaganda pamphlet *Facts About the United States*, and Radio Free Europe.[40] However, the many pressing social and economic problems facing the average Soviet citizen[41] certainly were the decisive factors in the Soviet Union's eventual failure.

In an insidious claim, *Project Russia* insinuates that the United States is biding its time, encouraging the former Soviet states to become completely independent of Russia, only to swoop in and take them over at a future date. The leaders of regional independence groups, for example Lech Wałęsa of *Solidarność* (Solidarity Movement),[42] sought to ally with the West and to break from Russia. *Project Russia* explains how this actually amounted to calculated exploitation *by* the West. Although the leaders of the newly independent, former Soviet states were typically very young and inexperienced, this does not mean they were inept. For instance, Mart Laar was only thirty-two when he became Estonia's first postcommunist prime minister in 1992. In 2006, the Cato Institute awarded him the 2006 Milton Friedman Prize for Advancing Liberty.[43] As stated in *Project Russia*:

> Emphasis is placed on the ambitions of a young person in power. He does not understand the overall situation, and therefore it is easy to instill the idea that to be the president of an independent state is better than being appointed by a ruler.[44] As a result, there is a whole army of freedom fighters. The trick is that they do not even finance [themselves]. They will go wherever a "carrot" has been hung. By reaching their goal, they unwittingly contribute to achieving the strategic goals of a stranger. Their hands, arms, and millions of other "fighters" are used blindly. The enemy realizes that its main task is to break Russia. Then, when it has removed this last major obstacle to world domination, the West will dissolve the "independent and sovereign" states.[45]

The implications are clear: *Project Russia* claims that the West has been at war with Russia for years. All the dysfunction in Russia has ostensibly been carefully engineered by the West, for that is how the so-called war is being waged. Supposedly, several planned and coordinated mechanisms run in parallel, leading to the destruction of the traditional national culture, religion, education, healthcare system, manufacturing industry, and the military. These coordinated efforts include the degradation of family, morality, and education. If one adds to this sex education, prostitution, drug abuse, and alcoholism, then the blame for Russian social problems is more or less complete.[46]

According to *Project Russia*, "Today, in so-called 'peacetime,' we lose more than during the Great Patriotic War. And these losses are growing like an avalanche. But instead of enemy soldiers in uniform and bombs falling from the sky, the population sees neon advertising, exciting TV series and glossy magazines."[47] *Project Russia* even creates spin for the conflicts in Georgia and the Ukraine:

> Where the West was able to break the continuity of government, as in the Ukraine, Georgia, and Kyrgyzstan, a period of active decay [set in]. "Rulers" appeared out of "nowhere," and will soon return "nowhere." They have been replaced by others who are the same, and so on, until the West decides that the desired condition is achieved. When the rough work is completed, the West will have new land to include in its sphere of influence. This is not going to happen by force. The free market is so constituted that anyone who enters that web will not be released. It drains his resources, leaving him without a chance. At the present stage of destruction of the system, Georgians, Ukrainians, and others fight "for freedom and independence," spouting beautiful, empty slogans. As a result people are deceived, wrecking their homes with their own hands. The new social order will have no place for either the Ukrainians, or the Georgians, or the Kyrgyz.[48]

Project Russia blames the West for social problems within the client states—again, these problems have supposedly been deliberately engineered in order to destroy those states and then redistribute their resources to the "Golden Billion."[49] The expression "Golden Billion" is used elsewhere in *Project Russia* in a passage that further illuminates the authors' thinking:

> If you talk sensibly, humanity has only two ways to live: either as one family, with one means, or with five billion providing the means for one-sixth: the "golden billion." But since so many "indentured servants" in an age of technological progress are not required, it turns out that these five billion people are just superfluous. [. . . so that] nowadays an active campaign has been launched for the final solution to the problem of "superfluous men" . . . "humane extermination."[50]

Later in the passage, the oft-quoted statistic on consumption in the United States—that the US population, about 5% of the world's population, consumes 40% of the earth's resources—is used to support its claim that America intends to sequester the world's resources for itself. Pointing out that earth's resources are

230   Lynn Corum

not sufficient to provide all 6 billion inhabitants a Western standard of living, *Project Russia* asks, "What will the [rest] of the world's population do? Live on Mars' resources?"[51]

The Coming World Collapse

As the flippant comment about "living on Mars' resources" illustrates, the assumption of *Project Russia* is that the world's resources are rapidly running out, while consumption of resources continues to climb, which will soon lead to economic collapse. Yuri Shalyganov was asked repeatedly by Larisa Kaftan, during his interview about *Project Russia*, about the "end of the world that world futurists promise." Clearly, this issue is considered to be central to the ideas in *Project Russia*. Here are his thoughts from that interview: "We believe that a new phase is coming in the development of human society. All will collapse—both Europe and America, and the U.S. dollar. It's a matter of time. By the way, if the dollar collapses, after that crashes the old-world order."[52]

Russia is apparently positioning itself for when the "inevitable" global crisis occurs. One gets the feeling that Putin must be rather looking forward to it as a chance to gain power, by being prepared to take over in the resulting chaos. *Project Russia* includes Putin's own speculations in this regard. For instance, "Russia still has sufficient resources to resolve the problem. The question is about their correct use. Not all the battles have been lost; the main battles are ahead. What their result may be, depends on how we are going to lead today."[53] As the passage continues, Putin stylizes himself after both Napoleon and Alexander the Great, preparing for battle. *Project Russia* muses, "Our goal is to get an idea of the strategic logic of the enemy . . . Think about how we would behave if we wanted to destroy Russia."[54]

Russia appears to already be "fighting the war." How? By attempting to sway public opinion in the West. Igor Sutyagin, the Russia specialist at the Royal United Services Institute maintains that Russia's propaganda machine is currently "very active," deploying what security experts call "hybrid warfare" that blends conventional military power with guerrilla tactics and cyber warfare: "The Russian campaign exists in a grey area, operating covertly—and often legally—to avoid political blowback, but with the clear aim of weakening Western will to fight, maturing doubts over NATO, the EU, Trident and economic sanctions."[55] According to Peter Pomerantsev and Michael Weiss of the Institute of Modern Russia, "The Kremlin exploits the idea of freedom of information to inject disinformation into society. The effect is not to persuade (as in classic public diplomacy) or earn credibility but to sow confusion via conspiracy theories and proliferate falsehoods."[56] As stated in *Project Russia* itself:

> The broad mass of the befuddled prefer to receive information from clips and slogans, specially created to impose on their consciousness posts that are not true, but false, and to provoke animalistic behavior . . . To bring these ideas to the masses, do not write books. It is necessary to turn to a more affordable way of feeding them thoughts. The method determines the flow of material related to the information. The masses need TV series, shows, cartoons, but not books. But today, the factory for the production of these products is in the hands of the market, and therefore will be stuffed with anti-human feeling.[57]

An entire "factory" has indeed been established by the Kremlin for this specific purpose. On June 2, 2015, *The Sunday Telegraph* published a highly illuminating interview with a brave Russian journalist who had successfully infiltrated the Kremlin propaganda establishment, the Troll Factory. Also known as the Internet Research Agency, the St. Petersburg firm pays computer bloggers very well to hourly churn out a minimum of 200 social media posts containing carefully crafted disinformation.[58]

Another major player in this effort is the Kremlin's primary propaganda organ abroad, *Sputnik International*, launched on November 10, 2014, by the Russian government–controlled news agency *Rossiya Segodnya* [*Russia Today*] as the successor to *RIA Novosti* (ria.ru). Headquartered in Moscow, this slick English-language media service has established modern multimedia centers in dozens of countries. *Sputnik* intends to broadcast in thirty languages, with over 800 hours of radio programming a day, covering over 130 cities and thirty-four countries. According to its chief, Dmitry Kiselyov, *Sputnik* intends to counter the "aggressive propaganda that is now being fed to the world." In its own words, it dedicates itself to "a multipolar world" ("multipolar" being a Russian catchphrase for a world in which Russia is again a major player, and the United States is diminished in influence).[59] As averred in *Project Russia*:

> Now we understand that there is a real war. We want to kill, but not with the force of a hand holding a sword, not with the force of gunpowder propelling a bullet, not even with atomic energy. We want to kill using social energy. Russia wants to destroy by manipulating the grievances and claims of the finely thinking elite. Sword against sword is effective, and gun against gun. But you cannot fight the weapon of the future with the weapons of the last war. Therefore, only

anti-social forces are effective against social forces. On the basis of this logic, our main task is to harness the power of protest.[60]

Shalyganov was asked during his interview, How likely is it that the world system would crash "in the next five years, or ten at most"? His answer was that "We think [the likelihood of a global crash] is so great that it cannot be ignored. According to optimistic forecasts, the probability of disaster is not less than 20%; according to pessimistic forecasts, more than 90%. Perhaps the tremendous acceleration of events will begin in the next year or two. Yet . . . none of the key political figures are aware of it."[61]

Not content with awaiting the alleged coming world collapse, Putin appears to be helping to bring it about by using current events to destabilize the West. According to US General Philip Breedlove, NATO's supreme allied commander in Europe, Putin, in concert with Syria's leader Bashar al-Assad, deliberately weaponized migration in 2016 in an attempt to overwhelm European structures and break European resolve.[62] Also, Putin openly provides financial support to radical opposition parties in order to polarize Western countries.[63] In 2016, Marine Le Pen's far-right National Front party was loaned €9.4 million (nearly $10.5 million) by the First Czech Russian Bank, a small bank with links to the Kremlin.[64] Georgia's far-right and anti-Western political party Alliance of Patriots is also said to be directly funded and guided by the Kremlin.[65] Other cases of possible Moscow-backed destabilization being monitored by diplomats involve extensive Kremlin links with Austria, including a visit by Austrian MPs to Crimea to endorse its annexation, as well as cases of Russian spies discovered using Austrian papers.[66] On May 17, 2019, *Der Spiegel* and *Süddeutsche Zeitung* published video footage of the extensive financial negotiations conducted at a luxury villa in Ibiza between Heinz-Christian Strache, the vice chancellor of Austria; Johann Gudenus, chairman of the Freedom Party of Austria; and a woman claiming to be Alyon Makarov, the niece of a Russian oligarch. The publication of the recordings led to the resignations of both Strache and Gudenus.[67]

There are a number of Russian nongovernmental organizations tasked with aiding and abetting antidemocratic groups in the West. One, the Kremlin-funded Antiglobalistskoye Dvizheniye Rossii (the Anti-Globalization Movement of Russia, or AGMR),[68] operates expressly to organize, train, and fund hard-left groups in the West. AGMR, which once chose Vladimir Putin as its "anti-globalization protester of the year," organizes publicity campaigns against the West as well as an annual conference in Moscow hosting a variety of Western hard-left groups and secessionists. The AGMR conference held on September 25, 2016, included representatives from Irish Republican Sinn Féin, Catalan separatists, and fringe American radical parties.[69]

Other initiatives of Putin intended to destabilize the West revolve around access to energy resources. Russia has long used access to Russian oil and natural gas as a political weapon. It is why Russia's Nord Stream 2 pipeline poses such a danger to the stability of Europe. Indeed, in response to sanctions levied over Russia's war with Ukraine, Russia's Nord Stream 1 pipeline reduced flows to Germany by 60%, leading German economy minister Robert Habeck to announce "We are in a gas crisis" at a news conference on June 23, 2022.[70] In a report for the Center for Strategic and International Studies, former US Ambassador to Lithuania Keith C. Smith had this to say:

> Imagine traveling in Latvia and Estonia during the unpleasant winter of 1992–1993, when Russia had cut off oil exports to those countries. Although Moscow claimed that the disruption was due to a conflict over pricing, the real reason was obviously political; to pressure the Baltic States into rescinding their demand that Russian troops be withdrawn from Estonia, Latvia, and Lithuania. This was my first experience with Moscow using its energy power to influence policies in neighboring countries.[71]

For this reason, securing other suppliers of energy, particularly to the sensitive Baltic states, has become highly important. Hydraulic fracturing, or fracking, is a technique designed to recover gas and oil from shale rock. Drilling companies suggest trillions of cubic feet of shale gas may be recoverable from underneath parts of the United Kingdom alone through the fracking process.[72] Unsurprisingly, Russian intelligence agencies appear to be covertly funding and working with European environmental groups to campaign against fracking and maintain EU dependence on Russian gas. Answering questions after a speech at Chatham House in London, NATO Secretary General Anders Fogh Rasmussen said that improving European energy security was of the "utmost importance" and accused Moscow of "blackmail" in its dealings with Europe. He averred, "I have met allies who can report that Russia, as part of their sophisticated information and disinformation operations, engaged actively with so-called non-governmental organizations—environmental organizations working against shale gas—to maintain European dependence on imported Russian gas."[73]

Russia's Future Role in World Leadership

Already in *Project Russia's* introduction, the authors prepare their readers for the book's actual project: "There is nobody to bring order to the 'kindergarten' because there is no prince with a team that can make sense of the situation and take appropriate action."[74] Tyranny is discussed as an attractive system that has—regretfully—fallen by the wayside: "The ancient ruler who held human power over society—be it the dictator, tyrant, the emperor, or the senate—was above the law . . . Now, sovereignty loses its human component."[75] The "prince" under discussion must be Putin himself; this ruler is described in great detail as *Project Russia* continues. *Project Russia* describes society's "natural" order as a pyramid with the "Prince-Monk" at the top. Thomas Aquinas is even trotted out, as if in agreement:

> At the top [of the pyramid] were the people of spirit, talent and will. The Prince-Monk was the Supreme Being. Next came the soldiers, willful but with great talent. At the bottom of the pyramid were the merchants, peasants and artisans, braving any risk [. . .] The robbers stood apart from society. It is interesting that to some thinkers, particularly Thomas Aquinas, the merchants also ranked as the robbers.[76]

In *Project Russia*, Putin is identified explicitly as Russia's salvation, the link binding modern Russia with the Soviet state. Putin is said to be the one bastion against social collapse: "Today we somehow exist only because the continuity of power is saved. CPSU[77]—Gorbachev-Yeltsin-Putin—all links in a chain, a continuation of Soviet power. The system decomposes rapidly, but it still exists." Clearly, implies *Project Russia*, Putin must stay in power in Russia because "when continuity disappears, the system will collapse."[78] In fact, in *Project Russia* Putin's continued presidency is described as Russia's "last stronghold":

> If the goal of the enemy is the *constant change of power*, i.e., the destruction of the structure, then our general goal is *the continuity of power*, i.e., the preservation of the structure. By itself, the understanding of this *fact* makes us stronger. At least we know that the fight is not over demagoguery concerning mythical freedoms and rights, nor for a place at the trough. We are fighting for the establishment of a permanent government. This is the last stronghold of Russia.[79]

But Putin is seemingly not content to rule only Russia. The lead-in to the Shalyganov interview (and remember—the article is entitled "What Awaits Us After the Presidential Election in 2012?") claims that Russia is awaiting the establishment of a supreme government that will be "beyond the state."[80]

The Color Revolution Theory

Putin's color revolution theory figures prominently in his state ideology as outlined in *Project Russia*. The idea of a color revolution was originally promulgated by the Kremlin as a means of explaining Ukraine's Orange Revolution in the wake of the 2004 presidential elections, a popular protest movement that successfully ended the pro-Russian Viktor Yanukovych government and ushered in pro-Western Viktor Yushchenko, the rightfully elected president. Yushchenko's supporters adopted the color orange as their symbol during visually arresting mass demonstrations featuring oceans of waving orange flags.[81] Soon, their movement came to be known as the Orange Revolution.[82] In *Project Russia*, it is claimed that the United States was behind the Orange Revolution and continues to use "these same methods" in Ukraine:

> If in a democratic society, a certain percentage of the voters treat the elections as a joke, this is a perfect environment for the "orange" technologies. One opposition government will be permanently replaced by another, and so on until it reaches the desired degree of chaos . . . An analysis of the situation shows that democracy is fundamental for destructive processes, for this is the basis of its doctrine and strategy of action. If you remove the foundation of democracy, destruction [of the system] becomes impossible.[83]

The events in Ukraine are linked to these ideas, and a volley is launched against the United States. It is significant that chapter 16 of *Project Russia*'s second volume ends as follows: "Look at the promoters of democracy, using big words to fool entire nations. One example: U.S. policy in Ukraine. Even before the announcement of the results of the election, America said that if they chose an objectionable candidate, the election would be undemocratic."[84]

The following quote from *Project Russia* implies that all involved were merely puppets in the hands of the Americans. An interesting passage is "if the candidate who wins is not to their liking"—to the liking of whom? It is being implied that the United States steps in unless the newly democratically elected leaders of other countries are its choice. In the Kremlin version of history, the United States has taken down governments with impunity, all over the world, via so-called color revolutions—including the Orange Revolution:

Let's start with the "orange" option [clearly referring to the Orange Revolution]. Essentially, it involves the recognition of non-democratic elections if the candidate who wins is not to their [?] liking. The weapon is to be the pressure and destabilization of the situation with simultaneous, secret negotiations conducted regarding terms for the handover of power. This methodology has been actively used in recent decades worldwide by the Americans. Such a scenario has been unfolding for several years in Ukraine. America hired the "revolutionaries" in the crowd. Meanwhile, backroom deals were held with the participation of the three parties concerned—Russia, the USA, and Ukraine. The U.S. advantage in such a situation is obvious.[85]

Realizing the effectiveness of the Orange Revolution in forcing a regime change, Putin's Kremlin analyzed the progress of the Orange Revolution and then refined their analysis into their color revolution theory. In the preface to volume 1, the *Project Russia* team speak in matter-of-fact terms concerning their "operation"—a "permanent change" of government—as having been laid upon the "foundation" of an "Orange Revolution." At first reading, the authors appear to be speaking about Ukraine and not the United States. But a closer reading strongly suggests that they are actually speaking in terms of eventually using the color revolution methods *ascribed* to the United States *against* the United States— where presidents can serve at most two terms of four-years, or eight years in total:

We figure that we are in the second phase of the operation. For the first phase— Setting up the system, announcing a permanent change of government—the prerequisites are now in place. The foundation for the "Orange Revolution" has been created. In four more years, a change of government will become possible; after eight years, it will be obligatory. While a change remains merely a possibility, there is a chance that things will remain the same. But at the critical juncture, when a change of government becomes mandatory, there will be no chance of keeping things the same.[86]

Putin the Would-Be Czar

In the context of what to expect after Putin's reelection in 2012, Shalyganov was asked by Kaftan, "Are you for a new monarchy?" Shalyganov replied, "No. Given that a monarchy is one of the best systems of government, in the current situation it is not possible." Asked about the aims of Putin's ideology as contained in *Project Russia*, Shalyganov explained, "Now, more and more people begin to dream of a strong hand."[87] Later in the interview, Shalyganov revealed what exactly the "Project" of *Project Russia* might be. Note that again, he speaks as "we"—seemingly to lend additional authority to the statement and to underscore that the statement does not originate as his personal idea: "We have come to the conclusion that the only structure that can replace a state is a supranational social system. To create a *defender*, you need to collect the *Cathedral*, which will answer all the accumulated problems. The force obtained at the time of the *Council*, will be the one supranational system. Everything will fall into place—at the top will be the one who has the most complete understanding of the world."[88]

Taken together, these are clearly ecclesiastical allusions. "Defender" recalls a defender of the faith. "Cathedral," to the Orthodox, designates a religious governing assembly, so that "collecting the cathedral" means convening an assembly of leaders. The "force obtained at the time of the Council" implies that this "supranational system" will be established at a "council," or meeting of these religious leaders. And they will endorse "the one who has the most complete understanding of the world" as leader. It would seem this pretentious description refers to Putin. As a "latter-day Czar," Putin desires to reclaim the leadership of the entire Orthodox world for Russia as the Third Rome.[89] The czars saw themselves as the "rightful heirs and guardians" of the "one true" (Orthodox) Christian faith.[90] During his third presidential term (2012–2018), Putin contrived to see the seat of the ecumenical patriarch of the Orthodox Church transferred from Istanbul to Moscow. This joint effort of Putin and Moscow Patriarch Kirill required commandeering control of the Pan-Orthodox Council, planned as the first Orthodox council of its kind since the Seventh Ecumenical Council held at Antioch in 787.

To ensure the Russian Orthodox would hold a numerical majority of clerics at this council, Kirill trebled the number of potential attendees by creating three new dioceses and appointing a mass of new vicars (bishops without sees)—those who might have been bishops if the dioceses existing prior to the years of persecution under the USSR still existed. Patriarch Bartholomew I of Constantinople himself resorted to extreme measures within the framework of church canons to successfully repel Moscow Patriarch Kirill's plans for dominating the proceedings.[91] In the end, the "Holy and Great Council" was held on Crete and not in Moscow, Istanbul remained the Second Rome, and Moscow lost its claim to be the Third Rome. The Russian Orthodox Church never even attended the Pan-Orthodox Council on June 19–26, 2016.[92]

238   Lynn Corum

But Putin is not finished with this project. His latest ploy involves Mount Athos.[93] Russian Orthodox monks worshipped there in their Monastery of St. Panteleimon for six centuries, and Tsar Nicholas II claimed it for Russia in 1835. Now Putin has reclaimed the place for Russia. Putin has refurbished the monastery,[94] and there has been a steady influx of Russians there ever since. Although Mount Athos has its own legislature and judicial bodies, it is legally part of the European Union like the rest of Greece. The monastic institutions there have a special jurisdiction, which was reaffirmed during the admission of Greece to the European community.[95] Executive power is vested in a sacred council of representatives of the twenty monasteries located on Mount Athos.[96] Their civil governor is Athanasios Martinos, Archon Offikialios.[97] As a theocracy, Mount Athos plays some yet-to-be-understood role in Putin's plans for world rule as a latter-day Russian emperor. But as Greek territory, Mount Athos is ultimately under the ecclesiastical authority of the Ecumenical Patriarchate of Constantinople, which is very hostile to Putin, so any takeover of Mount Athos by Putin is highly unlikely.

Putin's project revolves around the substitution of a belief system to take the place of the old system of Soviet Communism. As Shalyganov comments during his interview, "It's always easier and better to deal with someone who believes in God than an unbeliever. At the household level, this person is more predictable, adequate, he has a moral code . . . The ideology of the Soviet Union did not include God, but the people were better and the system, more robust."[98] Notice the sudden shift from a belief in God to a belief in Soviet ideology; they are treated as equivalent. Religion is seen merely as a highly useful tool for social control. As *Project Russia* laments, "The perplexing question for princes is how to create a hand-guided, controllable religion."[99]

Conclusion

Project Russia is not harmless agitprop. In the preface to volume 1, the authors state, "The aim of this work is to find people who will understand our message, then understand how it is implemented and will act according to the knowledge they have received. Whether with us, or independently, that is a separate question."[100] Nor is the plan to be implemented only within Russia. Later in the preface, an invitation is made to readers: "If you are ready to act on a global scale, and you do not mind a similar scale, let us unite. Because what we have is greater, and what they have less. In this is the key to success."[101] The invitation is repeated in the subsequent volumes. Most importantly, these actions are not limited to merely influencing public opinion. Yuri Shalyganov concludes his interview with Larisa Kaftan with this proposal:

> What to do until the end of the global system, while nothing is clear and we only wobble? Why not climb? . . . We propose to people of action to play by the rules of the real system . . . Get a job in government. Officials are elected at every level, from the rural to the federal . . . We, as a phenomenon, known today under the name "Project Russia" are not elected, and will not be elected anywhere. But we believe our supporters should use the system, and not [just] for their [daily bread]. Our interest: caring and daring, to become stronger due to the system. Very soon we will bring to the world what it has lacked for the last hundred years—a great idea. What, will be fully disclosed in the new project. For all questions we are ready to give advice, and in some cases, to unite and coordinate efforts.[102]

These words by Shalyganov reveal the lengths to which the "great idea" is intended to reach. The article even ends with contact information for readers who wish for help—including material assistance—and advice in achieving these aims. As revealed in *Project Russia* and detailed in this essay, the official Russian doctrine is that democracy does not work; all democracies are decadent; Soviet Russia was superior; its collapse was the fault of Western interference; and the Putin regime is its successor. The West is the enemy, and we are at war. The West will soon collapse, upon which Putin the "Prince-Monk" will establish a worldwide, totalitarian, "supranational" state, with a state religion to provide him with legitimacy and social control. Putin seems serious about pursuing the project outlined in *Project Russia*. Indeed, there are numerous indications that it is already being pursued. Familiarity with the outline of this plan as contained in the *Project Russia* book series has therefore become critically important.

NOTES

1. This and all subsequent translations are those of the author of this monograph. "Eto Proizvedeniye raskolet mir na dve chasti. Pobedit ta, chto budyet pravoy." Yuri Shalyganov et al., *Proekt Rossiya: Pervaya Kniga* [*Project Russia: The First Volume*] (Moscow: EKSMO Press, 2006), 3.

2. Walter Laqueur. *Putinism: Russia and Its Future with the West* (Thomas Dunne Books, 2015).

3. Philip Short, *Putin: His Life and Times* (Bodley Head, 2022); Steven Lee Myers, *The New Tsar: The Rise and Reign of Vladimir Putin* (Alfred A. Knopf, 2016).

240   Lynn Corum

4. For example, Stephen Kotkin, *Stalin: Paradoxes of Power, 1878–1928* (Penguin, 2015); Stephen Kotkin, *Stalin: Waiting for Hitler, 1929–1941* (Penguin, 2017); Stephen Kotkin, *Uncivil Society: 1989 and the Implosion of the Communist Establishment* (Random House, 2010); Stephen Kotkin, *Armageddon Averted: The Soviet Collapse, 1970–2000* (Oxford University Press, 2008).

5. Larisa Kaftan, "Chto Nas Zhdyet Posle Vyborov Prezidenta v 2012 godu?" [What Awaits Us after the Presidential Election in 2012?], *Komsomolskaya Pravda [Communist Truth]*, October 1, 2010, http://www.kp.ru/daily/24567/740255/.

6. IMDB, "Nikita Mikhalkov: Biography," accessed March 30, 2022, https://www.imdb.com/name/nm0586482/bio.

7. See the Labirint bookseller's book description for *Proekt Rossiya [Project Russia]*, http://www.labirint.ru/books/141082/.

8. Yuri Shalyganov, *Proekt Rossiya: Pervaya Kniga [Project Russia: The First Volume]*.

9. Yuri Shalyganov, *Proekt Rossiya Vibor Puti: Vtoraya Kniga [Project Russia, Volume 2: Path Selection]* (Moscow: EKSMO Press, 2007); Yuri Shalyganov, *Proekt Rossiya Tretye Tuicyacheletye: Tretye Kniga [Project Russia, Volume 3: The Third Millennium]* (Moscow: EKSMO Press, 2009); and Yuri Shalyganov, *Proekt Rossiya Bolshaya Ideya: Chetortaya Kniga [Project Russia, Volume 4: A Great Idea]* (Moscow: EKSMO Press, 2010).

10. Yuri Shalyganov, *Proekt Rossiya: Polnoye Sobranye [Project Russia: The Complete Collection]* (Moscow: EKSMO Press, 2014).

11. In fact, according to MoscowBooks.ru, the first edition of *Proekt Rossiya Tretye Tuicyacheletye: Tretye Kniga* ran to a million copies. See http://moscowbooks.ru/book.asp?id=456198.

12. Kaftan, "Chto Nas Zhdyet."

13. Kaftan, "Chto Nas Zhdyet."

14. Shalyganov, *Proekt Rossiya Vibor Puti: Vtoraya Kniga*, Part V, Chapter 5, 264.

15. Kaftan, "Chto Nas Zhdyet."

16. Shalyganov, *Proekt Rossiya Vibor Puti: Vtoraya Kniga*, Part II, Chapter 21, 167.

17. Kaftan, "Chto Nas Zhdyet."

18. Kaftan, "Chto Nas Zhdyet."

19. Shalyganov, *Proekt Rossiya: Pervaya Kniga*, 120–130.

20. Shalyganov, *Proekt Rossiya: Pervaya Kniga*, 125.

21. Shalyganov, *Proekt Rossiya: Pervaya Kniga*, 125.

22. Shalyganov, *Proekt Rossiya: Pervaya Kniga*, 32.

23. Shalyganov, *Proekt Rossiya: Pervaya Kniga*, 125.

24. "21 U.S. States Targeted by Russian Hackers, No Votes Changed," *Deutsche Welle*, March 25, 2022, https://learngerman.dw.com/en/21-us-states-targeted-by-russian-hackers-no-votes-changed/a-40650399#.

25. Wesley Bruer and Evan Perez, "Officials: Hackers Breach Election Systems in Illinois, Arizona," *CNN*, August 30, 2016, http://edition.cnn.com/2016/08/29/politics/hackers-breach-illinois-arizona-election-systems/index.html.

26. Kevin Corke, "Government Investigating Covert Russian Plot," *Fox News Special Report*, September 6, 2016, http://video.foxnews.com/v/5114712804001/growing-concerns-over-russian-interference-with-us-election/?#sp=show-clips.

Project Russia   *241*

27. Shalyganov, *Proekt Rossiya: Pervaya Kniga*, 125.

28. Shalyganov, *Proekt Rossiya: Pervaya Kniga*, 126.

29. Shalyganov, *Proekt Rossiya: Pervaya Kniga*, 123.

30. Scott Shane and Vindu Goel, "Fake Russian Facebook Accounts Bought $100,000 in Political Ads," *New York Times*, September 6, 2017, https://www.nytimes.com/2017/09/06/technology/facebook-russian-political-ads.html.

31. Donie O'Sullivan, "Facebook: Russian Trolls are Back. And They're Here to Meddle with 2020," *CNN Business*, October 22, 2019, https://www.cnn.com/2019/10/21/tech/russia-instagram-accounts-2020-election/index.html.

32. Shalyganov, *Proekt Rossiya: Pervaya Kniga*, 15.

33. Shalyganov, *Proekt Rossiya: Pervaya Kniga*, 13.

34. Shalyganov, *Proekt Rossiya: Pervaya Kniga*, 119.

35. Shalyganov, *Proekt Rossiya: Pervaya Kniga*, 127.

36. Shalyganov, *Proekt Rossiya: Pervaya Kniga*, 129.

37. Shalyganov, *Proekt Rossiya: Pervaya Kniga*, 67.

38. Larisa Kaftan, "Chto Nas Zhdyet."

39. Shalyganov, *Proekt Rossiya: Pervaya Kniga*, 27–29.

40. Kenneth Osgood, *Total Cold War: Eisenhower's Secret Propaganda Battle at Home and Abroad* (Lawrence: University Press of Kansas, 2006), 55.

41. Raymond E. Zickel and Eugene K. Keefe, *Soviet Union: A Country Study* (Washington D.C.: U.S. Library of Congress, 1991), 113–268.

42. Nancy L. Meyers, Ruud van Dijk, and Christian Ostermann, "Lech Walesa: Founder of Poland's Solidarity Trade Union," *CNN Perspective Series: Cold War*, Documentary, Knowledge Bank Profiles: The Cold Warriors, Cold War International History Project, 1998.

43. "Mart Laar: Winner of the 2006 Milton Friedman Prize," CATO Institute, May 2006, http://www.cato.org/friedman-prize/mart-laar.

44. Previously under the Soviet Union, leaders of the republics were selected by appointment. See Zickel and Keefe, *Soviet Union: A Country Study*, 312, on *Nomenklatura*.

45. Shalyganov, *Proekt Rossiya: Pervaya Kniga*, 33.

46. Shalyganov, *Proekt Rossiya: Pervaya Kniga*, 34.

47. Shalyganov, *Proekt Rossiya: Pervaya Kniga*, 36.

48. Shalyganov, *Proekt Rossiya: Pervaya Kniga*, 31.

49. Shalyganov, *Proekt Rossiya: Pervaya Kniga*, 34.

50. Shalyganov, *Proekt Rossiya: Pervaya Kniga*, 115.

51. Shalyganov, *Proekt Rossiya: Pervaya Kniga*, 115.

52. Kaftan, "Chto Nas Zhdyet."

53. Shalyganov, *Proekt Rossiya: Pervaya Kniga*, 40.

54. Shalyganov, *Proekt Rossiya: Pervaya Kniga*, 40.

55. Peter Foster and Matthew Holehouse, "Russia Accused of Clandestine Funding of European Parties as U.S. Conducts Major Review of Vladimir Putin's strategy," *The Telegraph*, January 16, 2016, http://www.telegraph.co.uk/news/worldnews/europe/russia/12103602/America-to-investigate-Russian-meddling-in-EU.html.

56. Peter Pomerantsev and Michael Weiss, "The Menace of Unreality: How the Kremlin Weaponizes Information, Culture and Money," *The Interpreter*, November 22, 2014, http://www.interpretermag.com/the-menace-of-unreality-how-the-kremlin -weaponizes-information-culture-and-money/.

57. Shalyganov, *Proekt Rossiya: Pervaya Kniga*, 140.

58. Tom Parfitt, "My Life as a Pro-Putin Propagandist in Russia's Shadowy 'Troll Factory,'" *The Telegraph*, June 24, 2015, http://www.telegraph.co.uk/news/worldnews /europe/russia/11656043/My-life-as-a-pro-Putin-propagandist-in-Russias-secret-troll -factory.html.

59. See Sputnik International's official website, https://sputniknews.com/.

60. Shalyganov, *Proekt Rossiya: Pervaya Kniga*, 71.

61. Kaftan, "Chto Nas Zhdyet."

62. Geoff Dyer, "NATO Accuses Russia of 'Weaponising' Immigrants," *Financial Times*, March 1, 2016, http://www.ft.com/cms/s/0/76a52430-dfe1-11e5-b67f -a61732c1d025.html#axzz4Jr8szlUh.

63. Foster and Holehouse, "Russia Accused of Clandestine Funding."

64. Gabriel Gatehouse, "Marine Le Pen: Who's Funding France's Far Right?", *BBC News*, April 3, 2017, https://www.bbc.com/news/world-europe-39478066.

65. "Opposition Demands Alliance of Patriots of Georgia Be Banned from October Elections due to Alleged Kremlin Support," *Agenda.ge*, August 25, 2020, https://agenda .ge/en/news/2020/2629.

66. Michael Weiss and Anton Shekhovtsov, "How a Soviet Triple Agent Recruited New Spies in the West," *The Daily Beast*, September 7, 2020, https://www.thedailybeast .com/leaked-kgb-manual-reveals-how-soviet-spies-recruited-in-europe?ref=scroll.

67. Piotr Andrzejewski, "The Freedom Party of Austria under Heinz-Christian Strache (2005–2019)," *Rocznik Polsko-Niemiecki [Polish-German Yearbook]* No. 29 (2021): 127. https://www.academia.edu/59996053/The_Freedom_Party_of_Austria_under _Heinz_Christian_Strache_2005_2019_.

68. The AGMR website address is http://anti-global.ru/.

69. Emmanuel Grynszpan and Samuel White, "Moscow 'Anti-Globalisation' Conference Stirs Up European and American Separatists," *Euractiv*, September 28, 2016, https://www.euractiv.com/section/global-europe/news/moscow-holds-conference -to-encourage-european-and-american-separatists/.

70. Nadine Schmidt and Mark Thompson, "Germany Declares Gas Crisis as Russia Cuts Supplies to Europe," *CNN Business*, June 23, 2022, https://www.cnn.com/2022/06 /23/energy/germany-russia-gas-alarm/index.html.

71. Keith C. Smith, *Russian Energy Politics in the Baltics, Poland, and Ukraine: A New Stealth Imperialism?* CSIS Report (Washington, DC: CSIS, December 2004).

72. "UK Shale Gas Resources 'Greater than Thought,'" *BBC News*, June 27, 2013, https://www.bbc.com/news/business-23069499.

73. Sam Jones, Guy Chazan, and Christian Oliver, "NATO Claims Moscow Funding Anti-Fracking Groups," *Financial Times*, June 19, 2014, https://www.ft.com/content /20201c36-f7db-11e3-baf5-00144feabdco.

74. Shalyganov, *Proekt Rossiya: Pervaya Kniga*, 25.

Project Russia   243

75. Shalyganov, *Proekt Rossiya: Pervaya Kniga*, 119.

76. Shalyganov, *Proekt Rossiya: Pervaya Kniga*, 75.

77. CPSU is the Communist Party of the Soviet Union, in Russian КПСС [KPSS], Коммунистическая партия Советского Союза [Kommunisticheskaya Partiya Sovyetskogo Soyuza].

78. Shalyganov, *Proekt Rossiya: Pervaya Kniga*, 30.

79. Shalyganov, *Proekt Rossiya: Pervaya Kniga*, 48.

80. Kaftan, "Chto Nas Zhdyet."

81. See Steve York, producer, "Photo Gallery," *Orange Revolution*, Documentary, accessed March 24, 2018, http://www.orangerevolutionmovie.com/photo-gallery .phphttp://www.orangerevolutionmovie.com/photo-gallery.php.

82. See "Orange Revolution Directory Page," *Encyclopaedia Britannica*, accessed March 19, 2018, https://www.britannica.com/topic/Orange-Revolution.

83. Shalyganov, *Proekt Rossiya Vybor Puti: Vtoraya Kniga*, 381–382.

84. Shalyganov, *Proekt Rossiya Vybor Puti: Vtoraya Kniga*, 277–278.

85. Shalyganov, *Proekt Rossiya Vybor Puti: Vtoraya Kniga*, 375.

86. Shalyganov, *Proekt Rossiya Pervaya Kniga*, 23–24.

87. Kaftan, "Chto Nas Zhdyet."

88. Kaftan, "Chto Nas Zhdyet."

89. In a propaganda piece by a Kremlin author, a thinly disguised "historical fiction," Putin is alluded to as Emperor Gabriel the Great, and his flag features the slogan, "Russia: The Third Rome. There can be no other." Mikhail Yuryev, *Tretiya Imperiya: Rossiya, Otoraya Dolzhna Byt* [*The Third Empire: What Russia Might Have Been*] (Saint Petersburg: Konstantin Tublin Publishing House, 2007). On the "Third Rome" concept, see *Radio Arzamas*, "Moskva—Tretiy Rim: Istoriya Spekulyatsii" [Moscow— The Third Rome: A History of Speculation], Course no. 10: *Genealogiya Russkogo Patriotizma* [*Genealogy of Russian Patriotism*], accessed July 7, 2018, https://arzamas .academy/materials/324.

90. Sebastian Lopez, "Church of the Tsars: Russian Orthodoxy's Role in Projecting State Power," *The Intelligencer*, October 7, 2016, https://www.phc.edu/intelligencer /church-of-the-tsars.

91. Oleg Kuznetsov, "Orthodoxy and Russian Foreign Policy: A Story of Rise and Fall," *Politics Today*, April 12, 2021, https://politicstoday.org/orthodoxy-and-russian -foreign-policy-a-story-of-rise-and-fall/.

92. Andrew Higgins, "Orthodox Churches' Council, Centuries in Making, Falters as Russia Exits," *New York Times*, June 14, 2016, https://www.nytimes.com/2016/06/15 /world/europe/orthodox-church-council-russia.html.

93. "Vladimir Putin Meets with Patriarch Kirill at St. Panteleimon Monastery (Athos)," *Katehon*, May 28, 2016, https://katehon.com/en/news/vladimir-putin-meets -patriarch-kirill-st-panteleimon-monastery-athos.

94. Jeremy Norman, "Mystery on Mount Athos," *The Spectator*, September 10, 2016, https://www.spectator.co.uk/article/mystery-on-mount-athos.

95. EUR-Lex, *Documents Concerning the Accession of the Hellenic Republic to the European Communities, Final Act, Joint Declaration Concerning Mount Athos*, OJ L 291,

November 19, 1979, 186 (DA, DE, EN, FR, IT, NL), accessed April 1, 2022, https://eur
-lex.europa.eu/legal-content/EN/TXT/?qid=1577994018803&uri=CELEX:11979H/AFI
/DCL/04.

96. "The Geopolitics of Athos," *Katehon*, May 28, 2016, https://katehon.com/en
/article/geopolitics-athos.

97. "The Civil Governor of Mount Athos Visited the Ecumenical Patriarch,"
Orthodox Times, March 19, 2022, https://orthodoxtimes.com/the-civil-governor-of
-mount-athos-visited-the-ecumenical-patriarch/.

98. Kaftan, "Chto Nas Zhdyet."

99. Shalyganov, *Proekt Rossiya: Pervaya Kniga*, 92.

100. Shalyganov, *Proekt Rossiya: Pervaya Kniga*, 5.

101. Shalyganov, *Proekt Rossiya: Pervaya Kniga*, 10.

102. Kaftan, "Chto Nas Zhdyet."

Chapter Nine

The Russo-Ukrainian War in the Historical Perspective

Serhii Plokhy

Russia's aggression against Ukraine and the start of the largest European conflict since the end of World War II came as a shock to the world at large. Despite continuing warnings from the White House, everyone asked the same question: Why in the world would Putin attack?

There was no good answer; hence, there was supposed to be no war. Vladimir Putin's own explanations about the threat posed to Russia by NATO—this at a time when NATO had no appetite for further expansion or intention of bringing Ukraine into its ranks—made no sense to the world in general. Putin's de facto declaration of war on Ukraine, delivered in conjunction with his official recognition of the independence of the puppet states created by Russia in eastern Ukraine, was dubbed a history lecture, and few observers outside Russia could make sense of it. Putin's accusations that Ukraine, led by the only Jewish president in the world outside Israel, was being ruled by Nazis and nationalists made even less sense.

Why, then, did Putin start the war, and why did it proceed in ways that no one could imagine, with the Ukrainians resisting, the West closing ranks, Russia becoming isolated, and a new Cold War knocking at the doors of politicians and taxpayers as Germany's defense budget and Poland's armed forces doubled? It has often been claimed that Putin wants to restore the USSR. This is a mistaken assumption. As Putin demonstrated in his war speech of February 2022, he is no follower of Vladimir Lenin, the founder of the Soviet state, since he rejects communist ideology and the pseudo-federal structure of the former USSR. Instead, he believes in the version of Russian imperial mythology that defines Russians, Ukrainians, and Belarusians as members of one big Russian nation.

Back in 1990, one of Putin's favorite Russian writers, Aleksandr Solzhenitsyn, proposed the creation of a new East Slavic state on the ruins of the USSR. That state, to be called Russia, was supposed to include Russia, Ukraine, Belarus, and parts of Kazakhstan. Putin's rhetoric about Russians and Ukrainians constituting one people fits Solzhenitsyn's vision of a future Greater Russia, helping to explain the thinking of the Kremlin's ruler and another important cause of the war. Putin's vision of Greater Russia finds a close parallel in Hitler's Greater Germany, while the annexation of the Crimea in 2014 is paralleled by the Austrian Anschluss of 1938.

During the last decade and a half, Russia has been waging open and hybrid wars, annexing territories, and using its virtual monopoly on energy supplies to the countries of Eastern Europe as a weapon, the object being to establish a much less costly and more flexible system of political control over post-Soviet space than was available either to the Russian Empire or to the Soviet Union. Yet many policies of the present-day Russian leadership have their origins in the last years and months of the existence of the USSR.

By far the most important of those policies has been the Russian leadership's early decision to maintain Moscow's political, economic, and military control over the "near abroad," as the Russian political elite and media dubbed the former Soviet republics. As early as the fall of 1991, advisers to Boris Yeltsin envisioned Russia gathering in the republics on its borders within the subsequent twenty years. Like many other former imperial powers, Russia opted out of the empire because it lacked the resources to keep the costly imperial project going. Unlike most of its counterparts, however, it took along the rich oil and gas resources of the empire—most of the Soviet oil and gas reserves were located in Russian Siberia. Thus, Russia had more to gain economically than to lose from the collapse of the USSR. Russian control over oil and gas resources made the divorce with the empire in 1991 easier in economic terms and prevented armed conflict between Russia and the republics that declared independence. We now know that such conflict was not eliminated but merely postponed. Over the last decade, rising oil and gas prices have made it possible for Russia to rebuild its economic potential and military might, allowing it to reopen the question of disputed borders and territories, and step up its efforts to gather back the Soviet republics more than twenty years after the Soviet collapse.

The Russo-Ukrainian War in the Historical Perspective   247

Ukraine, the second-largest post-Soviet republic, has played a crucial role in preventing successive Russian attempts to reintegrate the near abroad in economic, military, and political terms. Back in 1991, Russo-Ukrainian relations were the key factor in deciding the future of the Soviet Union. In August 1991, once the Ukrainian parliament declared the republic's independence, the Russian government of Boris Yeltsin threatened Kyiv with partitioning of its territory. Fingers were pointed specifically at the Crimea and the Donbas, which became a battleground twenty-three years later. Despite threats from Moscow, Ukraine pushed forward with its quest for independence, and in December 1991 the Soviet Union was replaced by the Commonwealth of Independent States, which was the result of a Russo-Ukrainian compromise. In his speech on the annexation of the Crimea, Putin claimed that many in Russia regarded the commonwealth as a new form of statehood. But that was not the position of the Ukrainian leadership, which took its own independence and that of the other Soviet republics with the utmost seriousness.[1]

In the 1990s, Ukraine turned the commonwealth into an instrument for a "civilized divorce"—a term coined in Kyiv—as opposed to one for Russian control over the near abroad. Ukraine worked hard to ensure recognition of its borders by Russia. In 1994, Kyiv gave up its nuclear arsenal in exchange for a guarantee of territorial integrity and independence given by Russia, the United States, and Great Britain. In 1997, the Ukrainian government agreed to lease the naval base in Sevastopol to the Russian fleet in exchange for a treaty that recognized the inviolability of Ukrainian borders. It took the Russian parliament two years to ratify the treaty that formally recognized the Crimea and Sevastopol as integral parts of Ukrainian territory. It seemed that the two countries had finally resolved all outstanding issues in their relations resulting from the Soviet collapse.[2]

The next decade demonstrated the limits of the Russo-Ukrainian understanding and the degree to which Russia was prepared to recognize Ukraine as an independent state. In the late 1990s, Ukraine began its drift toward the West, declaring integration into the European Union as the goal of its foreign policy and refusing to join Russia-led economic, military, and political institutions. Domestically, Ukraine managed to remain a much more pluralistic society than Russia, with a strong parliament, competitive politics, and an influential opposition. In 2004, Ukrainian civil society refused to accept the results of a rigged election and endorse the Russian-backed candidate, Viktor Yanukovych, as the country's new president. After a long and peaceful protest that became known as the Orange Revolution, the outgoing president of Ukraine agreed to a new round of elections that brought to power a pro-Western candidate, Viktor Yushchenko. From that time on, Moscow treated Kyiv's orientation on the West not only as a growing external danger but also as a threat to its own increasingly authoritarian regime. As far as the Kremlin was concerned, Ukraine's rejection of rigged elections and resistance to a corrupt regime was setting an example to Russia's own struggling civil society and had to be stopped at all costs.[3]

A major crisis in Russo-Ukrainian relations began on the night of November 21, 2013, with a Facebook post by a Ukrainian journalist of Afghan descent, Mustafa Nayyem. He was disturbed by news that the government of Viktor Yanukovych, who had come to power in 2010, had refused to sign a long-awaited association agreement with the European Union, which envisioned the creation of a free economic zone including Ukraine and the EU and stipulated bringing Ukrainian legislation, democratic procedures, and business practices in line with those of the EU. "Fine," wrote Nayyem on his Facebook account, "Let's be serious. Who is ready to show up on the Maidan by midnight tonight? 'Likes' will be ignored. Only comments on this post with the words 'I'm ready.'" There were 600 "I'm ready" responses. At 9:30 p.m., Nayyem typed another post: "Dress warmly, bring umbrellas, tea, coffee, a good mood, and friends." Shortly after 10:00 p.m., he was on Kyiv's central square, known in Ukrainian as the Maidan, where the Orange Revolution had begun ten years earlier. About thirty people had gathered by the time he arrived. By midnight, there were more than 1,000 young, educated urbanites. For them, the expected association agreement with the EU was the last hope that Ukraine might finally embark on a European course of development, overcome corruption, modernize its economy, and provide a decent standard of living for its people. Now those hopes were being crushed. Nayyem and his friends could not remain silent.[4]

The protest began like a festival, with singing and dancing to brave the cold weather of late November. It soon became known as the Euromaidan—the largest pro-European rally in history. President Yanukovych, for his part, had learned from the Orange Revolution of 2004 that the sooner one got rid of protesters, the better. Thus, in the early hours of November 30, riot police were ordered to attack the students camping on the Maidan. They did so with the utmost brutality under the pretext of clearing the square to allow the construction of a huge Christmas tree in preparation for New Year celebrations that were still one month away. Once images of police beating unarmed students were posted on the internet, dormant Ukrainian civil society reacted sharply. The next day was Sunday, and more than half a million people showed up in downtown Kyiv to protest police brutality. The

The Russo-Ukrainian War in the Historical Perspective   249

Euromaidan, which had begun with protests against the postponement of the signing of the EU association agreement, turned into what became known as the Revolution of Dignity. Hundreds of thousands of people would join the protests that continued through December 2013 into January and February 2014.

With the United States and EU countries applying pressure on President Yanukovych for a peaceful resolution of the crisis, Yanukovych turned to Russia. Ever since his election in 2010, the Kremlin had wanted him to stop Ukraine's drift toward the West, refuse to sign the association agreement with the EU, and join the Russia-led customs union, whose members included Belarus and Kazakhstan. Yanukovych was at first reluctant to do so, but the Kremlin raised the stakes by starting a trade war with Ukraine in the summer of 2013. In November, Yanukovych gave up. He refused to sign the agreement with the EU and went to Russia instead to negotiate a US$15 billion loan needed to keep his kleptocratic government afloat until the next presidential elections, which were scheduled for 2015. The Russian government granted the loan and delivered the first installment. The task now was to keep Yanukovych in power, and the Kremlin thought it could best be done by suppressing the Maidan protests—an option advocated publicly by Putin's adviser Sergei Glazyev. In January 2014, as protests continued, Yanukovych forced laws through parliament allowing him to do just that. But the new laws, condemned by the opposition as draconian, only brought more people onto the streets.

Clashes between protesters and police began in late January, reaching their peak on February 18, 2014, when dozens of protesters and policemen were killed by gunfire. That day, the government ordered snipers to shoot at the protesters, and fatalities among them soon exceeded 100. Those killed by the police and hired thugs became known as the "heavenly hundred." The European Union imposed sanctions, including travel bans and asset freezes, on members of the Ukrainian government responsible for the use of force against the protesters. The Ukrainian parliament, dominated by big-business oligarchs who did not want to lose access to money stashed in Western banks, passed a resolution prohibiting the government from using force against citizens. That was the end of the Yanukovych regime, which could not survive without reliance on brute force.

On February 21, 2014, EU delegates led by the Polish minister of foreign affairs, Radosław Sikorski, negotiated a deal between Yanukovych and the leaders of the opposition. One of its conditions was a new presidential election before the end of the year. But Yanukovych, who had no illusions about its outcome, fled his mansion near Kyiv the same night, taking reportedly hundreds of millions of dollars

250   Serhii Plokhy

and leaving behind a private zoo and a fleet of vintage cars. The next day, parliament voted to remove him from office. He drove with his bodyguards to the Crimea, and then, by some accounts, boarded a Russian ship to make his way to the Russian Federation, where he was granted citizenship.[5]

The Russian government was extremely displeased with the turn of events in Kyiv. On February 21, 2014, the Russian representative at the negotiations conducted by Sikorski refused to sign the agreement on behalf of his state, but after Yanukovych fled Kyiv, Moscow accused the West and the Ukrainian opposition of not honoring the agreement. It declared the Kyiv events a coup and branded the new Ukrainian government unconstitutional. As the world watched the closing ceremonies of the Sochi Winter Olympic Games on February 23, 2014, the corridors of European foreign ministries were rife with speculation about what Russia might do once the games were over. Vladimir Putin later admitted that on that day he gave his subordinates an order to begin the takeover of the Crimea. On February 27, four days after the end of the Olympics, Viktor Yanukovych, now safe on Russian territory, issued a statement claiming to be the legitimate president of Ukraine, and a detachment of heavily armed men in unmarked uniforms seized the buildings of the Supreme Council and government of the Crimea and flew Russian flags atop both centers of power.

On the same day, with the "green men" firmly in control, the Crimean parliament held a closed session that lacked a quorum, according to numerous reports, and dissolved the Crimean government. As the new prime minister, it appointed Sergei Aksenov, the leader of the Russian Unity Party, which had obtained only 4% of the vote in the Crimean parliamentary elections. On March 1, Aksenov appealed to Putin to help ensure "peace and order" on the peninsula. The next day, Russian military units moved out of their barracks in Sevastopol and, with the support of troops brought from Russia, seized control of the Crimea. They were assisted by specially trained groups of Russian Cossacks and mercenaries from Russia, as well as local militias. Putin and the members of his government, who had originally denied allegations of Russian military intervention in the Crimea, eventually admitted the participation of the Russian military in its takeover.

The Russian annexation of the Crimea was given a veneer of legitimacy by a referendum hastily organized on March 16, 2014. Officials declared that more than 83% of eligible voters had taken part in the referendum, with close to 97% voting in favor of joining Russia. Unofficial reports, including those from the Human Rights Council subordinate to the Russian president, cut both numbers almost in half, estimating the turnout at under 40% and the vote for joining Russia at under 60%. Those figures find support in a poll conducted in the Crimea in February 2014, when not many more than 40% of those polled were in favor of joining Russia.

But the new authorities clearly did not want to take any risks and went for outright falsification. In the city of Sevastopol, they reported a turnout that amounted to 123% of registered voters. The referendum was boycotted by the 250,000-strong Crimean Tatar community and declared illegal by the government of Ukraine. Its results were not recognized by the international community. But on March 18, 2014, Russia officially annexed the peninsula.[6]

In his speech on the occasion, in the tsarist-era St. George's Hall of the Kremlin, a venue for meeting foreign delegations and holding the most solemn ceremonies of state, Vladimir Putin claimed that the Crimean referendum had been held "in full compliance with democratic procedures and international norms." Putin hailed the annexation of the Crimea—an act undertaken in violation of the sovereignty of Ukraine, which had been guaranteed by Russo-Ukrainian treaties and ensured by the Budapest Memorandum of 1994—as a triumph of historical justice. Much of Putin's argument was historical and cultural in nature. Putin, who has never concealed his regret and even bitterness about the fall of the Soviet Union, referred specifically to the Soviet collapse in a speech delivered on the occasion of the Russian annexation of the Crimea in March 2014: "The Soviet Union fell apart. Things developed so swiftly that few people realized how truly dramatic those events and their consequences would be," said Putin, recalling the events of 1991. "It was only when the Crimea ended up as part of a different country that Russia realized that it had not only been robbed but plundered." He continued: "And what about the Russian state? What about Russia? It humbly accepted the situation. This country was going through such hard times then that, realistically, it was incapable of defending its interests." Putin's speech was meant to remove all doubt that the "hard times" were over and that Russia was back, prepared to undo the "injustice" inflicted on it by the disintegration of the USSR.[7]

What exactly would that mean, and how far was Russia prepared to go in order to undo perceived injustice? These were the questions on the minds of many world leaders. After a telephone conversation with Putin, Chancellor Angela Merkel of Germany said in apparent disbelief that he was living "in another world." The former US president Bill Clinton provided clarification of what world that was, suggesting that Putin wanted to reestablish Russian greatness in nineteenth-century terms. Prime Minister Arsenii Yatseniuk of Ukraine repeatedly accused Putin of wanting to restore the Soviet Union.[8]

It turned out that the annexation of the Crimea was just the beginning of Russian aggression against Ukraine. In April, veterans of the Crimean campaign from the ranks of the Russian Cossacks, nationalist activists, and undercover intelligence officers moved from the Crimea to the cities and towns of southern and eastern Ukraine. Their targets were government administration buildings, as well as headquarters of police and security services in the cities of Kharkiv, Luhansk, Donetsk, Mykolaiv, and Odesa, as well as in the smaller towns of southeastern Ukraine. The goal, many believe, was to proclaim a number of separatist republics that would then unite as one Russia-backed state of Novorossiia, or New Russia—the name originally used for one of the imperial provinces in southern Ukraine after the Russian annexation of the Crimea in the late eighteenth century. Participants in antigovernment rallies were often bused across the border from Russia and the Russian-controlled Transnistria region of Moldova.

The new revolutionary government in Kyiv was completely unprepared to deal with the Russian annexation of the Crimea and the hybrid war that the Kremlin had begun in the eastern Ukrainian Donbas (Donets Basin). For months, the leaders of the new government had led the opposition in its street war against the police and now could not rely on its support in dealing with the foreign-inspired insurgency. In fact, many policemen joined the Russian mercenaries and the local rebels. The Ukrainian army was virtually nonexistent. It was in transition from a conscript army to a professional one, severely underfunded, with no combat experience. The Russians had been fighting their war in Chechnya since 1991, and the Ukrainians were no match for the well-trained Russian regular troops and special forces. It soon turned out they had major problems in dealing even with Russian-trained local militias. The troops originally could not bring themselves to shoot at paramilitaries who were firing on them and taking over their barracks and equipment.

Kyiv began to put its act together only in mid-April. It was then that one of the leaders of the Maidan protests and the new minister of the interior, Arsen Avakov, managed to reclaim the regional administration building in his native Kharkiv, and Igor Kolomoisky, a Ukrainian oligarch, returned from de facto exile in Switzerland to lead the government of his native Dnipropetrovsk region. Avakov, an ethnic Armenian, and Kolomoisky, an ethnic Jew, emerged as the "saviors" of Ukraine from the Russian hybrid-war offensive, dispelling the myth of the nationalist or even fascist leanings of the new government in Kyiv and its supporters disseminated by Russian propaganda. By mid-May, it was clear that the Russian attempt to raise a revolt throughout southeastern Ukraine and create

Novorossiia, a state that would divide Ukraine in half and provide the Russian government with land access to the Crimea and Transnistria, had failed.

The Russian strategists of the hybrid war were much more successful in the Donbas industrial region on Ukraine's eastern border with Russia, where Russian-backed separatists declared the formation of the Luhansk and Donetsk People's Republics. On April 12, armed men led by Igor Girkin (*nom de guerre* Strelkov), a former colonel in Russian military intelligence and a veteran of the Yugoslav wars of the 1990s, seized the government and police headquarters in the city of Sloviansk in the northeastern Donbas. By the end of the month, militias led by the former Russian intelligence officers and reinforced by Cossacks, volunteers, and Chechen fighters brought in from Russia and funded with Russian money had seized administrative buildings in most cities and towns of the region, including its two major centers, the cities of Luhansk and Donetsk. They also seized radio and television stations, cutting off Ukrainian channels and bombarding listeners and viewers with misinformation about the new Kyiv government, which was called a "fascist junta," as well as its plans, which allegedly included the desire to ban the Russian language in the region. Viewers and listeners were promised Russian salaries and pensions, which were significantly higher than those in Ukraine, and citizenship either in Russia or in the new state of Novorossiia, which would include a good half of Ukraine.

The propaganda was effective: significant numbers of unemployed and semi-employed youth joined the rebel militias, where they were paid for their services. The resistance of the pro-Kyiv activists was crushed, and some of them were kidnapped and killed, while help from Kyiv failed to arrive. There were several reasons why the covert Russian invasion met little resistance in the Donbas. A major industrial powerhouse in Soviet times, it had become an economically depressed area with the switch from a command economy to the market after 1991. Like cities in rust belts throughout the world, Donetsk became a criminal capital. Many of its new elites had criminal backgrounds or connections, with the region's best-known politician, Viktor Yanukovych, having served two prison sentences in his youth. Although dependent on subsidies from Kyiv, the region had a strong sense of local pride and identity. Its ethnic composition differed from that of neighboring regions of Ukraine, with ethnic Russians constituting majorities in Donetsk and some other towns of the area. In 2001, only 24% of the inhabitants of Donetsk oblast and 30% of those in Luhansk oblast identified Ukrainian as their native language, compared with 67% in neighboring Dnipropetrovsk oblast. Although ethnic Ukrainians made up 47% of the population of Donetsk, only 27% of the city's children received their education in Ukrainian. Russian was the dominant language on the streets of the Donbas, and the local elites exploited that fact to mobilize their electorate, claiming that the new Kyiv government was a threat to the Russian language.

Despite their strong sense of local identity, in early April 2014, 85% of Donetsk residents were opposed to the seizure of government buildings and installations by militias, and more than 60% favored the arrest of separatist activists. But the local political and business elites refused to act against the Russia-led insurgents. They either remained neutral or even tacitly supported the protests in the hope that the new government in Kyiv would be more willing to make a deal with them if the region was in turmoil. It was a short-sighted tactic, and they would soon lose control over the rapidly developing crisis.

As the leaders of the Russian-inspired and funded insurgency took a page from the local elite's playbook and used the theme of protecting the allegedly threatened Russian language and culture, the region's political and business elites decided to go with the flow. In the local referendum that took place on May 11, 2014, and was not recognized by Kyiv, voters were asked whether they supported the *samostoiatel'nost'* of the republic—a term that could mean either autonomy or independence. The leaders of the Donetsk republic declared that 89% of voters favored independence, and the corresponding figure in Luhansk was 96%, but these figures were as fraudulent as the ones released in the Crimean referendum, and many of those who voted later claimed that they wanted broad autonomy, not independence. The referendum took place without the presence of international observers and was not recognized by the international community.

The Ukrainian government launched a counteroffensive against the separatist takeover of the Donbas in mid-April, without apparent success until after the presidential election of May 25, 2014. It brought to power one of the leaders of the Euromaidan protests, Ukrainian business tycoon Petro Poroshenko, who won more than half the vote in the first round. On May 26, the Ukrainian army recaptured the Donetsk international airport; on June 13, it took control of the port city of Mariupol on the Sea of Azov; on July 5, it took the city of Sloviansk, forcing the units of Colonel Igor Girkin, who by then had declared himself defense minister of the Donetsk People's Republic, to retreat to Donetsk. With the Ukrainian forces on the offensive, Russia increased its support for the separatist insurgents, now led by two Russian citizens with close links to the Russian government and security services—Colonel Girkin and the self-proclaimed prime minister of the Donetsk People's Republic, Aleksandr Borodai. In the second half of June, the

The Russo-Ukrainian War in the Historical Perspective   255

Ukrainian government claimed and NATO intelligence confirmed the continuing influx from Russia to Ukraine, not only of trained militants but also of heavy military equipment, including tanks and multiple rocket launchers.

On July 17, 2014, the war in eastern Ukraine became truly international as Russia-backed separatists shot down Malaysia Airlines flight MH17, killing all 298 people on board. The destruction of a civilian airliner produced a flood of protests throughout the world, forcing US and EU leaders to step up sanctions against Russian political and business elites associated with the undeclared war against Ukraine. But sanctions, which have an impact over time, had no immediate effect on Russian behavior. If anything, Russia increased its involvement in Ukraine. In July, Russian artillery and missiles began bombarding Ukrainian territory from the Russian side of the border, and in August regular units of the Russian army crossed the border not just to reinforce Russian mercenaries and local militias but also to take the lead in fighting the Ukrainian armed forces and volunteer battalions. Thousands of Russian regular troops took part in the offensive launched by the separatists during the last week of August 2014. Some of them were captured by the Ukrainian military and paraded before television cameras as proof of Russia's invasion of Ukraine. By sending regular troops into a battle previously fought under the command of Russian military officers and with Russian equipment, Moscow stopped the Ukrainian advance and saved the self-proclaimed Luhansk and Donetsk republics from imminent defeat.

In early September 2014, with the participation of Russia and the Organization for Security and Co-operation in Europe (OSCE), the two sides signed an agreement that resulted in a shaky ceasefire. In February 2015, a new ceasefire was negotiated in Minsk (the Minsk II agreement) by the leaders of Germany, France, Russia, and Ukraine, only to be violated in the next few weeks by the takeover by the Russia-backed militants of a strategic railway center of Debaltseve, previously held by the Ukrainian side. In 2015, despite the Minsk II agreement, Russia continued to provide military support for its puppet regimes in Donbas, sending not only supplies and weapons but also its military personnel, and causing the continuation of the sanctions introduced by the West to discourage Russia from the escalation of the conflict.[9]

The Russian Empire, the Soviet Union, and then post-Soviet Russia all associated international power and security with control over territories along their borders. If they could not control such territories completely, they would partition them and control what they could. This was the rationale behind the partitions of Poland in the second half of the eighteenth century and the division of Germany after World War II. The "New Russia" project, launched by the Russian government in 2014, had as its primary goal the partitioning of Ukraine and the creation of a Russian-controlled state in the southern and eastern parts of the country. That project failed, as Russia managed to destabilize and control only a small part of the projected state of New Russia. Although Crimea was annexed right away, the Russian covert war in the Donbas created conditions for the establishment of another enclave of "frozen conflict" unrecognized by the rest of the world, not unlike South Ossetia and Abkhazia in the territory of Georgia and Transnistria in the territory of Moldova. These enclaves are used to apply pressure to Western-leaning republics. Chances are that this will be the primary function of the new frozen-conflict area in eastern Ukraine.

Many in Russia and around the world believe that the crisis is far from over, mainly because Vladimir Putin did not achieve most of what he wanted when he began his aggression against Ukraine. "Putin wanted to tie Ukraine to Russia, to encourage its entry into the Customs Union. He got the exact opposite," wrote the Russian opposition leader Boris Nemtsov in October 2014:

> He wanted Ukraine to maintain a neutral status. He failed miserably . . . He wanted to win the respect of the Ukrainian people. He created a long-term enemy . . . Putin wanted a "Novorossiia" stretching from Donetsk to Odesa. He got a small section of the Donetsk and Luhansk oblasts . . . [H]e wanted a corridor to the Crimea via Mariupol. He raised awareness and resistance among the locals and spurred Russians residents in Mariupol to dig trenches around the city . . . He wanted to seize land without firing a single shot, as in the Crimea. He got 4,000 people killed on both sides . . . Putin wanted to be recognized as a strong leader in world politics. He became an outcast.[10]

Indeed, short of the annexation of the Crimea, few of the original goals set by the Russian leadership in the winter and spring of 2014 were achieved by the end of that year. And even that came with a huge cost to the Russian economy and international prestige.

In the wake of the Russian aggression against Ukraine, Vladimir Putin's (and, by extension, Russia's) stock in the West fell to an unprecedented low. Relatives of those who perished in the shooting down of Malaysia Airlines flight MH17 held him responsible for the deaths of their loved ones. But the damage goes far beyond Russia's loss of prestige. According to leaked Russian documents, Russia funds and runs in military, administrative, and economic terms the self-declared republics in the eastern part of Ukraine—an additional burden on the struggling Russian economy. In Ukraine, the cost is calculated not only in money and resources but also in human lives. The war has claimed more than 9,000 dead and at least twice as many wounded. Millions left the conflict zone, creating a refugee crisis in Ukraine that dwarfs the current refugee problem of the European Union.[11]

The hopes that the conflict could be resolved soon faded with every day of its continuation. The Minsk agreements reached between the Ukrainian government and the rebels in September 2014, after Russia's direct invasion of Ukraine and the Ukrainian defeat in the Battle of Ilovaysk, and then amended with the help of Germany and France and with the participation of Russia in February 2015, after the Russian-backed rebels violated the earlier agreement and seized the Ukrainian town of Debaltseve, now show little sign of life. The political solution as agreed in February 2015 included an end to hostilities; the withdrawal of all foreign military formations, including mercenaries, from the separatist republics; and the organization of local elections, which in turn should lead to the reestablishment of Ukraine's control over its borders with the Russian Federation. But the agreements failed to specify what comes first: the withdrawal of foreign military formations, which everyone understood are Russian, or the elections. Ukraine said sovereignty first. The Russian government and its proxies in eastern Ukraine disagreed.[12]

The realization of the "elections first" scenario would have ensured continuing Russian control over the region once it formally reenters Ukraine. A Russian-controlled Donbas, which the war has turned into a humanitarian disaster zone, would thus become a ball chained to Ukraine's leg, making economic and political reforms currently under way in that country all but impossible. The key precondition for the implementation of the Minsk agreements—the end to the military hostilities—remained an elusive target. August 2016 saw a significant increase of Russian troops on the borders with Ukraine, and the Ukrainian president Petro Poroshenko warned the world about Russia preparing a full-scale invasion of Ukraine. In October 2016, the leaders of the four countries that had participated in the Minsk negotiations in February 2015 (Minsk II) agreed on the creation of a road map for the implementation of the Minsk agreements, but privately few European officials expect the agreements to be implemented anytime soon.[13]

Vladimir Putin unilaterally abandoned the Minsk agreements in his televised speech to the nation on February 21, 2022, following the bizarre meeting of the Russian Security Council at which his sycophantic underlings assured their boss, in full view of television cameras, that they completely supported his denunciation of the agreements and de facto start of Russia's war against Ukraine. In his lengthy speech, which foreign observers called a history lecture, Putin laid claim not only to the Russian puppet dependencies in eastern Ukraine but also to Ukraine as a whole.[14]

The historical background to that claim had been laid out by Putin in a long historical essay published under his byline on the Kremlin website in July 2021. There he reaffirmed his imperial vision of the Russian nation. "I said that Russians and Ukrainians were one people—a single whole," asserted Putin in his opening statement. "These words were not driven by some short-term considerations or prompted by the current political context. It is what I have said on numerous occasions and what I firmly believe."[15]

While the article mainly emphasized developments in Ukraine and Russia in 1917, the historical portion of Putin's televised war speech of February 21 dwelled almost exclusively on the Soviet period. There, Putin declared the modern Ukrainian state to have been first and foremost a creation of Vladimir Lenin and the Bolsheviks. That theme was deeply rooted in the writings of Russian White Guard officers such as General Anton Denikin, who emigrated after the Bolshevik victory. It was also a prominent motif in the thought and published works of Aleksandr Solzhenitsyn. Putin decided to add historical gravitas to this argument, pointing out that he had studied the subject on the basis of archival documents. In his de facto declaration of war, Putin stated that "modern Ukraine was entirely created by Russia or, to be more precise, by Bolshevik, Communist Russia. This process started practically right after the 1917 revolution, and Lenin and his associates did it in a way that was extremely harsh on Russia—by separating, severing what is historically Russian land."[16]

Vladimir Putin launched his war with the declared intention of protecting the imagined unity of Russians and Ukrainians, who, as he had claimed repeatedly, were one and the same people. Relying on his own distorted version of history, he expected the Ukrainians to greet their Russian "liberators" with flowers. This delusion set up his army for defeat in the battle for Kyiv: the Russian troops were issued parade uniforms for a planned victory march on Kyiv's Khreshchatyk street but received no food rations and had enough fuel to last only two or three days. The botched invasion destroyed the last vestiges of any belief that Ukrainians and Russians are fraternal peoples, let alone the very same people.

In Ukraine, the rethinking of relations with Russia as a historically and culturally close neighbor began in 2014, after Russia annexed the Crimea and launched a hybrid war in the Donbas. The Ukrainians were mobilized by that first stage of

The Russo-Ukrainian War in the Historical Perspective   259

aggression and politically united to a degree that made it impossible for the Kremlin to destabilize Ukraine by exploiting differences in language and culture between the predominantly Ukrainian-speaking west and center of the country and the mainly Russian-speaking east and south.

Although it is much too early to predict what will happen in the days, weeks, and months to come, there can be little doubt that the current war has severed the last symbolic ties between the two peoples. It has produced the opposite of its authors' intended result. Instead of arresting the development of the Ukrainian nation and checking its drive for independence, Russia's unprovoked invasion, its loss of the battle for Kyiv, and the failure of its large-scale offensive in the Donbas have instead strengthened Ukraine's sense of identity and unity, endowing the country with a new raison d'être, new narratives, and new heroes and martyrs.

Far from promoting unity between Russians and Ukrainians, the current war has helped to destroy a number of Russian imperial and Soviet myths that underpinned the ties between the two nations in the course of the nineteenth and twentieth centuries. Cracks appeared even at the very top of the Orthodox Church, which serves as one of the last institutional and spiritual links uniting many Ukrainian citizens with Russia. As the war began, Patriarch Kirill of Moscow issued a statement calling on "all parties to the conflict" to overcome the "divisions and contradictions that have arisen and have led to the current conflict." But Kirill's formally loyal subordinate and ally in Ukraine, the head of the Ukrainian Orthodox Church (Moscow Patriarchate), Metropolitan Onuphry, showed little tolerance for his superior's refusal to name, blame, and condemn the aggressor. "Russia has launched military actions against Ukraine," declared Onuphry, all but accusing Putin of the "sin of Cain."[17]

The fate of Mariupol, the Russian-speaking city in Ukraine's southeast, almost completely razed by the Russian army, most vividly exemplifies the failure of the "one Russian nation" idea in Ukraine. Putin's utopian vision of a Greater Russia has brought more death and suffering to ethnic Russians and Russian speakers than to any other group of Ukrainians. The indiscriminate bombing of Mariupol and Kharkiv, as well as of Kyiv itself, to which Putin referred in one of his articles as the "mother of Russian cities," has buried his vision in ruined buildings and in makeshift graves, dug by citizens for their loved ones in children's playgrounds, for generations to come.

What makes the war look particularly senseless from Russia's point of view is that many of its negative outcomes were obvious long before it was launched. If it was anyone's guess whether the Ukrainians would resist, no one doubted that

Putin's demands on NATO to retreat to its pre-1997 borders would only strengthen the unity of the alliance and heighten Russia's security concerns. In fact, the war unified the West more than anyone could have predicted before it began. It brought together Republicans and Democrats in Washington and consolidated popular support for European leaders to a degree unprecedented since the end of the Cold War. In fact, the Cold War in Europe is back. It is also back in the Middle East.

Russia's complete isolation from the West and continuing drift toward China revives the Cold War alliance between Moscow and Beijing but reverses their roles, with Beijing now the senior partner. This is a major shift in international politics that is expected to last for decades. Although the old Cold War divisions in Europe are back, whether the new Cold War goes global will greatly depend on the outcome of the war in Ukraine. Russia's setbacks in Ukraine make Chinese military action against Taiwan less likely because they demonstrate how small but determined nations can effectively defend themselves. A strong Ukraine in alliance with the West will weaken, not strengthen, the Russo-Chinese alliance and will make future aggression anywhere in the world less likely.

Was the war in Ukraine and the world's slide into a new Cold War inevitable? This venture into history suggests that both were predictable but hardly inevitable. Russia's aggression against Ukraine did not start on February 24, 2022, when Russian missiles began to rain down on Ukrainian cities and towns. Russian military aggression in the post-Soviet space began in earnest with the two bloody wars against Chechnya in the 1990s, followed by the invasion of Georgia in 2008, the annexation of the Crimea in 2014, and the start of hybrid warfare in the Donbas in the same year. If the world had reacted to the use of ballistic missiles against Grozny in 1999 as it is reacting to the ballistic missiles fired on Kyiv in 2022, then Russia would not now be destroying Ukrainian cities and forcing millions of refugees to seek refuge in the European Union. But at that time, the world decided to wait and see.

The policy of Washington and its allies changed dramatically in the months leading up to the Russian invasion of 2022 and in the weeks that followed. After years if not decades of hesitation, Washington and other NATO capitals finally saw Russia's serial aggression during the Putin presidency for what it was—not merely a claim to regional hegemony but an assault on the international order and democratic institutions in general. The supply of Western arms and sharing of military intelligence helped to stop the Russian invasion in its first weeks, enabling numerous Ukrainian counterattacks and military accomplishments, from the killing of scores of top Russian commanders to the sinking of the *Moskva*, the flagship of the

Russian navy's Black Sea Fleet. The unprecedented sanctions imposed not only on the Russian political leaders responsible for the war, including members of Putin's family and entourage, but also on key sectors of the Russian economy, have crippled the country's ability to fight a successful war in the future.[18]

History, recent and more distant, provides a useful lens that helps to assess the importance of the Russo-Ukrainian war. The origins of the crisis that caught both Washington and Brussels by surprise and the all-out war that was predicted by the Western intelligence services lie in Ukraine's desire to transform itself by choosing a Western model of development and Russia's determination to stop that from happening and keep the former province in its embrace. To be sure, what happens in Ukraine depends mainly on the actions of the Ukrainians themselves. But historical contextualization of the current crisis suggests that Ukraine's desperate attempts to free itself from the suffocating embrace of its former master have a much greater chance of success with strong international support.

Ukraine's movement away from its former imperial master toward an international center of gravity finds numerous parallels in the history of the disintegration of empires and the emergence of national states. The French helped the British colonies of North America free themselves from London; the British, Russians, and French helped the Greeks free themselves from Istanbul; and in 1918, the Germans backed the Ukrainian nation-building project against Bolshevik Moscow. What makes the Ukrainian situation different is that the European Union, the pole that attracts Ukraine most, is not a united polity or a state at all. The strength and attractiveness of the EU lie in its values and in the models of political, economic, and social organization of its member states. Its weaknesses are its cumbersome structure and difficulty in formulating a coherent foreign policy. Nor is the EU equipped to deal with military threats and war situations like the one in Ukraine. The EU has the ability to attract—but currently no political will to accept—new members and no military muscle to defend those aspiring to join it.

The Russo-Ukrainian war reminded the world once again of the importance of the United States as a major stakeholder in European security and prosperity—the role it played for most of the twentieth century. The United States, whose involvement in East European affairs diminished significantly in the wake of Second Gulf War, began its return to the region's political scene with the start of the Euro revolution in Ukraine. Washington, whose relations with Moscow have been tarnished by tensions in the Middle East in the wake of the Arab Spring of 2010 and suffered a further setback with Putin's return to the office of Russian president in the spring of 2012, has provided leadership in formulating a joint Western response to the crisis. That response, which included diplomatic pressure and economic sanctions against Russia, as well as financial and limited military assistance to Ukraine, helped stop Russian aggression in the fall of 2014. It became absolutely crucial for helping Ukraine to stop the aggressor in 2022 and hold its ground in 2023.

The delays with providing military aid to Ukraine because of the deadlock in the US Congress in the winter and spring of 2024 put Ukraine in an extremely difficult position, raising the possibility of Russian strategic victory and dire consequences for Ukraine, Europe, and the world. The future not only of Ukraine but also of US leadership in the world depends on the outcome of the current war, the largest military conflict in Europe since 1945.

NOTES

1. On the history of the disintegration of the Soviet Union, see Stephen Kotkin, *Armageddon Averted: The Soviet Collapse, 1970–2000* (Oxford University Press, 2008); and Serhii Plokhy, *The Last Empire: The Final Days of the Soviet Union* (Oxford University Press, 2014).

2. On Ukraine in the 1990s, see Alex J. Motyl, *Dilemmas of Independence: Ukraine After Totalitarianism* (Council on Foreign Relations, 1993); and Bohdan Harasymiw, *Post-Communist Ukraine* (Canadian Institute of Ukrainian Studies Press, 2002).

3. On the Orange Revolution, see Andrew Wilson, *Ukraine's Orange Revolution* (Yale University Press, 2006); and Taras Kuzio, *Democratic Revolution in Ukraine: From Kuchmagate to Orange Revolution* (Routledge, 2013).

4. Oleksandr Zinchenko, "Shchodennyk Maidanu. Pro shcho my todi dumaly" [Diary of the Maidan. What I Was Thinking at the Time], *Ukrainska Pravda*, February 17 2015, http://www.istpravda.com.ua/articles/2015/02/17/147354/. (Unless otherwise indicated, all translations from Russian and Ukrainian are mine—S.P.)

5. For the overview of the events on Maidan, Kyiv's Independence Square, in November 2013 through February 2014, see Andrew Wilson, *Ukraine Crisis: What It Means for the West?* (Yale University Press, 2014), chapters 4 and 5.

6. "Putin rsskazal kak prinimalos' reshenie o vozvrashchenii Kryma" [Putin Shared How the Decision on the Return of the Crimea Had Been Made], *NTV*, March 10, 2015, http://www.ntv.ru/novosti/1356399/; Putin, "Obrashchenie Prezidenta Rossiiskoi Federatsii" [Address of the President of the Russian Federation], *Prezident Rossii*, March 18, 2014, http://kremlin.ru/news/20603. The Russian takeover of the Crimea is discussed in Wilson, *Ukraine Crisis*, chapter 6. On the prehistory of the Russian annexation of the peninsula, see Taras Kuzio, *The Crimea: Europe's Next Flashpoint?* (Brookings Institute Press, 2011); and Gwendolyn Sasse, *The Crimea Question: Identity, Transition, and Conflict* (Harvard University Press, 2014).

The Russo-Ukrainian War in the Historical Perspective   263

7. Vladimir Putin, "Obrashchenie Prezidenta Rossiiskoi Federatsii," *Prezident Rossii*, March 8, 2014, http://kremlin.ru/news/20603. Cf. "Transcript: Putin Says Russia Will Protect the Rights of Russians Abroad," *Washington Post*, March 18, 2015.

8. Peter Baker, "Pressure Rising as Obama Works to Rein in Russia," *New York Times*, March 2, 2014; Douglas Ernst, "Bill Clinton: Putin Trying to 'Re-establish Russian Greatness,'" *Washington Times*, May 14, 2014; "Yatseniuk: Putin mriie vidrodyty SRSR" [Putin Dreams about Restoring the USSR], *BBC Ukraine*, April 20, 2014, http://www.bbc.com/ukrainian/politics/2014/04/140420_yatsenyuk_putin_ok.

9. The Russian hybrid war in eastern Ukraine received extensive coverage in the rapidly growing literature on the Ukraine Crisis. Apart from the cited above book by Andrew Wilson, other monographic contributions to the field include Richard Sakwa, *Frontline Ukraine: Crisis in the Borderlands* (I. B. Tauris, 2014); and Rajan Menon and Eugene B. Rumer, *Conflict in Ukraine: The Unwinding of the Post-Cold War Order* (MIT Press, 2015).

10. "Al'fred Kokh i Boris Nemtsov o realiiakh Rossii i Putina" [Alfred Kokh and Boris Nemtsov on the Realities of Russia and Putin], *Krugozor*, October 2014, http://www.krugozormagazine.com/show/article.2370.html.

11. Julian Ropcke, "Secret Document Exposes Putin's Shadow Government for Donbass," *Bild*, March 29, 2016, http://www.bild.de/politik/ausland/ukraine-konflikt/donbass-shadow-government-45102202.bild.html; "UN Report Finds Impunity for Killings 'Remains Rampant' in Ukrainian Conflict," *UN News Center*, July 14, 2016, http://www.un.org/apps/news/story.asp?NewsID=54455#.WBY-1vkrLIU.

12. "Minsk Agreement on Ukraine Crisis: Text in Full," *Daily Telegraph*, February 12, 2015; "The *Economist* Explains: What Are the Minsk Agreements?", *Economist*, September 16, 2016, http://www.economist.com/blogs/economist-explains/2016/09/economist-explains-7.

13. Damien Sharkov, "Ukraine Reports Russian Military Activity on Crimea Border," *Newsweek*, August 8, 2016; Maryse Godden "Ukraine President Petro Poroshenko Says Russia Preparing for Full-Scale Invasion and EU Is Powerless," *The Sun*, September 7, 2016; "Little Optimism after Normandy Format Meeting," *DW*, October 20, 2016, http://www.dw.com/en/little-optimism-after-normandy-format-meeting/a-36106924.

14. Address by the President of the Russian Federation. February 21, 2022, 22:35; The Kremlin, http://en.kremlin.ru/events/president/news/20603; Putin, "On the Historical Unity of the Russians and Ukrainians," The Kremlin, July 12, 2021, http://en.kremlin.ru/events/president/news/66181.

15. Putin, "On the Historical Unity of the Russians and Ukrainians."

16. Putin, "On the Historical Unity of the Russians and Ukrainians."

17. Lena Rudenko, "Mitropolit UPTs MP 'poblagodaril' patriarkha Kirilla za prolituiu v Ukraine krov': vy otvetite pered Bogom," *Apostrof*, June 6, 2022, https://apostrophe.ua/news/society/2022-06-06/mitropolit-upts-mp-poblagodaril-patriarha-kirilla-za-prolituyu-v-ukraine-krov-vyi-otvetite-pered-bogom/271059.

18. "Fact Sheet: United States and G7 Partners Impose Severe Costs for Putin's War against Ukraine," The White House, May 8, 2022, https://www.whitehouse.gov/briefing-room/statements-releases/2022/05/08/fact-sheet-united-states-and-g7-partners-impose-severe-costs-for-putins-war-against-ukraine.

Chapter Ten

Russia, Demography, and Putin's Hidden Agenda

Andrew S. Natsios

> Russia's fate and its historical prospects depend on one thing: how many of us there are and how many of us there will be.
>
> VLADIMIR PUTIN, JULY 2020

Given the opaque nature of the Russian government and its obsession with secrecy, it has been challenging to understand all the factors that actually drove Vladimir Putin's invasion of Ukraine as opposed to his public justification, which is may obscure his real motives. This chapter reviews available evidence, which suggests the Kremlin's public statements on Ukraine ignore some hidden forces driving Russian behavior. Simply put, Moscow's objective has been the acquisition of strategically important new territory for a reborn Russian empire, the reengineering of the local population, the gutting of neighboring states, and the undermining of NATO and the European Union.[1] This reborn empire, for Putin and the Siloviki (the constellation of security services which help Putin control Russia), is necessary to stem Russia's ongoing demographic decline described earlier by Nicholas Eberstadt.[2] Russia is dying (a characterization first made by the Nobel Prize–winning Russian writer Aleksandr Solzhenitsyn in his address to the Russian parliament—the Duma—in 1994). Its mortality rates are among the highest in modern history for an educated industrial society, and its fertility rates are below maintenance level at 1.5 children (maintenance level is 2.1). Moscow's long-term strategy has been to absorb Ukraine and other neighboring states to address the threat Russia's shrinking population poses to its viability as a great power. Putin's insistence that Ukrainians and Russians are one people is a function of his need for Slavic populations to be added to the new Russian empire to stem this demographic crisis, even if the Ukrainian (and other Slavic) people militantly reject the notion they are ethnic Russians.

Moscow's initial strategy was to invade with massive force, decapitate Kyiv's government in a few days, and install a regime that would be subordinate to Russian interests and avoid the country's drift to NATO and the European Union, a drift that would have made Putin's annexation of Ukraine at some later date untenable. When that strategy failed because of Ukrainians' unified national resistance and the Russian military's initial poor performance on the battlefield, Moscow moved to a more realistic strategy of shrinking Ukraine as a nation-state, permanently damaging its economy, resettling Ukrainians deep into Russia and Siberia from conquered territory, and causing large-scale refugee flows to disrupt Ukrainian society and burden European countries, many of which are providing support to Ukraine.

The argument of this chapter contrasts with more common interpretations of Putin's motives. George Kennan and John Mearsheimer in the late 1990s argued (separately) that the expansion of NATO membership to former members of the Soviet bloc in Eastern Europe and the Balkans threatened Russia's interests and would eventually cause a Russian backlash.[3] Thus, they would blame the West for provoking the Russian invasion of Ukraine. Mearsheimer has famously argued that domestic imperatives do not drive the foreign policy of great powers. But in Russia, they do. Mearsheimer writes in *The Tragedy of Great Power Politics* that one of the critical elements of national power is demography, an argument that would support my thesis that Russia's demographic crisis is a major factor driving Putin's aggression. "Although there are always a variety of such resources," he writes, "the size of a state's population and its wealth are the two most important components for generating military might. Population size matters a lot, because great powers require big armies, which can be raised only in countries with large populations. States with small populations cannot be great powers."[4] And Putin desperately wants Russia to remain (or become) a great power.

Stephen Kotkin, the preeminent biographer of Stalin and historian of Russia, has argued that Mearsheimer and Kennan, although great scholars, are wrong about NATO being the cause of the Russian invasion of Ukraine. David Remnick of *The New Yorker* recounts his interview with Kotkin, writing, "Putin's aggression is 'not some kind of deviation from the historical pattern.'" Remnick references Kotkin again, quoting him as saying, "Russia in the nineteenth century looked much as it does today: It had an autocrat. It had repression. It had militarism. It had suspicion of foreigners and the West." Kotkin argued in a talk at Texas A&M University's Bush School on March 29, 2023, that Russia's war in Ukraine is a continuation of historical tsarist and Soviet expansionary strategies, which have nothing to do with NATO expansion. Finally, Remnick reports that "Kotkin describes how and why the Putin regime has evolved toward despotism, and he speculates that the strategic blunders in invading Ukraine likely resulted from the biases of authoritarian rulers like Putin, and the lack of good information available to them."[5]

Russian political scientist Sergei Medvedev, writing before the second invasion, argued that the Siloviki need an outside threat—in this case NATO—even if it is entirely invented, to justify their "bureaucratic domination" of the Russian system. The Siloviki, he argues, create nonexistent threats that later become crises because of their initial provocations.[6]

In a prescient book, *Putin's Wars: The Rise of Russia's New Imperialism*, published after the first invasion of Ukraine but before the second, Marcel H. Van Herpen argues that Putin and the Siloviki seek to reestablish the Russian empire. This vision—a throwback to tsarist and Soviet strategies—puts all countries within Russia's reach at risk of absorption, as the second Ukraine invasion demonstrates. Van Herpen describes in abundant detail Putin's overt long-term plan dating back to 2003 to absorb Belarus, which would realize his revanchist vision.[7] This chapter takes the Kotkin view and will connect Putin's current strategies with his and other Soviet leaders' previous actions to show historical continuity.

The Existential Crisis: Putin's Grand Strategy

While the United States and the European democracies focused on emptying the Russian treasury, crippling its economy, and paralyzing its sources of revenue, Russia was determined to acquire new territory and Slavic populations, beginning with the 2008 annexation of South Ossetia and Abkhazia from Georgia.

Moscow's strategy predating the second Ukraine war was to kill or displace the hostile population in neighboring states and then reengineer the ethnic and linguistic balance by moving Russians or their allies to repopulate the area. Suspected local populations were then resettled in Siberia or Central Asia. Russia sought to weaken any states within its reach, tie them to Russia, or make the survival of the elites entirely dependent on long-term Russian support. This had happened before under Stalin in the 1930s, and it happened again in 2014, when Russia annexed Crimea in eastern Ukraine and then absorbed Luhansk and Donetsk, and again in 2022, when it occupied the Ukrainian Black Sea coastline.[8] These events accompanied the largest forced migration of populations (westward to become refugees) in Europe since World War II. But although this has likely been Putin's strategy since the second stage of his war in Ukraine began, it does not mean he will be successful in carrying it out.

Putin's strategy has faced strong headwinds. Most of Europe has united in opposition to Russian aggression and welcomed millions of Ukrainian refugees, who escaped the violence by moving to EU countries, although many began returning in 2023. An expanded NATO alliance with the addition of Finland and Sweden is experiencing new energy and direction. The Ukrainian military initially performed admirably on the battlefield, while the Russian army appeared to be weaker than had been thought before the second invasion. Most importantly, Russian total combat casualties (dead and wounded) in the war were estimated by *The Economist* as of December 31, 2023, to be between 290,000 and 460,000, including deaths at 66,000 to 88,000—numbers that are four times greater than those the country suffered in Afghanistan during a twelve-year war in the 1980s and 1990s.[9]

That said, Russia's grand strategy in the second phase of the war has been refocused on east and south Ukraine along the Black Sea, one of the invasion's central objectives. In the third phase of the war, which began in May 2024, the Russian military massed 500,000 troops to take Kharkiv in the northeast region of Ukraine. Putin is playing a great game of empire building—he sees himself as a modern-day Russian tsar, and in June 2022 he compared himself to Peter the Great. In this effort, he is following the strategy of Joseph Stalin, one of his role models. His ambitions are expansive and reach far beyond Ukraine. Russia has troops in Libya supporting one faction in that country's civil war. Russia also tried to orchestrate a coup and assassinate the prime minister in Montenegro[10]—which has a coastline on the Adriatic Sea—when the country's leadership moved toward NATO membership. The Wagner Group—Russian mercenaries fronting for Russian intelligence—is moving across the African Sahel, shoring up failing dictators who will then be dependent on Moscow for survival. (After the death of Yevgeny Prigozhin in 2023, the group was renamed the Africa Corps—oddly enough, the name of the German army in North Africa during World War II.) Moscow's imperial ambitions have no bounds, even if its resources to carry them out are constrained.

In 2023, a Kremlin strategy paper was leaked to the media describing Russia's plan to absorb Belarus by 2030, which President Lukashenko said in an interview in November 2024 would mean war between Russia and Belarus if it was carried out.

Russia's Bleak Demographic Future

The question remains: Why did Putin invade Ukraine in the first place? The invasion carried a substantial risk of conflict with external actors such as NATO, a high potential cost in blood and treasure, Russia's isolation in the world order, and internal political fallout among Russian elites and eventually the public. Although these risks appear to be obvious now, given how poorly the Russian military performed during the initial invasion of Ukraine, Putin may have seen these risks as minimal because of the West's appeasement in the face of earlier Russian aggression. But could some other factors be driving Russian aggression?

Walter Laqueur, a keen analyst of Russia, predicts that Russia's dire demographic future would affect its foreign policy: "Discussions on demographic problems may seem not to belong to an analysis of (Russia's) foreign policy. But it appears likely that considerations of this kind will have a direct and decisive impact on Russian policy with respect to the near abroad."[11] Pessimistic estimates by the United Nations have Russia's population declining from 145 million in 2022 to 124.6 million by 2050 and 83.7 million by 2100. The UN's average projections have the population declining to 135.8 million by 2050.[12] Anatoly Antonov, a nationalist scholar at Moscow State University, is even more pessimistic: he estimates Russia's population could decline by 50% within fifty years to 73 million people.[13]

These are of course only forecasts, and if birth rates improve or adult mortality rates decline, they may not be realized. But these estimates were done before the COVID-19 pandemic, which caused a drop in Russian life expectancy by a year and a half and caused 1.2 to 1.6 million excess deaths, according to *The Economist's* modeling. (The number of excess deaths in Russia was proportionately twice the number in the United States, which itself had high COVID-19 mortality rates.) These estimates were also made before the war in Ukraine. It is not simply the net population decline, as many European states, South Korea, Taiwan, China, and Japan are suffering from a similar phenomenon of low fertility rates, but the pathologies in Russian society that have depressed life expectancy. Russia's below-maintenance fertility rates and very high mortality rates for an educated country combine to pose the greatest threat to Putin's ambition for Russia becoming a great power. Nicholas Eberstadt points out that:

> While death rates for Russian infants and children are close to First World, death rates for Russia's working age population are Fourth World. And generating Fourth World death rates in a literate urban society during peacetime

Russia, Demography, and Putin's Hidden Agenda 269

requires very different causes of death from those that impose brutal survival trajectories on Fourth World populations today . . .

In very poor countries, foreshortened life is typically due to the collision of malnutrition and communicable diseases. Although Russia's tuberculosis and HIV problems are very real, they account for only a tiny share—around one-fiftieth—of the vast gap separating all-cause, age-standardized mortality levels in Russia and the EU. Here's the surprise: Russia's terrible killers are cardiovascular disease (CVD) and injuries (homicides, suicides, traffic fatalities and miscellaneous accidents). For decades, Russia's death rates from CVD were higher than the highest levels ever recorded in any Western country (namely Finland, circa 1970). Indeed, in 2008, male CVD mortality levels for the Russian Federation were three and a half times higher than would have been predicted solely on the basis of the country's income. Age-standardized Russian CVD mortality has come down a bit since 2005. Even so, 2019 CVD mortality was two and a half times higher in Russia than in Finland and 3.2 times overall levels for the OECD.[14]

Even more surprising, the life expectancy of a fifteen-year-old Russian boy in 2019 was fifty-four years, comparable to mortality rates in South Sudan and Haiti, where they are even a bit lower than Russia's.[15] To repeat, these extraordinarily high Russian mortality rates for an educated, urbanized society are not a function of disease and malnutrition but of traffic fatalities, accidents, homicides, alcoholism, drug addiction, and suicides. Walter Laqueur reports that suicide rates among youth in Russia are three times higher than the highest rates in European countries. He writes that suicides are reported as accidents in nonurban areas of Russia, and so the actual suicide data are much higher than official statistics show.[16]

Putin himself has consistently focused on this human capital crisis facing Russia from early in his presidency. In his annual address to the Federal Assembly (the State Duma and Federation Council) on May 16, 2003, just three years after assuming the presidency of Russia, Putin stated:

> The [2002] Russian census showed that, according to preliminary data, the permanent population of the country is more than 145 million people. This is almost two million people more than current statistics showed, but also two million less than it was in 1989. What do these numbers say? Firstly, that the country's population continues to decline . . . Secondly, despite a certain increase in the birth rate, we nevertheless "grew" not thanks to the birth rate,

270 Andrew S. Natsios

but due to legal immigration. In total, over the past decade, about 7 million people have moved to us, mainly from the countries of the Commonwealth of Independent States.[17]

In his annual address on April 25, 2005, Putin said:

> I also believe that population growth should be accompanied by a meaningful strategy for immigration policy. We are interested in the influx of qualified legal labor resources. But still a considerable number of entrepreneurs in Russia enjoy the benefits of illegal migration, because a disenfranchised immigrant is especially convenient for unlimited exploitation . . . Ultimately, every legal immigrant should be given the opportunity to become a Russian citizen. The solution of such problems cannot be put off. Measures to create conditions conducive to childbearing, reduce mortality and streamline migration should be implemented simultaneously. I am sure that our society is capable of solving these problems and gradually stabilizing the size of the Russian population.[18]

In 2007, Putin endorsed a report on Russia's demographic crisis which recorded the low birth rates and high mortality rates, as well as the risks of an ever-increasing proportion of Muslims making up the population.[19] The report suggested pronatalist policies, which its authors thought would increase births, reduce premature deaths, and increase life expectancy. Later that year, Putin himself in a speech to the Civic Chamber of the Russian Federation revealed a three-stage plan to reverse the demographic slide into economic and political oblivion. He proposed substantial subsidies for women to have a second child, better housing, and an improved healthcare system.[20] These measures appear to have been successful over the short term (until 2020) in raising fertility rates closer to the European norm.

What is noteworthy about Putin's three speeches from 2003, 2005, and 2007 is his welcoming attitude toward legal immigration as one way of dealing with Russia's declining population and his concrete proposals to increase fertility rates. But Putin's mindset appears to have changed by 2014. According to Kimberly Marten, prior to the annexation of Crimea and the invasion of eastern Ukraine in early 2014, Putin did not use ethnic nationalist rhetoric in his public pronouncements on foreign policy. That changed with his victory speech to the Duma on March 18, 2014, after the annexation of Crimea, which he called "primordial Russian land," explaining that after 1991, "the Russian nation became one of the biggest . . . ethnic groups in the world to be divided by borders."[21] (This, of course, was a convenient fiction, as Crimea did not become part of the tsarist Russian

Russia, Demography, and Putin's Hidden Agenda 271

Empire until the eighteenth century under Catherine the Great, which would hardly make it primordial.)

Russian scholars and scholars of Russia have long debated the relative decline of the White Russian, Orthodox Christian population of Russia compared with that of the Central Asian and Caucasus Muslim populations. The Jamestown Foundation writes that Russian census figures from 2010 to 2021 reflect this decline of nearly 5 million people who identify as ethnically Russian.[22] A new chapter in this debate was opened when the Russian Institute for Strategic Studies (RISS) published a report in early 2014 on immigration to Russia, mimicking the one published in 2007 mentioned above.[23] One of the main authors of the report, Igor Beloborodov, in an interview[24] at the same time, claimed that 30 million immigrants, many illegal and many Muslim, had migrated from Central Asia to Russia, and that by 2050, a majority of the country's population would be Muslim. (During the 1990s, most immigrants to Russia were ethnic Russians from former Soviet republics, but this changed in the 2000s.) These statistics reflect the same predictions made in the 2007 report. If the 30-million-migrant figure is accurate (FSB estimates are much lower, although its data may be of legal immigration), it would mean that more than 20% of the Russian population were migrants, legal or illegal. By comparison, the United States had about 46 million foreign-born people in 2021, or about 12% of the country, approximately 25% of whom were undocumented.

The report goes into great detail on the nature of this avalanche of immigration and the threat it poses to Russian culture and language (and implicitly to Orthodox Christian Russia). One of the themes of the report is the fact that these immigrants do not speak Russian and are loyal to their home countries, not to Russia. Most notoriously, the report claims that mass immigration to Russia from central Asia is the most important long-term factor fueling Islamic radicalism in the Russian Federation. The RISS is an institute of the Russian government, and the last two appointments to its board of directors were from the Siloviki. It is unlikely the RISS would publish a report on such a controversial subject that Putin did not agree with, although he never quotes from the report in public. The report's very existence was not publicly known until it was communicated to the Russian news agency *Rosbalt* on February 27, 2014.

The timing of the release of the report is most instructive. The Revolution of Dignity in Ukraine, driven by the Euromaidan protests in Kyiv, took place February 18–23, 2014. Russian military operations in Crimea began February 22, 2014, five days before the RISS report was sent to *Rosbalt* for public distribution. On

April 7, Donetsk People's Republic declared its independence from Ukraine; the report was formally posted to the RISS website on April 9; and the puppet republic of Luhansk announced its independence from Ukraine on April 27. This timing is unlikely to be a coincidence.

Putin's shift to ethnic and nationalist rhetoric in 2014, the release of the RISS report on immigration, and the first stage of the dismemberment of Ukraine all within weeks of each other are no coincidence: the report likely drove the annexation of Crimea and eastern Ukraine with its largely Orthodox Slavic population. Although independent demographers would likely dispute the claim that Russia would be a majority Muslim country by 2050, the important thing to note is that policymakers themselves believed it, and they decided to write and then release the report at this critical moment in history because they feared the claim may become a reality.

Four years later, in his 2018 presidential decree, Putin made clear that Moscow's 2019–2025 strategy to address Russia's demographic problem had shifted its focus from immigration to natural reproduction (it is an update to the earlier 2012 decree): "The main source of replenishing the population of the Russian Federation and providing the national economy with labor resources should remain its natural reproduction. Migration policy is an auxiliary tool for solving demographic problems and related economic problems."[25]

During his campaign for president in 2018, Putin promised to spend $8.6 billion to encourage larger families through mortgage subsidies and payouts to families. Russia's net population (deaths over births) declined between 1992 and 2012, and it began to increase only to reverse into decline again in 2016.[26] Russia underwent its largest peacetime population decline in recorded history as a result of the COVID-19 pandemic and may have had the highest proportionate rates of any country in the world.[27]

In Putin's January 15, 2020, annual address to the Federal Assembly,[28] which he presented a month before the start of the COVID-19 pandemic (and thus could not have been driven by the disease's high mortality rates), his tone becomes much more ominous than in his earlier statements. He tells legislators from the State Duma and Federation Council that it is their "historic duty" to respond to the demographic crisis in Russia, challenging them with the task of increasing the fertility rates to 1.7 births per woman (interestingly, this was the US rate prior to COVID-19). He added: "Every step we take, every new law, or government program—we need to evaluate them primarily from the point of view of our highest national priority: the saving and increase of the Russian nation." Putin's use of the term "saving" implies Russia is at risk of decline or even state failure. Putin himself reported in the same address in 2020 (before COVID-19 and the second invasion of Ukraine) that the Russian population was once again declining demographically: "However, new families are being created now by the small generation of the 1990s. *And the birthrate is falling again* [my emphasis]. This is the main problem of the current demographic period in Russia."[29]

A full 40% of Putin's presidential address in 2020—the most important policy document of the year—was devoted to sustaining and expanding pronatalist policies and spending priorities. Thus, it can be concluded that Putin's concern with Russia's demographic "emergency situation" is not a rhetorical diatribe but a policy question on which he is focusing substantial state resources. Why would he do this if the problem were a contrivance?

More than a year later, on April 21, 2021—around the same time[30] that the Kremlin began ordering Russian troops to the Ukrainian border—Putin spoke once again to the same audience of policymakers, stressing the importance of solving Russia's demographic problems. He stated, "Today the situation in the sphere of demography is extraordinary."[31] He used the word чрезвычайная here, which can also be translated as "alarming" or "in an emergency state." In both speeches, he explains the demographic crisis first, before all other issues, and characterizes it as a question of national survival "with geopolitical consequences." He even quotes the very depressed Russian fertility rates of the past—from 1943, in the middle of World War II, where 27 million Soviet citizens lost their lives, and from 1998, at the peak of the economic collapse in Russia following the end of the Cold War—and compares the current demographic crisis to these two earlier periods, an extraordinary statement.

At his annual press conference on December 23, 2021—*two months prior to the invasion of Ukraine*—Putin once again emphasized the severity of the demography problem:

> We now have a little more than 81 million people of working age . . . We must seriously increase this by the year 2024, by the year 2030. This is one of the factors of economic growth. Not to mention—I want to emphasize this once again—*the geopolitical component of this most important issue* [my emphasis], and the humanitarian one. Therefore, the salvation of the nation, which Solzhenitsyn talked about, is becoming and is one of the most important tasks and one of the drivers of growth.[32]

When Putin uses the term "humanitarian," he is explicitly referring to the declining Russian life expectancy that the central government had tried to reverse through pronatalist policies and improved services to families with children. And it did, but only for a few years. When Putin says that the 81 million people of working age must be seriously increased by 2030, he is inadvertently (or perhaps not) embracing the notion of conquest as the only strategy for realizing that objective because the other alternatives he tried could not possibly achieve this by that date, if at all. Only conquest could.

Putin's reference here to Solzhenitsyn is also instructive. When Aleksandr Solzhenitsyn, the great Russian Nobel Prize–winning writer, returned to Russia after a twenty-year exile in Vermont, he was invited to speak to the Russian Duma in 1994. In his address, he criticized the widespread corruption in the Russian government, the country's demographic decline, the looting of the economy by the oligarchs, and the failure to establish strong local democratic government. But he also argued that Russians, Ukrainians, and Belarusians are of one kin and should be "together," implicitly in one country. In the same speech, he said, "Statistics show that today (and everyone in the world already knows this) the death rate has surpassed the birth rate [in Russia]. That is, we have begun to die out. Today, the birth of a child in Russia is already regarded almost as a feat." Putin was a great admirer of Solzhenitsyn and met with him just after becoming president, later giving him one of the highest awards of the Russian state. Quoting him suggests Putin had embraced Solzhenitsyn's dream of Greater Russia, though the author would likely have condemned Putin's establishing of it by military conquest. Putin's territorial ambitions appear to be far broader than Solzhenitsyn's given his comment to school children in 2016 that "the Borders of Russia Never End."[33]

Putin and the Siloviki have economic and military reasons for their obsessive focus on Russia's demographic decline. Putin says this plainly: Russia will not have enough workers to fuel economic growth, particularly in nonextractive industries. He has said publicly on many occasions that Russia must reduce its dependence on oil and gas revenues, and without workers, that will be impossible to accomplish. Russia has vast and rich agricultural land, but 100 million hectares out of 225 million have fallen into disuse as rural Russia loses 200,000 young people each year when they migrate to the cities. This leaves fewer and fewer people to grow food; mechanization can only go so far because even mechanized agriculture needs workers.[34] But the demographic decline has also reduced the pool of eligible young men to be recruited into the military, particularly given the high mortality rates of young men. This is what Putin means by the demographic "emergency situation" having geostrategic implications. Simply put, Russia does not have the population size to be a great power—at least not without the absorption of other Slavic (in Putin's mind, Russian) countries.

To summarize, Vladimir Putin has followed four strategies since he took office for addressing Russia's demographic crisis just described. The first was to increase fertility rates through pronatalist economic incentives to have more children; this strategy was tried, worked for several years, but now appears to have leveled off (the fertility rate in 2021 was 1.5 children, according to the Russian statistics bureau Rosstat). The second was to encourage immigration and facilitate new immigrants taking Russian citizenship. Again, this was tried but then abandoned when many of the immigrants turned out to be heavily Muslim from central Asia, which Putin and the Siloviki saw as threatening the survival of Russia's Orthodox Slavic culture.

The third was to increase life expectancy through health programs and lifestyle changes (the most difficult of the options). This strategy was tried, succeeded briefly, but leveled off until COVID-19 and the Ukraine war, when life expectancy declined. Although Russia's fertility rates are about equal to those of Europe, its adult mortality rates, despite slightly improving in the mid-2010s and rising again in the late 2010s, remain at "shockingly high levels," to quote Eberstadt, for an educated society. According to Eberstadt's analysis in chapter 6 in this book, Russia will suffer a net decrease in population for the next historical period. And the fourth and most ominous of the strategies has been the absorption of new territory and populations, such as the invasion and occupation of Crimea in 2014, the virtual occupation of Belarus by the Russian army in 2021–2022 (and absorption into Russia by 2030, as reported earlier in this chapter), and the military conquest of Ukraine, which is ongoing at the time of writing.

Putin and Solzhenitsyn have not been the only Russians concerned with the demographic crisis facing the country. Aleksandr Dugin, a far-right-wing (some argue a neo-fascist) intellectual who some have labeled "Putin's brain,"[35] has written about the demographic challenges facing Russia. In his 1997 book, *Foundations of Geopolitics*,[36] Dugin writes that "such a weak demographic position of Russians is especially alarming when compared with the demographic growth of the Eurasian South." He adds that "the implementation of geopolitical plans from the very beginning must be synchronously accompanied by actions aimed at the demographic growth of Russians." Even in the book series *Project Russia*, another far-right-wing bestseller of Putin's Kremlin (described by Lynn Corum in chapter 8 of this book),[37] the author says Russia "is going extinct" because of its population problem. Thus, among far-right-wing intellectuals, the demography crisis is increasingly apocalyptic. Whoever succeeds Putin will certainly be as focused on the depopulation of Russia as he has been. It is an existential threat to Russian survival, though a different leader could well try alternative means for confronting the challenge such as political and economic reform.

Although multiple reports suggest Putin is "haunted" by the shrinking size of Russia's population, his own retrogressive policies have made the decline much worse. According to a study[38] posted to the Moscow-based *Takie Dela* portal in October 2021, well before the Ukraine war, 5 million[39] well-educated, technologically skilled young Russians have emigrated to Western democracies since Putin took office in 2000, perhaps seeking a better life, greater personal freedom, and higher living standards.

Putin has also misjudged the absorption of Ukraine and Belarus as a solution to the Russian demographic crisis on another level because both countries face the same demographic makeup as Russia: low fertility rates and high adult mortality rates. But they would nevertheless add more than 40 million people to Russia's population.

Evidence for Demography Driving Russian Policy

Evidence of organized efforts by the Russian government to relocate Ukrainians deep into Russia comes from several sources. The International Criminal Court (ICC) charged Vladimir Putin with war crimes in Ukraine and issued an arrest warrant. The details are secret because the ICC fears that those who provided evidence would be in danger if the charges were made public. Specifically, Ukrainian children, many of whom appear not to be orphans, have been transferred to orphanages around Russia en masse. The Conflict Observatory at the Yale School of Public Health has documented at least 6,000 Ukrainian children from occupied territory being taken from their homes and potentially "forcibly deported or displaced" to Russia.[40] The observatory reported that the real number of children may be several hundred thousand.[41]

US Secretary of State Antony Blinken issued a statement on July 13, 2022, posted to the State Department website five months after the initial invasion, condemning the forcible relocation of Ukrainian civilians, calling it a grave breach of the fourth Geneva convention and a war crime. He said:

> Estimates from various sources, including the Russian government, indicate
> that Russian authorities have interrogated, detained, and forcibly deported

between 900,000 and 1.6 million Ukrainian citizens, including 260,000 children from their homes to Russia—often to isolated regions in the Far East. Moscow's actions appear pre-meditated and draw immediate historical comparisons to Russian "filtration" operations in Chechnya and other areas . . . Reports also indicate Russian authorities are deliberately separating Ukrainian children from their parents and abducting others from orphanages before putting them up for adoption inside Russia.[42]

The Russian strategy in Ukraine is not new. During the Greek Civil War after World War II, the Communist insurgency, backed by the Soviet Union in a strategy called "Paidomazoma," forcibly removed up to 30,000 Greek children from rural areas to destroy the villages' futures and demoralize the families. The children were sent to Moscow and orphanages in other areas to be brought up in socialist societies. They returned to Greece only after the collapse of the Soviet Union, when borders opened to foreign travel.

The composition of the 66,000 to 88,000 Russian combat deaths in Ukraine, reported earlier in this chapter, provides further evidence of Putin's hidden strategy. The Kremlin appears to be moving politically expendable troops—those recruited from prisons and non-Russian ethnic minorities (who make up 20% of the Russian population)—as cannon fodder to the front lines to wear down the Ukrainian army while protecting the ethnic Russian soldiers from combat. These include troops from Dagestan, Tuva, Tatarstan, Buryatia, Chechnya, and Krasnodar.[43] A former president of Mongolia (and leading figure in the human rights movement) said in September 2022, "I know since the start of this bloody war [in Ukraine], ethnic minorities who live in Russia suffered the most . . . They have been used as nothing more than cannon fodder."[44] The addition of 10,000 North Korean troops to the Russian front lines underscores this strategy of avoiding Orthodox Russian troops being put in harm's way.

This is not the first time Moscow used troops from non-Russian and Muslim areas of the country as cannon fodder; they followed the same strategy in Afghanistan in the 1980s, where most of their troops were from Soviet republics that were principally Muslim. In fact, the breakaway Soviet republics in central Asia that insisted on independence after the collapse of the Soviet Union in 1991 were motivated largely by popular "bitterness, frustration and contempt" because of this policy.[45] Additionally, the leader of the Wagner Group, Yevgeny Prigozhin, recruited prisoners to join his combat forces with the promise that if they survived, their sentences would be commuted. *Newsweek* reported that 40,000 of the 50,000

Wagner soldiers in the Ukraine war had been prisoners.[46] The White House briefed that the Wagner Group had suffered over 30,000 casualties, with 9,000 killed, a disproportionate number of casualties compared with the regular Russian army.[47] Thus, the assignment of combat troops to the most dangerous duty appears to have been based on demographic calculations to protect law-abiding ethnic Russian Orthodox troops in the regular army from suffering high casualty rates.

The departure of Russians who fled the country after the invasion further aggravated the population crisis. This flight accelerated when Putin made a national broadcast in March 2022 in which he called for "the self-purification of Russia from traitors and scum"[48] who have protested the Ukraine war. The FSB (the successor to the KGB) reports that 3.8 million Russians left the country in the first quarter of 2022 (although it is not clear from the data how many of these people are planning to return to Russia).[49]

Thus, the very war that was supposed to address the demographic crisis in Russia appears to have made it significantly worse. The commander of the Wagner mercenary group publicly urged Putin to stop any further out-migration of highly skilled Russians. Why has Putin allowed this? He cares for one thing more than Russia's human capital crisis: his own survival. According to a *Washington Post* article, many of the out-migrating Russians are the very people who have been in the streets protesting the invasion of Ukraine.[50] These are a young, well-educated, technocratic urban elite who despise Putin and might form the vanguard of an uprising against him (among those under thirty, Putin has had a 20% approval rating, which is four times higher among older people).[51]

The Demographic Vulnerability of Siberia

Russia faces one other existential threat (which is also not new), and that is its vast, empty interior. Siberia (a third larger in land area than the United States) has always been sparsely populated, but that will grow more extreme over the next several decades. In a widely read study, Lev Gudkov, one of Russia's leading sociologists, estimated that Siberia's population could decrease by 50% over the next fifty years—from 40 million to 20 million.[52] A separatist movement in Siberia has been growing for some time, fueled by Moscow's inaction on local issues. Moscow was forced to allow Siberians to identify themselves on their internal passports as Siberians rather than as Russians because of this separatist pressure.[53] Russia is home to a third of the planet's mineral, oil, and gas wealth, much of it in Siberia—an extraordinary national treasure if Russia can keep it.

It is China that Russia should be most worried about, not NATO, Europe, or the United States.[54] Putin's embrace of Xi Jinping is not because Russia and China are long-time brothers in arms—they nearly went to war in the 1960s and 1970s—but because it is better to embrace your potential enemies than confront them, particularly given Russia's vast Siberian vulnerability. In theory, Russia's alliance with China allows Putin to ignore the depopulation of Siberia—which may happen anyway—and resettle Siberian Russians in the new European territorial acquisitions without any immediate fear of China invading Siberia (as Moscow did in Crimea, as I will describe shortly).

The Ukraine war has provided Moscow with another solution to the depopulation of Siberia: the forced resettlement of Ukrainians. The Russian minister of defense Sergei Shoigu announced in late May 2022 that "more than 1.37 million people have been evacuated from the dangerous regions of the people's republic, as well as from Ukraine to Russia."[55] Human Rights Watch has reported that many have been exiled to Sakhalin, an island off the Pacific coast of Siberia. That Russia is doing this to "protect" the civilian population of Ukraine is not believable given that the camps have been built 10,000 miles away from Ukraine on Sakhalin, making it more difficult for people to return to Ukraine. The real reason for the relocation of 1.37 million people is likely the desire to bolster Siberia's declining population. This is a substantial amount of planned population reengineering—all in the first four months of the Ukraine war. What is even more troubling is that when the exiled Ukrainians arrive, they are sent to filtration camps, where Human Rights Watch reports that conditions are abysmal. In the camps, the Ukrainian displaced populations have their passports confiscated, which makes leaving Russia very difficult.[56]

Reengineering the Local Population

The latest stage of Moscow's imperial strategy, driven by this human capital crisis, was evident in the conquest of Mariupol, one of the most important Ukrainian ports on the Black Sea. That Mariupol was a Russian-speaking city historically oriented to Moscow was irrelevant to Putin. During the 2019 elections, the pro-Russian candidate Yuriy Boyko received 30% of the votes in Mariupol;[57] Volodymyr Zelensky, while getting 73% of the vote nationally, received only 29% in Mariupol. Mariupol had been a pro-Russian city, yet Russian missiles and artillery have destroyed 80%–90% of the city, which now likely has little remaining loyalty to anything Russian.

By appointing Russian general Aleksandr Dvornikov (who was later replaced in the constantly changing chain of command) to lead Russian forces in the second phase of the Ukraine campaign beginning in April 2022, Putin sent a clear and unambiguous message: we will crush all opposition to the new Russian empire even if it means laying waste to entire cities and regions. Dvornikov pursued such a strategy in Chechnya, where he leveled Grozny, the capital city.[58] He was known as the Butcher of Syria after leveling Aleppo, a center of opposition to Russia's ally President Bashar al-Assad in Damascus. Admiral James Stavridis, former supreme allied commander of NATO, told *NBC News*, "He [Dvornikov] has used tools of terrorism throughout that period, including working with Syrian forces, torture centers, systematic rape, nerve agents. He is the worst of the worst."[59]

What happened in Mariupol was also Russia's modus operandi in Chechnya and Syria. The civilian losses were substantial in both cases. The UN estimated that 350,000 civilians died in the Syrian civil war; other estimates go much higher—to 650,000. The death toll from two wars in Chechnya was in the range of 160,000[60] to 300,000[61] military and civilians—a remarkably high proportion of a prewar population of 2 million. In addition to deaths, the regions suffered massive displacement. More than 350,000 people[62] fled Chechnya for neighboring Ingushetia, other parts of Russia, central Asia, and central Europe, which means that half the population of Chechnya died or became permanent refugees.

To understand Putin's objectives for Mariupol, the case of Crimea is illustrative. The Russian army and navy razed Mariupol, a Ukrainian city, so Moscow can reengineer it as a Russian city with a Russian population. How do we know this? That is what they did in Crimea, but without destroying it first. Some 140,000[63] Ukrainians and Crimean Tatars were forced out of Crimea after 2014 and have been replaced by 250,000 Siberian Russians. Moscow favored Russians with no familial connections to Ukraine to avoid mixed loyalties, a problem Putin experienced within western Russia proper, where 11 million Russians had relatives in Ukraine. These incentives include $30,000 one-time payments[64] to the Siloviki to relocate.[65] Reliably loyal to Russia, the Siloviki would ensure control. Moreover, Russian banks organized large-scale remote mortgage programs[66] for Russians from Moscow, the High North, and Siberia to obtain financing for real estate purchases in Crimea. Russia also added thousands of military personnel to staff military installations in Crimea, along with the two new bases built since 2014.[67]

Putin's reengineering of Ukraine's population in Crimea echoes an imperial predecessor, Joseph Stalin, who did much the same thing. In 1944, Stalin forcibly relocated Pontic Greeks (who had lived in the Crimea and on the Black Sea coast since about 700 BCE) and Tatars (who had inhabited this peninsula since the thirteenth century CE)[68] from Crimea to central Asia, because he held their loyalty suspect. He then replaced them with ethnic Russians. Similarly, in the 1930s, he deported Koreans in the Soviet Far East, Meskhetian Turks, Kalmyks, Karachays, Poles, Estonians, and many other nationalities labeled as "anti-Soviet elements" to different parts of central Asia and Siberia. Hundreds of thousands of these people died during their brutal relocation.

Russian Acquisition of the Black Sea Coast and Moldova, and the Encirclement of Ukraine

Russia's conquest of Ukraine's entire Black Sea coast would give it control of Ukrainian grain exports—Ukraine is the world's fourth-largest exporter of corn and fifth-largest of wheat. The war has already interfered with the export of Ukrainian grain and sunflower oil, putting many countries at risk. Research shows that countries without seaports have much lower economic growth rates (and are poorer) than those with them. Thus, the Russian annexation of the Ukrainian coast would also permanently strengthen the Russian economy while ensuring the long-term weakening of Ukraine's.[69] It would also provide Russia a land route to Crimea from the formerly Ukrainian provinces of Luhansk and Donetsk, which Putin has declared independent republics.

Some argue that annexing these provinces would allow Russia to profit from its occupation. Currently, its occupation in Crimea and aid to separatists in the Donbas are loss leaders, costing Russia as much as $1.5 to $2 billion annually. Ukrainian officials estimate that Russia covers 50% of the budget for Donetsk People's Republic and 80% of the budget for Luhansk People's Republic. Run like neo-Stalinist states,[70] repressing and persecuting dissidents through secret police and "loyal" residents, these provinces are unlikely to become growth poles.

How do we know that Russia's conquest of the Ukrainian Black Sea coast is a foundational issue for Putin? Moscow has said that keeping Russia's new territory on the Black Sea is critical to its position on peace negotiations to end the war. Kremlin spokesperson Dmitry Peskov stated that Ukrainians "should recognize that Crimea is Russian territory and that . . . Donetsk and Lugansk are independent states. And that's it. [The war] will stop in a moment."[71]

But as President Zelensky made clear, the hope that Putin's aspirations would be satisfied by incorporating Crimea, Donetsk, and Luhansk is a thin reed on which to build a strategy. Ukraine's battle is one for European and Western values; if Ukraine fails, other bordering countries will be next. Putin threatened Estonia with invasion earlier in 2022 and said that Finland and Sweden would face severe consequences for joining NATO. Many believe that Moldova may be the next target. Arrows on a wall map behind Aleksandr Lukashenko, president of Belarus, during a televised briefing in March 2022 laid out a path for the Russian army to take Moldova. Maia Sandu, Moldova's young reformist president, anticipating the threat on March 3, signed a formal application for EU membership in 2022.[72] This decision was not welcomed by the government of Transnistria, a separatist region backed by Russia in eastern Moldova, which on March 4, 2022, demanded the Moldovan government recognize its independence.[73]

With Moldova, Russia will surround much of Ukraine with vassal states—having already quietly occupied Belarus, where President Aleksandr Lukashenko was saved by Russian power only after he was confronted with massive demonstrations following his theft of the previous election. Putin announced that the Russian troops sent to suppress demonstrations would be staying permanently in Belarus, and in March 2023, he announced that tactical nuclear weapons would be moved there. As mentioned earlier, the Kremlin's plan to absorb Belarus by 2030 was leaked to the press in 2023. Should Putin succeed in occupying southern and eastern Ukraine and in overrunning Moldova, 77% of Ukraine's border would be controlled by Russia and its neocolonial empire.

Putin announced on February 23, 2022, that Russia had no intention of "occupying" Ukraine over the long term, without defining what Ukraine he was referring to.[74] The Putin-appointed leader of Donetsk later announced that his "republic" would likely merge with Russia shortly. But in this case, Putin was probably accurate in saying Russia did not want to occupy historical Ukraine; in fact, it does not have the massive number of troops needed to hold a hostile country. Nor does Russia have the funds to feed the population, given the destruction of the Ukrainian economy, nor the will or finances to reconstruct the wasteland its missiles and field artillery have created. Russia could much more easily repopulate empty provinces (after they have been leveled) along the Black Sea coast and make them into Russian colonies, ending any evidence of Ukrainian nationality.

Weaponizing Refugees and Destabilizing Europe

Another element of the Russian strategy may be to cause chaos in NATO's eastern flank by weaponizing millions of refugees fleeing the destruction of Ukrainian cities. Although some observers see the refugees as a tragic but ancillary side effect of the war, these refugee flows may in fact be a weapon Putin deliberately

Russia, Demography, and Putin's Hidden Agenda   283

created as part of his arsenal of asymmetrical warfare pointed at Russia's perceived enemies in Europe, dividing and weakening NATO and the EU. At the beginning of the Russian invasion of Ukraine, the United Nations High Commissioner for Refugees estimated that 4 million people would become refugees.[75] That number was reached by the end of March 2022; by early June, refugees had risen to 7 million, with another 6 million internally displaced. Combined, that is 30% of the population of Ukraine in just the first four months of the war. Some of these refugees have even appeared at the southern border of the United States seeking asylum.[76]

The atrocities against unarmed civilians that Russian troops committed in Bucha may not have been a case of a breakdown of military discipline but a deliberate effort. Moscow ordered troops to terrorize the Ukrainian civilian population across the country to accelerate the refugee movement to Europe. When Putin awarded commendations to the Russian troops who occupied Bucha and committed the atrocities, he was sending a troubling message of deliberate intent.

Russia has weaponized refugees in other wars, well before the second Ukraine invasion. The Belarus government moved Iraqi, Syrian, Afghan, and Yemeni refugees to its border with Poland and forced them across in 2021. Belarusian authorities even provided refugees with wire cutters to destroy the fence Poland had erected on its border with Belarus[77] so they could pour into Poland. Polish Prime Minister Mateusz Morawiecki stated that these people are "being used as a tool by Lukashenko in order to create turmoil in Europe,"[78] while suggesting that Putin was responsible for orchestrating this refugee influx.[79] Putin's regime has pursued a similar strategy in Syria by indiscriminately attacking civilian facilities, such as bakeries and hospitals, "in an attempt to force the local population into capitulation and increase the flow of refugees towards Turkey and Europe."[80] Similarly, it has been reported that Russian buses have been bringing Syrian asylum seekers to the border with Norway,[81] where they eventually made their way into the Schengen member country by bike.[82]

The Soviet Union, through its indiscriminate bombing campaigns of population centers in 1979 and 1980 during the Afghan civil war, forced millions of Afghan refugees to seek shelter in Pakistan; the Soviets did this to pressure the Pakistani government. The Soviets later bombed these same Afghan camps when they became support centers for the Taliban insurgency. The Soviet military weaponized refugees in Afghanistan, and 4 million refugees lived in camps for two decades in Pakistan. It was in these camps, according to Ahmed Rashid in his book *Taliban*, where the Taliban was trained and nurtured.[83]

284   *Andrew S. Natsios*

For years, Putin laid the groundwork in Europe for his refugee weaponization strategy. He provided financial subsidies and social media support to the far-right, populist European parties (and some far-left-wing parties in Greece and the United Kingdom), giving them an issue to spur their rise to power—a flood of refugees. For example, Sweden's acceptance of 163,000 refugees[84] from Syria, Iraq, and Afghanistan led directly to the rise of the far-right-wing Sweden Democrats, boosting the party to 18% in the polls at one point. Marine Le Pen, the far right's candidate for president in France, received a $10 million loan for her 2017 campaign from a Cypriot bank fronting[85] for the Russian intelligence service. Le Pen and her party have been hostile to refugees and migrants, NATO, the EU, and the United States—but pro-Russia and pro-Putin. Thus, the Russian invasion of Ukraine served a secondary purpose beyond the acquisition of new territory; namely, it created a second, much larger refugee crisis as a political gift to nativist, pro-Russian political parties in Europe.

Finally, Putin knows that NATO country leaders have a limited time in office and that he doesn't. He will likely be around until he dies or is removed from office by an internal putsch and can outlast any Western leader to carry out his grand strategy: to undermine or destroy NATO and the EU, seize as much coastline of the Black Sea and Mediterranean Sea as he can with a minimum of resistance, and get the United States out of Europe. Russia will then become the dominant continental power. Even if Putin fails this time, he or his successor, likely from the Siloviki, will continue to pursue an empire and territorial acquisitions by whatever means the United States, the EU, and NATO allow by their vacillation and inaction. Unless the inherent fragility of Putin's Russia ultimately makes continuing the war in Ukraine untenable, which could well happen, or Russia collapses from the centrifugal forces pulling the country apart, as described earlier, this demographic strategy will likely continue. Or it could be the withdrawal of US support for Ukraine in a second Trump administration leads to its collapse, which will only accelerate Russian aggression against other countries.

Some unsolicited advice to the Ukrainian government: the Russian army will not voluntarily leave Ukrainian territory unless the Ukrainian military drives them out. Economic sanctions will not deter Russia, nor will the prospect of war crimes trials. Given the limitations of the other pronatal options, the conquest of new Slavic populations may be the only viable solution to Russia's demographic crisis, however dangerous, brutal, illegitimate, and illegal the solution may be. Given how much blood and treasure the second invasion of Ukraine has already cost Russia, Putin must show results in increased territory and population for his

Russia, Demography, and Putin's Hidden Agenda   285

very risky strategy to be seen as a success. Russia will not surrender its territorial and population gains willingly. Indeed, Ukraine will not be the last Russian attempted acquisition; it is only the beginning.

NOTES

1. Geir Hågen Karlsen, "Divide and Rule: Ten Lessons about Russian Political Influence Activities in Europe," *Palgrave Communications* 5, no. 19 (2019), https://doi.org /10.1057/s41599-019-0227-8.

2. A comment about the Siloviki is needed here. Michael Stuermer reports in his book *Putin and the Rise of Russia* (p. 73), "Much of the security forces, the government and the economy is now, directly or indirectly, under the control of the intelligence services. Three out of four senior Russian officials today were once affiliated with the KGB or related organizations." According to a 2006 study by Olga Kryshtanovskaya, the director of the Center of the Study of Elites at the Russian Academy of Sciences, 77% of the top 1,016 government positions in the Russian government were held at the time by Siloviki, which includes the Ministry of Defense, the FSB, the successor agency to the KGB, and GRU among many others. See Andrei Illarionov, "The Siloviki in Charge," *Journal of Democracy* 20, no. 2 (2009): 70. The majority of Russia scholars take the view the Siloviki are the dominant faction in Putin's patronal coalition. Some scholars such as David Rivera and Sharon Werning Rivera argue that the Siloviki's influence is half what Kryshtanovskaya estimates, but agree that in Putin's inner circle the Siloviki dominate. See David Rivera and Sharon Werning Rivera, "The Militarization of the Russian Elite Under Putin," *Problems of Post-Communism* 65, no. 4 (2018): 221–232.

3. See, for instance, George F. Kennan, "A Fateful Error," *New York Times*, February 5, 1997, https://www.nytimes.com/1997/02/05/opinion/a-fateful-error.html.

4. John J. Mearsheimer, *The Tragedy of Great Power Politics*. Updated Edition (W.W. Norton & Company, 2014), 60–61.

5. David Remnick, "Stephen Kotkin: Don't Blame the West for Russia's Invasion of Ukraine." *New Yorker*, March 14, 2022, https://www.newyorker.com/podcast /politics-and-more/stephen-kotkin-dont-blame-the-west-for-russias-invasion-of -ukraine.

6. Sergei Medvedev, *The Return of the Russian Leviathan* (Polity, 2020), 83–85.

7. See Marcel H. Van Herpen, *Putin's Wars: Russia's New Imperialism* (Rowman Littlefield, 2015), 62–70.

8. Taras Kuzio, "Inside Vladimir Putin's Criminal Plan to Purge and Partition Ukraine," *Atlantic Council*, March 3, 2022, https://www.atlanticcouncil.org/blogs /ukrainealert/inside-vladimir-putins-criminal-plan-to-purge-and-partition-ukraine/.

9. "How Many Russians Have Died in Ukraine?" *The Economist*, February 24, 2024, https://www.economist.com/graphic-detail/2024/02/24/how-many-russian-soldiers -have-died-in-ukraine.

10. "Montenegro Jails 'Russian Coup Plot' Leaders," *BBC News*, May 9, 2019, https://www.bbc.com/news/world-europe-48212435.

286   Andrew S. Natsios

11. Walter Laqueur, *Putinism: Russia and Its Future with the West* (Thomas Dunne Books, 2015), 205.

12. "UN Predicts Russia's Population Could Halve By 2100," *Moscow Times*, June 18, 2019, https://www.themoscowtimes.com/2019/06/18/un-predicts-russias-population -could-halve-2100-a66035.

13. See Laqueur, *Putinism: Russia and Its Future with the West*, 203.

14. See Nicholas Eberstadt, "Russian Power in Decline: A Demographic and Human Resource Perspective," American Enterprise Institute, August 2022.

15. Eberstadt, from the presentation: "Nicholas Eberstadt on the Demographics of Russia and China," *YouTube*, June 19, 2022, Program on Constitutional Government at Harvard. Time: 24:30. https://www.youtube.com/watch?v=Q7-fB_inNuw.

16. Laqueur, *Putinism: Russia and Its Future with the West*, 231.

17. Vladimir Putin, "Послание Президента Российской Федерации От 16.05.2003 г. б/н," *Президент России*, May 16, 2003, http://kremlin.ru/acts/bank /36352.

18. Vladimir Putin, "Послание Федеральному Собранию Российской Федерации," *Президент России*, April 25, 2005, http://kremlin.ru/events/president /transcripts/22931.

19. Michael Stuermer, *Putin and the Rise of Russia* (Pegasus, 2010), 124.

20. Stuermer, *Putin and the Rise of Russia*, 132.

21. Kimberly Marten, "Putin's Choices: Explaining Russian Foreign Policy and Intervention in Ukraine," *Washington Quarterly* 38, no. 2 (April 3, 2015): 189–204.

22. Paul Goble, "5 Million Fewer Than in 2010, Ethnic Russians Make Up Only 72 Percent of Russia's Population," *Jamestown Foundation*, January 10, 2023, https:// jamestown.org/program/5-million-fewer-than-in-2010-ethnic-russians-make-up-only-72 -percent-of-russias-population/.

23. Igor Beloborodov et al., "Политика Замещающей Миграции в России - Последствия и Альтернативы," Russian Institute of Strategic Studies, April 9, 2014, http://riss.ru/article/15524/.

24. Vitaly Slovetsky, "Тревожная Доля," *Novye Izvestia*, April 16, 2014, https:// newizv.ru/news/society/16-04-2014/200262-trevozhnaja-dolja.

25. "Указ 'О Концепции Государственной Миграционной Политики Российской Федерации На 2019–2025 Годы,'" Президент России, October 31, 2018, http://kremlin.ru/events/president/news/58986.

26. "UN Predicts Russia's Population Could Halve By 2100."

27. Paul Stronski, "Russia's Response to Its Spiraling COVID-19 Crisis Is Too Little, Too Late," Carnegie Endowment, October 18, 2021, https://carnegieendowment.org/2021 /10/28/russia-s-response-to-its-spiraling-covid-19-crisis-is-too-little-too-late-pub-85677.

28. Vladimir Putin, "Presidential Address to the Federal Assembly," January 15, 2020), http://en.kremlin.ru/events/president/news/62582.

29. Putin, "Presidential Address to the Federal Assembly."

30. Matthew P. Funaiole and Joseph S. Burmudez Jr., "Unpacking the Russian Troop Buildup along Ukraine's Border," Center for Strategic and International Studies, April 22, 2021, https://www.csis.org/analysis/unpacking-russian-troop-buildup-along -ukraines-border.

31. Vladimir Putin, "Послание Президента Федеральному Собранию," http://kremlin.ru/events/president/news/65418.

32. "Vladimir Putin's Annual News Conference," December 23, 2021, http://en.kremlin.ru/events/president/news/67438.

33. Yaroslav Trofimov, "How Far Do Putin's Imperial Ambitions Go?" *Wall Street Journal*, June 24, 2022, https://www.wsj.com/articles/how-far-do-putins-imperial-ambitions-go-11656085978.

34. Felix Light, "The Young People Don't Stay Here," *Moscow Times*, August 3, 2021, https://www.themoscowtimes.com/2021/08/03/the-young-people-dont-stay-here-depopulation-haunts-russias-breadbasket-a74683.

35. Ayesha Rascoe, "Russian Intellectual Aleksandr Dugin Is Also Commonly Known as 'Putin's Brain,'" *NPR*, March 27, 2022, https://www.npr.org/2022/03/27/1089047787/russian-intellectual-aleksandr-dugin-is-also-commonly-known-as-putins-brain.

36. See Aleksandr Dugin, *Foundations of Geopolitics: The Geopolitical Future of Russia* (Arktogeja Press, 1997).

37. See Lynn Corum, "Project Russia: The Bestselling Book Series of Putin's Kremlin," *South Central Review* 35.1 (2018): 74–100.

38. Artem Tinchurin et al., "Emigration of the 2000s: Where and Why Did They Leave Russia," *Если быть точным*, October 5, 2021, https://tochno.st/materials/emigratsiya-2000-kh.

39. Uliana Pavlova, "5 Million Russian Citizens Left Russia under Putin," *Moscow Times*, October 13, 2021, https://www.themoscowtimes.com/2021/10/13/5-million-russian-citizens-left-russia-under-putin-a75246.

40. "Russia's Systematic Program for the Re-Education and Adoption of Ukraine's Children," *Yale School of Public Health*, February 14, 2023, https://hub.conflictobservatory.org/portal/sharing/rest/content/items/97f919ccfe524d31a241b53ca44076b8/data.

41. Abigail Williams, "Thousands of Ukrainian Children Forced into Vast Russian Network of Russian Camps, Study Finds," *NBC News*, February 14, 2023, https://www.nbcnews.com/news/world/ukraine-children-russian-reeducation-camps-forcibly-moved-study-rcna70607.

42. Anthony Blinken, "Russia's 'Filtration' Operations, Forced Disappearances, and Mass Deportations of Ukrainian Citizens," Press Statement, U.S. Department of State, July 13, 2022, https://www.state.gov/russias-filtration-operations-forced-disappearances-and-mass-deportations-of-ukrainian-citizens/.

43. Amy Mackinnon, "Russia Is Sending Its Ethnic Minorities to the Meat Grinder," *Foreign Policy*, September 23, 2022, https://foreignpolicy.com/2022/09/23/russia-partial-military-mobilization-ethnic-minorities/.

44. Mackinnon, "Russia Is Sending Its Ethnic Minorities to the Meat Grinder."

45. Stuermer, *Putin and the Rise of Russia*, 121.

46. Thomas Kika, "Wagner's Convict Fighters Are Now Committing Murders in Russia: Reports," *Newsweek*, April 23, 2023, https://www.newsweek.com/wagners-convict-fighters-are-now-committing-murders-russia-reports-1796140.

47. "White House: Wagner Group Has Suffered over 30,000 Casualties in Ukraine," *Reuters*, February 17, 2023, https://www.reuters.com/world/europe/white-house-wagner-group-has-suffered-over-30000-casualties-ukraine-2023-02-17/.

48. "Putin Warns Russia against Pro-Western 'Traitors' and Scum," *Reuters*, March 16, 2022, https://www.reuters.com/world/putin-warns-russia-against-pro-western-traitors-scum-2022-03-16/.

49. "Nearly 4M Russians Left Russia in Early 2022—FSB," *Moscow Times*, May 6, 2022, https://www.themoscowtimes.com/2022/05/06/nearly-4m-russians-left-russia-in-early-2022-fsb-a77603.

50. Hannah S. Chapman, "Thousands of Russians Are Protesting Against the War with Ukraine. Putin's Not Likely to Listen," *Washington Post*, March 1, 2022, https://www.washingtonpost.com/politics/2022/03/01/thousands-russians-are-protesting-against-war-putins-not-likely-listen/.

51. Anthony Faiola, "Mass Flight of Tech Workers Turns Russian IT into Another Casualty of War," *Washington Post*, May 1, 2022, https://www.washingtonpost.com/world/2022/05/01/russia-tech-exodus-ukraine-war/.

52. Fred Weir, "Russia's Population Decline Spells Trouble," *Christian Science Monitor*, April 18,, 2022, https://www.csmonitor.com/2002/0418/p06s02-woeu.html.

53. Laqueur, *Putinism: Russia and Its Future with the West*, 203.

54. Bruno Tertrais, "Why Ukraine Matters to Russia: The Demographic Factor," Institut Montaigne, February 14, 2022, https://www.institutmontaigne.org/en/expressions/why-ukraine-matters-russia-demographic-factor.

55. Katie Bo Lillis, Kylie Atwood, and Natasha Bertrand, "Russia is Depopulating Parts of Eastern Ukraine, Forcibly Removing Thousands into Remote Parts of Russia," *CNN*, May 26, 2022, https://www.cnn.com/2022/05/26/politics/ukraine-filtration-camps-forcibly-remove-russia/index.html.

56. Lillid et al., "Russia is Depopulating Parts of Eastern Ukraine."

57. Grigory Pyrlik, "In This Frontline City in Ukraine, People Voted for Peace—But at What Price?", *OpenDemocracy*, April 23, 2019, https://www.opendemocracy.net/en/odr/mariupol-election-report-ru-en/.

58. Marat Iliyasov, "To Be or Not to Be a Chechen? The Second Generation of Chechens in Europe and Their Choices of Identity," *Frontiers in Sociology* 6 (2021), https://www.frontiersin.org/article/10.3389/fsoc.2021.631961.

59. Doha Madani, Courtney Kube, and Alexander Smith, "Russia Appoints General with Cruel History to Oversee Ukraine Offensive," *NBC News*, April 10, 2022, https://www.nbcnews.com/news/world/russia-appoints-general-cruel-history-oversee-ukraine-offensive-rcna23784.

60. "Chechen Official Puts Death Toll for 2 Wars at up to 160,000," *New York Times*, August 16, 2005, https://www.nytimes.com/2005/08/16/world/europe/chechen-official-puts-death-toll-for-2-wars-at-up-to-160000.html.

61. "Official: Chechen Wars Killed 300,000," *Al Jazeera*, June 26, 2005, https://www.aljazeera.com/news/2005/6/26/official-chechen-wars-killed-300000.

62. Tadeusz Iwinski, "The Humanitarian Situation of the Chechen Displaced Population," Committee on Migration, Refugees and Population, September 20, 2004, https://assembly.coe.int/nw/xml/XRef/X2H-Xref-ViewHTML.asp?FileID=10643&lang=en.

63. Steven Pifer, "Crimea: Six Years after Illegal Annexation," Brookings, March 17, 2020, https://www.brookings.edu/blog/order-from-chaos/2020/03/17/crimea-six-years-after-illegal-annexation/.

64. Alla Hurska, "Demographic Transformation of Crimea: Forced Migration as Part of Russia's 'Hybrid' Strategy," Jamestown Foundation, March 29, 2021, https://jamestown.org/program/demographic-transformation-of-crimea-forced-migration-as-part-of-russias-hybrid-strategy/.

65. Andrei Illarionov, "Reading Russia: The Siloviki in Charge," *Journal of Democracy* 20, no. 2 (2009): 69–72.

66. Hurska, "Demographic Transformation of Crimea."

67. "In Crimea, Russia Signals Military Resolve with New and Revamped Bases," *Reuters*, November 1, 2016, http://www.reuters.com/investigates/special-report/russia-crimea/.

68. Elmira Bayrasli, "Who Will Speak for the Tatars?", *Foreign Policy*, May 18, 2019, https://foreignpolicy.com/2019/05/18/crimean-tatars-ethnic-cleansing/.

69. Gordon C. McCord and Jeffrey D. Sachs, *Development, Structure, and Transformation: Some Evidence on Comparative Economic Growth*, No. w19512. National Bureau of Economic Research, 2013, https://www.nber.org/system/files/working_papers/w19512/w19512.pdf.

70. "Donetsk and Luhansk: What You Should Know About the 'Republics,'" *Al Jazeera*, February 22, 2022, https://www.aljazeera.com/news/2022/2/22/what-are-donetsk-and-luhansk-ukraines-separatist-statelets.

71. Catherine Belton, "Russia Will Stop 'in a Moment' if Ukraine Meets Terms - Kremlin," *Reuters*, March 7, 2022, https://www.reuters.com/world/kremlin-says-russian-military-action-will-stop-moment-if-ukraine-meets-2022-03-07/.

72. Alexander Tanas, "With War on Its Doorstep, Moldova Applies for EU Membership," *Reuters*, March 3, 2022, https://www.reuters.com/world/europe/moldovan-president-says-moldova-applies-eu-membership-2022-03-03/.

73. Radio Free Europe Romania, "Transnistria Cere Independenţa Faţă de Republica Moldova," *Europa Liberă România*, March 4, 2022, https://romania.europalibera.org/a/transnistria-independenta/31736497.html.

74. Nathan Hodge et al., "Russia Launches Military Attack on Ukraine with Reports of Explosions and Troops Crossing Border," *CNN*, February 24, 2022, https://www.cnn.com/2022/02/23/europe/russia-ukraine-putin-military-operation-donbas-intl-hnk/index.html.

75. United Nations Security Council, "Amid Violence, Mass Forced Displacement, 'Lives of Millions' of Ukrainian Civilians at Stake, Humanitarian Affairs Chief Tells Security Council," SC/14812, 8983RD Meeting, February 28, 2022, https://www.un.org/press/en/2022/sc14812.doc.htm; also see Mark A. Grey, a scholar of the weaponization of refugees, "The Big Exodus of Ukrainian Refugees Isn't an Accident—It's Part of Putin's Plan to Destabilize Europe," *The Conversation*, May 24, 2022, https://theconversation.com/the-big-exodus-of-ukrainian-refugees-isnt-an-accident-its-part-of-putins-plan-to-destabilize-europe-182654.

76. "Ukrainian, Russian Refugees Seeking Asylum at US-Mexico border." *ABC News*, March 18, 2022, https://www.youtube.com/watch?v=t_WNldiqXFY.

77. Jane Arraf and Elian Peltier, "Migrants Say Belarusians Took Them to E.U. Border and Supplied Wire Cutters," *New York Times*, November 13, 2021, https://www.nytimes.com/2021/11/13/world/middleeast/belarus-migrants-iraq-kurds.html.

78. "Belarus Creates Turmoil by Pushing Afghan Migrants to Pass Polish Border," *Schengen Visa Info News*, August 24, 2021, https://www.schengenvisainfo.com/news/belarus-creates-turmoil-by-pushing-afghan-migrants-to-pass-polish-border/.

79. "Belarus Migrants: EU Accuses Lukashenko of Gangster-Style Abuse," *BBC News*, November 9, 2021, https://www.bbc.com/news/world-europe-59215769.

80. Sam Jones, "Russia Accused of 'Weaponizing' Syria Refugees," *CNBC*, February 15, 2016, https://www.cnbc.com/2016/02/15/russia-accused-of-weaponising-syria-refugees-john-mccain.html.

81. Stine Jacobsen and Alister Doyle, "On Arctic Tip of Europe, Syrian Migrants Reach Norway by Bike," *Reuters*, September 3, 2015, https://www.reuters.com/article/us-europe-migrants-arctic-idUSKCN0R325N20150903.

82. Euronews with EBU, "Taking the Arctic Route: Migrants Cycle from Russia to Norway," *Euronews*, July 10, 2015, https://www.euronews.com/2015/10/07/taking-the-arctic-route-migrants-cycle-from-russia-to-norway.

83. Ahmed Rashid, *Taliban* (Yale University Press, 2000).

84. James Traub, "Even Sweden Doesn't Want Migrants Anymore," *Foreign Policy* (blog), November 17, 2021, https://foreignpolicy.com/2021/11/17/even-sweden-doesnt-want-migrants-anymore-syria-iraq-belarus/.

85. Suzanne Daley and Maïa de la Baume, "French Far Right Gets Helping Hand with Russian Loan," *New York Times*, December 2, 2014, https://www.nytimes.com/2014/12/02/world/europe/french-far-right-gets-helping-hand-with-russian-loan-.html.

Chapter Eleven

A View from Northeastern Europe

The Baltic States and the Russian Regime

James S. Corum

If one wants to understand what is going on in Russia and also to look at the main confrontation points between the West and Putin, the three Baltic states are the best place to start. The Baltic states of Estonia, Latvia, and Lithuania are not well-known to most Western leaders or academics, but these small countries are a special place to understand modern Russia and its politics. The Baltic republics were not only under Soviet domination, like so many new Eastern European NATO allies, but they were part of the USSR from 1940 to 1991. Baltic citizens had to learn Russian (in the Baltics, most people over forty are generally fluent in Russian), and the older generation had to serve in the Soviet military. As one Latvian general who listens to Russian news daily told me, "Unlike the Poles, Hungarians, and Czechs, who at least had nominal independence and some of their own institutions, we [Baltics] were part of the USSR—we were on the inside—and we KNOW these people."[1]

Only thirty-one years ago, the three Baltic states were impoverished republics of the USSR, and the historical memories of the USSR, the KGB, and the gulags are all very fresh. Although the Baltics suffered greatly, the people of Latvia, Estonia, and Lithuania were not crippled by their historical experience. The majority of the Baltic populations certainly have no liking for the Russians, but they coexist with them. Since independence, Baltic businesses have been focused on the West, but they still have considerable economic dealings with the Russians, especially in terms of importing energy and raw materials and serving as a transport conduit to Russia from the West. One of the most important events in Baltic–Russian relations since 2014 has been a policy of the Baltic governments to reduce their energy dependence on Russian oil, gas, and electricity. The Baltic populations coexist, generally peaceably, with large ethnic Russian populations that are a legacy of the Russian population movements after World War II. Finally, the Baltic populations feel considerable security in belonging to NATO and the European Union, and their attitude toward the Russians remains realistic. They know they have to exist as small democratic states next to a very large, aggressive, and dictatorial Third World (in most respects of living standards) neighbor.

English is now the common language of young people, businesspeople, and academics in the Baltics, but Russian is still widely understood and spoken among the over-forty generation, who had to learn it in school from a young age. Russian is widely taught in school, but today it takes a very second place to English in foreign language studies. Still, people in the Baltics read Russian books and follow the Russian media closely (when I lived in Tartu, Estonia, one hour from Russia, I had twelve Russian channels on cable TV). Many of the Baltic leaders travel to Moscow on business, and high school students travel as tourists to nearby St. Petersburg. The Baltic states have world-class universities (Tartu University, Tallinn University of Technology, University of Latvia in Riga, and Vilnius University, among others, are exceptional modern universities with very high entry standards) with some of the top Russian studies faculties in Europe.

After more than five years of living in the Baltics and working with their governments, I can say that the Baltic political leaders are highly realistic. Unlike the other Soviet republics that became independent with the breakup of the Soviet Union in 1991, the Baltic states have been remarkably effective in becoming economically prosperous and politically stable. In terms of dealing with Russia, they understand that Russia is, by its nature, economically a fragile state beset by social problems and overwhelmingly dependent on oil and gas exports. At the same time, they also understand that Russia is a revanchist state with a huge military and has never fully accepted the fact of the Baltic states' independence. They know that in order to survive, small democratic nations like theirs need allies. The Baltic populations believe, for good reason, that they face an existential threat from Russia, whose leaders are working to restore a new version of the Soviet empire in which the Baltic states and all former republics will have a place clearly subordinate to Russian interests. This chapter will examine the view of Russia and the Putin government from the perspective of the Baltic states and focus on the key

A View from Northeastern Europe   293

areas of friction between the Baltics and Russia and how the former continue to manage their relations with the latter.

The Weight of History

History is key to understanding the Baltic and Russian relationship and the Baltic peoples' relationship with the West. First of all, although the Baltic states are geographically in Eastern Europe, in terms of culture, economic relationships, religion, and political development, they are thoroughly Western European. The Baltics' relationship with the West began in the late twelfth century with the arrival of merchants, missionaries, and crusaders from Germany, Denmark, and Sweden. The Baltic region was inhabited by pagan tribes divided into two major ethnic/linguistic groups: the Baltic peoples (ancestors of the Latvians, Prussians, and Lithuanians) and Finno-Ugric peoples (ancestors of the Finns and Estonians). By the 1240s, Danish and German crusaders had established small states and dioceses in Latvia and Estonia (Livonia) as the local tribes converted to Christianity (some voluntarily, some not). A German-speaking upper class, including assimilated local rulers, governed the small states, and the establishment of the Hanseatic League (Europe's first free-trade organization) brought extensive Western European trade to the Baltics and Latvia and prosperity to Estonia. Lithuania developed separately and remained Europe's last pagan kingdom until it accepted Catholic Christianity in 1386 and aligned itself by marriage with the Polish dynasty. Along with Finland, the Baltic region developed as an integral part of the West in the Middle Ages in terms of religion (Catholic, not Orthodox), political relationships (tied to the Swedish and Danish kingdoms and German Empire), and economics, with the German language as the lingua franca of the Baltic states.

After the State of the Teutonic Order dissolved in the early sixteenth century, Estonia and Latvia became Lutheran under the Swedish Empire. In the eighteenth century, Czar Peter the Great conquered Estonia and Latvia and absorbed them into the Russian Empire. Later that century, Lithuania was conquered by Russia, and the Duchy of Kurland (Kurzeme in modern Latvia) was taken into the Russian Empire. However, under the czars, the Baltic countries developed very differently from the rest of the Russian Empire.

From the beginning of the Russian takeover, the provinces of Estonia and Latvia were granted autonomy under the czar, with a council of ethnic German barons ruling the region. When the Russians took Finland from Sweden in 1809, Finland was granted autonomy as a grand duchy and ruled by an indigenous nobility.

Both Finland and Livonia, as Lutheran and culturally Western, looked to the West in terms of trade and culture. Estonia and Latvia became the richest and most advanced provinces of the Russian Empire, with universal literacy in the region by 1800 (150 years before Russia had universal literacy) and with serfdom abolished more than forty years earlier than in Russia. Lithuania remembered its long history as an independent state and duchy associated with Poland and, along with the Poles, initiated several major nationalist rebellions in the nineteenth century. These were, of course, suppressed with utter ruthlessness by the Russians, but this suppression failed to quench the desire for independence. Under self-rule, Estonia and Latvia developed more peacefully, and by the nineteenth century, the Baltic provinces and Finland had an indigenous middle class and extensive trade networks with the West. It was also the first region of the Russian Empire to industrialize.

However, through the era of the Russian Empire, there was constant friction between the Baltic peoples and the Russians caused mainly by the prosperity of the Baltic peoples vis-à-vis the generally poorer Russians and the very important role that the Baltic nobility played in running the empire. One only has to read *War and Peace* to see the friction between the ethnic Russians and the Baltics. The commander of the Russian army in 1812 was Field Marshal Barclay de Tolly, an ethnic German from Estonia with a staff of mostly German-speaking officers who were viewed by the ethnic Russian officers with distrust as "Germans" and, as such, not fully committed to the preservation of Russia.[2]

Latvia and Estonia, along with Finland, became the most modern, literate, and advanced regions of the old Russian Empire. In the nineteenth century, the Baltic peoples developed a strong sense of nationalism. The Baltics retained their languages and national culture as separate from the Russian culture and created sophisticated national literatures. With the collapse of the Russian Empire in 1917, the three Baltic states and Finland quickly established Western-style governments and, with Western help (mostly German and British), decisively defeated the Red Army in a series of bloody independence wars.[3] Russia, soon to become the Soviet Union, reluctantly accepted reality and recognized the three Baltic states and Finland as independent nations. However, the Soviets remained bitter and hostile toward the Baltic republics, and the interwar period saw blatant acts of aggression against the Baltic countries that included a failed attempt by Soviet agents to overthrow the Estonian government by a coup during Christmas 1924.

In the twenty years of peace following the end of the independence wars, the three Baltic nations evolved as modern Western countries with some measure of prosperity, in contrast to the violence, collectivization, and poverty prevalent in Russia under Stalin. However, in August 1939, the fate of the small republics was sealed by the Molotov–Ribbentrop Pact, which divided Europe into spheres of influence to be controlled by Stalin and Hitler. The three Baltic states were designated as a Soviet sphere of influence, along with eastern Poland, part of Romania, and Finland. The Soviet Union was given the green light by Hitler to annex those regions. Stalin immediately invaded Finland in November 1939, and after a brief and bloody war, succeeded in annexing a major part of Finnish territory. At the same time, Stalin pressured the Baltic states into allowing large Soviet military bases in their countries. The West, at war with Hitler and fearful of antagonizing Hitler's key ally, did nothing to counter this naked aggression against small democratic states. In June 1940, the neutral and militarily weak Baltic states were invaded and occupied by Stalin's forces.

The Baltics as Western Nations

In the summer of 1940, after phony elections, the three nations were annexed and became republics of the Soviet Union.[4] Under Soviet domination, the three Baltic states suffered horrendous oppression as the national elites were either murdered or sent to the gulags. Collectivization of farms and nationalization of industries and businesses were imposed. Large sectors of the population, including priests and ministers, businessmen, many professionals, intellectuals, military officers, and landowners, were identified for mass arrest and deportation.[5] The only respite came from the German invasion of the Soviet Union in June 1941, which quickly overran the Baltic states and placed the countries under German control until 1944. The Baltic peoples, who had long resented German rulers and kicked the Germans out in 1919, viewed the Germans as the lesser of two evils, and a considerable number of Latvians and Estonians fought alongside the Germans during World War II.[6] The fact that the Baltics had fought eagerly, and very well, against the Soviet state remains one of the main points of friction between the Baltic states and Russia today.

After the Soviets reestablished power in the three Baltic states in 1944, there were massive waves of repression lasting until the death of Stalin in 1953.[7] This period was characterized by the imprisonment or forced exile of hundreds of thousands of Lithuanians, Latvians, and Estonians either to the gulags or Siberia.[8] The Baltic peoples strongly resisted, and large nationalist resistance movements were formed in the Baltics. For almost a decade after the end of World War II, the Soviets faced anti-communist guerrilla forces, called the "Forest Brothers," in the rural areas of the Baltic states. Not until 1953, after major efforts by the KGB and military, were the Forest Brothers effectively suppressed.[9] Repressing the Baltics was a bloody conflict that lasted for years and resulted in tens of thousands of casualties. The waves of Soviet repression in the 1940s and 1950s touched virtually every family in the Baltic states. Most Baltic families can recall a father who was jailed, an uncle who disappeared in the gulags, or a grandfather who was sent to Siberia. The memories are still fresh.

Although repression became less brutal after Stalin's death in 1953, the rest of the Soviet era was still a gray dictatorship maintained by a harsh criminal code that punished any expression of dissent and was backed up by the ever-present KGB. The Baltic states became a center for Soviet high-tech and military industries, and thousands of Russian workers were brought into Latvia and Estonia to work in the military complexes. The northeastern corner of Estonia was declared an area of military industry and cleared of Estonians, who were deported and replaced by Russians. Large numbers of Russians were also settled to work in industries in Latvia. Lithuania was the only Baltic nation that did not experience a large influx of Russians because the Forest Brothers caused so much trouble in rural areas that Stalin's plan to settle Russians on collectivized land was foiled.[10]

After Stalin's death in 1953 and until the 1980s, Soviet policy was to Russify the Baltic republics and Sovietize the national culture. On the surface, the Baltics were "good Soviet citizens," but under the surface, the Baltic peoples worked to preserve their languages, literatures, and unique national identities. It was an impressive effort of peoples who never forgot their history or identity as independent nations. For example, throughout the Baltic states, monuments to Baltic victories over the Red Army in 1919–1920 were carefully hidden in houses and barns or buried in fields, only to reappear in the 1990s after more than fifty years of Soviet rule. The US policy of never recognizing the Soviet annexation of the Baltic states as legitimate served as a beacon of hope to the Baltic peoples. The Helsinki Accords (1975) also put international pressure on the Soviet Union to reduce the persecution of dissidents.

With the difference in freedoms and standards of living between East and West so glaring, even the Soviet leaders could not maintain the façade of communist success. In the late 1980s, when First Party Secretary Gorbachev announced reforms in the Soviet Union, the Baltic peoples responded by organizing noncommunist political parties (quite illegal even under Gorbachev) and initiating mass demonstrations opposing Soviet rule. The most dramatic expression of Baltic nationalism and yearning for democracy came in August 1989 when, on the fiftieth

A View from Northeastern Europe   297

anniversary of the Molotov–Ribbentrop Pact, more than 2 million Baltic citizens formed a human chain 500 kilometers long through the three states. The chain began in Tallinn, Estonia, wound through Riga, Latvia, and ended in Vilnius, Lithuania. On that day, the Baltic peoples celebrated their national pride, and thousands flew their secretly made national flags, even though it was a criminal act under Soviet law. It was the largest peaceful mass demonstration in history. Whatever the local communist leaders had told Moscow, the Baltic human chain was clear proof that most Baltic peoples saw the Soviet Union as an occupying force.

The desire for the Baltic peoples to have an honest account of their relationship with the USSR resulted in the Soviet government agreeing in 1989 to a commission of Baltic and Russian historians to examine the events of 1939 and 1940. The joint commission acknowledged the existence of the secret clauses of the Molotov–Ribbentrop Pact, and in December 1989, the People's Congress of the USSR voted to denounce the secret Soviet/Nazi protocols as unjustified and invalid under international law.[11] This resolution completely undercut any legal or moral foundation for the Soviet Union to retain the Baltic states as subject republics, and the independence movement in the Baltics progressed to open calls for the renewal of their independence.

In defiance of the USSR, Lithuania declared its independence in 1990 and held free elections even as KGB troops tried to suppress the new government in Vilnius in January 1991. Bloody repression attempts in Latvia and displays by Soviet forces in Estonia were met with overwhelming public mobilization against the Soviet government. In the Baltic nations, militia units were formed and deployed to guard newly elected national parliaments, town councils, and other democratic institutions. Free elections were held and resulted in democratic and anti-communist governments. National referenda in all three countries overwhelmingly supported full independence. With the failed coup of August 1991 and the collapse of the Soviet Union, the three Baltic states all officially proclaimed independence and were soon recognized by the Western nations.

The Baltic States Opt for the West

The reform government in Moscow under Boris Yeltsin that followed the 1991 coup recognized the Baltic states as independent nations, and for a brief period, Russia and the Baltics tried to establish friendly state-to-state relations. The chief priority for the new Baltic democracies was to negotiate the withdrawal from the Baltics of all Russian military bases, of which there were many. The complex negotiations resulted in the withdrawal of the Russian forces and the turnover of bases to the national governments in 1994.

In 1997, Russia attempted to negotiate a long-term arrangement with the Baltic states that offered security guarantees and economic ties to Russia in an attempt to keep the Baltics neutral and far away from NATO. Given the unhappy history of past Russian guarantees, the Russian proposals were rejected out of hand, and this resulted in considerable diplomatic and economic friction between Russia and the Newly Independent States.[12] Yet, from the Baltic viewpoint, Russia had nothing positive to offer. In the 1990s, Russia was bankrupt and suffering from economic and social crises and was openly developing into an authoritarian mafia state run by oligarchs. The idea of relying on security and protection from a government that had recently killed unarmed Baltic citizens in the independence demonstrations of 1990 and 1991 was ludicrous.

The Baltics saw nothing from the old Soviet system worth retaining, and the only thing that the new Russian Federation could offer them was cheap energy. So when the Baltic states regained independence, they immediately chose a path of Westernizing their politics, economics, and defense, and this approach was overwhelmingly supported by the people. Estonia, Latvia, and Lithuania adopted democratic constitutions and parliamentary states and opted for capitalist market economies with laws modeled after the United States and Western Europe. They also created new armed forces from scratch, all based on a Western/Nordic model, equipped with Western weapons, and informed by Western doctrine.

What the Russian Federation offered the Baltics in the 1990s was nothing less than maintaining an illusion of a lost empire, and this had no appeal to the Baltics. That the Baltic policy of turning to the Western model of government and economics was a wise one is evident from the dramatic economic and social progress made after the fall of the Soviet empire. Countries that decided in 1991 to move to a fully Western model (Poland, Hungary, the Czech Republic, Slovakia, and the three Baltic states) have become stable and prosperous. Countries that were unwilling to take the plunge toward full democratization and Western economics and that retained a close association with Russia remain mired in authoritarianism and poverty. Starting from a relatively equal level of per capita income in 1991, Eastern European and Baltic states have since enjoyed high economic growth rates and made rapid progress toward a Western European living standard, while Russia-aligned nations continue to lag in every standard. One can simply compare the World Bank data (from 2020) on per capita income (gross national income, GNI): GNI for Poland was $15,742; for Estonia, $23,054; for Latvia,

A View from Northeastern Europe   299

$17,736; and for Lithuania, $20,232. Contrast this with the GNI for Russia's close ally Belarus ($6,424) or Ukraine ($3,724), a country that came very late to Westernization. Even oil-rich Russia lagged behind the three Baltic states with a GNI of $10,126.[13]

The desire to rejoin the West was not a rejection of their history, but a fulfillment of it, as the Baltic states see themselves as fundamentally Western in national culture. Still, with Russia on their borders, the Baltics proceeded cautiously in the area of national security policy. The Baltic states maintained an official policy of neutrality until the withdrawal of the last Russian forces from the Baltic nations in 1994. At that time, all three nations proclaimed their goal of complete political and economic integration with the West and announced their intention to join the NATO alliance as soon as possible.[14] The goals of joining NATO and the EU were treated with considerable skepticism in the United States and Western Europe, but from the mid-1990s, the Baltic states made a concerted effort to develop economic and security policies and institutions that met the NATO and EU standards.[15]

Most significantly, the Baltic states have made an impressive effort to visibly support the West in military operations. All three Baltic countries have sent troops to operate under US and NATO command in the wars in Iraq and Afghanistan. Unlike some other NATO allies and major US partners, the Baltic states have sent combat troops and have not placed caveats on the use of their forces in combat. In Afghanistan, the commitment was significant, with more than 750 Baltic personnel serving there in 2010, including Estonian and Latvian infantry companies and Lithuanian special forces, as well as support personnel and personnel to staff a provincial reconstruction team. The Baltic states have also suffered casualties while fighting at the side of the American forces.[16] The competence of the Baltic forces in Afghanistan won praise and respect from coalition allies and demonstrated that the Baltic states were willing to pay a price in blood to demonstrate the depth of their commitment to the West.

Putin's Russia Tries to Rewrite History—Again

Any chance for positive developments in Russian–Western relations ended in 2000 with the rise of Vladimir Putin as leader of the Russian state. Liberalization measures and tentative steps toward open government and democracy were systematically quashed. One of Putin's priorities is supporting a new Russian nationalist version of history, following essentially the old Soviet line. Under the current regime, history is again relegated to the role of glorifying the state. The tone and substance of Russian state history publications since 2000—and almost all scholarship in Russia is under the control of the state and state-allied agencies—is one of aggressive nationalism.[17] This aggressive nationalism also includes a virulent anti-Baltic theme and a resounding defense of the Soviet takeover and occupation of the Baltic states after 1940.

Since the beginning of Putin's tenure as Russia's leader, an extremely nationalist history of Russia has been officially promoted to uphold Russia's historical right to rule the entire region constituting the Soviet empire. One common theme is an appeal to the history of the old czarist empire. One 2007 history book that was published "With the blessing of His Holiness Patriarch of Moscow and All Russia Alexey II" noted that Georgia, Ukraine, and the Baltic states had a centuries-old tradition of being tied to Russia. Thus, it is only natural that Russia should play the lead role in governing those regions.[18]

In the history now promoted by the Russian government under Putin, the official view is that the Soviet occupation of the Baltic states was fully justified and those Baltic claims of Soviet crimes against humanity, which are carefully documented and detailed by national commissions in the Baltics, are exaggerated. The Russian historical approach under Putin is to portray the Baltic peoples as enthusiastic Nazi supporters in World War II, and any critique of the Soviet Union and its role in the Baltics is a "revival of fascism."[19] In 2014, Putin stated that an "open neo-Nazism" has become "commonplace" in Latvia and the other Baltic nations, as well as in Ukraine.[20] History is now a major battlefield between Russia and the West.

Beginning in 1988, all three Baltic states created historical commissions composed of top academics to document the extent of human rights abuses in the years of Soviet occupation. One helpful circumstance was the rapid abandonment of regional headquarters of the KGB in the Baltics and the large number of files left behind. Since the 1990s, the Baltic governments have published extensive historical studies carefully documenting Soviet-era arrests, mass deportations, and mass murder in the Baltic states. Attempts to publish accurate histories and gain international recognition of the crimes committed against the Baltic peoples have been challenged by Russian propaganda aiming to discredit the Baltic states internationally.[21]

In 2005, the Kremlin's European affairs chief, Sergei Yastrzhembsky, rejected the findings of the 1989 Baltic/Russian historical commission and the subsequent resolution of the Soviet government on the legality of the Soviet occupation of the Baltic states in 1940. The Kremlin insisted that the Soviet occupation of the three states was done with the approval of the Baltic governments.[22] The attack

A View from Northeastern Europe 301

on the legal existence of the Baltic states as independent countries has even accelerated. In 2015, the office of the Russian attorney general issued a decision that the United Russia government that had recognized the Baltic states as independent nations was, in fact, an unconstitutional body, and therefore, the recognition of Baltic independence was illegal and invalid.[23]

Since 2007, the Putin government has worked incessantly to rehabilitate Stalin and his actions. Russian history books have been systematically rewritten to minimize the crimes of Stalin and the Soviet regime and to extol Stalin's accomplishments.[24] In 2009, Prime Minister Dmitry Medvedev set up a commission to combat "falsification of history"—which means any account that shows the Soviet regime in a negative light.[25] This fits with the new Russian history that now presents Stalin in a positive light as a great national leader and military commander. Putin's new education minister, Olga Vasilyeva, has stated publicly that Stalin was a "blessing for the state" and staunchly argues that Stalin's repressions and the gulag state were all necessary actions to protect Russia.[26] Her statements accompany a wave of official historical revisionism that whitewashes the labor camp system and mass executions under Stalin and insists that events such as the Ukrainian famine were the exaggerated product of Western propaganda.[27]

A constant theme of official Russian media is to depict the Baltic peoples of the 1930s and 1940s as Nazis and insist that the Baltic peoples remain deeply Nazi today, thus legitimizing overt Russian hostility in the past and present. Western support for the Baltic states can therefore be interpreted as open support for the return of Nazism. For example, a Russian news service's denunciation of a film about the Latvians in World War II states, "One wonders if the filmmakers stressed the fact that ethnic Latvians were amongst the most enthusiastic and willing collaborators with the Nazis during World War II . . . The US government is supporting Nazi revisionists in Riga (and in Tallinn, Kiev, and Zagreb as well). How low have we fallen?"[28] Russian media cartoons from 2014 show depictions of Latvia with a Hitler and Nazi flag, and the Russian state media runs articles such as "Estonia could become a haven for Nazis around the World."[29] The characterization of all Eastern Europeans, and especially the Baltics, as Nazis is a regular theme stressed by Putin.

In October 2014, in reply to Putin's campaign, the Latvian foreign ministry commented that Putin was waging an "information war" against the Baltics and other European states.[30] Only Ukraine has received more attention as being an essentially "Nazi" regime and culture. Indeed, in the last fifteen years, a whole genre of books describing former Soviet republics as Nazi regimes has appeared

302   James S. Corum

in popular history and political science. One recent book by Sergei Glazyev, a close Putin adviser, describes the United States as being the primary culprits behind the effort to place a Nazi regime in place in Ukraine.[31]

Putin's feelings about the interpretation of history are not a new development. At a meeting in Hamburg, Germany, in 1994, long before Putin came to power, the Estonian president Lennart Meri referred to the Russians as "occupiers," at which point Putin dramatically stood up and led the Russian diplomats out of the conference.[32] Russia's policy to style itself as the protector of ethnic Russians outside of Russia is one of the major themes in the books of *Project Russia*, the ideological expression of the Putin regime.[33] Today, the state-supported Russian media publishes books insisting that the occupation of Lithuania under Stalin was a voluntary act endorsed by Lithuanians and that the occupation of Lithuania in 1940 and after World War II was legal and proper. These blatant falsifications of historical events that included mass murder and deportations are clearly irritating to the Lithuanian and Baltic peoples. But the Baltic governments also understand that the actions by Russia are essentially part of a long-term information campaign to delegitimize the Baltic states in the eyes of the world, to whip up the feelings of the ethnic Russian population in the Baltic states against the Baltic governments, and to encourage the belief among the Russian population that the Baltic states are an imminent threat to Russia. Finally, the Putin regime's media campaign pushed the view that the Baltic threat can be properly resolved only if the Baltics come under the Russian sphere of influence as a subject state— something similar to the status of Belarus.

Today, Russia generously subsidizes ethnic Russian groups, political parties, and local Russian television programs within the Baltic states. Russian regime propaganda is prominent in all three Baltic nations, where it is seen by the Russian minorities, who often refuse to assimilate as Baltic citizens. Information warfare, conducted over the long term, is a Russian specialty, and many of the old Soviet propagandists are now working in the service of the Russian state. Indeed, the old Soviet media and propaganda organizations simply changed their names and operate today much like in the Soviet era—down to many of the old Soviet propaganda themes. These include an emphasis on Russian glory in World War II and labeling all who opposed the Soviet Union as fascists and Nazis. Russia has conducted media campaigns against Georgia, Moldova, and Lithuania in times when Russia wanted to coerce those countries to accept Russian policies.[34] The non-Russians are fully aware of the content of the Russian press and programming because Baltic people over the age of forty generally speak fluent Russian.[35]

Russia and the Ethnic Russians in the Baltics

When the USSR occupied the Baltic states, it initiated a policy of mass deportations of Baltic peoples and the resettlement of ethnic Russians into Latvia and Estonia especially. In the 1960s and 1970s, many ethnic Russians moved into the Baltic states to work in the military industries. In 1940, the populations of the Baltic states were almost all indigenous, but by the end of Soviet rule, large Russian minorities had been established. For example, in 1935, Latvia had a population of 1.48 million ethnic Latvians and 206,000 Russians; in 1989, the population was 1.38 million ethnic Latvians and 909,000 Russians.[36] Estonia, which had only a handful of ethnic Russians in 1940, had a Russian ethnic population of 23% by 1991. Almost all ethnic Russians remained in the Baltics after those countries declared independence in 1991, preferring life as noncitizens in the Baltics to life in Russia. Currently, Latvia and Estonia have significant Russian ethnic minorities.[37] Although ethnic Russians in Latvia and Estonia can become full citizens through a simple naturalization process that requires only a five-year legal residency and a basic knowledge of the national language, many ethnic Russians still refuse to accept citizenship.[38]

History plays a big role in ethnic tensions. The Baltic governments, representing the feelings of the great majority of their citizens, have taken down or moved communist-era memorials that represent the most horrible events of their history. For the Russian ethnic minority, however, the memorials to the Red Army and its occupation of the Baltic states are a reminder of the glory days of Soviet history. In 2007, the Estonian government's attempt to move a memorial commemorating the Red Army in Tallinn provoked a violent response from mobs of ethnic Russians. Both Tallinn and the heavily Russian northeast region witnessed days of violent demonstrations that resulted in one death.[39] In Latvia and Estonia, there have been other incidents of mob violence connected with the Russian minorities. Lithuania is peaceful in this regard, as only 6% of its population is ethnic Russian. However, the interpretation of history also plays an important role in Lithuania's relationship with Russia, and there is considerable bitterness between Russian and Lithuanians over the period of Soviet occupation.[40]

Unfortunately, several Russian opinion polls show that Putin's propaganda portraying the Baltic states as a threat to Russia is succeeding among the Russian population. According to Russian polls, Latvia and Lithuania are seen as two of the three nations most hostile to Russia. For example, the 2007 polls showed that 42% of Russians saw Lithuania as "very hostile" to Russia.[41] On the other hand, Putin

304   James S. Corum

is likely to be fooling himself if he believes that the ethnic Russian populations in the Baltics might actively serve to help Russian ambitions to neutralize or reoccupy the Baltic states. Although ethnic Russians in Estonia and Latvia might take pride in Putin and voice support for the Russian invasion of Ukraine, few would choose to live in Russia or see their present situation changed.

The decision of all three Baltic states upon gaining independence to strive to join the EU, a goal that was attained in 2004, has a great deal to do with effectively managing the issue of large numbers of ethnic Russian noncitizens living within their borders. Since 2004, even those ethnic Russians who do not opt for full citizenship have the status of EU residents, which means they have full rights to travel, work, study, and do business within the EU—opportunities and freedoms they would never have as Russian citizens. Ethnic Russians in the Baltic states enjoy a far higher living standard, better social services and benefits, more political freedom, and better pay and opportunities than they would in an economically depressed, authoritarian Russia. Although Putin might command some admiration among Baltic ethnic Russians, there are no indications that the ethnic Russian communities would ever be willing to risk their enviable status quo as EU members to side with Russia against the Baltic states. Over time, the ethnic tensions in the Baltics will diminish with the aging of the large Russian work force that was brought into Latvia and Estonia during the Soviet era and the ongoing assimilation of their children, who, unlike their parents, learn the national languages and are more integrated into the social and economic life of the country.[42]

Recent developments show that the large ethnic Russian populations of Estonia (about 23%) and Latvia (over 30%) are moving more toward assimilation and accommodation after thirty years of living in the West. In 2018, Latvia passed a law limiting the use of Russian in schools and making Latvian the prime language of instruction in all the nation's schools. This action would have caused riots in the 1990s, but there was little protest from the Russian community in Latvia over the measure.[43] Putin's invasion of Ukraine in February 2022 found little open support among the ethnic Russians of Latvia, with the younger ethnic Russians, born in Latvia, showing little if any inclination to support Putin's aggression.

Indeed, the Russian invasion of Ukraine emboldened the Latvian parliament to pass a law to remove the large monument to the Soviet Army that "liberated" Latvia in 1944.[44] This monument has been resented by most Latvians for decades but allowed to stand for fear of provoking Putin and the local Russian community. Again, Putin's open aggression has pushed the Baltic peoples to assert their sovereignty and national identity more openly with strong public support, even from a great part of the ethnic Russian community that Putin has tried to court since taking power in 2000.

Security Concerns

All three Baltic states have faced aggressive and coercive actions from Russia in the last fifteen years. In April and May of 2007, Estonia faced a large-scale, highly organized cyberattack that was designed to take down government websites as well as the websites and communications of banks and large businesses. This coordinated attack was most likely the work of Russian groups, although the Russian government denied any involvement.[45] The Baltics also face aggressive economic pressure from Russia. Lithuania, almost completely dependent on Russian energy supplies, was made to pay the highest energy costs in the European Union.

What is most disconcerting is the ratcheting up of open hostility against the Baltic states expressed in the highest levels of Russian leadership. In 2013, Vladimir Zhirinovsky, deputy speaker of the Russian Federation State Duma, stated, "Let the puppies [referring to Latvia] bark in the world, eventually they will be occupied . . . The entire Baltics will be either occupied or destroyed . . . definitely."[46] Aleksandr Dugin, professor at Moscow State University and a leading ideologue of the Russian regime, referred to the Baltic states in a recent interview and noted, "Russia considers them an enemy, and makes no special distinctions between them. This view is shared by the elite, including the liberals, and general population. Russia is waiting for a global redistribution of power [in the world]. For example, should something happen to the U.S., we will immediately re-occupy these countries. We will accomplish this either peacefully or by force. We have already applied some of the methods to create serious internal problems in Estonia and Latvia."[47]

The aggressive Russian statements against the Baltics are being followed up by various legal harassment actions. In 2014, the Russian state prosecutor, a major tool of Russian policy today as it was under Stalin, reopened the case against more than 1,500 Lithuanians who refused to serve in the Soviet Army after Lithuania declared independence in March 1990. The ruling, acting as if the Soviet occupation of Lithuania were legal, means that warrants have been issued against the Lithuanians who refused service. The Lithuanian government has advised those Lithuanians not to travel outside the EU or NATO countries.[48]

The Baltic nations have responded to such open threats to their independence with restraint, partly because they are members of NATO and the EU, and partly because they know that as small countries, they should perhaps refrain from criticizing the United States or Western Europe until it really matters. Unlike the US or Western European governments, the Eastern European and Baltic countries realize that there was never any "reset" with Russia.[49] In fact, after the US government announced that relations with Russia had been "reset" in 2009, the Baltic security situation worsened. Although the United States and NATO talked of closer cooperation with Russia from 2009 to 2014 and NATO refrained from listing Russia as a threat, the last four Russian military doctrines promulgated since 2003 (the last was approved in 2014) all explicitly state that NATO is Russia's enemy. Russian doctrine states that the expansion of NATO into the Baltic states constitutes a grave threat to Russia.[50]

But even while NATO and the West were looking to seek accommodation with Russia in matters of trade and security after 2009, the Baltic countries were working quietly to reduce their vulnerabilities to Russian pressure. The greatest success of the Baltic states has been in dealing with their dependence on Russia for energy. Since regaining independence in 1991, the Baltic states have been overwhelmingly dependent on Russia for oil and gas, with Lithuania also dependent for electricity. When disputes arose, Russia was not slow to turn off the gas or oil to the Baltic countries for brief periods just to show what Russia could do to their economies if crossed. Lithuania, the state most energy dependent on Russia, went ahead and financed and built a modern liquefied natural gas (LNG) post in Klaipėda, completing the project in 2014. The complex was developed to further transship gas to Poland, Latvia, and Estonia through regional pipelines. Lithuania went from getting most of its electricity from Russia in 2010 to buying only 10% of its power needs from Russian companies in 2022. When Russia invaded Ukraine in February 2022, the Baltic states immediately cut their energy imports from Russia. All three Baltic nations now rely on Lithuania's LNG port to meet their needs, and Lithuania is also able to supply some gas to Poland.[51]

Yet within the European Union and in some major NATO nations, there has been a reluctance to challenge Russia's aggressive actions between 2014 and 2021 in any meaningful way. Generally, the three Baltic states have refrained from speaking up in NATO and EU councils for fear of upsetting the larger Western European nations, notably Germany, who are still committed to a closer relationship with Russia. Within the European Union, the three Baltic states want to be viewed as modern and cooperative nations, and for this reason have been muted in pushing the EU to stronger actions against Russia since this would lead to increased friction with Germany, which is also a key Baltic trading partner.[52]

There is an almost universal consensus among the Baltic political and military leaders that Russia is a direct threat to their existence and that, as small nations, the only assurance of their freedom is the defense guarantee of the United States through NATO. On the other hand, there has been a fear of sounding alarmist and thus irritating the US administration by any overt critique of US policy, or lack of policy, toward Russian aggression in Eastern Europe.[53] Therefore, the Baltic states have quietly worked through NATO to lobby for a more realistic view of Putin's Russia. In the run-up to NATO's publication of the new NATO strategic concept in 2009 and 2010, the three Baltic states, along with the Eastern European NATO members, mounted a quiet but effective lobby to influence the new NATO strategic concept. This lobbying effort worked to see that NATO officially recognized the strategic threat of Russia and would maintain its focus on conventional military deterrence.[54] In the NATO strategic concept document adopted by the member states at the Lisbon conference, NATO reaffirmed territorial defense of the member states as a core mission of NATO. However, the United States was turning its focus away from Europe and greatly reducing its forces there in the face of major Russian military increases from 2009 to 2014—and leaving the Baltic nations very worried about the long-term commitment of the United States.

However, the Russian seizure of the Crimea in 2014 and the initiation of a Russian-supported insurgency in Ukraine's Donbas region pushed the Baltic states to begin increasing their defense expenditures to meet NATO's 2% of GDP standard. NATO had previously questioned the real need for the "air policing" operation, where top squadrons of fighter planes from NATO member nations are rotated though the Šiauliai Air Base in Lithuania (extensively rebuilt and modernized by the Lithuanians) to protect Baltic air space from Russia. But Putin's increasingly aggressive posture ended the debate and ensured that NATO would provide even more open support and troops for Baltic defense.

Both the Obama administration and Trump administration in the United States had started out skeptical of the need to keep large numbers of US forces in Europe, and both began by hoping there could be better relations with Russia. But both administrations then changed their course in terms of evolving a stronger approach to military deterrence of Russia. During his 2016 election campaign, Trump had been very critical of NATO over the failure of most member states to meet NATO's goal of 2% of GDP for defense. However, after the election, he changed his position, and when meeting with NATO Secretary General Jens Stoltenberg in April 2017, Trump praised the alliance and stated that it was not obsolete.[55] Since

308   *James S. Corum*

then, there has been consistent support within NATO for a visible and improved deterrent force in the Baltic states.

After failing to find a diplomatic solution to the Russian aggression in Ukraine and reluctantly recognizing that Russia poses a military threat to NATO's eastern members, NATO responded in 2016 to the request of the three Baltic states and Poland for a permanent NATO military force in the region by stationing 3,000 to 4,000 NATO troops (including 1,000 US troops) in the Baltics and Poland on a rotating basis, as well as stepping up NATO's air and naval presence in the Baltic Sea region. This action was supported by the United States specifically to serve as a deterrent to Russia's increased military forces in the region.[56] By 2021, four well-armed and well-trained NATO multinational battle groups (brigade-sized forces) were now committed to Baltic defense by NATO, with the United States as the lead nation for the group based in Poland, Germany as the lead nation for the group in Lithuania, Canada as the lead nation for the group in Latvia, and the United Kingdom as the lead nation for the group in Estonia.[57]

When Russia initiated an all-out attack on Ukraine in February 2022 with the stated intent of eliminating Ukraine as an independent state, the Baltics were less surprised than the Western Europeans. They understood the Russian leadership's thinking far better than any Western European did. Even before the accession of Vladimir Putin to power in 2000, the Russian state had worked to reestablish some kind of control over the Baltic states, generally along the lines of Russia's relationship with the former Soviet republics in central Asia, with Russia de facto directing control of their economies, foreign relations, and security. With an official state ideology laid out in the volumes of *Project Russia*, Putin concocted a toxic mixture of old czarist and Soviet rhetoric to justify the reestablishment of empire and aggressive diplomatic, economic, informational, and, finally, military action to meet that goal.

The Baltic states showed considerable wisdom in recognizing the character of Putin and the Russian leadership when they joined NATO in 2004. Moreover, by steadily reducing Russian economic influence, especially in the key area of energy supplies, the Baltics are in a sound position to maintain their security and economies within NATO and the European Union. Traditionally moderate and neutral, neighboring Sweden and Finland decided to join NATO in response to Putin's threats. (Finland officially joined in 2023 and Sweden in March 2024.) The expansion of NATO in northeastern Europe adds some very modern and capable ground, air, and naval forces into play in the immediate region that will serve as a NATO deterrent to Russia. Most importantly, the addition of the well-trained and well-

A View from Northeastern Europe   309

equipped Swedish and Finnish air forces into direct NATO command would give NATO likely air superiority over the Baltic region in case of any hostile Russian moves.[58] Ironically, Putin's move against Ukraine was a signal event that has immediately and significantly improved the military deterrence position of the Baltic states against any Russian revanchist inclinations. Thus, the Baltic states are today in an even stronger position to maintain their independence and Western identity.

NOTES

1. I worked in and for the Baltic States from January 2009 to June 2014 as dean of the Baltic Defence College, the higher military education college of the three Baltic States. In that position, I worked closely with senior military and political leaders and academics of the three Baltic States. I lived and worked in Estonia, but my job took me regularly through all parts of the Baltic States. Much of this article is based on my personal experience working for and with the Baltic armed forces.

2. See Leo Tolstoy, *War and Peace* (London: Classic Books Edition, 2013), books 9–12. Barclay de Tolly's 1812 strategy of avoiding battle with Napoleon's army at the start of the invasion, when the French Army was at is strongest and close to its bases of supply, was ridiculed by the Russian generals who wanted immediate aggressive action. Yet de Tolly's plan to avoid battle until the French were deep into Russia almost certainly saved the Russian Army, and the Russian Empire, from a catastrophic defeat. The Russians never gave de Tolly full credit for their eventual victory because of de Tolly's Baltic ethnicity.

3. Andres Kasekamp, *A History of the Baltic States* (London: Palgrave, 2010), 99–105. Kasekamp provides the best general history of the Baltic States in English.

4. Kasekamp, *A History of the Baltic States*.

5. All the Baltic States have established historical commissions to document the victims of the Soviet period of occupation. All three states have published extensive detailed studies of the Baltic citizens killed, exiled, arrested, or sent to prisons. In many cases, the outcome is fuzzy with a known arrest date but nothing thereafter. Nevertheless, the enormous scale of Soviet repression and crimes against humanity committed against the Baltic States over fifty years has been very well-documented. For details on the Soviet repression in Estonia in 1941–1945, see Estonian International Commission for the Investigation of Crimes Against Humanity, *Estonia 1940–1945* (Tallinn: Estonian Foundation for the Investigation of Crimes Against Humanity, 2005).

6. Latvia provided two divisions to the German Army, the 15th and 17th Waffen SS Divisions, and the Estonians manned the 20th Waffen SS Division. The Western Allies after the war during the Nuremberg Trials determined that the Baltic military formations were not criminal organizations and had not committed war crimes.

7. Kasekamp, *A History of the Baltic States*, 141–146.

8. In one wave of deportations in three days in March 1949, 43,000 Latvians, including women and children, were rounded up and deported to Siberia, where many perished. In just this one wave of deportations, 92,000 Baltic people were sent to Siberia. In all,

310   *James S. Corum*

hundreds of thousands of people from these small states were sent to the gulags and to settlements in Siberia and Central Asia. See Paul Rothenhäusler and Hans-Ueli Sonderegger, eds., *Errinerung an den Roten Holocaust* (Stäfe: Rothenhäusler Verlag, 1999), 58–69.

9. For details on the suppression of the Latvians, see Janis Straume, *Lettland im 2. Weltkrieg* (Riga: Nacionālais Apgāds, 2007), 41–46.

10. For a detailed analysis of the largest and most effective resistance movement in the Baltics, see Vylius Leskys, "'Forest Brothers' 1945: The Culmination of the Lithuanian Partisan Movement," *Baltic Security and Defence Review* 11.1 (2009): 58–86.

11. On the history commission that revised the Soviet history of the 1939 Pact, see Heike Lindpere, *Molotov-Ribbentrop Pact: Challenging Soviet History* (Tallin: Estonian Foreign Policy Institute, 2009); on the Soviet denunciation of the treaty's legality, see 173–195.

12. See Zaneta Ozolina, "Crisis Prevention or Intervention: Latvia's Response to the Proposed Russian Security guarantees," in *Crisis Management in a Transitional Society: The Latvian Experience*, eds. Eric Stern and Dan Hansen (Stockholm: Forsvarshogskollan, 2000), 188–215.

13. See "GDP Per Capita (US$)," World Bank, https://data.worldbank.org/indicator /NY.GDP.PCAP.CD.

14. On Baltic States economic reforms in the 1990s, see Kasekamp, *A History of the Baltic States*, 181–183.

15. Kasekamp, *A History of the Baltic States*, 183–185.

16. For a study of the deployments of the Baltic forces in service of NATO, see James S. Corum, *The Development of the Baltic Armed Forces in Light of Multinational Deployments* (Carlisle: U.S. Army War College Strategic Studies Institute, 2013).

17. In Russian history today, the history of the gulags is being suppressed. The death of approximately 5 million Ukrainians in the forced collectivization of the 1930s is downplayed. Stalin is presented in a positive light, and the Russian invasions of Finland and the Baltic States are justified as necessary to oppose Nazism. The Baltics are portrayed consistently as enthusiastic Nazis during World War II.

18. I. M. Strizhova and N. M. Terekhova, eds., *Rossiya I Yeyo 'Kolonii': Kak Gruziya, Ukraina, Moldaviya,Pribaltika iSrednyaya Aziya Boshli v Sostav Rossi* (Moscow: ROC Publishing, 2007).

19. Kasekamp, *A History of the Baltic States*, 196.

20. Damien Sharkov, "Putin Warns of Neo-Nazism in Ukraine and Europe Ahead of WW2 Memorial," *Newsweek*, October 15, 2014, https://www.newsweek.com/putin -warns-neo-nazi-rise-ukraine-and-baltics-latvia-responds-look-mirror-277710.

21. On the activities of the Baltic Historical Commissions, see Eva-Clarita Pettai, "The Convergence of Two Worlds: Historians and the Emerging Histories of the Baltic States," in *Forgotten Pages of Baltic History*, eds. Martyn Housden and David Smith (Amsterdam: Rodolpi, 2011), 262–280.

22. "Russia denies Baltic 'Occupation,'" *BBC News*, May 5, 2005, http://news.bbc.co .uk/2/hi/europe/4517683.stm.

23. *КомсомольскаяПравда*, *Komsomolskaya Pravda*, "Генпрокуратура РФ пров еритзаконностьвыходаПрибалтикиизСССР" ("The Prosecutor General's Office of the Russian Federation will check the legality of The Baltics SSR"), July 1, 2015.

A View from Northeastern Europe   311

24. On the rewriting of history texts in Russia and the movement to put up new statues to Stalin, see Hannah Thoburn, "For Putin, For Stalin," *Foreign Policy*, January 25, 2016, https://foreignpolicy.com/2016/01/25/for-putin-for-stalin-russia-propaganda/.

25. Kasekamp, *A History of the Baltic States*, 197.

26. Halya Coynash, "Putin Appoints Apologist for Stalin as Russia's Education Minister," *Khpg.org*, August 25, 2016.

27. See Ola Chichowlas, "The Kremlin is Trying to Erase Memories of the Gulag," *New Republic*, January 23, 2014, https://newrepublic.com/article/118306/kremlin-trying-erase-memories-gulag; and Shaun Walker, "Russia's Gulag Camps Cast in Forgiving Light of Putin's Nationalism," *The Guardian*, October 29, 2015, https://www.theguardian.com/world/2015/oct/29/russia-gulag-camps-putin-nationalism-soviet-history. On denying the Ukrainian famine, see Ekaterina Blinova, "Holodomor Hoax: Joseph Stalin's Crime That Never Took Place," *Sputnik International*, September 8, 2015, https://sputniknews.com/20150809/1025560345.html.

28. *Voice of Russia World Service*, December 4, 2008, http://www.ruvr.ru/main.php?lng=eng&q=25586&cid=59&p=12.04.2008.

29. "Эстония может стать прибежищем для нацистов со всего мира. Маргелов подбивает Эстонию дать убежище уцелевшим нацистам со всего мира" [Estonia can become a refuge for Nazis from all over the world. Margelov encourages Estonia to give refuge to surviving Nazis from around the world], *NewsRU*, October 30, 2011, https://www.newsru.com/russia/30oct2011/margelov.htm. English translation is the author's.

30. "Estonia can become a refuge."

31. For an example, see a book by one of Putin's leading advisors: Sergei Glazyev, *Ukrainskaya Katastropha. Ot Amerikanskoy Agressii k Mirovoy Voyne?* (Izborsk Club Collection: 2017)

32. Masha Gessen, *The Man without a Face: The Unlikely Rise of Vladimir Putin* (London: Granta, 2012), 133.

33. See Lynn Corum's article on *Project Russia* in this book.

34. For an analysis of Russia's media campaign against small neighbors, see Nerijas Maliukevicius, "Russia's Information Policy in Lithuania: The Spread of Soft Power of Information Geopolitics?" *Baltic Security and Defence Review* 9 (2007): 150–170, https://community.apan.org/wg/tradoc-g2/fmso/m/fmso-monographs/243743.

35. On Russia's approach to soft power and information, see Robert Orttung, "Russia's Use of PR as a Foreign Policy Tool," *Russian Analytical Digest* 81 (June 2010): 7–10. See also "'Russia's World'—Russia's Soft Power Approach to Compatriot's Policy," *Russian Analytical Digest* 81 (June 2010): 2–4.

36. Valters Nollendorfs, Dzintra Burg, Gundega Michele, and Uldis Neiburgs, *The Three Occupations of Latvia 1941–1991* (Riga: Occupation Museum Association of Latvia, 2008), 37.

37. See the *CIA World Factbook* for recent statistics on the ethnic makeup of the Baltic States. In Latvia the population is 59.3% ethnic Latvian, 27.8% Russian, 3.6% Belarusian, and 2.5% Ukrainian; 37.5% of Latvians are Russian speakers. In Estonia, 68.7% of the population is ethnic Estonian, and 25.6% are Russian or Russian speakers.

312 James S. Corum

38. On the citizenship issue and ethnic friction, see Andris Runcis, "The Citizenship Issue as a Creeping Crisis," in Stern and Hansen, *Crisis Management*, 61–97.

39. Heiko Pääbo, "'War of Memories': Explaining the 'Memorials War' in Estonia," *Baltic Security and Defence Review* 10 (2008): 5–28.

40. Ceslovas Laurinavicius, "The Role of History in the Relationship between Lithuania and Russia," in *Lithuanian Annual Strategic Review 2005* (Vilnius: Strategic Research Center, 2006), 109–125.

41. Leonid Karabeshkin, "Russian-Lithuanian Relations: Between Negative Perception Stereotypes and Pragmatic Cooperation," in *Lithuanian Annual Strategic Review 2006* (Vilnius: Strategic Research Center, 2007), 65–83. See p. 82.

42. As a teacher at Tartu University in Estonia, I can add some of my own experience. From 2011 to 2014, I taught every year a graduate class of approximately forty-five students who are mostly Estonian and include ethnic Russians as well as ethnic Estonians. The ethnic Russians can speak Estonian (although their English tends to be more fluent than their Estonian) and also tend to be employed by Estonian firms. That many ethnic Russians are able to meet the very high entrance standards of Tartu University shows that the Estonian education system has not failed the ethnic Russian population. The ethnic Russians are fully included in the university life. Some of my ethnic Russian students have told me of visiting their relatives in Russia, but they seem to have little interest in becoming Russian citizens or to hold a deep attachment to the Russian state. The ethnic Estonian relationship to Russia seems to be more of a connection with their cousins back in the old country. Sometimes, my ethnic Russian students note that they have been brought up to speak a Moscow (more educated) form of Russian, while their relations in Russia sometimes speak local dialects that are hard for them to understand.

43. "A New Law in Latvia Aims to Preserve National Language by Limiting Russian in Schools", *National Public Radio*, October 28, 2018, https://www.npr.org/2018/10/28/654142363/a-new-law-in-latvia-aims-to-preserve-national-language-by-limiting-russian-in-sc.

44. "Latvian Lawmakers Approve Bill Allowing Removal of Soviet Monument in Riga," *Radio Free Europe, Radio Liberty*, May 12, 2022, https://www.rferl.org/a/latvia-soviet-monument-removal-ukraine/31846730.html.

45. On the cyber attacks on Estonia, see Robert Ashmore, "Impact of Alleged Russian Cyber Attacks," *Baltic Security and Defence Review* 11 (2010): 4–39.

46. Session of the Russian State Duma, *ITAR-TASS*, April 9, 2013.

47. Alexandr Dugin, from an interview with the Russian DELFI in Lithuania. November 2010.

48. "Russia Reopens Case Against Lithuanians who Refused to Serve in the Soviet Army," *Baltic Times*, September 9, 2014, https://www.baltictimes.com/news/articles/35526/.

49. On March 6, 2009, the U.S. Secretary of State presented Russian Foreign Minister Sergei Lavrov with a large "reset" button as the Obama administration announced that it would lift various sanctions and restrictions placed on Russia for its invasion of Georgia only a few months before. A new era of good relations and cooperation with Russia was expected by President Obama and Western leaders.

50. See *The Military Doctrine of the Russian Federation*, Approved by Russian Federation Presidential Edict on February 5, 2010. Translation by the SRAS-School of Russian and Asian Studies. The main external threats to the Russian Federation are as follows: (1) the desire to endow the force potential of NATO with global functions carried out in violation of the norms of international law and to move the military infrastructure of NATO member countries closer to the borders of the Russian Federation, including by expanding the bloc; (2) the attempts to destabilize the situation in individual states and regions and to undermine strategic stability; and (3) the deployment (buildup) of troop contingents of foreign states (groups of states) on the territories of states contiguous with the Russian Federation and its allies and also in adjacent waters. The 2014 Military Doctrine condemns the expansion of NATO in harsh terms. See Margarete Klein, "Russia's New Military Doctrine" *SWP Comments 9*, Stiftung Wissenschaft und Politik, February 26, 2015, https://www.swp-berlin.org/en/publication/russias-new-military -doctrine.

51. Jeane Whalen, "A History of Russian Oppression Fueled Lithuanian Energy Independence," *Washington Post*, May 6, 2022, https://www.washingtonpost.com/world /2022/05/06/lithuania-russia-oil-gas/.

52. Gediminas Vitkus and Jurate Novagrockiene, "The Impact of Lithuania on EU Council Decision-Making," in *Lithuanian Annual Strategic Review 2007* (Vilnius: Strategic Research Center, 2007), 91–123.

53. For a detailed overview of the Baltic leaders and their view on security, see James S. Corum, *The Security Concerns of the Baltic States as NATO Allies* (Carlisle: U.S. Army War College, Strategic Studies Institute, 2013).

54. The Baltic Defence College was part of this lobby effort in hosting a workshop on the New NATO strategic concept that featured leading Baltic politicians and academics. The proceedings of the workshop featured the need to maintain collective security as the key NATO strategy and discussed the perception of the Russian threat to NATO. See *Proceedings of a Workshop on NATO's Strategic Concept*, October 15–16, 2009, Tartu Estonia. Published in the *Baltic Security and Defence Review* 12.1 (2010).

55. Spencer Ackerman, "'No Longer Obsolete': Trump Backtracks on NATO with Russia Tensions Rising," *The Guardian*, April 12, 2017, https://www.theguardian.com /world/2017/apr/12/trump-nato-meeting-russia-syria-missile-attack.

56. Robin Emmott and Sabine Siebold, "NATO Sends Troops to Poland, Baltic States to Face Off with Russia," *Christian Science Monitor*, July 9, 2016, https://www .csmonitor.com/World/2016/0709/NATO-sends-troops-to-Poland-Baltic-states-to-face -off-with-Russia.

57. Jens Stoltenberg, *NATO Secretary General's Annual Report*, NATO, March 31, 2021, https://www.nato.int/nato_static_fl2014/assets/pdf/2022/3/pdf/sgar21-en.pdf.

58. Alia Shoaib, "Norway, Sweden, Finland, and Denmark Struck a Deal to Run Their 200+ Advanced Fighter Jets as a Single Fleet, Creating a New Headache for Russia," *Business Insider* March 25, 2023. https://www.businessinsider.com/norway -sweden-finland-denmark-fighter-jets-one-fleet-2023-3.

Chapter Twelve

Economic Implications of the Russian Invasion of Ukraine

Todd J. Lefko and Raymond Robertson

The February 24, 2022, invasion of Ukraine was not unanticipated, but predictions of the economic effects seemed to imply that it caught most forecasters by surprise. Both the invasion itself and the economic sanctions imposed by Western countries on Russia were a measured, nonmilitary response that had significant effects on Ukraine, Russia, Europe, developing countries, and the United States. In March 2022, a poll of economists suggested that nearly 75% of respondents expected a global economic slowdown in 2022 and over 90% believed that the imposed sanctions would induce a deep recession in Russia.[1] In fact, both the Russian and global economies proved more resilient than expected. The Russian economy contracted by only 2.1% in 2022, and global growth reached 2.4%. The goal of this chapter is to assess the short-, medium-, and long-run impacts of the Russian invasion, explain why predictions proved overly pessimistic, and provide economic policy recommendations to mitigate adverse economic impacts in the medium and long runs.

Russia's attack occurred just after the International Monetary Fund (IMF) cut its 2022 global growth forecast.[2] The IMF reduced growth expectations in January 2022 because of supply chain disruptions, new COVID-19 variants, and an economic slowdown in China. Subsequently, rising COVID-19 cases in China and the ongoing lockdown in Shanghai further disrupted both finance and supply chains. In April 2022, the World Economic Forum reduced growth projections published in *World Economic Outlook*.[3] The report predicted only 3.6% growth in both 2022 and 2023, contrasting sharply with 6.1% growth in 2021, and predicted a falling gross domestic product (GDP) in emerging and developing Europe and an 8.5% decrease in growth in Russia.

These pessimistic predictions had a strong foundation in economic statistics. As a large developing country that relies primarily on commodity exports, Russia plays a significant role in global commodity markets. Wheat and fuel play a leading role, but significant increases in other commodity prices quickly followed Russia's invasion of Ukraine.[4] Supply chain disruptions directly affected Europe—especially in fuel markets—and threatened developing countries by disrupting food supplies. The United States, meanwhile, struggled with unusually high inflation rates in 2022 that were exacerbated by invasion-induced supply chain disruptions. What seems to have been unexpected was the Russian understanding of Keynesian economic policies, the resilience of highly integrated global commodity markets, and simple good economic luck. The remaining sections of this chapter illustrate how these factors supported the economic resilience of Ukraine, Russia, Europe, developing countries, and, finally, the United States.

The Future of Ukraine

It is obvious that the invasion has destroyed much of Ukraine's productive capacity—in both cities and fields. In April 2022, the World Bank predicted a 4.1% economic contraction in Europe and central Asia, which contrasted sharply with the previous prediction of 3.1% growth.[5] The World Bank also predicted that the Ukrainian economy would shrink by 45.1% in 2022.

There were several obvious reasons for the pessimistic predictions. Unplanted crops and bombed cities had the same economic effects in Ukraine as they would have everywhere. By nearly every measure, the human toll was greater than the loss of land and capital. By May 2022, the United Nations reported that 6.4 million refugees had fled Ukraine (the majority left in March 2022).[6] Over 3.4 million went into Poland and nearly another million entered Romania and the Russian Federation. According to *The Economist*, in 2022, the number of refugees from Ukraine was nearly three times the number of Syrians who had entered Europe in 2015.[7] The loss of human capital to Ukraine was significant.

Although the post-conflict economy is difficult to predict, one of the less appreciated aspects of the invasion is likely to have permanent effects. Russia's pattern of invasion implies that an immediate goal was to control access to the Black Sea. Successful Russian occupation or control of Crimea, Kherson, and territories farther west along the coast could transform Ukraine into a landlocked country.

Landlocked countries export 27%–41% less than other countries.[8] Significant reduction in exports would have significant implications for long-run growth because it is well established that exporting contributes to economic growth.[9]

The predicted economic contraction of 45.1% overstated the actual loss in 2022, which was 29.2%. In April 2023, predictions for Ukraine in 2023 were a *positive* 0.5%. Why did the economy perform better than expected? Several factors fell in favor of Ukraine: First, dire predictions for global food prices and for developing countries dependent on Ukraine grain helped generate successful negotiations for a grain deal that resumed shipments in 2022.[10] Second, nearly 4 million migrants returned to Ukraine. Third, the Ukrainian government successfully leveraged both the skillful macroeconomic management that maintained price stability and the significant inflows of foreign aid to support government expenditures.

The Russian Economy

Predictions for Russia's economic performance in 2022 were also overly pessimistic. In April 2022, the World Bank's revised economic forecast for the Russian economy predicted a contraction of 11.2%.[11] The IMF and others had similar predictions. The Institute of International Finance in Washington, DC, estimated that Russia's GDP might fall by up to 15% in 2022 and 3% in 2023.[12] Goldman Sachs predicted the Russian economy would decrease by 10% in 2022, replacing their past prediction of a 2% increase,[13] and the World Bank predicted a Russian economic contraction of 11.2% in 2022.[14] The *Financial Times* estimated that per capita income would drop to under $10,000 by the end of 2022,[15] falling from a 2016 peak of $16,000 to $12,000 before the invasion.[16]

The overly pessimistic predictions for the Russian economy were no less well-founded than the overly pessimistic predictions for Ukraine. After all, the loss of trade and diplomatic relations threatens growth in a number of specific ways. Western sanctions isolated Russia from the international financial system, making access to capital uncertain for the near future. The loss of access to relatively low-cost capital increases the costs of investment. Rising investment costs reduce investment and, in the medium and long terms, economic growth. In addition, the loss of trade and diplomatic relations prevented Russia from accessing the latest technologies. Writing for *Forbes*, Bill Conerly argued that the invasion would isolate Russia for years to come, resulting in lower economic growth.[17] In other words, the sanctions and injured diplomatic relations with wealthy Western countries would hurt trade and, by extension, economic growth.

But as we mentioned above, contrary to predictions, the Russian economy contracted by just 2.1% in 2022.[18] The World Bank predicted only a 0.5% contraction for 2023. In retrospect, it seems reasonable to believe that Russia anticipated the Western response and that forecasters underappreciated Russia's preparation (especially in energy markets), as well as its ability to implement a Keynesian response to the expected contraction.

In terms of energy markets, Russia's plan was to mitigate the (anticipated) Western economic response by dominating energy sourcing, distribution, and processing. By purchasing European pipelines and processing systems, Putin, in effect, gained significant control over heat and lights in Europe. The break-even point for Russian oil was $42–$43 per barrel. As the price per barrel rose to $100 and beyond, Europe was funding Putin's war with at least $500 million in oil revenue flowing in each day. Russia strongly desired the rapid rise in cost per barrel, as it provided additional budget and military support. The system paid into Russia's plan for the short term. Even if Europe transitioned out of fossil fuels, Russia had correctly assumed that other friendly nations would continue to trade and that the large Chinese and Indian markets would mitigate the loss of European sales.

Russia's war spending was complemented by additional countercyclical spending that stabilized and supported the Russian economy, which is a textbook Keynesian response to an expected economic contraction. Although these moves increased the budget deficit in an environment where access to loanable funds was increasingly difficult, Russian deficit levels of 2.2% of the GDP were still much lower than in some Western countries (5.4% in the United States in 2022, for example).

Russia also benefited from some good economic luck, including a record-high grain harvest in 2022[19] and growth in other domestic sectors. Although the longer-term predictions are still not very positive, the predictions of steep recession seem to have receded.

European Tensions

Europe relied heavily on fuel exports from Russia, which provided at least 40% of gas and 33% of oil coming into the European Union (EU). Figure 12.1 uses data from the United Nations Comtrade database to illustrate the importance of Russian and Ukrainian fuel exports. It graphs all countries that import more than 10% of their total fuel and related imports (Harmonized System [HS] code 27: mineral fuels, mineral oils, bituminous substances, and mineral waxes) from Russia and

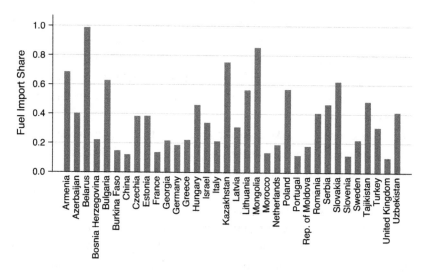

Figure 12.1 Share of Fuel Imports from Ukraine and Russia, 2018. *Note:* Fuel is represented by Harmonized System Code 27: Mineral Fuels, mineral oils, bituminous substances, and mineral waxes. *Source:* Authors' elaboration using data from COMTRADE, https://comtradeplus.un.org/.

Ukraine. Russia supplied about 10% of the global oil and natural gas supply, but this influence was outsized in the region Russia considered most essential. Some countries, like Belarus, imported nearly all of their fuel and related materials from Russia.

The financial news website 24/7 Wall St. reviewed data on export and import values reported to the Trade Statistics Branch of the United Nations Statistics Division. These data were curated by the Observatory of Economic Complexity, an online data visualization and distribution platform. The data are from 2020 and show that former Soviet Union members from central Asia were the most dependent on Russian energy.[20] In particular, 83.5% of Kyrgyzstan's oil imports and domestic production were tied to Russia, one-tenth of its population (650,000 people) worked as laborers in Russia and sent remittances back to their families, and 73% of Tajikistan's total oil imports and domestic production were tied to Russia. Other nations tied to Russian oil imports included Armenia at 72.1%, Belarus at $3.6 billion a year for Russian oil imports, North Korea at 67.9%, Mongolia at 66.4%, Uzbekistan at 40.9%, Hungary at 31.7%, Georgia at 28.8%, Ukraine at 27.7%, Czechia at 26.3%, and Greece and Slovakia each at 21.7%. The Baltic states and neighboring countries were also dependent on Russia for oil imports and domestic oil production, with Latvia at 64.1%, Finland at 57.6%, Poland at 54.9%, Lithuania at 45.6%, and Estonia at 43.6%.

Germany, France, Sweden, the United Kingdom, and other European countries are also listed in figure 12.1. Studies from top German think tanks[21] predicted that a full EU embargo on Russian energy would produce a major German recession, dropping its GDP by 2.2% in one year and destroying over 200,000 jobs. It was one thing to ban coal imports, which the EU planned to begin in August 2022, but banning oil and gas was a whole other topic. Many European nations were dependent on Russia for oil imports and domestic production, including Poland at 54.9%, Malta at 53.5%, Bulgaria at 43.8%, Turkey at 30.0%, the Netherlands at 28.0%, Ukraine at 27.8%, Germany at 23.6%, and Slovenia at 21.7%.[22]

The EU received 37% of Russia's global trade, mostly in energy, before the second Ukraine invasion in 2022.[23] Nearly 12% of Russian oil went to Europe, and Russian thermal coal constituted 70% (36 million tons) of the EU coal imported in 2022. These numbers are being sharply reduced, but not without significant adjustment costs.

German analysts initially assumed that an immediate shift away from Russian energy would cause Germany to lose 400,000 jobs and reduce its economic output by 2.2% in 2023. But in 2023, the IMF predicted an *increase* in Germany's GDP of 1.7%. Germany seemed to have avoided the major industrial slowdown that could have occurred if supply shifted away from industry to provide for home heating and personal use. Before the invasion, in 2021, one-half of Germany's natural gas and thermal coal imports came from Russia, as well as one-third of its oil imports, but Berlin hoped to diversify away from Russian oil by the end of 2022 and gas by 2024. Also in 2021, Russia provided almost 70% of the EU's thermal coal imports, but the EU subsequently banned the import of Russian coal beginning in August 2022. Because about 16% of the EU's total electricity was expected to be produced from thermal coal in 2022, this ban was a major change requiring time, investment funds, and political ability to withstand popular anger. It also required a plan for spreading the costs; without one, short-term reliance on Russian energy would remain a salient issue for Europe.

Another key variable creating tension in Europe was migration. Most of the academic literature clearly establishes that the net benefits of immigration are positive.[24] Immigrants are associated with new ideas, complementary labor-market skills, increased demand for local and imported goods and services, innovation, and, although less appreciated, an increased demand for native workers. Nevertheless, immigration fuels political discontent as opportunistic politicians take advantage of natives' often misplaced resentment toward immigrants. Such policies feed political discontent, which can potentially have adverse effects on economic growth.

The EU's March 3, 2022, directive welcomed Ukrainians by giving them access to benefits and allowing them to both live and work in twenty-six of twenty-seven EU member countries.[25] The directive contrasted with the 2015 policies that made adjustment more difficult for refugees. In 2022 and 2023, the governments of Poland and Great Britain offered households temporary cash payments for hosting refugees. *The Economist* reported that some cities were strained because of large concentrations of migrants, but dispersion, along with the return of many Ukrainians, apparently helped mitigate the strain.

Developing Countries: Rising Starvation Risks

Although it is a large commodity-exporting developing country, Russia is a significant supplier for much of the developing world. Figure 12.2 draws on Comtrade data from before the COVID-19 pandemic to illustrate Russia's importance for many developing countries. The countries shown import more than 10% of their total imports from Russia and Ukraine. Many of these are former Soviet republics that are relatively close to Russia, but these countries are in a precarious position with respect to global supply chains, which were revealed to be not especially resilient during the COVID-19 crisis.

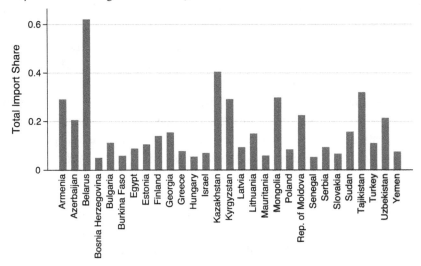

Figure 12.2 Share of Total Imports from Ukraine and Russia, 2018. *Source*: Authors' elaboration using data from COMTRADE, https://comtradeplus.un.org/.

Of all the commodities imported from Ukraine and Russia by developing countries, cereals are especially concerning. Figure 12.3 shows all countries in the Comtrade database that import more than 10% of their total cereal imports (HS 10) from Russia and Ukraine. This list is long, and at least seven countries import more than 60% of all cereals from Russia and Ukraine.

By 2022, the world had become dependent on the region for other needs. In the previous five years, Russia and Ukraine had provided 17% of global corn exports, 32% of the world's barley exports, and 75% of sunflower oil exports.[26] There would be major secondary impacts from any shutdown. Ukraine produced one-third of the wheat going to Egypt, Indonesia, and Bangladesh, and without wheat to make inexpensive bread, hunger and political instability would develop in other nations.

The United Nations Global Crisis Response Group on Food, Energy, and Finance noted, "The war in Ukraine is setting in motion a three-dimensional crisis—on food, energy and finance—which is producing alarming cascading effects on the world economy already battered by COVID-19 and climate change."[27] The USDA Foreign Agricultural Service also illustrated how the rise in commodity prices would contribute to rising food insecurity.[28]

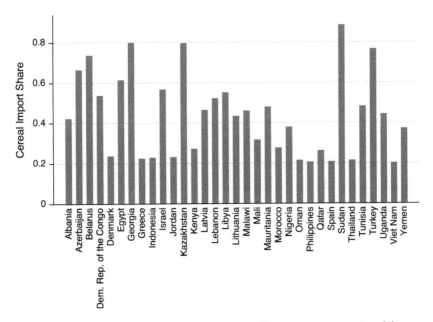

Figure 12.3 Share of Cereal Imports from Ukraine and Russia, 2018. *Note*: Cereal data are represented by Harmonized System Code 10. *Source*: Authors' elaboration using data from COMTRADE, https://comtradeplus.un.org/.

With Ukraine's Black Sea port shut down by a Russian blockade, wheat was still exported by rail but represented only a small fraction of past sea exports.[29] One-third of the world's population "relies on wheat as a dietary staple," according to David Beasley, executive director of the UN World Food Program.[30] Political anger from rising food prices has often produced civil unrest. Ukraine produced about 20% of the world's high-grade wheat and 7% of all world wheat. The World Food Program had previously purchased half of its grain from Ukraine, but then the country's most productive agricultural regions fell to Russian control. Major canals were damaged. Diesel for tractors and other farming equipment was in short supply, and the agricultural calendar was disrupted by fertilizer shortages and delayed tilling, and planting.

This change in food supply for many of the most food-insecure people was now added to the war-related fertilizer shortage and rising fuel costs that were expected to decrease yields and increase hunger globally.[31] In Ukraine, the Russian strategy seemed eerily reminiscent of the Holodomor of the 1930s, when Stalin's starvation-based genocidal policies resulted in the death of at least 3.9 million people. In 2022, the Russian strategy of starving Mariupol residents repeated the past. As John Rash of *The Minnesota Star Tribune* stated, "The longer the war continues, the higher the chance it becomes even more of a profound geopolitical event." Ukraine's export numbers were dramatically reduced immediately after the invasion, supporting dire predictions.[32]

Direct food imports were only part of the problem. Russia and Ukraine were also significant sources of fertilizers. The World Bank's 2022 report *Commodity Markets Outlook* shows that the prices of fertilizers rose by 220% between April 2020 and March 2022 (the largest increase over the same time period since 2008).[33] The price increase for fertilizer was especially sharp during the first quarter of 2022, which represents several key concepts illustrating the complicated implications of the Russian invasion. The fertilizer prices rose because the immediate conflict both restricted supply and increased the price of fuel. The compounded effects of the rising prices of both energy and fertilizer contributed to sharp increases in food prices that went beyond the direct effect of the loss of Russian and Ukrainian supplies.

As a result, it is not surprising that the World Bank predicted higher commodity prices for 2022. In particular, the 2022 *Commodity Markets Outlook* predicted a 50.5% increase in energy prices and a 69.3% increase in fertilizer prices. Overall, the report predicted that food prices would increase by 22.9%, with a 20.4% increase in the price of grains.[34]

Given the limited global food supply, the expected lack of resilience in global supply chains, rising food prices, falling food supplies, and rising input costs, the main economic risk from Russia's invasion of Ukraine in these developing countries was reasonably predicted to be starvation. The starvation-weary nation of Sudan, for example, imported more than 80% of its cereals from Russia and Ukraine. Already plagued by drought and a civil war that had lasted since 2013, South Sudan faced a pending humanitarian crisis made much worse by the invasion.

Again, however, the dire predictions proved somewhat overestimated. The Sudan crisis exploded in early 2023 but seemed to have been driven more by domestic politics than by external pressure. Oil prices fell in the second half of 2022. The 2023 *Commodity Markets Outlook* report predicted that commodity prices would fall by 21% and energy prices in particular would be 23% lower than in 2022. Commodity prices, including of energy, fell sharply in the last quarter of 2022, suggesting that forecasters significantly underestimated the resilience of commodity markets.[35]

The United States: Supply Chains and Inflation

The United States relies much less on Russian oil than European countries do, and unlike the developing countries that must import Russian and Ukrainian cereals, the United States is a food exporter. In addition, the US economy in 2022 performed extremely well and continued to experience falling employment and moderating inflation into 2023. Using data from the US Bureau of Labor Statistics, figure 12.4 shows the evolution of the US unemployment rate—a main indicator of macroeconomic health. By late 2022, the US unemployment rate had almost fully recovered from the COVID-19 pandemic, which caused short-lived but record-high unemployment rates.

Unemployment fell dramatically after the initial spike caused by COVID-19, and this impressive drop was largely attributed to generous government support programs that resulted in an unusual shift from services to goods spending. This increase in consumer spending generally, and the shift from services to goods in particular, contributed to supply chain shortages that, in turn, contributed to inflation.

Russia's invasion of Ukraine contributed to a wide range of supply chain disruptions. Other secondary impacts included oceangoing workers: 15% of the world's 1.9 million seafarers were either Russian or Ukrainian, often in leadership positions.[36] Many of these workers found difficulty returning home. When trained

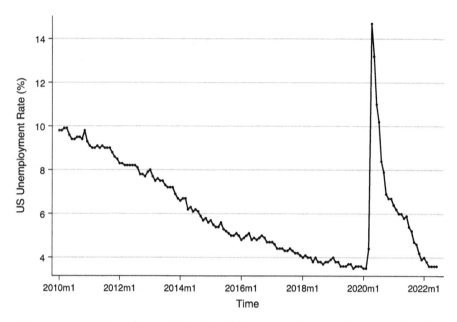

Figure 12.4 US Unemployment Rate. *Note*: Data represent the unemployment rate for all workers between eighteen and sixty-five. *Source*: Authors' elaboration using data from the United States Bureau of Labor Statistics, https://www.bls.gov/.

personnel leave their jobs, replacing them can take years. Before the invasion, Russia controlled 10% of global copper reserves and was a major producer of aluminum, platinum, and other precious metals that are essential for microchip processing and thus integral to everything from kitchen appliances to laptops and mobile phones. Ukraine is a major global supplier of neon for technology, as well as cobalt and gold. Russia is the second-largest supplier of cobalt for rechargeable batteries and the second-largest provider of vanadium, which is used for large-scale energy storage and steelmaking. It is also the sixth-largest supplier of gold and the tenth-largest supplier of lead.[37]

The World Bank's April 2022 *Commodity Markets Outlook* notes that Russia is also the world's largest exporter of pig iron, natural gas, and nickel, and the report documents significant increases in a wide range of commodity prices that year.[38] For instance, the price of potassium chloride, coal, nickel, and vegetable oils all increased significantly during the first quarter of 2022 but then moderated and fell by the end of the year.

The war contributed to price increases in products such as batteries and slowed the production of semiconductors, jet engines, automobiles, and some medicines in the short term. Because natural gas is a critical input for fertilizer, which is used in world food production, the energy shortage guaranteed an increase in world food prices at a time of global food shortages, major migration growth, and widespread famine. The world markets, however, proved to be more resilient than expected, with other producers stepping up to fill the gaps left by Russia and Ukraine.

Using data from the Federal Reserve Economic Data (FRED) database at the Federal Reserve Bank of St. Louis, figure 12.5 shows the path of the US consumer price index, both with and without food and energy. Both series show a dramatic spike during the COVID-19 recovery. One of the main economic problems for the United States related to the Russian invasion of Ukraine was the resulting supply chain disruption and fuel price increase that contributed to inflation. The US Federal Reserve Bank, however, exercised great care and skill in managing inflation by indicating that rising interest rates were on the horizon. Inflation in 2023 continued to fall, possibly leading to a very rare "soft landing" for the US economy.

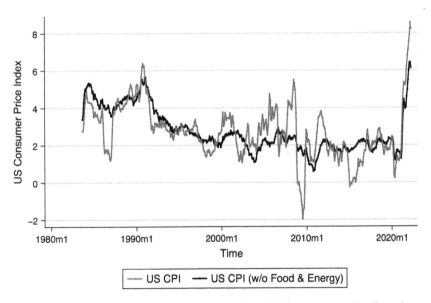

Figure 12.5 US Consumer Price Index. *Source*: Authors' elaboration using data from the St. Louis Federal Reserve FRED database, https://fred.stlouisfed.org/.

Outlook and Policy Responses

Vulnerability to disaster is one of the most significant barriers to achieving sustainable development goals.[39] Typically, developed countries rush to disaster-stricken countries shortly after disaster hits. Understanding the economic implications of the Russian invasion of Ukraine offers unique foresights as to the true resilience of the global economy. Given that we expected increases in the prices of food and fertilizers and could identify which countries were especially dependent on food imports from Russia and Ukraine, developed countries took the opportunity to anticipate the pending food crisis and support global markets that were more resilient than expected. Sudan, Egypt, and other developing countries, in desperate need of alternative food supplies and support from developed countries, were able to draw upon integrated global markets and mitigate the adverse impacts of the war.

The war in Ukraine will not end with any cessation of bombing. Although initial predictions seemed overly pessimistic, the economic, social, and political impacts are still likely to be felt for years because externalities will linger. The economic costs will be calculated in financial data. The social and political costs will be felt but often not reflected in the data. These costs will be a growing reality of social inequality, leading to political change. They will be a loss of faith in democracy and a desire for quick, simple, and authoritarian answers to complex issues. They will be a renewed impulse to question systems of capitalism, courts, the press, information, and governance. The war once again raises the nuclear threat, which the world felt was resolved for the present.

The war in Ukraine has increased the demand for global answers to global issues, such as food security, water, and adequate distribution of medicines and financial support. The war has produced another cost. Existential threats such as climate change and pandemics have lost attention and investment as the immediacy of the war shifted the political pressures for resolution. But these challenges remain and have been made more immediate by the focus on the war. What Ukraine represents is not simply a battle over land. It is, for some, the end of globalization in the form of worldwide supply chains. For others, it represents the end of US hegemony and the beginning of shifts in global power. The war will also speed the demand for alternatives to fossil fuels. The process had begun before the invasion, but the timeline for realization has been shortened. The war will not have winners, only losers. Russia may gain limited land by brute force, but will lose its future in terms of technology and trained personnel. Ukraine will survive, but

Economic Implications of the Russian Invasion of Ukraine   327

it will require years to restore infrastructure and an economic base. For Ukraine, their symbolic victories will be tested by the long-term patience of the West to support the reconstruction of a destroyed economy. The image of a powerful Russia has been destroyed. What the war demonstrates is that corruption in Russia and Ukraine limits the potential of a growing economy.

NOTES

1. Romesh Vaitilingam, "Economic Consequences of Russia's Invasion of Ukraine: Views of Leading Economists," *Vox EU*, March 10, 2022, https://voxeu.org/article/economic-consequences-war-ukraine-igm-forum-survey.

2. "The IMF Cuts Its Global Growth Forecast for 2022," *The Economist*, January 25 2022, https://www.economist.com/graphic-detail/2022/01/25/the-imf-cuts-its-global-growth-forecast-for-2022?utm_medium.

3. "War Sets Back the Global Recovery," International Monetary Fund, April 2022, https://www.imf.org/en/Publications/WEO/Issues/world-economic-outlook-april-2022.

4. John Baffes and Peter Nagle, "Commodity Prices Surge due to the War in Ukraine," *World Bank Blogs*, May 5, 2022, https://blogs.worldbank.org/developmenttalk/commodity-prices-surge-due-war-ukraine.

5. "Russian Invasion to Shrink Ukraine Economy by 45 Percent this Year," World Bank, April 10, 2022, https://www.worldbank.org/en/news/press-release/2022/04/10/russian-invasion-to-shrink-ukraine-economy-by-45-percent-this-year.

6. United Nations High Commissioner for Refugees, "Ukraine Refugee Situation," March 14, 2022, https://data.unhcr.org/en/situations/ukraine.

7. "How the Ukrainian Refugee Crisis Will Change Europe," *The Economist*, March 25, 2022, https://www.economist.com/europe/2022/03/25/how-the-ukrainian-refugee-crisis-will-change-europe.

8. A. J. Moore, "Quantifying the Landlocked Trade Penalty Using Structural Gravity," *Journal of Quantitative Economics* 16.3 (2017): 769–786, https://doi.org/10.1007/s40953-017-0106-3.

9. Jeffrey A. Frankel and David Romer, "Does Trade Cause Growth?", *American Economic Review*, 89.3 (1999): 379–399; Marta Noguer and Marc Siscart "Trade Raises Income: A Precise and Robust Result," *Journal of International Economics* 65.2 (2005): 447–460.

10. World Bank, "Global Economic Prospects," January 2023, www.worldbank.org.

11. "Europe and Central Asia Economic Update: War in the Region," World Bank, https://www.worldbank.org/en/region/eca/publication/europe-and-central-asia-economic-update.

12. Institute for International Finance, Macro-Notes: "Russia: Economy to Contract Sharply in 2022," Publicity Brief, March 30, 2022.

13. Elliot Smith, "Russia's Economy Is Beginning to Crack as Economists Forecast Sharp Contraction," *CNBC*, April 4, 2022, https://www.cnbc.com/2022/04/04/russias-economy-is-beginning-to-crack-as-economists-forecast-sharp-contractions.html#.

14. World Bank, "Latest Economic Update," Press Release 2022/EC/79, April 30, 2022

15. Ruchir Sharma, "How Putin Aged into a Classic Oil State Autocrat," *Financial Times*, April 10, 2022, https://www.ft.com/content/ff617dd8-e713-48ef-bd07-efb5fb725d50.

16. Sharma, "How Putin Aged into a Classic Oil State Autocrat."

17. Bill Conerly, "Long-Term Economic Effects of the Ukraine War," *Forbes*, March 30, 2022, https://www.forbes.com/sites/billconerly/2022/03/30/long-term-economic-effects-of-the-ukraine-war/?sh=7a6b4bdc10fa.

18. World Bank, "Global Economic Prospects."

19. World Bank, "Global Economic Prospects."

20. John Harrington and Douglas A. McIntyre, "This Is the Country That Is Most Dependent on Russian Oil," 24/7 Wall Street, May 8, 2022, https://247wallst.com/special-report/2022/05/08/this-is-the-country-that-is-most-dependent-on-russian-oil/.

21. Arnold Martin, "EU Ban on Russian Energy Would Spark Recession in Germany," *Financial Times*, April 13, 2022, https://www.ft.com/content/2f5d17aa-fc3d-4184-ba83-3fea862a3875.

22. John Harrington, "Countries Most Dependent on Russian Oil," 24/7 Wall Street, April 6, 2022, https://247wallst.com/special-report/2022/04/05/countries-most-dependent-on-russian-oil/.

23. Patricia Cohen and Stanley Reed, "Why the Toughest Sanctions on Russia Are the Hardest for Europe to Wield," *New York Times*, February 25, 2022, https://www.nytimes.com/2022/02/25/business/economy/russia-europe-sanctions-gas-oil.html.

24. J. Portes, "The Economics of Migration," *Contexts* 18.2 (2019): 12–17.

25. "How the Ukrainian Refugee Crisis Will Change Europe."

26. Jack Nicas, "Ukraine War Threatens to Cause a Global Food Crisis," *New York Times*, March 20, 2022, https://www.nytimes.com/2022/03/20/world/americas/ukraine-war-global-food-crisis.html.

27. United Nations Global Crisis Response Group, "UN Brief on the Global Impact of War in Ukraine on Food, Energy, and Finance Systems," Brief Number 1, April 13, 2022, https://unipd-centrodirittiumani.it/en/news/UN-brief-on-the-Global-Impact-of-war-in-Ukraine-on-food-energy-and-finance-systems/6204#:~:text=According%20to%20the%20new%20findings,COVID%2D19%20and%20climate%20change.

28. See "The Ukraine Conflict and Other Factors Contributing to High Commodity Prices and Food Insecurity," USDA, April 2022, https://www.fas.usda.gov/sites/default/files/2022-04/22%2004%2006%20Food%20Prices%20and%20Food%20Security_0.pdf.

29. Max Bearak, "Ukraine's Wheat Harvest Which Feeds the World Can't Leave the Country," *Washington Post*, April 7, 2022, https://www.washingtonpost.com/world/2022/04/07/ukraine-wheat-crop-global-shortage/.

30. Bearak, "Ukraine's Wheat Harvest Which Feeds the World."

31. Joe McCarty. "The Global Hunger Crisis Won't End Within Our Current Food System: UN," *Global Citizen*, July 2, 2022, https://www.globalcitizen.org/en/content/state-of-food-security-report-2022/.

Economic Implications of the Russian Invasion of Ukraine 329

32. John Rash, "World Food Supply May Be the Next War Casualty," *Minneapolis Star Tribune*, April 15, 2022, https://www.startribune.com/world-food-supply-may-be-the-next-war-casualty/600165364/.

33. "Commodity Markets Outlook: The Impact of the War in Ukraine on Commodity Markets," World Bank, April 2022, https://openknowledge.worldbank.org/bitstream/handle/10986/37223/CMO-April-2022.pdf.

34. World Bank, "Commodity Markets Outlook: Pandemic, War, Recession: Drivers of Aluminum and Copper Prices," October 2022, https://openknowledge.worldbank.org/bitstream/handle/10986/38160/CMO-October-2022.pdf.

35. World Bank, "Commodity Markets Outlook: Under the Shadow of Geopolitical Risks," October 2023, https://thedocs.worldbank.org/en/doc/4df0850dcb2a5a9b7260e65863c1cd63-0350012023/original/CMO-October-2023.pdf.

36. International Chamber of Shipping, "Russian and Ukrainian Seafarers Make Up 14.5% of Global Shipping Workforce—According to ICS." Press Release, February 24, 2022.

37. Douglas Broom, "What Else Does Russia Export, Beyond Oil and Gas," World Economic Forum, March 18, 2022, https://www.weforum.org/agenda/2022/03/russia-gas-oil-exports-sanctions/.

38. World Bank, "Commodity Markets Outlook: Special Focus: The Impact of the War in Ukraine on Commodity Markets," April 2022, https://openknowledge.worldbank.org/server/api/core/bitstreams/c7f65ff2-9e31-5b2a-9ceb-ed37900e8223/content.

39. Tarek Ghani and Grant Gordon, "Predictable Disasters: AI and the Future of Crisis Response," chapter 6 in Homi Kharas, John W. McArthur, and Izumi Ohno, eds., *Breakthrough: The Promise of Frontier Technologies for Sustainable Development* (Washington, DC: Brookings Institution Press, 2021), https://www.brookings.edu/wp-content/uploads/2021/12/Chapter-Six_Breakthrough.pdf.

CONTRIBUTOR BIOGRAPHIES

Andrew Natsios is an executive professor and the director of the Scowcroft Institute at the Bush School of Government at Texas A&M University. Formerly a distinguished professor at Georgetown University and USAID administrator (2001–2006), he also served as the US Special Envoy to Sudan in 2006–2007. A retired Lt. Colonel from the US Army Reserve, Natsios is a Gulf War veteran. He is the author of four books and a contributor to thirteen others, and his research focuses on North Korea, Sudan, food security, famines, humanitarian assistance, civil wars, human rights, and foreign aid.

Anders Åslund is a senior fellow at the Stockholm Free World Forum and adjunct professor at Georgetown University. A leading specialist on the East European economies, he has authored fifteen books, most recently *Russia's Crony Capitalism: The Path from Market Economy to Kleptocracy* (Yale University Press, 2019). He has advised the Russian and Ukrainian governments and earned his DPhil from Oxford University.

Alexandra Chinchilla is an assistant professor at the Bush School of Government & Public Service at Texas A&M University and a core faculty member of the Albritton Center for Grand Strategy. She is a 2024 nonresident fellow with the Irregular Warfare Initiative, a joint production of Princeton's Empirical Studies of Conflict Project and the Modern War Institute at West Point. Previously, Chinchilla was a Niehaus postdoctoral fellow at the John Sloan Dickey Center for International Understanding at Dartmouth College. Her research examines international security, with a focus on security cooperation and its effectiveness—especially within NATO, Russia, and Eastern Europe.

James S. Corum is a military historian with twelve books and more than seventy major journal articles and book chapters

332   Contributor Biographies

published in military history and strategic studies. Corum taught at US staff colleges from 1991 to 2008 and from 2009 to 2014, and was dean of the Baltic Defence College in Tartu, Estonia. He is currently head of the MA in Terrorism and Security Program at Salford University in Manchester, UK.

Lynn Corum is a freelance Russian translator and analyst educated at Brown University (BA) and Exeter University in the UK (MA). She has taught for thirty years, first as a language instructor at St. Lawrence University, and finally as the international teacher at Miina Härma Gümnaasium in Tartu, Estonia. Her daily monitoring of Russian media and Kremlin publications, begun in Estonia, is her window into the ideology of Putin's Kremlin.

Nicholas Eberstadt holds the Henry Wendt Chair in Political Economy at the American Enterprise Institute in Washington, DC, and is senior adviser to the National Bureau of Asian Research in Seattle, WA. He is author or editor of over twenty books and monographs, including *Russia's Peacetime Demographic Crisis: Dimensions, Causes, Implications* (National Bureau of Asian Research, 2010). He earned his AB, MPA, and PhD from Harvard and his MSc from the LSE.

Raymond C. Finch III is a Eurasian military analyst for the Foreign Military Studies Office (FMSO) at Fort Leavenworth, Kansas. He has produced analytical studies dealing with the Russian military and society. Prior to this he worked as the assistant director in the Center for Russian, East European, and Eurasian Studies at the University of Kansas. Finch spent twenty years in the US Army, first as a field artillery officer and then as a Eurasian foreign area officer. He earned both his BA and master's at the University of Kansas.

Paul Gregory is a research fellow at the Hoover Institution. He is the Cullen Professor Emeritus in the Department of Economics at the University of Houston, a research fellow at the German Institute for Economic Research in Berlin, and emeritus chair of the International Advisory Board of the Kiev School of Economics. Gregory has held visiting teaching appointments at Moscow State University and the Free University of Berlin.

Scott Jasper, CAPT, USN (ret.), is a senior lecturer at the Naval Postgraduate School, specializing in defense strategy, hybrid warfare, and cyber operations. With a PhD from the University of Reading, UK, he authored *Russian Cyber Operations* and *Strategic Cyber Deterrence*. Editor of multiple works, he contributed to various handbooks and publications on cyber security. A sought-after commentator, he has spoken on defense and cyber issues in national media outlets, including NPR, and provided commentary in international newspapers such as the *Los Angeles Times* and *Daily Express UK*.

Todd Lefko, president of the International Business Development Company, has thirty-four years of experience in Russia. With over 680 published articles in various publications, including *Rossiske Vesti*, he serves on the editorial board for the *Russian Historical Reporter*. Lefko is the English editor for four Russian books and also chairs the East-West Connections. His extensive lecturing spans universities in Russia, Germany, China, Belarus, Kazakhstan, and Turkmenistan. Holding a BA in history and an MA in public administration, Todd pursued PhD coursework in urban history at the University of Minnesota, complemented by studies at Harvard University and the University of Manchester, UK.

Serhii Plokhy is the Mykhailo Hrushevsky Professor of Ukrainian History and the director of the Ukrainian Research Institute at Harvard University. His interests include the intellectual, cultural, and international history of Eastern Europe. A leading authority on the region, he has published extensively in English, Ukrainian, and Russian. His numerous books and other scholarly work deal with the history of religion, origins of East Slavic nations, history of the Cold War era, and collapse of the Soviet Union, and they have been translated into a number of languages and won numerous awards. He is the author, most recently, of *Lost*

Contributor Biographies

Kingdom: The Quest for Empire and the Making of the Russian Nation (Basic Books, 2017).

Roger R. Reese is a professor of history at Texas A&M University, where he has taught courses on European, Russian, Soviet, and military history since 1990. His research specialty is the social history of the Soviet Red Army. He has authored numerous articles and four books on the Red Army: *Stalin's Reluctant Soldiers*, *The Soviet Military Experience*, *Red Commanders*, and most recently *Why Stalin's Soldiers Fought* (University Press of Kansas, 2011).

Raymond Robertson holds the Helen and Roy Ryu Chair in Economics and Government in the Departments of International Affairs at the Bush School of Government & Public Service and is the director of the Mosbacher Institute for Trade, Economics, and Public Policy. He is a research fellow at the Institute for the Study of Labor in Bonn, Germany, and a senior research fellow at the Mission Foods Texas-Mexico Center. He was named a 2018 Texas A&M Presidential Impact Fellow.

Kathryn Stoner, Mosbacher Director at the Center on Democracy, Development, and the Rule of Law at Stanford University, is also a professor of political science and senior fellow at the Hoover Institution. Formerly at Princeton University, she has authored or coedited six books and numerous articles on contemporary Russia. Her latest work, *Russia Resurrected: Its Power and Purpose in a New Global Order*, was published by Oxford University Press in 2021.

Index

Abkhazia region (Georgia), 126, 133, 256, 266
Abramovich, Roman, 30, 55–56
Afghanistan: Baltic soldiers in NATO deployments in, 299; life expectancy in, 154; refugees from, 283, 284; Russian veterans of Soviet war in, 194; Soviet War (1979–1989) in, 267, 277; Taliban regime in, 283; US war (2001–2021) in, 9, 98, 299
Africa Corps, 267. *See also* Wagner Group
Aksenov, Sergei, 250
Alabama, 168, 169*f*
Aleppo (Syria), siege (2012–2016) of, 280
Alliance of Patriots party, 232
Antiglobalistskoye Dvizheniye Rossii (Anti-Globalization Movement of Russia), 232–33
Antonov, Anatoly, 268
Applebaum, Anne, 3, 9
Aquinas, Thomas, 234
Arab Spring uprisings (2011), 34, 98, 261
Armenia, 318
al-Assad, Bashar, 14, 74, 280
Astashov, Alexei, 208–9
Austria, 232, 246
Avakov, Arsen, 252
Azerbaijan, 212

Bakhmut (Ukraine), 15, 83
Baltic states: birth rates in, 150; democratic and capitalist systems created after 1991 in, 298; economic performance after 1991 in, 124*f*, 292, 298–99; English language in, 292, 312n42; ethnic Russian populations in, 302–5; European Union and, 196, 292, 299, 304, 305, 306, 308; First Ukraine War and, 307; Forest Brothers insurgency (1945–1953) in, 295–96; Germany and, 293, 295, 306; Gorbachev era political reforms and, 296–97; Helsinki Accords and, 296; "human chain" demonstra-

tions (1989) in, 297; human rights abuses during Soviet era in, 300, 309n5; independence after 1991 of, 297; independence (1919–1940) of, 294–95; KGB (Soviet secret police) in, 291, 296, 297, 300; medieval era in, 293; Molotov-Ribbentrop Pact and, 295; North Atlantic Treaty Organization and, 72, 292, 298–99, 305–8; participation in operations in Afghanistan and Iraq by soldiers from, 299; Putin and, 300–302, 303–5, 307; removal of Communist-era memorials in, 303–4; Russian charges of "fascism" in, 300–302; Russian imperial era and, 293–94; Russian language in, 291–92, 302, 304, 312n42; Russian military presence (1991–1994) in, 233, 297–98; Russian oil and gas exports to, 292, 305, 306, 318–19; Russian propaganda in, 302, 303; Russia's economic relationship with, 291–92; Russia's revisionist foreign policy aims and, 3, 9, 15, 292, 300, 302, 306–7, 309; Second Ukraine War and, 306, 308–9; Second World War and, 196–200, 212, 295, 300–301, 302–3; Soviet annexation (1940) of, 295, 300; Soviet army veterans living in, 200; Soviet deportation of people from, 295, 303, 309n8; United States and, 301, 306–8; universities in, 292. *See also* Estonia; Latvia; Lithuania
Bandera, Stepan, 197
Bangladesh, 156, 159, 321
Barclay de Tolly, Michael Andreas, 294
Barro, Robert, 158–59
Bartel, Fritz, 8
Bartholomew I (Orthodox Church patriarch), 237
Belarus: economic performance since 1991 in, 299; election protests (2020–2021) in, 282; Eurasian customs union and, 249; net mortality rates in, 149, 150*t*; refugee flows

336   Index

Belarus (cont.)
  weaponized by, 283; Russian oil and gas
    exports to, 318; Russia's revisionist foreign
    policy aims and, 246, 266, 267, 275–76;
    Russia's sphere of influence and military
    presence in, 275, 302
Belgium, 144, 159, 169–70, 170t
Belgorod (Russia), 81
Beloborodov, Igor, 271
Belousov, Andrei, 84
Belton, Catherine, 58
Berezovsky, Boris, 29, 30
Berserk Bear cyber warfare group, 107
Beslan terrorist attack (2004), 31
Bick, Alexander, 75
Biden, Joseph R., 11, 60, 106
Black Lives Matter movement, 225
Black Sea: grain exports from Ukraine and,
    281, 322; land routes to Crimea on coast of,
    281; "Putin's Palace" on, 52–53, 55–56;
    Russia's revisionist foreign policy aims and,
    279, 282, 284; Second Ukraine War and, 80,
    261, 266, 267, 281, 315, 322
Blinken, Antony, 276–77
Borodai, Aleksandr, 254
Bortnikov, Alexander, 33, 50
Boyko, Yuriy, 279
Brazil, 123, 125–26, 181f
Breedlove, Philip M., 14, 232
Brezhnev, Leonid, 8, 187, 188–89
BRICS countries, 123, 126
British Virgin Islands, 49, 53
Bronze Soldier of Tallinn statue, 197
Browder, Bill, 57
Bucha massacre (2022), 80, 283
Budapest Memorandum (1994), 247, 251
Bulgaria, 149, 150t, 152f, 319, 320f
Burt, Tom, 94
Bush, George W., 67

California, 168, 169t
Canada, 57, 60–61, 308
Cayman Islands, 49–50, 59
Central Asian countries: Afghan War veterans
    in, 277; Chechen refugees in, 280; collapse
    of Communist regimes in, 10; immigration
    to Russia from, 271, 275; Russian oil and gas
    exports to, 318; Russia's revisionist foreign
    policy aims in, 308. See also specific countries
Central Asian regions of Russia, 269, 271, 281
Central Bank of Russia, 59–61, 129, 130

Central Museum of the Great Patriotic War
    (Moscow), 194
Chechnya: birth rates in, 151, 152; casualties
    from wars in, 133, 280; displaced persons
    and, 280; Grozny siege (1999) in, 260, 280;
    Kadyrov regime in, 6; Moscow apartment
    bombings (1999) and wars in, 133; Putin
    and, 133; Russian military's use of conven-
    tional weapons in, 98, 260; Russian
    veterans of wars in, 194; Russia's deporta-
    tion of local populations from, 277; Russia's
    revisionist foreign policy aims and, 260;
    soldiers in Second Ukraine War from, 277
Chernomyrdin, Viktor, 51
China: birth rates in, 268; COVID-19
    pandemic and economic slowdown in, 314;
    foreign direct investment levels in, 27;
    Global Financial Crisis and, 126; Great Leap
    Forward and mortality rates in, 148; highly
    educated working-age manpower and, 179;
    military spending levels in, 73; patents
    awarded to innovations in, 170, 171t; as
    revisionist power, 1; Russian military
    procurement and, 82; Russian oil and gas
    exports to, 131, 317; Russia's alliance with,
    1–2, 3, 66, 120, 130, 260, 279; state-owned
    companies in, 125; Taiwan and, 260
Clinton, Bill, 251
Clinton, Hillary, 12–13, 37
Cold War: arms race during, 11; client states
    and, 7; Communist Europe's public health
    outcomes during, 163; nuclear brinkman-
    ship during, 2; psychological warfare
    campaigns during, 227–28; Russia's
    revisionist history regarding, 68
Collier, Paul, 4
Combating America's Adversaries with
    Sanctions Act (CAATSA), 57
Commonwealth of Independent States, 247, 270
Communist Party: as opposition party in Putin
    era, 31–32; Second World War and, 187–88,
    194–95; Yeltsin economic reforms opposed
    by, 25
Computer Emergency Response Team of
    Ukraine (CERT-UA), 105, 106, 108
Conerly, Bill, 316
Corporate Transparency Act of 2020 (United
    States), 58–59
Cossacks, 250, 252, 253
COVID-19 pandemic (2020–2021): cyber
    warfare and disinformation regarding,

108–9; demographic decline in Russia and, 146, 148, 150, 151, 154, 162, 179, 268, 272, 275; excess death totals in Russia and, 148, 154, 268; global economic slowdown and, 314–15, 321; United States and, 148, 268, 315, 323–25; vaccines for, 108–9

Cozy Bear cyber warfare group, 100, 105

Crimea: demographic decline in Russia and Russian annexation of, 145, 146f, 275, 280; dissolution of parliament (2014) in, 250; financial costs of Russia's occupation of, 281; First Ukraine War and Russia's annexation of, 11, 12, 23, 57, 68, 72, 99, 120, 127, 134, 145, 146f, 196, 201, 246, 250–52, 256, 260, 266, 270, 307; land routes along Black Sea coast to, 281; referendum (2014) in, 250–51; Sevastopol naval base in, 247, 250; Siberian Russians resettled after 2014 in, 280; Stalin's resettlement of "suspect populations" from, 280–81; Tatar community in, 251, 280–81; tsarist era in, 270–71; Ukraine's early era of independence during 1990s and, 247

Cruz, Ted, 13

cyber warfare by Russia: civilian volunteers engaging in, 95; COVID-19 disinformation and, 108–9; critical infrastructure targeted by, 100, 104–5, 107, 110; data degradation as goal of, 102–4; disinformation and propaganda spread through, 95, 99, 108–9; distributed denial-of-service (DDoS) attacks and, 102, 112; Estonia as target of, 94, 110, 305; European elections as target of, 13; fake social media pages and, 13, 225–26; Georgia targeted by, 94–95, 101–2; hybrid war concept and, 98–99, 109–10; influence operations and, 94, 97, 99; information collection goals and, 106–7; "living off the land" operational paradigm and, 105; malware and, 102–6, 112; military personnel's participation in, 95, 100; opposition parties in Russia targeted by, 38; phishing emails and, 101, 106, 108; Poland targeted by, 103–4, 110; Russian military doctrine and, 96–98; Second Ukraine War and, 94–96, 99–105, 108, 109–12; security and intelligence agencies' participation in, 95, 100–103, 105–6, 107; *Tallinn Manual 2.0* and, 111; United States targeted by, 13–14, 95, 101, 103, 105, 110, 224–26; websites as target of, 101–2

Cyprus, 48–49

Czechoslovakia, 227

Czech Republic (Czechia), 3, 298, 318

Dawisha, Karen, 2, 33–34, 122

Day of Memory and Sorrow (Russia, anniversary of 1941 German invasion), 189

Debaltseve (Ukraine), 255, 257

Delaware, 49, 215

Democratic National Committee cyberattack (United States, 2016), 101, 105–6

demographic decline in Russia: Africa's demographic trends compared to, 154, 155t, 156, 156f, 157t, 159; age-standardized mortality rates and, 162–65, 163f, 164f, 269; agricultural sector and, 274; birth rates and, 147–54, 147f, 151f, 171, 173, 175, 181, 264, 268, 269, 270, 272–73, 275; "brain drain" and, 276; cardiovascular disease and, 165–66, 166f, 167f, 269; COVID-19 pandemic and, 146, 148, 150, 151, 154, 162, 179, 268, 272, 275; Crimea annexation as means of reversing, 145, 146f, 275, 280; death rates and, 147f, 148, 154, 156, 173, 175–76, 177f, 181, 264, 268, 270, 275; elderly population and, 9, 175–76; gender discrepancies and, 156, 157t, 160, 165, 167f; highly educated working-age population and, 179, 180f, 181f; human capital levels and, 156, 158–59; immigration and, 145, 178, 269–72, 275; infectious and parasitic diseases' limited role in, 165, 269; injury and poisoning death rates and, 165–66, 167f, 269; knowledge economy deficits and, 167–73, 168t, 169f, 170t, 181–82; life expectancy and, 154, 155t, 160–62, 160f, 161f, 176, 178f, 181, 182f, 268, 274; military readiness and, 274–75; modest reversals (2005–2019) of, 145, 164–66, 164f; Muslim population and, 152–53, 270–72, 275; net mortality rates and, 147–48, 147f, 149t, 150t, 178–79, 179f, 181, 272; projected population decline and, 178–79, 180f, 268, 275; pronatal policies and, 145, 150, 270, 272–75; public health programs and, 275; Putin on, 269–70, 272–76; regional discrepancies and, 151–52; Russian Orthodox Church and, 271–72, 275; Russia's revisionist foreign policy aims as means of addressing, 9, 12, 264–65, 268, 275–78; Second Ukraine War and, 150, 271–72; Siberia and, 278–79; Solzhenitsyn on, 264, 274, 275; women ages twenty to thirty-four and, 175, 176f; working-age population and, 162, 173, 174f, 175f, 177f, 179, 180f, 181, 181f, 268, 273–74

338   Index

Denikin, Anton, 258
Denmark, 110, 293
Deripaska, Oleg, 30
Digital Army of Russia, 109
Donbas region (Ukraine): civilian casualties in, 206; economic decline after 1991 in, 253; ethnic Russian population in, 253; First Ukraine War and, 72, 74, 76, 80, 99, 120, 134, 191–92, 196, 201, 206, 252–58, 260, 266, 307; land routes to Crimea from, 281; Orthodox Church and, 272; referendum (2014) in, 254; Russian language in, 254, 259; Russian support for proxy forces in, 281, 307; Second Ukraine War and, 65, 77, 80–81, 97, 109, 259; Ukraine's early era of independence during 1990s and, 247. *See also* Donetsk People's Republic; Luhansk People's Republic
Donetsk People's Republic (DPR): financial costs of Russia's support to, 281; political opponents repressed in, 281; Putin and, 245, 282; referendum (2014) in, 254; Russian-backed separatists' declaration of, 253, 272; Russian economic and military support for, 255, 256; Russian popular opinion regarding, 202, 208; Russian propaganda operations in, 109. *See also* Donbas region (Ukraine)
Dragonfly cyber warfare group, 107
Dubai (United Arab Emirates), 59
Dugin, Aleksandr, 275, 305
Duma (Russian parliament): anti-LGBTQ+ legislation and, 37; constitutional powers of, 30; demographic decline in Russia and, 272; election (2000) for, 28; election (2011) for, 37; establishment (1993) of, 25; legislation on Second World War legacy in, 198–200; religious legislation and, 37; as "rubber stamp" for Putin's policies, 24; United Russia's dominant role in, 28, 31
Dvornikov, Aleksandr, 280

Eastern Europe: collapse of Communist regimes in, 10, 187, 227; democratic and capitalist systems created after 1991 in, 298; economic performance after 1991 in, 124*f*; European Union expansion into, 10; NATO expansion in, 8–10, 265–66; Putin's charges of "fascism" in, 301; Russia's oil and gas exports to, 246; Second World War and, 187, 188, 198; Soviet hegemony (1945–1989) in, 200, 291; Warsaw Pact and, 10. *See also specific countries*

Eberstadt, Nicholas, 4, 9, 268–69
economy of Russia: agricultural sector and, 274; asset stripping and, 51–52, 53, 55, 122, 125; banking system and, 50, 53; coal exports and, 319; commercial service exports and, 170, 172*f*, 181–82; computer and information service exports and, 172*f*; corruption and, 125; COVID-19 pandemic and, 315; cronyism and, 32–34, 48, 50, 52–56, 122; economic inequality and, 39; First Ukraine War and, 128; foreign direct investment levels and, 27, 48; Georgia War (2008) and, 122, 123*f*; Global Financial Crisis (2008–2009) and, 126, 134; government debt levels and, 7; grain exports and, 315, 317, 321, 321*f*; import-substitution models and, 125–26; inflation and, 121, 130, 131; international patent awards and, 168, 168*t*, 169*f*; international reserve currency holdings and, 130–31; international sanctions and, 6, 7, 30, 33, 38, 57–61, 82, 84, 85, 121, 126, 129–30, 210, 249, 255, 261–62, 284, 314, 316; knowledge economy deficits and, 167–73, 168*t*, 169*f*, 170*t*, 181–82; offshore wealth and, 49–50, 54–55; oil and gas sector and, 2, 4–5, 27, 28, 30, 36, 51–52, 61, 67, 124–25, 126, 127, 128, 131, 246, 274, 292, 317–19, 318*f*; oligarchs and, 2, 4, 5, 12, 26, 28–30, 32, 48–50, 53–61, 129; precious metals and, 324; Putin era performance of, 121–28, 123*f*, 124*f*, 131, 133; Putin's political legitimacy and, 6, 28, 36, 41, 67, 120, 123, 134; "resource curse" and, 4–5; Second Ukraine War and, 121, 129–30, 314–17; size of, 144; standards of living and, 8, 27, 67, 121, 131; Ukrainian oil and gas exports to, 317; Yeltsin era and, 122, 123*f*
Ecumenical Patriarchate of Constantinople, 238
Edmonds, Jeffrey, 75
Egypt, 34, 320*f*, 321, 326
Eisenhower, Dwight D., 227–28
Energetic Bear cyberattack group, 100, 107
Estonia: cyberattacks by Russia in, 94, 110, 305; defense industries during Soviet era in, 296; democratic and capitalist systems created after 1991 in, 298; economic performance since 1991 in, 298; ethnic Russian population in, 303–4, 312n42; "human chain" demonstrations (1989) in, 297; independence after 1991 of, 297; medieval era in, 293; net mortality rates in, 150*t*; Putin's threat to

invade (2022), 282; removal of Soviet monuments in, 94, 197, 303; Russian imperial era and, 293–94; Russian media in, 292; Russian oil and gas exports to, 233, 319; Russian troops after 1991 in, 233; Second World War and, 196–97, 198, 295, 309n6; Soviet coup attempt (1924) in, 294; Soviet deportation of political opponents from, 295. *See also* Baltic states

Eurasianism, 221–22

Euromaidan protests (Ukraine, 2013–2014), 248–49, 271

European Union (EU): age-standardized mortality rates in, 162–63, 163f, 165; anti–money laundering legislation in, 58, 60; Baltic states and, 196, 292, 299, 304, 305, 306, 308; birth rates in, 152, 152f; COVID-19 pandemic and economic slowdown in, 314–15; Eastern Europe expansion by, 10; far-right political parties in, 11, 14, 232, 284; First Ukraine War and, 255; lack of military capacity of, 261; net mortality rates in, 149; refugees from Middle Eastern countries in, 14, 232, 257; refugees from Ukraine in, 260, 265, 267, 282–84, 315, 320; Russian oil and gas exports to, 233, 317–18, 318f, 319; Russia's coal exports to, 319; Russia's revisionist foreign policy aims and, 10, 188, 264; sanctions against Russia and, 57, 249; Second Ukraine War and, 15, 60, 262, 319; Ukraine's moves toward membership in, 247, 248–50, 261, 265; Ukrainian oil and gas exports to, 317–18, 318f. *See also specific countries*

Fak, Alex, 52

Fancy Bear cyberattack group, 100, 101

Federal Agency of Government Communication and Information (FAPSI), 107

Federal Security Bureau (FSB): coordination with other security forces by, 71; cyber warfare conducted by, 100, 107–8; Moscow apartment bombings (1999) and, 133; Putin's support from, 5, 67; Putin's tenure as director of, 2, 33; Russian constitution and, 25; Second Ukraine War and, 77, 109. *See also* Siloviki

Federation Council (upper house of Russian Parliament), 31

Financial Action Task Force (Organization of Economic Co-operation and Development), 59

Financial Crimes Enforcement Network (FinCEN, United States), 58–59

Finland: medieval era in, 293; Middle Eastern refugees in, 14; Molotov-Ribbentrop Pact and, 295; North Atlantic Treaty Organization and, 12, 130, 267, 282, 308–9; patents awarded to innovators in, 168; Putin's threats against, 282; Russian imperial era and, 293–94; Russia's oil and gas exports to, 319; Soviet Union and, 294–95

First Czech Russian Bank, 232

First Ukraine War (2014): airborne military forces and, 72; Baltic states and, 307; casualties in, 134, 256–57; charges of Ukrainian "fascism" during, 201, 252–53; Crimea annexed by Russia during, 11, 12, 23, 57, 68, 72, 99, 120, 127, 134, 145, 146f, 196, 201, 246, 250–52, 256, 260, 266, 270, 307; displaced persons and, 134, 257; Donbas region and, 72, 74, 76, 80, 99, 120, 134, 191–92, 196, 201, 206, 252–58, 260, 266, 307; economy of Russia and, 128; hybrid warfare concept and, 98–99, 134; international sanctions against Russia and, 6, 33, 38, 57, 60, 129, 130, 255, 262; Malaysian Airlines downing and, 255, 256; Minsk Agreements and, 255, 257–58; missile and artillery attacks from Russian territory during, 255; Nemtsov's report regarding, 6, 256; North Atlantic Treaty Organization and, 9, 128, 134; Orange Revolution and, 98, 127, 134; Putin and, 23, 47, 98, 120, 127, 134, 247, 250–51, 256; referendums in Crimea and Donbas during, 250–51; Russian-backed separatist militia forces and, 6, 250, 252, 253, 254–55, 257; Russian military forces and, 6, 87n21, 127, 250, 252, 255; Russian nationalism and, 35; Russian propaganda and, 38, 127, 134, 253; Russia's revisionist foreign policy aims and, 143, 246, 251, 255–56, 260; Second World War and, 196; Ukrainian armed forces and, 252, 254; United States and, 134, 255, 262

Foreign Agents Registration Act (FARA, United States), 13–14

Foreign Intelligence Service (SVR, Russia), 25, 33, 100, 105–7. *See also* Siloviki

foreign policy of Russia: Baltic states and, 3, 9, 15, 292, 300, 302, 306–7, 309; China and, 1–2, 3, 66, 120, 130, 260, 279; decline in Russia's international status and, 1–2, 143,

340 Index

foreign policy of Russia (*cont.*)
187; Iran and, 1, 3, 120, 130; "Near Abroad"
and, 246; North Korea and, 1, 3, 120, 130;
nuclear weapons and, 2, 11, 109, 143; oil
and gas exports as tools in, 233, 246;
revisionist goals and, 1, 3, 7, 10–11, 16, 23,
128; Second World War and, 188; support
for far-right parties in Western Europe and,
11, 14, 232, 284
Forest Brothers, 295–96
For Faith and Fatherland party, 195
France: arms procurement levels in, 73; cyber
warfare attacks by Russia in, 13, 101, 103;
far-right politicians with funding from
Russia in, 232, 284; First Ukraine War and,
255, 257; human capital levels in, 159; life
expectancy in, 154; Muslim population in,
152t; Russian oligarchs' mansions in, 56;
Russia's oil and gas exports to, 318f, 319;
Victory in Europe Day in, 212
Fridman, Mikhail, 30

G7 countries, 59
G8 countries, 2–3
Gaddafi, Muammar, 34
Galeotti, Mark, 69
Gamaredon cyber warfare group, 100, 101,
107–8
Gazprom: asset stripping at, 51–52, 53, 55, 122,
125; corporate governance of, 51; gas
pipeline companies and, 51, 52; Gusinsky's
expulsion from Russia and, 29; international
sanctions against Russia and, 61; monopoly
power of, 51; petrochemical industry and,
52; Putin's cronies as leaders of, 33, 51; Sochi
Olympics funding from, 125
Georgia: Abkhazia region of, 126, 133, 256,
266; cyberattacks by Russia after 2008 war
in, 101–2; far-right political parties with
Russian funding in, 232; *Project Russia* on
the politics of, 229; Rose Revolution (2003)
in, 98; Russian oil and gas exports to, 318;
Russian propaganda in, 302; South Ossetia
region of, 95, 133, 256, 266; Soviet
monuments removed from, 198. *See also*
Georgia War (2008)
Georgia War (2008): airborne forces and, 72;
cyberattacks by Russia and, 94–95;
international sanctions against Russia and,
126; military draft in Russia and, 190; North
Atlantic Treaty Organization and, 128; Putin

and, 2–3, 47, 120, 133, 134; Russian military's
poor performance in, 68, 84; Russia's
economy and, 6, 126, 127, 134; Russia's
revisionist foreign policy aims and, 9, 47, 143,
260, 266; US-Russian relations and, 67
Gerasimov, Valery, 15, 75, 84, 98
Germany: arms procurement and defense
spending levels in, 73, 245; Baltic states and,
293, 295, 306; Cold War and, 254–55; cyber
warfare attacks by Russia in, 13; demographic
trends in, 145, 149t; First Ukraine War and,
255, 257; Muslim population in, 152t; North
Atlantic Treaty Organization and, 308;
reunification (1991) of, 7; Russian oil and gas
exports to, 9, 233, 318f, 319; Second World
War and Nazism in, 3, 187–88, 195, 197,
198–200, 222, 227, 246, 295
Girkin, Igor, 253, 254
Glavnoye Razvedyvatel'noye Upravlenye (GRU).
See Main Intelligence Directorate (GRU)
Glazyev, Sergei, 125, 249, 302
Global Financial Crisis (2008–2009), 36, 126,
134
Gorbachev, Mikhail: Baltic states and,
296–97; economic and political reform
initiatives of, 24, 25, 66, 227, 296–97;
German reunification (1991) and, 7;
patronal system of Soviet Union and, 4;
Second World War and, 187, 196
Great Britain. *See* United Kingdom
Great Patriotic War. *See* Second World War
Greece, 238, 261, 277, 284, 318
Greene, Samuel, 35, 37
Gref, German, 50–51
Grozny, siege (1999) of, 260, 280
Gudenus, Johann, 232
Gudkov, Lev, 202, 204, 278
Guliaev, Roman, 207
Gumilev, Lev, 48
Gunvor, 52
Gusinsky, Vladimir, 29–30, 51

Habeck, Robert, 233
Haiti, 154, 269
Hale, Henry, 34
Hanseatic League, 293
Harris, Kamala, 225
Helsinki Accords (1975), 296
Hostomel Airport, battle (2022) of, 72
Hungary, 149, 150t, 298, 318, 320f
Hussein, Saddam, 61

Iceland, 58

Ilovaysk, battle (2014) of, 257

Ilyin, Ivan, 48, 222

Immortal Regiment marches, 206

India: COVID-19 pandemic in, 148; economic liberalization in, 125; Global Financial Crisis and, 126; highly educated working-age manpower in, 179; military spending levels in, 73; Russian oil and gas exports to, 131, 317

Indonesia, 321

informatsionnoye protivoborstvo (information confrontation doctrine, IPb), 97

International Criminal Court (ICC), 122, 276

International Republican Institute, 39

Internet Research Agency (Russian cyber warfare unit), 13, 225, 231

Iran: economic sanctions against, 57, 59; as revisionist power, 1; Russian military procurement and, 82; Russia's alliance with, 1, 3, 120, 130

Iraq: Baltic soldiers in NATO forces in, 299; international sanctions against Saddam Hussein's regime in, 61; refugees in Europe from, 14, 283–84; US war (2003–2011) in, 67, 98, 261, 299; violent death rate during wars in, 165

Iridium cyber warfare group. *See* Sandworm cyber warfare group

Islamic State, 74

Ivanov, Sergei, 50

Japan, 27, 145, 149*t*, 159, 177*f*, 181*f*, 268

A Just Russia party, 32

Kadyrov, Ramzan, 6

Kaftan, Larisa, 223, 230, 236, 239

Kara-Muraza, Vladimir, 57

Katyn massacre (1940), 194

Kazakhstan, 212, 246, 249

Kennan, George, 8, 265

Kerimov, Suleiman, 53

KGB (Soviet secret police), 50–51, 291, 296, 297, 300

Kharkiv (Ukraine), 208–9, 252, 259, 267

Khodorkovsky, Mikhail, 29–30

Khrushchev, Nikita, 227

Kinzhal missiles, 12, 73–74

Kirill (Russian Orthodox Church patriarch), 237, 259

Kiselyov, Dmitry, 231

Klaipėda liquefied natural gas project (Lithuania), 306

Kofman, Michael, 75

Kohl, Helmut, 7

Kolbin, Petr, 52

Kolesnikov, Sergei, 52–53, 54, 55

Kolomoisky, Igor, 252

Koneva, Elena, 204

Kononov, Vasily, 197

Konstantinov Palace (Saint Petersburg), 53

Kosach-Kvitka, Larysa, 213

Kosmodemianskaia, Zoe, 196

Kotelnikova, Anna, 52

Kotkin, Stephen, 8, 15, 222, 265–66

Kovalchuk, Yuri, 32, 50–51, 54, 57, 61

Kyiv, battle (2022) of, 65, 76–77, 80, 85, 259

Kyrgyzstan, 229, 318

Laar, Mart, 228

Laqueur, Walter: on Putin and Russian nationalist philosophers, 47; on Russia's demographic decline and foreign policy, 268; on state ideology under Putin, 221–22; on suicide rates in Russia, 269

Latvia: cyber warfare attacks by Russia in, 103; defense industries during Soviet era in, 296; democratic and capitalist systems created after 1991 in, 298; economic performance since 1991 in, 298–99; ethnic Russian population in, 303–4; "human chain" demonstrations (1989) in, 297; independence (1990–1991) of, 297; Latvian language legislation in, 304; medieval era in, 293; net morality rates in, 149, 150*t*; North Atlantic Treaty Organization and, 308; removal of Communist-era memorials in, 304; Russian imperial era and, 293–94; Russian oil and gas exports to, 233, 319; Russian troops after 1991 in, 233; Russia's charges of "fascism" in, 301–2; Second World War and, 196–97, 198, 200, 295, 301, 309n6; Soviet deportation of people from, 295, 309n8; Soviet monuments removed in, 197. *See also* Baltic states

Lavrov, Sergey, 5, 312n49

Ledeneva, Alena, 34

Lee, Jong-Wha, 158–59

Lenin, Vladimir, 245, 258

Leningrad, siege (1941–1944) of, 189–90

Le Pen, Marine, 232, 284

LGBTQ+ population in Russia, 37, 134

342 Index

Liberal Democratic Party (Russia), 31–32
Liberation Square (Tallinn), 197
Libya, 34, 98, 267
Liechtenstein, 58
Lithuania: cyber warfare attacks by Russia in, 103; democratic and capitalist systems created after 1991 in, 298; economic performance since 1991 in, 299; ethnic Russian population in, 303; "human chain" demonstrations (1989) in, 297; independence after 1991 of, 297; liquefied natural gas projects in, 306; medieval era in, 293; military service in Soviet army after Lithuanian independence and, 305; NATO deployments at air base in, 307; Nazi and Soviet symbols banned in, 198; net mortality rates in, 150t; Russian imperial era and, 293–94; Russian propaganda in, 302; Russian troops after 1991 in, 233; Russia's oil and gas exports to, 305, 306, 319; Second World War and, 196, 200, 302; Soviet deportation of political opponents from, 295; Soviet occupation (1940) of, 302. *See also* Baltic states
Luhansk People's Republic (LPR): financial costs of Russia's support for, 281; political opponents repressed in, 281; Putin's official recognition of, 245; referendum (2014) in, 254; Russian-backed separatists' declaration of, 253, 272; Russian economic and military support for, 255, 256; Russian popular opinion regarding, 202, 208; Russian propaganda operations in, 109. *See also* Donbas region (Ukraine)
Lukashenko, Aleksandr, 267, 282, 283
Luxembourg, 49
Lysenko, Trofim, 125

Macron, Emmanuel, 9
Magnitsky, Sergei, 56–57
Main Intelligence Directorate (GRU), 100–103, 109–10
Makarov, Alyon, 232
Malaysian Airlines downing (2014), 255, 256
The Maldives, 59
Malta, 319
Mariupol (Ukraine): elections (2019) in, 279; First Ukraine War and, 254, 256; Russia's revisionist foreign policy aims and, 279–80; Second Ukraine War and, 80, 259, 279–80, 322

Markwick, Roger, 186
Marten, Kimberly, 270
Martinos, Athanasios, 238
Matovski, Aleksandar, 28
McFaul, Michael, 127–28
Mearsheimer, John, 8, 265
Mediterranean Sea, 284
Medvedev, Dmitry: commission on Soviet history established by, 301; presidency (2008–2012) of, 23, 121, 126; as prime minister of Russia, 36; Second World War and, 198–99; wealth of, 39
Medvedev, Sergei, 8, 11, 266
Memorial civil rights organization, 194, 199
Menzel, Ken, 224
Meri, Lennart, 302
Merkel, Angela, 251
Meskhetian Turks, 281
Mikhalkov, Nikita, 222–23
military forces of Russia: advanced weapons systems and, 73–74; air force and airborne forces of, 71–72, 78, 80; arms procurement and, 72–73; Baltic states presence (1991–1994) of, 233, 297–98; command and control structure of, 71; conscript soldiers and, 69–70; contract soldiers and, 69, 70–71, 78; corruption and, 72, 79, 85; cyber warfare by members of, 95, 100; demographic decline in Russia and, 274–75; discipline in, 69–70, 80; draft evasion and, 191–92; education and training of, 70, 78–79; force structure of, 71–72, 78–79; Georgia War (2008) and, 68, 84, 190; law banning criticism of, 199; missile arsenal and, 73–74; number of soldiers in, 69; personnel management and promotion in, 70–71, 83–84; professionalization of, 69–70; reform initiatives in, 68–74; Russian public opinion regarding, 68, 69–70; Russia's revisionist foreign policy aims and, 69, 74; Second Ukraine War and, 9, 11–13, 41, 65–66, 75–82, 84–86, 128, 265, 267, 268; Syria and, 71, 75
Miller, Alexei, 33, 50–51, 56
Milošević, Slobodan, 61
Milov, Vladimir, 51, 52, 53, 54, 55
Ministry of Internal Affairs, 71
Minsk Agreements (2014–2015), 255, 257–58
Minyaylo, Alexey, 202, 204, 207–8
Moldova: European Union and, 282; First Ukraine War and, 252; Russian propaganda

Index

in, 302; Russia's revisionist foreign policy aims and, 3, 9, 15, 282; Transnistria separatist conflict in, 256, 282

Molotov-Ribbentrop Pact (1939), 198–99, 295, 297

Monastery of St. Panteleimon (Mount Athos, Greece), 238

Mongolia, 318

Montenegro, 59, 267

Morawiecki, Mateusz, 283

Moscow apartment bombings (1999), 133

Moscow Patriarchate (Russian Orthodox Church), 7, 259

Mount Athos (Greece), 238

Mubarak, Hosni, 34

Mueller, Robert, 13

Muslim population in Russia: birth rates and, 152–53; immigrants from Central Asian countries and, 271, 275; size of, 152, 152*t*, 272; soldiers during Afghanistan War drawn from, 277

Muzhenko, Viktor, 76

Myers, Steven Lee, 222

Nakasone, Paul, 100

Naryshkin, Sergei, 33, 50

Nashi (Russian nationalist youth organization), 38, 94

National Democratic Institute, 39

National Endowment for Democracy, 39

National Front Party (France), 232

National Unity Day (November 7, Russia), 188

Navalny, Alexei, 6, 39–40, 122, 129

Nayyem, Mustafa, 248

Nemtsov, Boris: assassination of, 6, 57; asset stripping analyzed by, 51, 52, 53, 54, 55; First Ukraine War and, 6, 256; Sergei Magnitsky Rule of Law Accountability Act and, 57

neo-Nazi parties in Russia, 195, 212

The Netherlands, 13, 144, 319

Neuberger, Anne, 102, 106

Nicholas II (tsar of Russia), 4, 238

Nobelium cyberattack group, 100, 105, 106–7

Nord Stream gas pipelines, 233

North, Douglass, 4

North Atlantic Treaty Organization (NATO): Afghanistan War (2001–2021) and, 299; Article 5 collective security obligation of, 15–16; Baltic states and, 72, 292, 298–99, 305–8; Eastern European expansion by, 8–10, 265–66; Finland and, 12, 130, 267,

282, 308–9; First Ukraine War and, 9, 128, 134; Georgia War (2008) and, 128; risk of Russian accidental escalation with, 74; Russia's revisionist foreign policy aims and, 8, 10, 15–16, 264; Second Ukraine War and, 9, 11, 84, 86, 97, 121, 129–30, 136, 201, 206, 245, 260, 265–66, 268; Sweden's entry into, 11–12, 130, 267, 282, 308–9; Syria and, 128; Trump and, 307; Ukraine's long-term relationship with, 265

North Korea: economic sanctions against, 57, 59; as revisionist power, 1; Russian military procurement and, 82; Russian oil exports to, 318; Russia's alliance with, 1, 3, 120, 130; Second Ukraine War and soldiers from, 16, 277

Norway, 14, 58, 168, 283

NotPetya malware, 102–3, 109–10

Novatek, 52

NTV television station, 29, 51

Obama, Barack, 11, 67, 307, 312n49

Ocasio-Cortez, Alexandria, 225

October Revolution (Russia, 1917), 188, 258

oligarchs in Russia: elections of 1996 and, 26; insecure status and illegitimate nature of power of, 12; international sanctions against, 57–61, 129; libel suits against Western journalists and, 58; media companies owned by, 26, 28–29; offshore wealth held by, 5, 49–50, 54, 59–61; oil and gas sector and, 5, 30; palaces and mansions owned by, 56; Putin's political and legal attacks against, 29–30, 32, 48, 50; Putin's support from, 2, 30, 53–54; Second Ukraine War sanctions and, 30; state sector control held by, 4; yachts and private jets owned by, 55–56; Yelstin era and consolidation of economic power by, 26

Onuphry (Ukrainian Orthodox Church leader), 259

Open Society Institute, 38–39

Operation Ghost cyber warfare campaign, 105

Orange Revolution (Ukraine, 2004): First Ukraine War and, 98, 127, 134; *Project Russia* series' description of, 235–36; Putin's denunciation of, 201, 221; United States and, 235–36; Yushchenko's ascent to presidency following, 235, 248

Organization for Security and Co-operation in Europe (OSCE), 198, 255

344   Index

Organization of Ukrainian Nationalists (OUN), 200
Orthodox Church. *See* Russian Orthodox Church
Otkritie, 53

Pakistan, 283
Panama Papers, 53, 54, 55, 57–58
Pandora Papers, 54, 55, 58
Panfilov Twenty-Eight Guardsmen (Second World War), 196
Pan-Orthodox Council (2016), 237
Paradise Papers, 55
Patent Cooperation Treaty, 169, 170*t*, 171*t*
The Path Home (anti-war movement in Russia), 210
Patriot Act (United States, 2001), 60
Patrushev, Nikolai, 33, 50
Pereverzeva, Natalia, 190
Peskov, Dmitry, 99, 281
Peter the Great, 293
Poklonnaia Gora War Memorial (Moscow), 194
Poland: armed forces expansion after 2020 in, 245; birth rates in, 150; cyber warfare attacks by Russia in, 103–4, 110; democratic and capitalist systems created after 1991 in, 298; Lithuanian natural gas exports to, 306; North Atlantic Treaty Organization and, 308; partition during eighteenth century of, 255; refugees from Middle East in, 283; Russia's oil and gas exports to, 319; Russia's revisionist foreign policy aims and, 3, 15; Second World War and, 212
politics in Russia: authoritarian and patronal nature of, 3–4, 11, 24, 83–85, 121; civil society restrictions and, 2, 3, 4, 5, 24, 37–39, 41, 121; constitution (1993) and, 25, 30; democratic decline and, 24; election (1996) and, 25, 26; election (2000) and, 2, 27–28; election (2011) and, 37, 67; election (2012) and, 5, 12, 36, 122, 127–28; election (2024) and, 24; gubernatorial elections cancellation after 2004 and, 31; judicial system and, 3, 67; LGBTQ+ population and, 37, 134; political prisoners and, 38, 39–40; Russia as "fragile state" and, 1, 4, 12, 16, 23, 34, 41, 83, 284, 292; Russia as "revisionist" power and, 1, 3, 7, 10–11, 16, 23, 128
Pomerantsev, Peter, 230–31
Pontic Greeks, 281

Poroshenko, Petro, 254, 257
Potanin, Vladimir, 30
Prigozhin, Yevgeny: death under suspicious circumstances of, 83, 267; First Ukraine War and, 127; Internet Research Agency and, 13; march on Moscow and rebellion (2023) led by, 15, 83–84, 122; prisoners recruited to serve as soldiers in Ukraine by, 277; Wagner Group and, 83
Primakov, Yevgeny, 135
Project Russia book series: authors of, 224–25; autocracy endorsed and democracy criticized in, 7, 224–26, 234–39; color revolution theory in, 235–36; commercial success and popularity of, 7, 221, 223; on demographic decline in Russia, 275–76; The "Golden Billion" described in, 229; political ideology of Putin's Russia described in, 7, 221–23, 230, 234–36, 302, 308; propaganda strategy described in, 231; Russian Orthodox Church and, 7, 237; Russia's revisionist foreign policy aims and, 221, 234–35; Shalyganov on the goals of, 239; US political system described in, 224; Western countries viewed as decadent and hostile in, 221–22, 226–30; world collapse predicted in, 230–32
Prokhorov, Mikhail, 30
protests in Russia: against pension reform (2018), 35; against Putin (2011–2012), 12, 36–37, 38, 121–22, 134; against Second Ukraine War, 36, 210, 212–13, 278; against social benefit reforms (2005) in, 35
Putin, Vladimir: anti-LGBTQ+ legislation supported by, 37; assassination of political rivals of, 6, 39–40, 57; autocratic and patronal regime of, 4, 5, 6, 23–24, 32–41, 66–68, 85, 222; Baltic states and, 300–302, 303–5, 307; Black Sea palace of, 52–53, 55–56; Chechnya War (1999–2002) and, 133; civil society restrictions implemented by, 2, 23–24, 28, 37–39, 41; cronyism under, 32–34, 48, 50, 52–56, 122; cyber warfare and, 11; democratic institutions in Russia destroyed by, 3, 15, 23, 31; demographic decline in Russia and, 269–70, 272–76; Duma address (2020) by, 36; economic basis of political legitimacy and, 6, 28, 36, 41, 67, 120, 123, 134; economic performance under, 121–28, 123*f*, 124*f*, 131, 133; economic reform initiatives during early years of presidency

of, 2, 48; election (2000) and, 2, 27; election (2012) and, 12, 36, 122, 127–28; election (2024) and, 24; far-right political parties in Europe funded by, 232, 284; federalist system in Russia undermined by, 31–32; as Federal Security Service director, 2, 33; First Ukraine War and, 23, 47, 98, 120, 127, 134, 247, 250–51, 256; Georgia War (2008) and, 2–3, 47, 120, 133, 134; immigration policy under, 270; International Criminal Court indictment against, 276; international sanctions against Russia and, 57; judicial system in Russia and, 67; media restrictions implemented by, 2, 5–6, 24, 28–29, 68, 134; military leadership of, 66, 67–68, 73, 84, 191; Moscow apartment bombings (1999) and, 133; nationalism and, 35, 38, 48, 133, 190, 194–95, 205, 222, 272, 300; nostalgia for Soviet era of imperial power and, 27, 47, 143, 251, 299–300; nuclear brinkmanship and, 109; oil and gas sector and, 5, 6, 11, 27, 28, 67, 124, 127, 233, 274, 317; oligarchs as subject of political and legal attacks by, 29–30, 32, 48, 50; oligarchs' support for, 2, 30, 53–54; Orange Revolution denounced by, 201, 221; organized crime and, 47–48; political ideology of, 7, 221–23, 230, 234–36, 302, 308; as prime minister of Russia, 48; protests (2011–2012) against, 12, 36–37, 38, 121–22, 134; public uprisings feared by, 5, 24; refugee flows weaponized by, 283–84; revisionist foreign policy aims of, 3, 10–11, 23, 47–48, 68, 109, 120, 128, 143, 222, 245–46, 251, 258, 264–67, 275, 284, 302; Russian Orthodox Church and, 221–22, 237–38; Russian public opinion regarding, 30, 35, 37, 68, 126–27, 131–35, 135*f*; Saint Petersburg municipal government and power base of, 2, 32–33, 47, 50, 54, 67; Second Ukraine War and, 8, 11, 12–13, 14, 15, 23, 41, 47, 59, 77, 84, 97, 109, 112, 120–21, 128–30, 134–36, 202–5, 208–10, 212, 245, 257–60, 264; Second World War and, 8, 84, 129, 133, 186, 187–88, 190–91, 192, 194–95, 197, 198, 199, 206–9, 211, 212; secret police work during Soviet era by, 2, 10, 32, 66–67; Siloviki support for, 2, 5, 16, 33, 50–51, 67, 285n2; Sochi Winter Olympics (2014) and, 133; Soviet Union's collapse and, 10, 66–67; Stalin and, 129, 194–95, 267; succession questions regarding, 14–15, 40–41, 284;

United Russia Party and, 31; wealth of, 51–55, 67; Yeltsin's selection for presidency (1999) of, 2, 23, 26–27, 33

Radio Tavria, 109
Rashid, Ahmed, 283
Rasmussen, Anders Fogh, 233
RCB Bank, 53
Reagan, Ronald, 11
Rebuilding Economic Prosperity and Opportunity for Ukrainians Act (United States, 2024), 60
Remnick, David, 265–66
"resource curse," 4
Roberts, Matthew, 224
Robertson, Graeme, 35, 37
Roldugin, Sergei, 53
Romania, 150, 295, 315
Rosneft: asset stripping at, 122; cyberattacks on, 103; international sanctions against Russia and, 61, 130; libel suits against Western journalists and, 58; Putin cronies as leaders at, 33
Rostec, 61
Rotenberg, Arkady and Boris: companies owned by, 51–52; economic sanctions and, 57, 61; Putin's cronyism and wealth held by, 33, 50, 52, 54; Sochi Winter Olympics construction and, 52
RT America media outlet, 109
Rubio, Marco, 13
Russian Orthodox Church: demographic decline in Russia and, 271–72, 275; Pan-Orthodox Council (2016) and, 237; *Project Russia* book series and, 7, 237; Putin and, 221–22, 237–38; Second Ukraine War and, 7, 259, 278; Second World War and, 195, 212
Russian Unity Party, 250
Russia Today news agency, 231

Saakashvili, Mikheil, 102
Saint Petersburg (Russia): Baltic tourists in, 292; Kostantinov Palace in, 53; organized crime in, 47–48; protests in, 196, 210, 213; Putin's time in municipal government and base of power in, 2, 32–33, 47, 50, 54, 67; Victory Day celebrations in, 189
Salye, Marina, 47–48
Sanders, Bernie, 13
Sandu, Maia, 282

Index

Sandworm cyber warfare group, 100, 101–5, 110, 112

Saudi Arabia, 170

Sberbank, 129

Schulmann, Yekaterina, 204

Sechin, Igor, 33, 50–51, 56

Second Ukraine War (2022–): aerial bombardment of Ukraine and, 80–81; airborne military forces and, 72; anti-war movement in Russia and, 36, 210, 212–13, 278; assassination of political opponents in Russia during, 6, 129; casualties among Russian soldiers in, 16, 41, 65, 80, 85, 128, 136, 267, 277–78, 284; charges of Ukrainian "fascism" during, 201–2, 203, 205, 207, 208, 209, 210–11, 213, 245; civil society restrictions in Russia and, 39, 41; cyber warfare by Russia and, 94–96, 99–105, 108, 109–12; desertion by Russian soldiers in, 211; Donbas front and, 65, 77, 80–81, 97, 109, 259; Donetsk People's Republic and, 109, 202, 208, 245, 253–56, 272, 281–82; Eastern Front and, 201; economy of Russia during, 121, 129–30, 314–17; economy of Ukraine during, 282, 315–16, 322; emigration from Russia during, 172–73, 209–10, 278; enlistment bonuses for Russian soldiers in, 211; equipment losses by Russian military in, 85–86, 128; ethnic minority soldiers among Russian armed forces in, 277; European security system threatened by, 1–2; financial costs for Russia of, 7, 16, 85, 284; global economy during, 314, 323–26; global food insecurity and, 321–23, 325–26; grain exports and, 316, 321–22; international humanitarian law and, 111; international sanctions against Russia and, 7, 30, 57, 59–61, 82, 84, 85, 121, 129–30, 210, 261, 284, 314, 316; Luhansk People's Republic and, 109, 202, 208, 245, 253–56, 272, 281; Mariupol siege (2022) and, 80, 254, 256, 259, 279–80, 322; military contracts in Russia and, 41; Minsk Agreements (2014–2015) abandoned by Russia in, 257–58; missile attacks from Russia and, 73–75, 81, 279; North Atlantic Treaty Organization and, 9, 11, 84, 86, 97, 121, 129–30, 136, 201, 206, 245, 260, 265–66, 268; North Korean soldiers in, 16, 277; nuclear brinkmanship and, 109; popular support in Ukraine for resisting Russian invasion and, 13, 77, 128, 265; prisoners in Russia conscripted as soldiers for, 130, 136, 277–78; Putin and, 8, 11, 12–13, 14, 15, 23, 41, 47, 59, 77, 84, 97, 109, 112, 120–21, 128–30, 134–36, 202–5, 208–10, 212, 245, 257–60, 264; refugees from Ukraine and, 260, 265, 267, 282–84, 315, 320; reparations for Ukraine and, 60–61; return of refugees to Ukraine during, 316; Russian National Guard troops and, 210–11; Russian Orthodox Church and, 7, 259, 278; Russian public opinion regarding, 68, 192, 201–6, 208–9; Russian territory targeted by Ukrainian forces in, 81; Russia's media restrictions and propaganda during, 5, 12, 79, 83, 84, 97–98, 109, 202, 205–6, 210; Russia's revisionist foreign policy aims and, 10, 15–16, 23, 109, 143, 258–59, 264–66, 268, 276, 278, 284–85, 326; Second World War compared to, 84, 129, 186, 196, 204–9, 211–13; strategic adjustments by Russia after initial battlefield failures in, 82–85, 265; strategic miscalculations and poor military performance by Russia in, 9, 11–13, 41, 65–66, 75–82, 84–85, 265, 267, 268; training of Ukrainian soldiers by Western militaries in, 81; Ukraine's air defense forces during, 12, 73, 75–76, 78; Ukraine's military performance in, 76–77, 79–82; Ukrainian civilian casualties in, 80, 213; Ukrainians deported to Russia during, 276–77, 279; United Nations and, 110–11; United States and, 9, 15, 60, 75, 81–82, 99, 121, 129, 130, 136, 260–62, 284, 326; unmanned aerial systems and, 81–83, 105; Wagner Group mercenaries and, 83, 277–78; war crimes committed by Russian forces during, 80, 283; Western governments' miscalculations regarding, 82–83; Western military assistance to Ukraine and, 129–30, 136, 260, 262

Second World War: Baltic states and, 196–200, 212, 295, 300–301, 302–3; casualties among Soviet soldiers in, 187; First Ukraine War and, 196; foreign policy of contemporary Russia and, 188; gender imbalance in Soviet population following, 187; major battles in Russia during, 189–90; Molotov-Ribbentrop Pact and, 198–99, 295, 297; popular culture in Russia and depictions of, 193–94; Putin's invocations of, 8, 84, 129, 133, 186, 187–88, 190–91, 192, 194–95, 197, 198, 199, 206–9, 211, 212; Russian nationalism and, 8, 133, 188, 191, 195; Russian Orthodox Church and, 195,

212; Russian public opinion regarding legacy of, 189; Second Ukraine War and, 84, 129, 186, 196, 204–9, 211–13; Soviet monuments in Baltic states and, 197, 212; Soviet territories devastated during, 187; Ukraine and, 196, 197–98, 200, 202, 212; veterans in Russia from, 192–93, 200, 206, 208; Victory Day celebrations in Russia and, 187, 189, 191–92, 196, 206–8

Security Assistance Group–Ukraine (SAG-U), 81

Security Council (Russia), 33, 77, 107, 257

Serbia, 61, 98, 149, 150*t*

Serdyukov, Anatoly, 69

Sergei Magnitsky Rule of Law Accountability Act (United States, 2012), 56–57

Sevastopol naval base (Ukraine), 247, 250

Seventh Ecumenical Council (787 CE), 237

Shalyganov, Yuri: democracy criticized by, 224; on goals of *Project Russia*, 239; "supranational social system" endorsed by, 237; on theism *versus* atheism, 238; world collapse predicted by, 230, 232

Shamalov, Nikolai, 52–53

Shcherbakova, Irena, 207

Shevchenko, Taras, 213

Shoigu, Sergei, 15, 69, 83, 84, 126, 279

Short, Philip, 222

Šiauliai Air Base (Lithuania), 307

Siberia: China and, 279; demographic vulnerability of, 278–79; natural resources in, 127, 246, 278; resettlement of Ukrainians and other "suspect populations" in, 265, 266, 276, 279; separatist movement in, 278; Soviet deportation of political opponents to, 295

Sibur, 52

Sikorski, Radosław, 249–50

Siloviki (military and security officials in Russia): anti-Semitism among, 222; Crimea resettlement and, 280; demographic decline in Russia as source of concern among, 274, 275, 280; insecure status and infighting among, 12, 14–15; outside threats as source of legitimacy for, 8, 266; Putin's succession and, 15, 284; Putin's support from, 2, 5, 16, 33, 50–51, 67, 285n2; Russia's revisionist foreign policy aims and, 264, 266, 284; Second Ukraine War and, 16

Singapore, 49

Slovakia, 3, 298, 318

Slovenia, 319

Sloviansk (Ukraine), 253, 254

Smith, Keith C., 233

Snyder, Tim, 16

Sobchak, Anatoly, 32–33, 67

Sochi Winter Olympics (2014): construction bonanza prior to, 52; financial cost of hosting, 5; Gazprom's financial contributions to, 125; Putin and, 133; Russian nationalism and, 191; Russia's release of political prisoners prior to, 30

SolarWinds cyber warfare campaign (2020), 106

Soldat veterans' organization, 194

Solzhenitsyn, Aleksandr, 246, 258, 264, 274, 275

Soros, George, 12, 38–39

South Africa, 123, 126, 170

South Ossetia region (Georgia), 95, 133, 256, 266

South Sudan, 323

Soviet Union: Afghanistan War (1979–1989) and, 283; armed forces of, 189–90, 193, 195, 197–98, 200, 212, 294, 296, 303, 304–5; Baltic states annexed (1940) by, 295, 300; collapse (1990–1991) of, 6, 7–8, 10, 24, 66, 68, 186, 187, 211, 228, 247, 251; commodity trade in, 48; Gorbachev's reform initiatives in, 24, 25, 66, 227, 296–97; Greek Civil War and deportation of Greek children to, 277; nostalgia in contemporary Russia for imperial power of, 6, 27, 47, 143, 227, 251, 299–300; oil and gas sector in, 27, 48, 246; as patronal state, 4; prison camps in, 38; Russian revisionist history regarding, 68; Second World War and, 8, 186–89, 194–202, 212, 302; standards of living in, 8

Spain, 154, 222

Sputnik International news service, 231

Sputnik V COVID-19 vaccine, 108–9

Stalin, Joseph: agricultural policy under, 125, 295; Baltic states and, 295, 302; death of, 35, 295–96; expansion of Soviet federal power under, 266; Holodomor and forced collectivization in Ukraine under, 322; Putin and, 129, 194–95, 267; repression of political opponents by, 189, 194, 199, 200, 212; resettlement of "suspect populations" by, 280–81; Russian nationalism and, 194–95; Russian revisionist history accounts of, 301; Second World War and, 188, 189, 194–95, 212, 302; totalitarian nature of regime of, 5

348   Index

Stamos, Alex, 225
State of the Teutonic Order, 293
Stavridis, James, 280
Stoltenberg, Jens, 307
Stoner, Kathryn, 127–28
Strache, Heinz-Christian, 232
Strontium cyberattack group, 100, 101
Stuermer, Michael, 10
Sudan, 159, 323, 326
Surovikin, Sergei, 83–84
Sutyagin, Igor, 230
Sweden: Baltic states and, 293; medieval era
    in, 293; North Atlantic Treaty Organization
    and, 11–12, 130, 267, 282, 308–9; Putin's
    threats against, 282; refugees from Middle
    Eastern countries in, 284; Russia's oil and
    gas exports to, 318f, 319
Sweden Democrats Party, 284
Switzerland: death rates in, 156; European
    Union anti–money laundering regulations
    and, 58; Russian offshore wealth held
    in, 50, 59; Russian oligarchs' mansions
    in, 56
Syria: advanced weapons used by Russian
    forces in, 73–74; Aleppo siege (2012–2016)
    in, 280; civilian deaths and war crimes
    during civil war in, 280; Islamic State
    forces in, 74; refugees in Europe from, 14,
    232, 283, 284, 315; Russian mercenary
    forces in, 120; Russian military's force
    structure in, 71; Russia's military
    successes in, 75; Russia's revisionist foreign
    policy aims and, 9, 11, 23, 66, 84; US
    military engagement in, 74

Taiwan, 260, 268
Tajikistan, 212, 318
Taliban regime (Afghanistan), 283
Tallinn Manual 2.0 on the International Law
    Applicable to Cyber Operations, 111
Tallinn University of Technology, 292
Tartu University, 292, 312n42
Taylor, Brian, 34
Thatcher, Margaret, 49
Timchenko, Gennady: companies owned
    by, 52; economic sanctions and, 57, 61;
    Putin's cronyism and wealth held by, 33, 50,
    54–55
Transnistria region (Moldova), 256, 282
Trump, Donald, 11, 13, 225, 284, 307
Turkey, 59, 74, 283, 319

Ukraine: air defense systems in, 12, 73, 75–76,
    78; Budapest Memorandum's guarantee of
    independence (1994) to, 247, 251; cyberattacks
    by Russia before 2022 in, 102–3; election
    (2004) in, 235, 247–48; election (2014) in, 254;
    election (2019) in, 279; Eurasian customs
    union proposal and, 249; European Union
    and, 247, 248–50, 261, 265; grain exports
    from, 281, 316, 321–22, 321f; Holodomor
    famine and forced collectivization during
    1930s in, 322; independence declaration (1991)
    by, 247; military modernization in, 66, 76; net
    mortality rates in, 149, 150t; North Atlantic
    Treaty Organization and, 265; nuclear arsenal
    surrendered to Russia (1994) by, 247; oil and
    gas sector in, 317–18, 318f; precious metals in,
    324; Project Russia on the politics of, 229;
    Russia's charges of "fascism" in, 200–202,
    203, 205, 207, 208, 209, 210–11, 213, 252–53,
    302; Russia's forced resettlement of children
    from, 276; Russia's oil and gas exports to, 128,
    319; Second World War and, 196, 197–98, 200,
    202, 212; Soviet era in, 258; Victory Day
    celebrations in, 200. See also First Ukraine
    War (2014); Second Ukraine War (2022–)
United Arab Emirates, 49, 59
United Kingdom: anti–money laundering
    legislation in, 58, 60; arms procurement
    levels in, 73; "Big Bang" financial deregula-
    tion (1986) in, 49; Budapest Memorandum'
    (1994) and, 247; cyberattacks by Russia in,
    110; fracking in, 233; Muslim population in,
    152t; North Atlantic Treaty Organization
    and, 308; Putin's support for far-left political
    parties in, 284; Russian oligarchs'
    residences and offshore wealth in, 29, 49,
    56; Russia's oil and gas exports to, 318f, 319
United Nations, 110–11
United Russia Party: Baltic states and, 301;
    Duma dominated by, 28, 31; election (2000)
    and, 28; election (2011) and, 67; election
    (2012) and, 36; Putin and, 31; regional
    governments in Russia dominated by, 32
United States: Afghanistan War (2001–2021)
    and, 9, 98; anti–money laundering legislation
    in, 58–61; Baltic states and, 301, 306–8; birth
    rates in, 272; Budapest Memorandum (1994)
    and, 247; COVID-19 pandemic and economic
    slowdown in, 148, 268, 315, 323–25; cyber
    warfare attacks by Russia in, 13–14, 95, 101,
    103, 105, 110, 224–26; election (2016) in,

13–14, 101, 105, 224–25; election (2020) in, 225–26; election integrity in, 225; financial markets in, 49–50; First Ukraine War (2014) and, 134, 255, 262; foreign aid to Russia from, 7–8; foreign-born population in, 271; highly educated working-age manpower and, 179; high-tech economic sector in, 27; inflation levels in, 325, 325f; International Emergency Economic Powers Act of 1977 in, 60; Iraq War (2003–2011) and, 67, 98, 261, 299; military spending levels in, 11, 73; *Project Russia* book series' description of, 224–28, 229–30; Russian elections and, 37; Second Ukraine War and, 9, 15, 60, 75, 81–82, 99, 121, 129, 130, 136, 260–62, 284, 326; Sergei Magnitsky Rule of Law Accountability Act and, 56–57; Syria and, 74; Ukrainian refugees and, 283; unemployment rate in, 323, 324f; US Army Europe and, 72
Unity. *See* United Russia Party
University of Latvia, 292
US Agency for International Development (USAID), 5
US Computer Emergency Readiness Team (US-CERT), 107
Usmanov, Alisher, 55
US Russia Foundation, 39
Uzbekistan, 198, 212, 318

Vakhshtayn, Victor, 206–7
Van Herpen, Marcel H., 266
Vasilyeva, Olga, 301
Veblen, Thorstein, 56
Velvet Revolution (Czechoslovakia, 1991), 227
veterans in Russia: cemeteries for, 193; Chechnya Wars and, 194; government benefits for, 193; National Unity Day celebrations and, 188; Second Ukraine War and, 196; Second World War and, 192–93, 200, 206, 208; Soviet-Afghan War and, 194
Vike-Freiberga, Vaira, 196
Vilnius Declaration (2009), 198
Vilnius University, 292
Vlasov, Andrey, 195
VTB Bank, 53
Vyakhirev, Rem, 51

Wagner Group, 13, 15, 83, 267, 277–78
Wałęsa, Lech, 228

Wallis, John Joseph, 4
War and Peace (Tolstoy), 294, 309n2
Warren, Elizabeth, 225
Warsaw Pact, 10
Weber, Max, 83
Weingast, Barry, 4
Weiss, Michael, 230–31
West Germany, 7
World Cup Tournament (Russia, 2018), 133
World Food Program, 322
World War II. *See* Second World War

Xi Jinping, 279

Yanukovych, Viktor, 201, 235, 247–50, 253
Yastrzhembsky, Sergei, 300
Yatseniuk, Arsenii, 251
Yeltsin, Boris: Baltic states and, 297; civil society organizations and civil rights expanded under, 25, 28; Communist Party opposition to reforms of, 25; Congress of People's deputies dismissed (1993) by, 25; economic performance under, 122, 123f; economic reforms promoted by, 24–25, 28, 30; election (1996) and, 25, 26; federalism in Russian system under, 31; oligarchs' consolidation of economic power under, 26; political reforms promoted by, 24–25; Putin named as president (1999) by, 2, 23, 26–27, 33; Russian foreign policy in "Near Abroad" and, 246; "shock therapy" economic reforms under, 25–26, 120; Ukraine and, 247
Yemen, 154, 159, 283
Yukos, 29–30, 125
Yushchenko, Viktor, 235, 248

Zaluzhny, Valery, 82
Za! TV, 109
Zelensky, Volodymyr: approval rating in Ukraine for, 13; election (2019) and, 279; election of, 134–35; Putin's label of "fascist" for, 202, 245; Russia's attempt to overthrow, 41, 134–35, 281; Waffen-SS celebration marches in Ukraine opposed by, 198
Zhirinovsky, Vladimir, 305
Zhora, Victor, 105, 110
Zucman, Gabriel, 49
Zvonsovsky, Vladimir, 202
Zyuganov, Gennady, 25, 27–28

Explore other books from HOPKINS PRESS

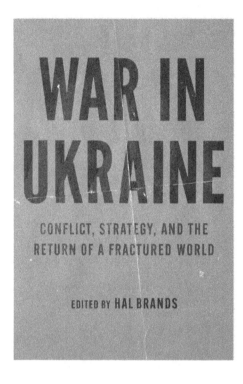

"An indispensable resource for navigating the complexities of a turning point in the post–Cold War order."

—*Parameters*

"The most definitive and authoritative work ever presented on higher education in Russia."

—Sir Malcolm Grant, Former President, University College London

JOHNS HOPKINS UNIVERSITY PRESS | PRESS.JHU.EDU |